Ma, Now I'm Goin Up in the World

Ma, He Sold Me for a Few Cigarettes
Ma, I'm Gettin Meself a New Mammy
Ma, It's a Cold Aul Night and I'm Lookin for a Bed

Ma, Now I'm Goin Up in the World

MARTHA LONG

PUBLISHING

EDINBURGH AND LONDON

This edition, 2011

First published in Great Britain in 2010 by
MAINSTREAM PUBLISHING COMPANY
(EDINBURGH) LTD
7 Albany Street
Edinburgh EH1 3UG

ISBN 9781845967031

This book is a work of non-fiction based on the life, experiences and
recollections of the author. In some cases, names of people, places, dates,
sequences or the detail of events have been changed to protect the privacy
of others. The author has stated to the publishers that, except in
such respects, not affecting the substantial accuracy of the work,
the contents of this book are true

A catalogue record for this book is available
from the British Library

Typeset in Caslon and ParmaPetit

Printed and bound by
CPI Group (UK) Ltd, Croydon, CR0 4YY

5 7 9 10 8 6 4

ACKNOWLEDGEMENTS

IN MEMORY OF ELLEN

Through those dark lonely days of my early childhood, when I tried to find something to hang on to, your lovely kind face appeared in my mind's eye. Then I would remember. You reached out the hand of comfort, soothing my mother as she sat weeping and desolate, crying for the want of a bit of human kindness, someone who cared whether she lived or died, a little shelter from the elements, a bed to lie down for a bit of comfort.

I stood watching, feeling very afraid. Trying to make sense of why my world was such a frightening place. Then you turned your attention on me, making me feel safe for a while with your tender loving care.

You filled my empty belly with a hot meal, covered me tenderly with a blanket as I lay dozing on your bed, listening to your gentle voice as you quietly murmured words of comfort to my mother.

You are my earliest memory of kindness, showing me the world can be a kind place. The few early treasured memories of a world that brought mostly pain. That great gift you had, Ellen, of a big heart, filled with kindness and gentleness, left a tremendous impression on me.

I always promised myself one day we would meet again. I wanted you to hear me say, 'Thank you, Ellen. Your kindness to me and my mother stayed with me all the days of my life.' Now, my deepest regret is I never found you again. I was too late. You were gone. Taken much too soon to your eternal rest.

When I did catch up, I heard you had searched for my mother, then later for me, in the hopes you would both meet again. It broke my heart. Yet, every now and then, your gentle face will appear in my mind's eye. It is then, somehow, I sense your presence is close by, particularly when I am most in need. You are letting me know I am not alone. Just like that time so long ago when me and the ma were lost in an uncaring world.

My deepest sympathy to your family, Ellen. They know who they are. May you rest in peace.

To the lovely Sangita. Thank you, Sangita. I am so very honoured by your tribute. Truly, it has meant the world to me. You are a very special lady.

To Bill, my publisher, without whom these chronicles marking my early life may never have seen the light of day. They perhaps may have lain in some dark hidden drawer, gathering dust as its edges curled, growing yellow through the long mists of time, making a meal for the bookworms.

To my editor, the lovely Ailsa Bathgate, whose eagle eye misses nothing, brooks no nonsense and sends me smartly packing back from the path where I am quite happily treading, but understood only by me and God, and the brightest of all bright editors! Ailsa!!

Last but not least, our faithful little mongrel, half-Tibetan, half-Yorkshire terrier. You were only a little ball of fluff, but you strutted your stuff, parading the length and breadth of the garden, watching and seeing off cats and rats and foxes three times the size of yourself! From your six inches off the ground, you were master of all you surveyed. Oh! We miss you terribly! Sometimes, in the quiet still of the dead of night, your ghostly bark can still be heard. Now you rest in a sunny spot in your beloved garden, under the shade of your favourite tree.

Lynkey, February 1997 – February 2010

I

I sat in the bath up to me neck in hot water. Ooh, lovely! That's one of the great things about this place – they never spare the hot water. No, I would be lost without it. I grabbed up the big bar of carbolic soap slipping around the bath. Got it! Pity, I thought, holding it up to examine it. It's only really for scrubbing the floors. That will take half me skin off! I managed to rob that out of the cleaner's bucket when she wasn't looking.

Right! Beggars can't be choosers! I rubbed it into me washcloth until I was satisfied, then lifted me leg to give it a good wash. 'Ohhhh! Grafton Street's a wonderland! DERE'S MAGIC IN DE AIR!'

I suddenly felt a draught and whipped me head around. An old woman came wandering in, looking at me confused.

'Where's Dickie? Where's me husband?' she moaned, sounding like she was near to crying.

'Eh? Oh, he's gone next door. Close the door quick, Missus! I'm getting an awful draught here.'

'Wha? I want Dickie!'

'Mrs Kelly! What are you doing out of bed? Get back quickly before Sister catches you.'

'Nooo! Let me go!'

The nurse tried wrestling the old woman out the door, but she was having none of it.

'You have to stay in bed! Now come on like a good girl . . . Who are you?' she suddenly asked, letting go of the woman's arm and coming at me.

Oh, Jaysus! I'm done for. I hid me face, ducking me head under the water. Then lifted it back, nearly suffocating. I let the wet hair streel around me face, hoping to hide it. I couldn't hear her right with all the water rolling around in me ears.

'What's this?' she roared, whipping me head around and pointing at me suitcase standing up against the wall. 'Are you a new patient?'

'Eh, yeah.'

'What's going on here? Wait a minute! You're that young one going around eating up all the patients' dinners, causing mayhem!'

'No, I most certainly am not!' I snorted, lifting me face and looking at her squarely in the eyes. 'I'm a hospital visitor. I come here visiting the poor patients who have no visitors whatsoever. And furthermore, they are always delighted to see me!'

'Yes! At lunchtime, when they are having their dinner, which you sit eating!'

'EXCUSE ME! I'm only helping them out! They don't want it, and it's a sin to be wasting good food.'

'I . . . this . . .' she said, lost for words, with her head whipped around making her hat spin, and her eyes crossed in her head. She was outa breath from trying to understand all the confusion.

'Look!' I said, snorting air up through me nose, hoping the bit of air would make me brain think, then getting on with me washing, playing for time.

'How did you get in past the porters' desk?' she asked, trying to keep her voice calm. Then she suddenly let rip, before I could get a word out, 'You know full well you are barred from entering this hospital, Miss! Your antics are well recorded. You even had the cheek to make yourself right at home one night in an empty annexe right next door to the morgue! The porter went down with a corpse and had to hunt you out! You gave the poor man the fright of his life!'

'Well, the dead don't need it!' I shouted. 'But I did!' I said, thumping me chest.

'This is preposterous! It is an absolute outrage!'

'Excuse me! I did no such thi—' I said, getting ready to deny everything else, before she opened her mouth again.

'This is not a hotel,' she interrupted.

'Well, really!' I gasped, sounding just like Sister Eleanor. Hoping to make meself sound respectable.

'Not to mention it is not even visiting time!' she spluttered, gasping for the want of a bit of air, with her face turning purple from all her outrage, as she calls it.

Suddenly I heard a man's voice whistling. I looked over, seeing a porter stopping his whistling, leaning his head down to get a good look at me through the open door. His mouth looked like he was blowing something and his eyes leapt outa the back of his head he was so intent at getting a good look at me. He even forgot about the patient moaning on the trolley that he was supposed to be pushing.

I let out a scream, grabbing me washcloth to hide meself. 'Aaaahhh! Nurse! Ye're lettin that man look in at me!'

'What?' she screamed, sending the door flying shut with a bang.

'Ooooh!' a voice moaned. Then the door whipped open again.

'Staff Nurse! Have you seen Mrs Kelly? She's gone missing.' Then the young nurse's eyes peeled on me, hoping to see I might be Missus Kelly. 'Doctor's on his rounds!' she gasped.

'What?' Staff Nurse puffed, whipping her head around in even more confusion. 'She was here a minute ago! Ohhhh! This is too much, Nurse! Can you not keep your eye on the patients even for one minute?'

'But, Staff Nurse, I was taking temperatures!'

'Stop prattling, girl, and go and find her! Quickly!'

I watched as they flew out the door with their heads going in one direction and their bodies in another, not able to decide which way to go first. Then they crashed into each other as the staff nurse made back in for me.

'Oh, for heaven's sake, Nurse! Pull yourself together! Go that way!' she pointed, waving her arm down the passage. Then she leapt back into me. 'Out, you! And if I see sight or hair of you again you will be in major trouble. Very big trouble,' she snorted, rattling her head like mad, making the cap shake as if she was having some kind of a fit.

'Certainly! I have no intention of staying here to be insulted!' I snorted back.

I shuffled me way down O'Connell Street, then stopped, trying to get a look at meself in a big plate-glass shop window. Me hair was standing up in all directions. Jaysus! The state of me! I thought, gaping at meself. I plastered it down with me two hands, yawning the face offa meself. Ohhh! Me neck. Me bloody neck! I have a crick in it. I walked on, rubbing it. That's the last time I am ever sleeping in a confessional box. I woke up in the middle of the night gasping for me life. The bloody air was all gone! I nearly suffocated meself. Then when I pushed open the door, crawling out of the box, I got an awful, terrible fright. I even started screaming me head off for all I was worth. It was the sudden shock of seeing all them statues staring down at me, an me still half asleep. I didn't recognise them for a minute, with their faces all lit up and their eyes glowing red in the dark. Jaysus! I didn't know what I was looking at! There they were, all standing up in the dark corners of the church, with the little red lights burning underneath, making me think they were a load of ghosts coming to get me. Gawd, Mammy! I'm still not the better of that! I thought, giving a shiver at the memory. That must have come outa me sleeping in the empty room next to the morgue. Never again!

I looked back, throwing me eye up at Cleary's clock, seeing the time was ten to eleven. Right! Just in nice time. I turned left, heading down Abbey Street, then crossed the road to the hotel. I peeked in the door, seeing the aul fella, the porter. He was stretched in his chair at the desk, scratching himself. Then he picked his nose, looking at his finger to see what he got. Ah, bloody hell! I have no chance getting past him! Think, Martha.

I straightened meself, getting ready, then moseyed in, sliding past the desk. I held me breath and kept one eye on him. I had just made it to the stairs, with one foot on the step, when I heard the roar.

'Eh! EXCUSE ME! Where do you think you're goin?'

I took in a big breath, letting it out, saying, 'Oh, I'm all right thanks, Mister! I'm, eh, just heading up the stairs!'

'I can see that! But wha business have ye in comin in here?' he barked, waving his hand around the place and landing it on his hips. 'You're no payin guest! I don't know wha yer game is, but ye can take yerself and yer bloody suitcase!' he said, waving his finger down at me suitcase and twisting his nose outa shape like he was getting a bad smell from it.

'Eh, excuse me, Mister! You are barking up the wrong tree if you think I'm only here to get up to no good! I'll have you know I am looking for me granny. Where is she?' I roared.

'Wha in the name a Jaysus are ye on about? There's no granny of yours staying here!' he said, slamming his fists on his hips.

'What! Then you must be blind, Mister! She came in here to use the toilet an she hasn't come back. So would ye mind goin an lookin for her!' I snorted, losing me rag.

'Listen!' he barked, shaking his head, with the pockmarked face on him turning red. 'Don't come in here tellin me my job! I am sittin at tha desk since half past eight this mornin!' he roared, bending his back and head, pointing in at the desk like he was bowing to it. 'An nobody, but NOBODY, has got past me fittin tha description. Now get out before I call the manager. You have no rights te be comin in here unless ye're a payin patron!'

'Right! But at least go and check the toilet! She could be lying in there now, dead. Dead as a stone corpse!'

'I will do no such thing. Eh, wha are ye talkin about? Stone corpse?! Wha the hell is tha, I ask you?'

I thought for a minute, hearing the words again. Then roared, 'You know what I mean! Stone dead!' I shouted, annoyed at making a fool outa meself.

He let a big breath outa his nose, shaking his head at me, then asked me patiently, 'Now, are ye goin to leave peacefully, or do I have to call the guards to remove you?'

'Huh! Bloody aul culchie! Only an aul culchie would be fond a callin the coppers!' I roared, knowing that insult would get a rise outa him.

'Get out! Before I raise me boot and send you flyin out tha door!' he roared, making to grab a hold of me.

I ducked under his arm, making to fly out the door, and went headlong straight into a man coming in wearing a long check apron, carrying a big tray of sausages and black and white puddings and chops. The lot went up into the air, and as I skated over the sausages, me eye lit on them for a minute! No good. They're raw! Then I was out the door like greased lightning.

'You whore's melt!' the sausage man roared.

'I'll fuckin brain you if I ever get me hands on ye again!' roared the porter as I looked back.

Then I shot me head forward just in time to see the bus barrelling down on me. I stopped dead, frozen for one second, doing a see-saw, rocking on me feet. Back? No! I leapt forward, tearing for the footpath. Made it! Phew! Nearly got me last gasp there!

The bus driver lashed open his little side window, roaring his head off at me, 'Get off the road, you stupid, dirty-looking pile a shite!'

'Ah, go on now,' I said, grinning and lifting me chin slowly. 'Ye're just jealous cos ye look like the back a yer bus! But that's a grand horn ye have there. Did you gerrit for yer birthday?' Then I turned tail and headed back up to Cleary's, making me getaway.

I better get meself a squirt of scent. It doesn't look like I'm going to be getting a bath today. Pity! I liked that place. The hotel bathrooms were nice and handy to get at. Just up the stairs and along the corridor. And it even had a thing on the bath for holding me soap and washcloth and Palmolive shampoo. Yeah! And I could take hours if I wanted, with nobody to bother me. Hmm, I had all me comfort there. Pity I couldn't get in today. I was looking forward to using me nice clean fresh towels I managed to grab off the nurse's trolley before I got thrown out.

I wandered back out of Cleary's smelling of Lavender Water. I sniffed the air, that's a bit strong. I put too much on. You can smell me a mile away. I stood looking up and down. It was drizzling down with the rain. And the wind blew me coat up around me legs. I pulled the collar of me coat up. Brrr! It's bloody freezing. I looked up at the clock. Half past twelve. Time for din-dins up at the hospital. Wonder what they're getting to eat for the dinner today? Never mind. I better keep me nose outa there for a while. Pity! Poor Arabella, Lady Arabella. She will miss me today. The poor thing gets no visitors. Imagine! Ending up in a paupers' hospital, left lying, dumped in a ward with no one to care whether she lived or died, and she the daughter of an 'aristocrat', as she called it. Her family owned half of the best parts of Dublin city in the old days!

I met her on me travels around the hospital. I do wander around, stopping to smile and chat to the patients, especially the old ones, when there's no one bothered with them at visiting time. It can be very lonely watching other people getting fussed over, and you lying there like a spare part. I know what that's like meself. Anyway, it's a grand way to pass the time.

The first time I wandered into the ward, I made straight for her because she was looking at me very intently with a big smile on her face. 'Hello! How are you?' I said. 'Would you like me to sit down for a chat? I'm a hospital visitor.'

That's what I call meself, I thought.

'I visit people for a chat,' I said to her. 'Me name's Martha. What's yours?'

'Arabella, Lady Arabella. How do you do, Martha? What a wonderful idea! Oh, how lovely, you are so kind! Yes, please, do sit down, dear,' she beamed up at me, patting the chair beside her bed, wanting me to sit down.

We talked for hours, with me listening to all the great balls, parties, dinners and dances they had in the big house over on the south side of the Liffey. She even got to meet the King and Queen of England – the old one, not the new one – when she was eighteen, for her 'Coming Out', she called it.

But the other patients are very good to her. 'Here, Missus!' – they call every woman that, even though she's not married. 'Have them few aul biscuits.' 'Would you like a bit of that cake?' 'Take them aul oranges. I have too much stuff.' 'Them relations of mine are tryin to start me up in me own sweet shop judgin by the amount of stuff they're bringin me in.'

Then they clap eyes on me, too. 'Ah, it's too much for me. Here, love, come over to me, an I'll give you a bit of stuff for yourself. I want to clear out some of this stuff! Me locker's collapsin wit the weight!'

Yeah, they're very good to me, too. There's eating and drinking in the place and all the entertainment I could want.

Right, I'm starving. So, what have I got left for eating? Hmm. Two oranges and a couple of custard-cream biscuits. That won't get me far. And I need to save them for later. By tonight, when it gets really cold, I may be falling off me feet with the hunger!

I could get the lovely smell of chips pouring out of Caffolla's café up the street. Pity I have no money. I would love to get me jaws into a big plate a chips! So, what now? Think! A big bowl of steaming hot soup would be even better. Bewley's! I'm desperate. I better get moving. I want to get there before the dinner-hour rush starts or I won't get a seat.

2

I could smell the lovely scent of coffee before I even hit the place. I rushed in the door, getting the lovely blast of heat straight away. I stopped to look. Self-service downstairs? No! You need money for that. Waitress service upstairs? Me eyes peeled into the women busy rushing around carrying trays held high in the air. They were piled up with plates of steaming grub. Me belly rumbled and me mouth watered. They were wearing white frilly aprons over black skirts, with matching white-and-black striped caps on their heads. They had pencils stuck behind their ears and notebooks hanging out of their pockets. Waitress service! That's better.

I rushed in, then stopped, looking for the best spot to sit.

'Are you looking for a table, dear?'

'Yes, please, I am,' I said quietly to the grey-haired woman with the hair coming out of her chin. I could feel meself rattling inside but hoping for the best.

She walked me over to a table and chairs against the wall beside the stairs leading down to the other eating place and the toilets. Good! I will be able to make me escape that way!

She handed me a white piece of paper showing what today's grub was. 'I'll be back for your order in a few minutes, love. OK?'

'Oh, yeah. Thanks very much, Missus.' Me eyes landed on the big silver thing sitting in the middle of the table. It was weighed down with cakes. You can help yerself to as many as you like then tell them how many you had. Gawd! Poor aul Mister Bewley! He's very trusting! Yeah, everyone talks about him. Mister Victor Bewley is a very good man they say. He does an awful lot for charity. He even gave all his workers

15

a share in all the cafés! Whatever that means. I suppose everyone owns a bit of the place they work in. I heard he was a Quaker. I read about them down in the library. They believe in peace. They have nothing to do with rowdy people or get involved in wars. They used to shake at the mention of someone threatening them in the old days. Quake, shake – that's what it means! I read up all about it.

Hmm! Me eyes whipped back to what's on offer for the dinner.

'Are you ready to order?'

Me head shot up, seeing the waitress whipping out her notebook and grabbing the pencil from behind her ear. I took in a deep breath. 'Yeah, thanks. I'll have the kidney soup and rolls with plenty a butter. Then I'll have the, eh, shepherd's pie. No! Give me the lamb chops and peas and mash potatoes and gravy. Then after that—'

'Right! That will do to be getting on with!' she puffed, losing patience with me, snapping the notebook shut. 'I'll get you your soup,' she said, giving me half a smile.

'Thanks very much,' I said.

I pushed the plate away feeling I couldn't eat another cake even if I got paid for it. Me belly felt like a cement bloke.

'Everything OK?' the waitress asked, appearing back beside me, whipping out her notebook. 'Now let's see,' she said, tapping the list in her notebook with the pencil. 'Soup, rolls, butter, lamb chops, peas, mash, two helpings of apple tart and ice cream! Did you have any cakes?' she asked, letting her eyes light on the empty silver cake holder. Then she whipped them over to the old woman sitting in front of me. She was wearing a big hat with a fancy scarf wrapped around her shoulders. The face on her was so painted and powdered she must have put the stuff on with a shovel. Me and the waitress watched, waiting for her answer. She put down her knife after using it for the last half hour to cut her cake into tiny little bits, then chewing for so long I was blue in the face watching. I wanted to see when and if she would ever swallow it.

She kept us waiting as she wiped an imaginary crumb off her mouth with the linen napkin. Then she lifted her baldy eyebrows.

They were marked in with a brown pencil. That was to show where they used to be. Then she stretched her eyeballs and curled down her mouth, flicking her eyes shut, much as to say, No! I would not be so common as to make such a glutton of meself! Then she finally opened her mouth and we held our breath.

'I have partaken of one, my dear,' she announced, making my Lady Arabella sound common.

'Oh, yeah, thanks very much,' I said. 'That was lovely altogether. I, eh, had the rest a them.'

'How many was that?' the waitress said, looking down at me belly bulging outa me skirt. I had to open the zip!

'Eh, I think it was five.'

'Let me see,' she said, thinking. 'We generally put out a dozen. I think that cake stand was just put out when you sat down.'

'Was it?' I puffed, feeling shocked I had eaten so many.

She peeled off the bill and plastered it down on the table. 'Glad you enjoyed yourself!' she said, smiling. 'Now! Here's the bill,' then took off to serve more customers.

The place was filling up fast. People were crowding in, looking hungry and wanting somewhere to sit. Jaysus! How am I going to get outa here? I picked up the bill without looking at it. Me eyes were flying around the room, watching and waiting. I was looking to see if the aul fella, the manager in the suit, was standing outside the door. He watches like a hawk, seeing everything that goes on. His sharp eyes took everything in at once, missing nothing. He was busy rushing in and out, leading people by the arm then pointing them to a vacant seat. Fuck! He's looking over at me, seeing the two free chairs next to me. I kept me eyes down, pretending to be busy examining the batch of new cakes that just appeared on the table.

'Are you all right, dear?' the waitress asked, wanting me to get going.

'Oh, I'm grand, thanks,' I muttered, me insides rattled with the nerves.

Two women made for my table. I watched the waitress head over to take an order in the far corner, then me eyes flew to the aul fella in the suit. He was watching me and the two people heading over to the free chairs beside me. Then his head was out the door again, making to ask the next batch of people to wait for a seat.

Suddenly I was up standing on me feet and lifting me suitcase from under the table and making me way over for the back stairs. I walked down without rushing, then past the toilets and the self-service and up the other stairs. I stopped before I got to the top, then lifted me head to see where the aul fella in the suit was. The cash desk was just to me left. I would have to pass that. But the aul fella was over to me right, standing just outside the dining room. He was keeping the people on the queue moving in as soon as someone left and, more importantly, making sure they went to the cash desk to pay the bill.

I held me breath, moving back down the stairs again. He only has to catch one sight of me and I'm done for! I wouldn't be able to turn back. I would have to go to the cash desk and then the game would be up! Jaysus! Pity I ate so much! When they see the bill . . . Wonder how much it is? Oh, bloody hell! Me nerves are gone! I moved up again, seeing him disappear into the dining room.

Right! Now's the time to move. I was up the stairs, turning the corner, then walking past the cash desk with the woman looking out at me through her glass box. I kept me eyes peeled ahead like I hadn't a care in the world, and walked on, looking into the distance, feeling me back prickle. I was waiting for the shout and the tap on the shoulder. I was out the door, turning left down Grafton Street, walking quickly now, trying to get lost in the dinner-hour rush. I turned left on to Wicklow Street and sat meself down on the side entrance to Switzer's, managing at last to be able to let me breath out, knowing I was free and clear, for the moment.

Jaysus! Enough of that! I may be starving be times, maybe even most of the time, but that is pure stupidity! I got carried away and nearly ate them outa the place. My intention by going there was only to get meself a hot bowl of soup. That way, if I was caught, they might have let me go. But, oh no! I had to go and lose the run of meself. Jaysus! It goes to show, Martha, if you give yourself an inch, you take a mile. Hunger is one thing but that is bleedin sheer madness! Imagine the bill if I ended up in court! *Two pounds ten shillings, your honour! That is what the bill came to for the amount of food she ate!* Well, it must have been near it anyway. That place is very dear. No, let that be the end of it. One more time doing that, I would be right back where I started. No, better to starve than that. Robbing is only for mugs. I'm at rock bottom now, just living on me wits, with no money, no job, no place to live and not one soul in the world to turn to. So, there's only one place I can go now and that's up!

'Would you move, please!'

I stood up, grabbing me suitcase outa the way, looking at the woman standing well back, waiting for me to give her plenty a room.

'Sorry, Missus,' I muttered, giving her a bit of a smile. She ignored me, just lifted her face and turned away, then started sniffing air up through the two narrow slits punched into the middle of her hatchet face. Then she rushed past, pulling her big fur coat well away from me, giving me a smack in the face with the big black leather handbag swinging on her arm. I rubbed me cheek, waiting for her to say sorry. But she was gone! Straight through the door leaving it swinging open. Then she stopped dead in the middle of the shop, making the big fur hat on her mallet head fly in all directions because she was so worked up about buying herself something she didn't know where to start first.

I could still feel the stinging in me cheek. Suddenly I put me head in the door, letting out a roar. 'Dyin lookin, aul cow! I hope you die roarin! Yeah!' I muttered. 'An I hope the pickpockets get their hands on all yer money!' I sniffed, rubbing me cheek. Bleedin hell! The cheek a her treating me like dirt. You wait, Missus! One day I will have the likes of you rushing and gushing all over me, wanting to know me. I will be somebody then. Because I am going to make it right to the bleedin top! I'll be the best at whatever I do. I don't care how long it takes me. But one day I am going to walk through this door here wearing a fur coat and a matching fur hat, then have them carry all me boxes over to Brown Thomas for another spot a shopping. Then they can deliver all me parcels to me mansion in its own grounds! It may take me years and years, I may starve, but I will get there. 'Yeah! So fuck off!' I muttered, nearly crying with the rage as I stood just inside the door, watching them all rushing around, trying to outdo each other spending money. One thinking they are better than the next.

Then I spotted the store detective flying her head in my direction. She stood watching, with her little beady eyes taking me in from head to toe. I moved back. Fuck! Them aul fuckers are still on the mooch. I remember that one. But she never got her hands on me! I was always too wide awake for her. But they're great gas to watch. Sneaking around the shop holding tight to their handbags, pretending to be shoppers. Then when they get the sniff of a robber, the chase is on, with you flying ahead, then stopping to see where they are before dropping something into your shopping bag then pretending to be intent on looking at something. They do the same thing. The pair of us giving sneaky looks to see what the other one is doing. I used to double back on them then come up behind them when they were peeping around the corner, intent on trying to spot where you'd gone without them being seen themself.

Yeah! These days that's great gas. I can have many happy hours giving them the run around, knowing I don't have to rob any more. Bleedin gobshites. They're not that good at the job. I can spot a robber a mile away just by seeing the shifty look on their face. You can smell the fear! Only last week up in Dunnes Stores, I came face to face with an aul one after wrapping half the shop around her body. She got an awful fright when our eyes locked on each other. There she was, hiding herself under all the coats in the back corner of the shop. I felt sorry for her. She probably had ten kids waiting at home, starving with the hunger. The husband was probably drinking all the money and wouldn't work in a good fit! I could tell by looking at her she was desperate.

'The store detective is on my tail,' I muttered.

The poor woman's eyes nearly leapt outa her head, whipping it around so fast, trying to spot them. I gave a big wink to the detective, grinning like mad, then headed meself over in her direction. The detective got such a fright I was on to her, she turned her back, pretending to be examining the ladies' jumpers. The poor aul woman spotted her too and took off in an awful hurry, shuffling like mad, desperate to make it out the door but getting herself slowed up with the amount of stuff weighing her down. Meanwhile the detective was raging! Now she knew she wouldn't get the glory of catching me robbing because I was on to her. While the real robbers had been cleaning the place out! Yeah, culchie eejits! They're not wide enough for us Dubliners.

Right! I looked around, shaking meself, then let out a big breath, thinking it's getting late. It's definitely time I got moving. Now, where will I go to get meself changed into me good clothes? I better wash me face and clean meself up. But I'm not too bad. I had that grand bath yesterday over in the hospital. OK! I'll head down to the quays. There's a nice hotel there just opposite the bus I need to take. Bus? I haven't got the fare! Never mind. They can't throw you off if you give them your name and address. Any address. I'll make up one. Now, what will I tell this aul one looking for the mother's help? Ah, play it by ear, let her do the talking. Lucky for me I spotted it in that newspaper dumped on the ground. I even managed to get tuppence for the phone call outa that culchie in the GPO. 'Ah, here, keep the thruppence,' he said after getting fed up waiting for me rooting in me coat pocket looking for the thruppenny bit I didn't have.

'Are you sure, Mister?' I said, pushing me luck! Sometimes I can be a right gobshite!

3

I walked up the short path of the house in a nice quiet cul de sac and rang the doorbell, planting me suitcase down beside me. Jaysus! I forgot about that! One look at that case and she'll think I really am very forward, expecting to get the job before she even decides to take me. Think!

If we don't suit each other, I'm taking the boat to England tonight. I have a job lined up there with me big sister, working in a pub. No, too young! Jam factory. So I have me suitcase all ready. Right! That is what I will tell her. Yeah, that will do.

I stood looking around at the nice trees along the footpath, taking in all the high hedges along the low walls of the houses. One house had a black Ford Anglia parked outside. Jaysus! That's a very old-fashioned car. A couple of houses down they had a little Mini parked outside. There's not too many cars around here. They must not be very well off. I turned around to press the bell again and the door flew open. I stared into the lovely made-up face of a woman with a huge belly. She's expecting!

'Are you Missus O'Brien?'

'Yes. Are you the girl come about the job?' she smiled.

'Yeah! Yes, I am.'

'You're the girl that phoned yesterday.'

'Yes! Martha is my name.'

'Right, come in. I had quite a few phone calls. I'm getting a bit muddled now about who is who,' she laughed, as I followed her into the hall and turned into a small sitting room. It was a bit dark and depressing looking, like nobody really came in here, and it had a musty smell, like the room never had a window opened.

'Now,' she said, sitting down, folding her hands in her lap, then trying to pull down the hem of her very short maternity frock. 'I need someone to help me around the house. You would have to do all the cleaning, washing up and anything else that needs doing. I have six children, all boys. The eldest is nine. Sam. And the youngest is a toddler. You will have bed and board, and I will pay you three pounds ten shillings a week, every Friday. Do you have any experience working with children?'

'Oh, ye—'

Before I could answer, she said, 'Mind, you won't really have much to do with them. I take care of all their needs. Now it is very important that you rise early. I need you up and downstairs by 7 a.m. sharp! My husband is a stickler for time. You will have to help me in the mornings with the children's breakfast and my husband's. You always serve him first. He does not eat with the children. They eat in the breakfast room. Well, it's really the kitchen, too! But my husband eats alone in the dining room. So you will have to look after him. Make sure he has everything he wants. He's very particular about his fresh grapefruit. It has to be just so. Not too much sugar.'

I kept nodding. 'Oh, yes! Of course!' I agreed, desperate in case she might not give me the job. But me heart kept sliding deeper into me belly the more she talked. I didn't like the sound of the husband. It looks like he might be a bit peculiar.

'What age did you say you were?'

'Eh—'

I started to think. But before I could get a word out she said, 'Oh, another thing! You have Sunday off and one night a week.'

Me mouth dropped. Fuck! I knew there was a catch!

'How soon can you start?' she suddenly asked, beaming at me.

'Eh, right away,' I said.

'Fine! Come on, I will show you your room. Then you can help me to get the tea. Evenings are always very busy what with having to supervise the boys' school homework. Oh, a woman's work is never done!' she sighed, trying to drag herself up the stairs.

I concentrated on carrying me suitcase up. I didn't want to look up and see any more of her white knickers than I already saw. I had an uneasy feeling in me guts. I couldn't decide whether I had lost or won. This is the easiest job I ever walked into. She seemed even more desperate to get me than I was to get the job, even though me life depended on it! Now, God, just let me keep this job and I promise to make it up to you for burning all them candles when I was sleeping in the church!

'Wake up! For goodness' sake, get up quickly! Noel is waiting for his breakfast.'

I managed to get one eye open and squint it up at Mary.

'Get out of that bed!' she shouted, putting the fear of God into me with all the excitement she was in. I yawned and stretched, still not able to take in what all the fuss was about, waiting to figure out why I was feeling so worried. She turned back at the door, shouting and nearly grinding her teeth. 'You are late! Hurry! It is already five past seven and here you are lying in bed.'

Oh! Then it hit me. Jaysus! Me new job! Me eyes spun around, taking in me new living quarters. I'm in a bed. 'Oh, right, sorry, Mary! I'm flying now.'

I dived outa the bed straight into me knickers, brassiere, vest, skirt, blouse and cardigan, slipping on me shoes after sending me pyjamas flying through the air. I took the stairs two at a time, fixing me hair up into a ponytail and buttoning up me cardigan at the same time. I blew into the kitchen, seeing Mary going mad, red in the face, trying to get stuff on a big wooden tray covered with a white linen cloth.

'Here, take this,' she said, pointing at the tray and landing down a glass bowl with a big yellow grapefruit cut in half. Me eyes landed on the blue flower sitting in a tiny little vase, then peeled onto the boiled egg sitting snug under a teenie-weenie little knitted hat right in the middle of a blue little plate with a silver spoon next to it. Then came a row of toast, all lined up in a silver rack, with the butter waiting next to it in a glass bowl. He even has for himself a china teapot covered with a tea cosy, a blue teacup and saucer with a matching side plate, then, for his extra enjoyment, marmalade in a little glass jug, with a silver cover and a tiny silver spoon sticking out.

Jaysus! This fella really gets himself minded, I thought, staring with me mouth open at the style of it all.

'Please take this tray into Noel. He is furious you are late. I even had to take the trouble to go up and get you,' she whispered, pushing the tray down for me.

'Oh, I am very sorry, Mary,' I whispered, feeling very nervous and shaky inside. I picked up the tray and she held open the door for me.

'In there,' she pointed, aiming her finger at the door off the hallway. She leapt ahead and opened the door for me, then closed it behind me and disappeared. A tall, thin, pasty-face man with thin brown hair was sitting at a round mahogany dining table reading the *Times* newspaper. He rattled the paper, snapping it into shape, then folded it very quickly and slammed it to one side as I made me way over. Then he started drumming his fingers on the table and tapping his shiny black shoes on the polished floorboards, making them rattle with his impatience. He turned his head away as I neared the table and stared out the window into the cold, frosty garden.

'Eh, good morning, Mr O'Brien,' I whispered, afraid of me life he was going to snap the head off me. I put the tray at the other end of the table and started to put out the dishes. Then he let out a bark.

'Leave it! Go!'

I looked at him, not sure what was happening.

'Out!' he said, waving his hand at me, then waving it at the door.

'Oh, sorry! Right!' I said, turning slowly then hurrying to get out of the room. I closed the door behind me and felt meself shudder with nerves and fear. Jesus! That man is a demon! This is not a place to be living. I took in a deep breath and walked back into the kitchen instead of making for the front door.

'Hurry! We are running well behind time,' the woman snorted, trying to spoon porridge, land it into bowls, and grab toast burning in the toaster. The kettle gave a piercing scream on the gas stove with smoke pouring out of the spout, and the lid started hopping. I didn't know what to go for first. Me head was whirling on me shoulders.

'Here! Take these and hand them out to the boys.'

I grabbed two bowls of porridge and whipped over to an alcove with two long leather padded seats facing each other and a table in the middle. Six pair of eyes all looked up at me, then down at the porridge, waiting patiently to be served.

'Hello! Will I serve you first?' I said to a little fella of about three. He shook his head and pointed to the biggest one. 'Oh! Right! Here you are! You must be Sam,' I said, smiling and handing a bowl to a thin, paled-face little fella that was the image of his father. He barely looked at me and took the bowl without saying a word. None of them spoke!

Jaysus! This is like a prison, I thought to meself. The kids are afraid to open their mouth. I rushed back, bringing the food as quickly as I could, then I got to the youngest, a little blondie boy of about two. 'Now! And that's yours,' I said, putting the bowl in front of him and lifting the spoon ready to give him some.

'No,' he moaned quietly, taking the spoon out of me hand and managing to get it the right way up then straight into his mouth.

Jesus! Even he is well trained. And he doesn't mind waiting till last. Because you have to serve them in order of their age. Jaysus! Even Jackser could learn a few things from the aul fella in this house! Then it hit me. I don't have to take blackguarding from this aul fella. He has no control over me. I am only selling him me labour. I can walk out of here any time I want! I felt meself lifting, a warm feeling of contentment spread through me. I started to feel easier in meself.

I dragged the vacuum cleaner, as she calls it, over to put it under the stairs. I made sure to wrap the cord around properly and not let it get tangled, or Mary will go mad. 'Right! That's all finished,' I said, walking into the kitchen as Mary was taking a casserole out of the oven.

'Really?' she said, raising her eyebrows.

'Yeah! Everything is done, Mary. I changed all the bed sheets and cleaned every room, including polishing and scrubbing the bathroom until you can see your face in it.'

She whipped open the door and stopped, staring down at the well-worn hall carpet, then threw her eye up at the carpet on the stairs. 'No! You better get the vacuum out again and give it another going over. I can see it still needs cleaning properly!'

'But, Mary, that is the very best I can do with that carpet. That is as clean as you will get it,' I said, staring at the bald carpet that should by rights be thrown out.

'Don't argue with me, Martha. Just do it!' she said, then marched back to the kitchen and slammed the door.

I cleared the last of the dishes off the kitchen table, bringing them over to stack beside the sink, then rinsed out the cloth under the hot tap and went back, wiping down the table. I gave the seats a wipe then swept under the table. Right, that's done, I thought, looking back and heading for the long press in the corner to put the brush away. Now for the dining room. I was just heading back out the door, holding on tight to 'Hitler's' tray, when a little pair of legs skidded past, nearly tripping me up.

'Ahh! Ohh! Take it easy!' I laughed, watching Cormac flying past hanging on to his helmet!

'Hurry! Everyone is in the car!' shouted Mary, grabbing him by the neck and hauling him out the door.

I could hear the daddy shouting, 'You need order! Discipline, young man! Preparation, preparation! This is what I keep trying to instil in you!'

I stopped to listen, hearing but not daring to move and get a better look out through the half-open door. The voices faded, leaving only a muffled sound as the car door slammed shut. I moved off into the kitchen, landing the tray down and sorting the stuff out for washing. Poor little mite! He's only a fuckin babby! Order! I'll give him 'Order' one of these bleedin days. Yeah! I know what that aul bastard needs. An 'Order' for a red-hot poker to be shoved up in his arse!

* * *

I just finished the last of the dishes and was wiping around the sink when Mary appeared. 'Martha. We have a busy day today!'

'Yeah!' I said, smiling up at her painted face. No matter what time of the day it is, she always has her face done up. Noel likes her to look her best, she told me one day!

'Yes, indeed we do! Come into the front room and collect all the clean washing. You can start ironing it in the kitchen.'

Merciful hour! I thought, landing me eyes down on the basket of washing filled to the brim. Then me eyes slid along the sofa, seeing even more of it. Jaysus! The couch is collapsing with the amount of stuff waiting to be ironed. I heaved up the basket of washing and swung it from side to side trying to get it down the hall and into the kitchen. 'It's heavy,' I laughed, landing it down in the middle of the floor.

'Oh, it has to be done! The children need clean clothes for school and Noel needs a fresh shirt at least once a day. Two if he has an evening business meeting! Then he may have to go out to dinner. Some days he has three! If he has to stay over for dinner in the evening, with his golfing partners in the club. But it's all business,' she sighed, sounding weary, but as if now she's gotten used to it.

'Right, let's get started. We don't have much time for chit-chat, Martha! It's going to be a busy day!' she said, whipping open the long press. 'Here! Take out the ironing board and set it up there. You can put all the ironed clothes on the table,' she said, pointing her pink fingernails plastered with nail varnish. 'I'm going to start preparing the evening meal. What day is it?' she asked the wall.

'Tuesday, Mary. Tonight I'm going into town to me shorthand and typing class. So I, eh, need to get into town early. I don't want to be late and miss the beginning of the class!'

I waited for her to say something. But she ignored me and started opening a recipe book. 'I'm looking for something special,' she muttered to herself, flying through the pages.

'The beginning of the class is very important,' I muttered to meself. 'I don't want to lose me place where they're at. I won't be able to catch up! Anyway! I want me money's worth!' I mumbled, wanting to talk about it, but there was no one to tell.

She looked over at me, staring at the iron, not really seeing me, then flew out the door. She was back in a flash swinging a pile of wooden hangers. 'Don't fold the shirts. When you have them done, hang them open on the hanger. Just button the three top buttons, to keep the shirt in place,' she said, hanging them on the knob of the long press.

'OK, Mary! So will I still fold down the collars after ironing them?'

'Yes, of course! Goodness! What else would you do?' she said, getting back to her cookery book and sniffing out a smile, shaking her head like I was a complete eejit!

'Ohh! Finished! That's the lot, Mary,' I said, wriggling me shoulders and letting out me breath, then rubbing me neck.

'Oh, good!' she said, looking up at the clock, seeing it was nearly half past two. She peeled her eyes along the pile of trousers, shirts, pyjamas, socks and a whole lot of other stuff all folded neatly and piled high on the table, covering every inch of space. Then along the seats. They were covered from one end to the other with even more stuff.

'Let's get these upstairs,' she said, grabbing hold of the shirts hanging on the doorknob on their hangers. She examined them carefully, one by one, making sure they were done to perfection. I held me breath, not wanting to do them again.

'Fine! Let's go!' she puffed, taking off with them while I grabbed up a pile from the table and followed her upstairs.

She went into her own room, closing the door over so I wouldn't see in, and I heard her opening the wardrobe. I went into the children's room, landing their clothes on the bed. They all slept in here, squashed into this little room with just enough space to squeeze in three bunk beds, one in front of the window, and a big press with a single wardrobe stood against the back wall. I had the third bedroom, the little box room, all to meself.

'Hurry up, Martha. Get all that stuff put away and come downstairs quickly. We need to keep going!' She was making a pot of tea and

I could smell toast. Me belly rumbled. I was always hungry in this house. When she wasn't looking. I would sometimes empty the whole box of Weetabix. Well, nearly! I had to leave something or she would get suspicious.

'Would you like jam or marmalade?' she asked me, whipping the toast out and spreading soft butter on it. It looked suspiciously like margarine to me. I hate that stuff! I would rather starve than eat that!

'Eh, jam, Mary. I don't like marmalade.'

'Hmm! It's good for you,' she muttered, landing two slices of bread and jam on me plate. 'When you are finished your lunch,' she said, trying to swallow half a sandwich stuffed with good ham, 'I want you to wax the dining room floor.'

I looked at her, feeling meself getting worried. That will take me the rest of the day and bloody night! I need to get out after tea, as soon as I finish up washing the dishes, I thought, feeling me heart sink and losing the hunger for me jam and bread. I put it down, deciding to get started straight away. Then the sooner I will be finished.

Her face creased up in a frown. 'Martha,' she said, trying to think of the best way of telling me something, 'Noel has decided to dock some of your wages this week.'

'WHAT?' Me heart leapt with fright and annoyance. 'But, Mary, he has already docked one pound ten shillings for that alarm clock he bought for me! Why didn't he tell me what I should get? I could have bought me own! That was an awful price to pay for a little clock! You can get them for five bob!'

'Martha, you were late for work! Noel runs a tight ship! You know that now.'

'And what about the other money he docked from me? I have hardly enough left to buy me few cigarettes after I pay for me lessons at the secretarial college! I can't afford to go out on a Sunday, Mary! I know I stay in to learn me shorthand but it would be nice to have me own money that I work hard for. I'm entitled to spend it the way I want!'

'Martha, you need to buck up with your work! Now! He has

complained about that dining room table. He says it is a disgrace. He wants you to polish it properly!'

'What! Mary, I use nearly half a tin of polish cleaning that table.'

'Well, you better use the whole tin if that's what it takes,' snorted Mary. 'It should be polished to a high finish. It should glow and shine like glass!' she growled, getting up and putting the plates and cups in the sink.

'Ah, fuck!' I moaned, wanting to scream and cry and dance up and down on the belly of that Noel bastard. Tear him limb from limb.

'His mother set high standards,' she mumbled, looking at me, making it sound like she wanted to make peace. 'I should know!' she said, giving a half laugh. 'I have to follow them, or, well . . . Marriage is not always easy,' she murmured, staring out into the miserable-looking garden, with the wind blowing rain and bare trees in all directions.

'But tomorrow is my birthday!' she said, snapping her head back to me, letting a smile come to her face. 'On Saturday he is going to take me to get my face done.'

'Yeah?' I said, opening me mouth staring at her. Wondering what she was talking about.

'Oh, yes! They have special make-up people. They show you how to put on your make-up,' she laughed, seeing me confusion. 'Look! See my eyebrows, they pluck them, give them a nice shape. Then I can keep them neat myself. They are marvellous! They say the American women are wonderful with putting on their make-up. They can see through their fingers! Now, tomorrow I am going to cook him a special dinner. It will be just the two of us! In there!' she pointed. 'I will be eating in the dining room with him.'

'Lovely!' I said, wondering if she was all there. 'But isn't that very good of him, letting you eat with him?' I said, dropping me head sideways, looking into her face, waiting for her to roar at the cheek of me.

'Oh, he is a wonderful man, really! You have no idea how thoughtful he can be. Like now, for example. I don't have to take the children on the bus any more. For the last month I have been able to take it easy. He takes them all in the car. Even the two youngest are dropped over to his mother! How many men would be that thoughtful?' she snorted, thinking about all the other bowzies out there making their wife's life a misery by having to walk miles to the shop! Well, we do that too – walk the long miles to the shops, but then she has me to carry the messages back!

'How well off can you get?' I said, thinking he put an awful lot of thought, too, into how much he can stop outa me wages! Fuck, he's messing with me. Now he has it coming!

I flew into the kitchen, hearing pots banging and Mary moaning, trying to shush one of the kids crying, and little Paddy keening. Another day in this mad house, I thought, stopping dead, taking a bit of a yawn and scratching me head, wondering what to dive into first. Me head shot over to little Paddy holding his hands up to his eyes, keening. He was afraid to let rip, knowing his aul fella would march in letting a roar outa himself.

'Ah, what's the matter?' I said to him.

'Here! Stop dallying there and give me a hand,' snapped Mary. Her face red, with the fear of God in her eyes, trying to do a hundred things at once.

'Oh, sorry, Mary. What's wrong with little Paddy?' I whispered, looking over at him, seeing him lift his head to look over at the mention of his name.

'He's not well! Look! Get on with the work. Take the tray and get Noel's breakfast set. Here! Put the sugar on his grapefruit. Only a half-teaspoon, mind!'

'OK, Mary!'

She grabbed the burning toast, staring at it, then decided to butter it anyway and put it on the children's plate. I watched as she belted over to the table carrying bowls of porridge. She wasn't looking!

I grabbed out the two sachets of powder from the apron pocket Mary let me wear and sprinkled the powder onta the grapefruit, then dumped the rest into the teapot, including the second packet. I put the lid back on and dumped the tea cosy on top just as she hurried back.

'Right! Ready!' I said, picking up the tray and marching out the
door. She opened the door then banged it shut behind me. I walked
across the room, keeping me eyes peeled on his white shirt with the
gold studs in the cuffs, then lifted me eyes to follow the rest of him
up to his face. He was staring in shock at the white watermark stain
in the middle of the table. He lifted his eyes, looking at me like he
couldn't believe what he was seeing.

'What on earth is that?' he roared, but not too loud, because he
kept it down into his chest.'

'Wha?' I said, knowing it would annoy him. He told Mary I had
to improve me diction, I was a bad example to the boys and so I
wasn't to speak to them until I had improved! Fuck that!

'Oh, that was only an accident, Mister O'Brien. I knocked over
the vase a flowers when ye were letting Mary, eh, the wife eat, eh,
the special dinner youse had the other night! It happened when
I was cleaning up after ye's,' I said, throwing one eye at the table
and the other on his face, seeing him staring in shock at his lovely
dinner table. 'Tsk, tsk,' I muttered, shaking me head in sorrow. 'Aw,
Gawd! Isn't tha just terrible now! It looks like it's destroyed for life,'
I moaned.

Then he came back to his senses. 'How dare you?' he roared. 'What
my wife and I do is most certainly none of your business!'

'I was only sayin! You asked me!' I said, sticking up for meself.

'You will have little or no wages this week!' he shouted. 'The quality
of your work is very poor! Very poor indeed!' he snorted, grabbing
the tray and snapping his fingers at me. 'Now get out!' he roared,
waving his hands in the air at me and snapping them at the door.

'Certainly!' I said, raging in me heart at him but not one bit afraid.
'Enjoy your breakfast, Mister O'Brien,' I breezed, holding me hand
on the doorknob and throwing me head to the tray.

'What? Did you say something? Come back here! Take this tray!
Now! One other matter. Has my wife told you all your duties when
she goes to the nursing home?'

I hesitated, wondering about this.

'You will have to take over her duties, Miss! It is expected she may

go in any day next week,' he said, taking in a deep breath, looking like
he was happy at the idea. Then his eyes peeled on me. From me feet,
they moved slowly, taking in me bare legs, then up the rest of me,
stopping on me chest. I felt sick watching his eyes narrow, looking
like he was thinking what use he could make of me. I waited until he
had his fill, then his eyes landed on me face, seeing I was watching
him, staring with me face turned to stone and me eyes letting him
know I knew exactly what he was thinking. I turned around taking
the empty tray with me and walked out of the room. He didn't say a
word. Poor fucking Mary! What a blind stupid cow she is! That rat
bag is nothing but a chancer. A good bang of this tray on his mallet
fucking head would smack sense into him! And she needs a good kick
up the arse! I really feel sorry for them poor kids in there. So! Jacksers
are not just the only wasters. The educated are just as fucking bad!

I was polishing away at the dining room table, rubbing white spirits
mixed with other stuff to get the white watermarks off. Which I did
on purpose in the first place! Nope! Certainly no accident! I knew that
would get a rise outa Mister fucking would be, if he could be, Adolf
fucking Hitler! 'Ohhh, you are my hearttt's deelight!' I sang happily,
murmuring to meself, when the front door suddenly flew open.

'Mary! Mary! Where the blazes is that woman?'

I stopped me singing, holding the cloth halfway to the table. Ohhh!
That sounds like himself. He's back! That was quick!

'What? What's the matter, Noel?' I heard Mary keen, sounding
shocked and worried.

'Telephone for the doctor quickly!' He flew up the stairs and straight
for the toilet before she could get another word out. I listened, then
went back to me cleaning. Yeah! It must be good stuff! I told that
fella in the chemist me ma said she needed something strong – extra
strong, the strongest stuff he had in the place – because me granny
hadn't had a good shit for weeks! We needed to clean her out! Lovely!
It's working! A doze of the scutters should put a stop to his gallop for
a while! I nipped out the back door for a quick smoke while Mary
clucked and the doctor fussed upstairs with the quare fella.

I sucked on me cigarette, letting the smoke out through me nose, then taking in the cold, damp February air up though me nostrils, giving me a sharp pain through me head and stinging me lungs. Still, it's nice to be out of that house, even if it's only for a few minutes. I feel like I'm in prison in this place. It would put years on you!

The kitchen door opened and I stamped on the end of the cigarette butt, flying in and closing the back door and locking it. Mary didn't notice. She was too busy wringing her hands, looking very worried. I said nothing, just stood waiting for her to tell me what she wanted me to do next.

'He looks very grey,' she said, looking at me like someone had told her he was on death's door!

'Oh! What did the doctor say?' I asked, knowing full well what was wrong.

'He said it was probably something he ate. Hmm, Martha,' she said, clearing her throat. 'You prepared his breakfast—'

'His grapefruit,' I interrupted. 'You did the rest, Mary.'

'Yes, I did, didn't I?' she said, thinking, looking a bit lost with all the worry. 'He, eh, thinks it may have been the way you handled his food. Did you wash your hands this morning?'

'Ah, Mary! For the love a God! You know only too well I'm always washing me hands when I'm handling food. Anyway, I never touch food with me hands if I can avoid it. Haven't you seen me often enough? I am only too aware of not spreading me germs onta food, Mary! I'm well trained at that. The nu—'

I shut up. Nearly walking meself into it by mentioning about the bloody nuns!

'No, that's not the problem,' I said, shaking me head.

'Well, I better bring him up a hot drink. Get the bottle of milk out of the fridge there,' she said, looking very tired. 'I will boil some of that and put ginger into it. Maybe some dry toast will help.' She shook her head, looking very fed up at this interruption to her routine and worrying about that gobshite, who will be right as rain as soon as he gets rid of all that pile of shit blocking his brain!

* * *

I sat working at the kitchen table, trying to learn me shorthand. Thick lines, thin lines. Ch J d a. I practised, writing and learning, trying to learn the letters and how they go. I lifted me head, thinking, looking over at Mary supping a cup of tea before she goes to bed and standing dreaming, looking out the window into the dark, icy-cold night. Her belly was nearly hitting the floor. She will be going in to have the new baby any day now. I can't stay here. As soon as she's gone out that door, that rotten aul bastard will be straight after me! No. Tomorrow's Friday. Let's hope I get some money in me wage packet. That aul bastard has been finding one excuse after another to stop most of me wages. As it is, I am now practically working only for me bed and board. Miserable aul fucker! No. I won't say anything until she hands that to me. Then I'll tell her I'm leaving, straight away. If I tell them now, well, I wouldn't get a penny. Anyway, there's no telling what might happen to me with that aul fella. He is even vicious enough to try and give me a bit of a hammering. Especially if Mary is not here. I can tell by the look of him. He would like nothing better than to let fly with his fists. I've seen him leathering the arse off the kids when they fight or make too much noise. Yeah, I can even see the mad glint in his eye when he's doing it. Like he is really enjoying himself. No. I'll go up and pack me case now. I haven't much to pack anyway. Just me one set of good clothes and me night things. Then I'll get to bed. Pity I have no other job lined up. But I never got the time. I was barely out the door except on Tuesdays to go to me night classes. Please God I will find a job straight away. Otherwise . . . Well, I'm barred nearly everywhere. They all get to know you after a while. Dublin is a very small place. Everyone recognises everyone else. Even if they don't know who you are, they know the face.

4

I stood staring up at the church, seeing it all shut up for the night. So that is that. Now what am I going to do? I left it too late. I turned me head, walking away not really able to think or feel or care any more. I walked on, sitting meself down on the steps of the big church house next door. A car pulled up at the footpath and a man jumped out, locking the car. I took no notice.

'Hello! What are you doing sitting there in the cold?' he laughed, looking down at me.

I lifted me head as far as his shoes, working me way up to his heavy, long black wool coat, with a scarf wrapped around his neck. Then ignored him, dropping me head back to stare at the ground again. I just don't have the energy to bother about anyone or anything. Nothing is of any interest to me. I'm too weak and tired.

'What's this? Don't you have a home to go to?' he laughed, waiting for me to answer.

I said nothing.

'Have you left home? Run away? Look, come with me.' He bounced up the steps and put a key in the door, opening it, then stood, waiting for me to move.

I looked up at him.

'Come on. It's OK. We can have a little chat.'

I still didn't move.

'You can't stay there all night,' he laughed. 'Do you need help? Perhaps there is something I can do to help. It's late now, so we better be quick.' Then he suddenly bounced down the steps again and whipped up me suitcase and took my arm. 'Come with me. I don't bite!' he laughed quietly, giving me a gentle tug and pulling me up the steps.

I followed him in the door and reached over, taking his hand off me, brushing it away. I didn't want anyone touching me. He looked down and laughed. I stood for a minute watching him shut the big heavy door, then he was off, flying down a big corridor, switching on lights as he went.

'Come on, follow me,' he said, nodding his head in the direction he was going.

We went into a huge old parlour room with big pictures of saints on the wall. 'Take a seat,' he said, pulling out a chair from around a big mahogany table. He sat down opposite me and stared, thinking what he wanted to say.

I watched him, looking at him suddenly sweeping back his big head of silky brown hair that collapsed in a wave covering his left eye.

'So! What is the problem?' he said, folding his hands on the table and leaning across to me.

'I have nowhere to stay,' I muttered quietly, feeling me face stiff from the exhaustion and the hunger and the cold. Just like the rest of me. Everything inside of me had frozen solid from living on the streets, walking day and night.

'Why? Do you live in Dublin? Where are you from? Where is your family?'

'I just left a convent,' I muttered.

'What were you doing after you left the convent?'

'I was working.'

'Do you not have a job now?'

'No.'

'How old are you?'

'Sixteen.'

'Very young. You can't possibly be roaming the streets at your age. OK! Let us go,' he said, standing up.

I stood up, half standing, wondering where he was taking me.

'Come along! I shall take you to a bed and breakfast for tonight.

Then in the morning you can come and see me. Then we will talk. See what we can sort out.'

I listened, saying nothing.

'Is that OK with you?'

'Yes. Thanks.'

'Right! Let's go,' he said, whipping the door open and waiting with his hand on the doorknob.

I picked up me case and walked out the door. He shut it behind me and followed, putting out lights as we went back out to the front door.

I trailed him down the steps as he bounced ahead of me, opening the car door. 'It's not far but it's much too late to walk. Come on, hop in and we'll drive there.' He reached over and grabbed me suitcase, flinging it onto the back seat, and hopped in the driver's side, leaving me to make me way around to the other side. We took off heading down towards the quays. I could feel me eyes closing with the sleep.

I shifted meself for more comfort and lay me head back on the seat, barely taking in where we were going.

'OK! You sit here,' he muttered, and leapt out of the car.

I shot up in the seat and watched him heading up the steps of an old two-storey house with a basement and railings all round. A big sign outside swinging on a pole said 'St Christopher's B&B'. He waited, moving himself up and down with impatience after ringing the bell, then leaned over to give it another ring, and the door suddenly opened, leaving him swinging back on his leg cocked out behind him, trying to get his balance. I watched as he said something, and the woman looked from him to me. Then he shot down the steps and grabbed me suitcase.

'Come along. You can stay here for the night and come and see me in the morning around nine o clock.'

'What! So you can give me a good talking to about not hanging on to me job?'

'No, that is up to you,' he said, shaking his head and grinning at me.

'Fine, so long as we know where we stand!' I muttered, stepping into the dim hall with the musty smell of years of damp and landing meself just inside the door, standing on the shiny brass metal to hold down the carpet. I looked back, seeing him fly down the steps and jump into the car. Then he was gone, vanishing down the icy road in a puff of blue smoke.

I'm not having him think he can tell me what to do just because he's paying for me bed and breakfast! But I'm desperate. With every day that passes now, me luck seems to get less and less. I can't seem to get back on me feet with finding a job and somewhere to live. Jesus! Imagine being able to climb into a warm bed at night and feel safe. It seems like years now, not only just weeks since I last had that kind of life. But I keep coming up against a blank wall whichever way I turn. Me heart isn't even in it any more. I'm too run-down looking. I could be mistaken for a beggar. I feel like one and it must show on me face. Yeah, and in me voice. I walk around asking in shops, and even the dealers in Moore Street, if they know of any jobs going. They all give me funny looks after skinning me from head to toe with their tired weary eyes. The eyes that show they are all-knowing. See everything, say nothing. Then they give me a shrug of the shoulders that says, *Sure, everyone has their troubles! I have me own worries!* So they just mutter, 'No, love. Sorry! I wouldn't know anythin about tha kinda thing.' Then look away like I was someone mental they didn't want to know. Their heads shaking at each other in confusion. *Can't make that young one out at all! Wha kinda carry-on is tha? Walkin aroun the streets in threadbare order carryin a suitcase! Don't I do be seein her wit me very own two eyes day after day, Missus! An she from Dublin! What's all tha about? I don't know. Must be somethin wrong wit her. Ah, God love her! An she's harmless, the poor thing! Ah, well, we shouldn't talk bad about the afflicted. God bless the mark! We shouldn't be sayin things like tha. It might come back on us!*

Fuck! There has to be a way! There is! But what? The priest might know someone. Still and all, I could be walking meself into trouble, getting mixed up with nuns and priests again. Asking them for help only puts me back in their clutches. Jaysus, yeah! If I'm not careful,

I could end up being put away in a bloody convent again, scrubbing floors and stuck behind barred windows.

This time it would be in one of them places where they lock up the women. The aul nuns don't need much excuse to get their hands on you. I know that only too well! How many of them have they whipped back and locked up in the country? Even some of the kids got sent away to the reformatories because they were giving trouble! Fuckers wanted to do that to me too. Only the courts wouldn't let them. Jaysus! They could say I'm not fit to be let loose! I'm not able to look after meself. I might get into trouble! That's all the excuse they need. Only this time, they would be the ones able to decide when and if it suits them to let me go. Now they have a record of me, because I was in their care.

Fuck! If only I could go back to the ma. Then they couldn't touch me. No, not with someone to claim me. I could feel me heart flying with the pain of the worry of it all. Always watching out to make sure no one was ready to pounce on me while I dozed against the back door of a café or a factory hidden up a back lane in the pitch black at the dead of night. Me heart lepping into me mouth at a sudden noise, expecting someone to jump at me with a knife. Then letting me breath out, feeling it warm me face, and the pain hitting me from the icy-cold frost as I watched, seeing only a black cat streak out of the dark, making a flying leap for the rubbish bins, pouncing on the back of a rat sniffing around the rotten leftovers.

I sat hunched one night, me legs up around me, trying to keep warm, listening and watching with me stomach turning in disgust as the rat twisted and squealed, mad with the fear and pain, desperate to get away, fighting for its life. The cat screamed with rage as it tore into the rat, lifting one claw while the other gripped, pinning the rat down, and sinking its claws deeper, then lowering itself, covering the rat with its body, sinking razor-sharp teeth down on the head of the helpless rat. I dropped me head down into me lap, not able to look any more. That could be me if I came face to face with a madman.

The sudden thought that I'm still safe hadn't made it to me chest.

Me heart kept lepping with the fright. I listened to it thump in me ribcage, then ease off as the relief slowly smothered the fear, melting into just one long ache that shuddered out in a deep sigh. Me chest jerking with every breath as I slowly got over the fear that someone was going to do me harm. What will I do? Take a chance or turn me back on his help? Ah, no! Take it easy, Martha. They would only do that if I was stupid enough to let them. I just need to keep me guard up, that's all.

'Are you coming in or not? You're letting out all the heat! And get off me brass!'

I looked up into the grey wrinkly face of an aul one gripping a tight hold of her dressing gown. She was trying to keep the collar wrapped around her neck to keep out the cold.

'Look! You're destroying it!' she roared, pointing down at me feet planted on her bit of brass.

'Sorry, Missus!' I muttered, shifting meself off her brass. Then I let me eyes slowly peel up to her bony head. I was looking at the few bits of hair she had. It was stone grey mixed with a bit of blue. The hair was all wrapped up in tight curlers, and the lot kept together with a black net. I stared at her white shiny skull with all the hair missing.

'What's the matter with you? Are you simple or what?' she suddenly roared, losing patience with me standing here waiting for her to tell me what to do.

She leant her face into me, trying to see if I really was stupid. I leapt with the fright, shaking me head and blinked, trying to wake meself out of me doze and bring meself back to me senses. I could hardly stand up with the tiredness. The weeks living on the streets with no sleep has caught up with me.

'Come on! I haven't got all night to stand here watching you gaping!' she snorted, grabbing me inside and slamming the door shut with an almighty bang. 'I want to get me night's sleep!' she huffed, grabbing the nightgown tighter around her neck and taking off in a hurry.

I trailed after her, dragging me suitcase as she puffed, trying to gallop herself down the dark hall in an old man's pair of slippers twice the length of herself. We got nowhere. I kept bumping into her when she stopped to pick up the slippers. Jaysus! Why can't she buy herself a new pair with all her money? She makes walking in them flippers look like she is trying to make her way through heavy weather. Or she could be mistaken for one of them deep-sea divers without the suit!

I followed her up the stairs, then waited, standing on a little landing while she stopped for breath, hanging on to the staircase. Then we were off again. She swung open a door at the end of the passage, smacking on the light. I crept in past her while she stood holding the door open, watching me with a suspicious look. She could tell by the state of me I was living on the streets. I could see her counting up the money for me night's bed and wondering if I was worth it after all. She probably thinks she will have to spend half of it anyway buying a box of DDT to fumigate the place. Me eyes landed on a big bed weighed down with heavy eiderdowns and blankets. I stared at the two white fluffy pillows sitting on top of the lovely white sheets. Me heart gladdened and I suddenly let out a big sigh, dropping me shoulders, and smiled happily up at her. 'Thanks, Missus!' I muttered, making me way over to the bed.

'Now! I want you gone out of here by nine o clock, or earlier if it suits you!'

Me heart slipped. Ah, Jaysus! I was hoping for a long sleep. That's very bleedin early! I stared at her, letting her see me face drop, hoping she could see I thought she was a miserable aul cow.

She lifted her nose, dropping her mouth in disgust, looking like she was wondering why she was so kind-hearted to be putting up with the likes of me. 'Now! I like to be gone meself out of the house by half nine. I'm a busy woman! I intend to be first on the queue down at that butcher's. I want to get me hands on a nice bit a tripe for me lodgers' dinner. Or maybe instead I might get a bit of that neck a lamb. Hmm, that comes in on a Tuesday,' she muttered to herself.

I stood by the bed still holding me suitcase, waiting for her to go and close the door. She didn't move. I let go of the suitcase and sat meself down on the side of the bed, letting out big sighs, hoping she might notice.

'Hmm,' she muttered, getting lost thinking about all her doings for the next day.

Ah, Jaysus! Will she ever stop? I let out another huge sigh, collapsing me face onto me hands, waiting patiently for her to stop her rambling and let me get into the bed.

'I could do that for tomorrow's dinner,' she muttered, slapping her mouth with her finger, her eyes blinking up at the ceiling, forgetting all about me sitting here dying to leap into the bed. 'Tuesdays. Yes! That's definitely the best day for getting the nice cheap cuts of meat.'

'Eh, Missus!' I interrupted. 'Can I, eh, get into the bed?' I whispered, afraid she might turn on me and throw me out, but still wanting to get me money's worth.

'What?' she roared, blinking like mad, trying to clear her eyesight, then looking at me like I was asking her to give me something for nothing.

'Can I just—'

'Yes! I heard you! I'm not deaf!' she roared, rushing over to drag me off the bed. 'Don't be sittin on the side of me good bed. You'll sag the mattress! And here! Don't destroy that good eiderdown.' She whipped it off the bed, folding it, and rushed over to put it sitting on the floor of an empty wardrobe. I was left looking at a thin aul thing that was eaten alive by moths and had definitely seen her through the Boer War.

'Eh, sorry! But excuse me, Missus,' I said, gritting me teeth in annoyance. 'I'm going to need that heavy eiderdown to keep me warm. It's bloody freezing.'

'Beggars can't be choosers,' she moaned, whipping down the blankets and sheets so that I couldn't do any more damage to her stuff.

'But what about the quilt? Why did you put it on the bed if you don't want people to use it?' I roared, nearly crying at me loss. I was looking forward to getting buried under that.

'There's no need to be impertinent!' she sniffed, lifting her chin at me like she had a bad smell under her nose.

'But what about the quilt?' I snorted, losing me patience.

'That's only for show,' she explained, leaning into me, trying to be patient with me ignorance. 'To make the room look nice. Well-reared, decent people would know that straight away,' she moaned, folding her arms, daring me to contradict her.

Jaysus! This aul one is stone mad, I thought to meself, looking away from her in disgust.

'This is my house, you know! I don't normally take in the likes of you. So be thankful! I'm only doing this because that lovely priest, Father – what's his name? – himself asked me to. Now get into that bed and don't go rambling around this house! I'm a very light sleeper and I can hear a pin dropping. And switch off the light! I don't want no big electricity bills left after you. I'll give you five minutes. No more than that, mind!' she snorted, waving her bald head up and down, shaking the hell out of her finger, threatening me.

Suddenly I had enough. Me chest started heaving up and down with all the annoyance wanting to erupt outa me. Before I knew what was happening, I lost the rag. Without even thinking, I heard meself say, croaking and squealing with the exhaustion, 'Ah, listen! Fuck off, Missus!', me face going red with the rage. 'Stick you an yer so-called bed and breakfast right up yer fuckin arse! I'm goin!' I whipped up me suitcase, making for the door, trying to push past her.

'Here! No! You stay here,' she roared, grabbing me shoulders and steering me back into the room, her bony fingers digging into me like steel rods, poking the life out of me.

I moved back over to stand beside the bed, rubbing the pins and needles flying up and down me shoulders. Jaysus! That aul one is made a steel, vicious aul cow. I glared back at her, ready to tell her in even more no uncertain terms what I thought about her and her bleedin B&B.

'Father brought you to stay here for the night and here you'll stay. Now get into that bed and don't let me hear any more cheap aul guff out of you. Ye're disturbing all me lodgers! Now ye better be aware of this. Like I said, I start all me cleaning exactly at eight-thirty. Well, maybe a quarter to nine. I won't be washing me kitchen floor tomorrow. That's not due until Thursday,' she muttered to herself. 'So you better be down in the kitchen no later than eight o'clock. Or you won't be gettin any breakfast outa me!' she snorted, tightening her mouth and waving the finger at me, really losing the run of herself after now forgetting she was supposed to be all grand and respectable.

'Oh, God! Please make her stop,' I moaned, burying me head in me hands. I only want a night's sleep in peace and quiet. No, I'm saying nothing. I'll doze here and let her go as mad as she wants. Even this is better than nothing. Right! That's what I'll do, even as me temper started to rise again. Right! No losing the rag!

I started snorting air in and out of me mouth fast. That's supposed to keep you calm. 'Thanks, Missus!' I squeaked, gasping on me temper, making me voice sound like I was being strangled, feeling desperate to get the satisfaction of screaming every curse I could think of right into her hatchet face, then rush out the door, telling her to wipe her arse on her aul eiderdown. But then I would only have to face another cold dark night sleeping up a godforsaken, pissy, rat-infested alleyway, at the mercy of the world and the fucking weather, with the rain, snow, sleet, and icy winds trying to lift me off me feet and blow me away. No! Not on yer nelly!

I started humming a tune in me head. Ohhh! Yes it is grand to be beside the seaside! The door suddenly slammed shut while I was lost in me own world. I stared, listening to the silence. Me head whipped around the room in case she was hiding. She's gone! I held me breath in case she came back. 'No! Definitely gone!' I muttered out in a big breath. I listened, just in case. But all I could hear were the traces of her voice still rattling around in the cold air of the room. Jaysus! That aul one is stone mad! The neck of her to treat paying customers like that! Well, the priest is. Then it hit me. Did he say he would pay? Oh, holy Jesus! Did I tell him I have no money? I can't remember! Maybe he thought I was paying. Right! I better make meself scarce as soon as I wake up. Just in case. I won't wait for the breakfast.

I clamped me eyes on the lovely bed waiting for me and felt a surge of heat flying up me chest, and I smiled happily, rubbing me hands with the happiness. This is all mine! Then it hit me. I rushed over to the wardrobe, whipping it open, and grabbed up the eiderdown, feeling the weight of it, and threw it over the bed, wanting nothing but the best of comfort. I pulled open me damp wool coat and left it on the bed, peeling off the rest of me clothes. They were warm and damp. Even me skin felt cold and damp. That's from all the wetting I got. I shivered in me skin as I opened me suitcase, grabbing out me pyjamas. At least these should be OK. I haven't worn them since I got fired from me last job. No! Fuck! They're damp too. Must be because the suitcase got soaked with all the rain and snow. Me eyes landed on the hot water bottle. Pity I can't ask that aul biddy to give us a sup of hot water. No! Not on yer nelly, Martha. I've had enough madness for one night, I laughed, tearing into the bed and grabbing up all the bedclothes. The sheets were a bit damp, but who cares? This is better any day than a kick up the arse!

Ohhh! I shivered with the happiness tingling all through me body as I slid up and down and all around, trying to bury meself deep down into the soft mattress, feeling the lovely heavy weight of the bedclothes snuggled all around me. Ohhh! This is lovely. I'm in the height of comfort. Gawd, Missus! Am I glad you didn't throw me out on me arse after losing the rag. Ah, maybe that's just her way. It's being old and ailing that makes her very cranky. She likes to keep busy but can't do as much as she wants. Yeah, that's it. She probably has a heart of gold! Ohhh! This is heaven, and the lovely peace.

I heard only the quiet of the room and the sound of a car backfiring in the distance as I gently wriggled me head on the pillow, looking for the deepest and softest part. Me eyes started to feel very heavy and I could feel a smile on me face of deep contentment. It's just for one night. But for now I'm safe! Nothing and nobody can get me now. I won't come to any harm this night. 'Ohhh! Thanks, God!' I muttered. It's so lovely to feel safe and warm, and have the lovely buzzing sound of peace and quiet all around me.

5

I woke suddenly with the fright. What is that? Where am I? I lifted me head off the pillow, looking around the half-dark room. I stared over at heavy curtains covering a big window, trying to come to me senses. I could hear a cat crying, coming from somewhere close, and the sound of pots and dishes banging. Am I sleeping outside a kitchen café?

Then I heard footsteps passing outside the door. I listened, holding me breath, then heard a door slamming. Suddenly I woke up. Oh! The B&B! I'm in a bed! I stretched, feeling the lovely heat and softness, and wriggled over on me side, snuggling down, burying meself deep into the mattress, laughing, delighted with me comfort. Hmm, lovely. I could feel meself dozing off into another sleep. I yawned hard, feeling exhausted, then started to sink back into a deep sleep. Then it hit me. I got a sudden electric shock running through me with the fright and I turned icy cold. I could feel me heart slowly dropping into me belly with the thought. I better get up! I have to get out. It must be early morning, judging by whoever it was that went out the front door. They've probably gone off to work.

I turned over slowly, lifting the warm blankets, and swung me feet out of the bed, landing them on the black varnished floorboards. The cold in the room hit me straight away and I grabbed for me clothes sitting on the back of the chair, wanting to get dressed and get it over with. I'll leave on me pyjama top. It's nice and dry now. That will keep the rest of me damp clothes off me skin. That way I should keep lovely and warm. I wonder what time it is? It still sounds very early. I don't hear the sound of many people on their way to work yet, or even the noise of much traffic coming from the street.

I walked over to the window and pulled back the curtains, letting in the grey early-morning light. Then me eyes clapped on the street outside! Ah, Jaysus! Would you believe that? More fucking snow! I looked over at a woman wrapped up in a black heavy coat with a scarf and woolly shawl covering her shoulders and mouth. She was staring down at the thick snow, taking little steps in her brown boots, trying not to break her neck. I looked up and down the street, seeing thick heavy snow covering all the roofs of the shops and houses; even the road was thick with it. I stared at the tyre marks made by a big lorry, and it glittered shiny and white, making the road look very treacherous altogether. Not another car or soul in sight. Jaysus! I'm going to have to go out again in that! I gave a shiver, feeling suddenly tired and weak, and even old.

I turned away from the window, landing me eyes on the bed. It looks so warm and cosy! I wonder if that old woman needs a bit of help. I'll tell her I'll work just for me keep. She won't have to pay me anything. No! We would only end up killing each other! I wouldn't last a day with her. Jaysus! I'm not in the mood to face her. She better not be looking for any money outa me. Ah, to hell with it! I'll tell her the priest said he would pay. Right! Better get moving. I put the bottom of me pyjamas in the suitcase and took off out the door, wondering if I should chance going down for me breakfast. No harm in trying me luck! Even if he's paying. I wonder if it's extra for the breakfast?

I could murder a pile a rashers and half a dozen eggs and a plate of fried bread with six sausages! That would keep me going for a while. Well, he did say bed and breakfast, so that means I get the two, even if you do have to pay extra. Jaysus! Wish I knew more about these things. No wonder half the people think I'm stupid!

I crept down the stairs, not wanting the aul biddy to hear me yet. Not until I found me bearings. Wonder where the kitchen is? I heard a door opening then footsteps coming up the stairs. It's her! I recognise the heavy breathing!

'So! You managed to get yourself outa the bed then?' she roared, coming up the stairs of the basement, catching me unawares as I landed in the hall. 'Do you want a wash?'

'Eh! Wha, what do you mean?' I asked, not knowing what she was talking about. Gettin outa breath at the shock of her appearing outa nowhere.

'A bath! A bath! Surely you have come across one of them in your time?'

'Eh, is the water hot?' I whispered, afraid to annoy her.

'Of course it's hot! What kind of house do you take this for? And while I'm at it, if you don't mind me saying, you could do with a good wash before you expose the poor unfortunate public to the smell of ye!'

'What?' I screamed, me heart hammering in me chest with rage at the terrible insult she just landed me with. Ah, enough is enough! 'Well, Missus! You can go and fuck yourself! Shove your bath up your skinny arse! Yeah!' I snorted, trying to get more wind into me lungs. 'But before you do that, why don't you go and drown yourself in it first? You would probably be doing the public, especially the butcher and yer bleedin lodgers, a big favour!'

Her chin dropped down to her skinny chest and her eyes bulged outa her head while she busied her hands, wiping them like mad on the tea towel she carried. Then she stuck it inside the apron strings wrapped around her belly and asked me, 'But, sure, how could I stick the bath up me if I've already drowned in it? Sure, you make no sense at all! I knew as soon as I laid eyes on you, you hadn't your wits about you!'

Me mouth hung open trying to take in what she was saying. 'Ah, to hell with you!' I roared, picking up me suitcase and marching off down the hall making for the front door, feeling too tired to argue any more. Somehow I knew she was right. I didn't have me wits about me, as she called them. I seemed to be going around like I'm not half all there! But still an all, it did hurt to hear her say that. She is a vicious aul cow!

I opened the front door, slamming it shut behind me, taking me time going down the stone steps. They are all covered in thick inches of snow. 'Fuck you, Missus!' I muttered to meself, creeping along the icy path, making me way off this street. Of course I would have loved a nice big hot bath. Who wouldn't? So how did that all go wrong? Why didn't I get one? Oh, yeah! She insulted me! Bleedin hell! I think I'm losing me marbles. I'll be forgetting me own name next. But I'm so bloody tired!

I walked up the steps of the house holding on to the railings and grabbing hold of me suitcase in the other hand. Me bloody hands are frostbitten. They're locked solid around the handle of the case. OK! Here we go! Hope this priest doesn't start asking too many awkward questions. Gawd! I wonder if he can help me? What can he do? Know of a job somewhere? They know everyone and know everything that's going on. Hmm, that's the problem. They know too much about people's bleedin business!

Right! Just tell him to get stuffed if he starts making a fuss. Maybe he will start telling me I would be better in a home. 'For a little while,' I can hear him saying, 'until you get a bit older then find your own feet.' Fuck, yeah! No! I won't bother with him. It's better not to take the chance.

I turned, heading down the steps, and walked on, looking up at the big church next door. Maybe I should go in there and have a little rest. I'm still feeling worn down even though I managed to get meself that bed last night. Yeah. Good idea. Wish I had something to eat. Haven't had much at all really for weeks now. Except the few apples I managed to pick up off the ground without the dealers catching me down on Moore Street. I walked into the church, seeing the lights glowing in the lamps all around the statues. It felt warm and peaceful, and I could smell the incense from the benediction. They must have had that last night.

I noticed the coffin up the top of the chapel with the purple cloth wrapped around it. They do that for the dead. I wandered up to take a look. Flowers and wreaths were lined all round the coffin and memoriam cards stood on top. I leaned over to get a look. See who it was.

'In memory of Jim, from all your friends in the Seamen's Mission.'

Poor Jim, whoever you were! Ye're all gone now; it's over for you! I knelt down and said a little prayer for him. God, look after Jim. I hope he had a good life. May he rest in peace.

I looked around, seeing me and Jim were the only ones in the chapel. Well, I'm sure he's still hanging around waiting, watching to see what happens to his body. Not feeling like? . . .Well! He's in no hurry, eternity will wait for him. I can sense things – people, things they don't want you to know. Or even things they don't know themselves. I can tell sometimes when they're sick and they're not aware of it. Sometimes even what is making them sick. Yeah, even places, especially when something bad has happened in it. Sometimes I turn up when someone is not expecting me but somehow I know they are in trouble. Yeah, it has happened to me time and time again. I was always like that. Ever since I was a little child. It's a sixth sense or something. The old people were always telling me I had it. I know and see things, they said, that other people don't know. They used to laugh and say, 'Oh, that one was born before! This is not her first time round.' I think maybe lots of people do have that. But they don't notice.

I started to feel meself doze off and jerked me head up. I looked around, seeing I was in the middle of the chapel. People can see me straight away when they walk in. I got up and headed meself over to the other side, the dark part, and sat down in a little alcove. Not too many people bother coming up and around here. It's too far when the church is empty. I rested the suitcase down on the kneeler and lay down on the bench. I put me arms under me head, resting me face in me hands, and started to doze off. Me chest shuddered with a sudden breath. I got the lovely feeling of rest and peace, with the bit of heat coming from the candles burning rosy red in their lamps.

I woke up, lifting me head. Ohh! Me bloody head hurts and I'm stiff all over. I wriggled, trying to stretch the pain out of me neck and back. Me eyes felt red and sore, and it's freezing with the cold. I sat up and watched an old woman with a black shawl wrapped around her head and shoulders, kneeling in front of the statue of Our Lady. The statue had a wreath of little golden lights burning around her head and a long blue flowing robe painted in gold around the sleeves and hem.

The old woman was whispering her prayers, holding up a black pair of rosary beads. She moved them slowly around her fingers as she got to the next prayer. I feel weak with the hunger. What will I do now? I better get something to eat. Where? How will I do that? Ahh, God almighty, I'm not in the mood to move anywhere. Jaysus! I better do something, though. Sitting here is not going to get me anywhere.

The priest! To hell with it. I'll go and see him. It can't really do me any harm. I can always walk out. Yeah!

I rang the doorbell and waited. Me heart is in me mouth. Supposing he doesn't have any time for me? Ah, stop moidering yourself, Martha. Jaysus! I wouldn't have any of these problems if I was still robbing me butter. Think of all the money I made over the years!

'Yes?'

I looked up into the face of a fat man bursting outa his trousers and half the dinner poured down the front of his jumper. 'Eh, can I see the priest, please? He told me to come and see him this morning.'

'Well, you're more than a bit late for morning time. He's not in. He's away.'

'Oh,' I said, feeling the life go outa me.

'Come back tomorra.'

I watched as he was just about to slam the door in me face. 'Eh, excuse me,' I said, waking up and putting me foot in the door, 'is there another priest here? I want to see someone.'

'No! They're all busy. Now would you mind taking your foot outa the door and move off.'

'No!' I said, getting me other foot in the door and staring him in the face. 'I want to see the priest with the shiny brown hair.'

'Which one? There's tons of them!'

'With goldie brown hair?' I asked.

'Yeah! That's just what I said,' he moaned.

'The one with the big mop of goldie brown hair,' I said, trying to remember if he gave me his name. 'He told me he would be here. Look, Mister! I need to see him! Now I'm prepared to sit out here all night if that's what it takes. I want to see him. Are you going to let me in?' I stood me ground, with our eyes locked on each other. Him trying to decide if I was important enough for him to go and bother himself getting the priest for me. I could get the stale musty smell of dinner and years of not bothering to change his clothes.

'Come in and I will see what I can do. They're at their dinner. So you'll just have to wait.'

'OK! Thanks, Mister,' I said, happy I might be getting somewhere.

'Wait in here,' he said, showing me into a very old-fashioned parlour with a big white marble fireplace and pictures of saints and an old big press with a big statue of St Anthony sitting on top. I pulled out one of the chairs pushed under a long wide mahogany table and sat down. It feels nice and comfortable. The chair was padded and covered in old black leather that was all cracked from years of wear and tear. There was a very heavy musty smell in the room, like it hadn't been dusted for years and years. Jaysus! The nuns would never stand for this! They have nightmares about dust. They wake up screaming about it. Everything in the convents is polished within an inch of its life. I suppose men are different. They don't notice. They're much more out and about. Nosing into people's business. Taking charge of everything! Well, anything to do with money!

The door flew open, making me jump with the fright. 'Well, well! If it isn't the little waif!' he roared, staring at me with a big smile on his face. Then he shut the door and sat down opposite me on the other side of the table.

'So! You decided to come back then,' he said, speaking in a very grand accent. He pulled out a packet of Carroll cigarettes and took one out. 'Would you like one?' he said, holding out the packet to me.

I moved me head up and down slowly without saying anything, and reached over, taking one before he changed his mind. Hmm, so he doesn't mind me smoking! Most people ate the head offa ye. 'Put tha cigarette out before you kill yerself! Ye're too young to be smokin!' they roar. Maybe yer man is not so bad after all!

'So! What is the problem?' he said, leaning back in his chair, making smoke rings and watching them curl around his head.

I said nothing, just sucked on me cigarette, watching him and keeping meself to meself. I don't trust him! There's something about him. He's wanting me to like him, make me let down me guard. I'm supposed to be thinking I can trust him. Yeah, and even though he's an aul fella, well in the thirty mark I would say, he reminds me of a young fella somehow. The way he acts and bounces when he walks or moves. Still, beggars can't be choosers!

'Oh, bother!' he suddenly said. 'Wait here. I have something I must do first. I won't be long.' Then he sprang out the door, leaving a draught behind him.

I sat waiting, watching the cars and people going past the window. The cars were going very slowly, keeping well back from each other. The dark was beginning to come down already and the snow had hardened into shiny ice on the road. With the really bad cold coming down for the night, people were keeping their heads down, pushing to get going faster, intent on getting in out of it. But they had to watch every step. Especially the old people. I watched an old woman make her way along the railings of the house, holding on to the black bars tight. She kept stopping to get her breath, then moved on slowly, after fixing the scarf tight around her head, shoving it well down inside the collar of her coat. She looked like she was afraid of her life of slipping. I pulled me coat collar tighter around me, glad to be in out of it. I felt more content now. Maybe that priest will help me. He seems very nice, really friendly.

The door shot open and he was back, stopping to turn a sign on the door that said 'Do Not Disturb'. Then he slammed it shut and came rushing over to the fireplace. He dropped on his knees and plugged in an electric fire sitting in front of the fire grate. 'Awfully cold in here! Brrrr! It's absolutely freezing weather,' he said, rubbing his hands together. 'Are you cold?' he said, making it sound like I had done something wrong the way he creased his eyebrows.

'Yeah, a bit,' I murmured.

He grabbed a chair from under the table and pulled it over beside the fire. Then he dragged my chair, with me still sitting in it, and put it sitting next to his and planked himself down, stretching out his long legs. 'Now!' he said, grabbing me around the shoulders and pulling me close to his chest. 'Tell me! What has happened?' he whispered, breathing down me neck.

I could smell his dinner and the cigarette smoke off his breath. There was a faint smell of aftershave off his skin and even mothballs off his suit. I suddenly felt meself curling up inside. I pulled me shoulders together, tightening meself inside, trying to make meself smaller and move away from him. I wasn't expecting that. Priests don't do that! Not in my life anyway. The ones I always met gave me and the ma the run out the door because we were begging, with me ma hoping to get a few shillings. They didn't really see me. I was scruffy and dirty, with me head walking with lice. They were always glad to see the back of us. But priests are supposed to be holy. They are supposed to keep their distance. Like the nuns did in the convent, and all the other nuns and priests I met in me life. But this priest is different. He doesn't act like a priest. Maybe that's because he's very posh! He sounds very like my friend Lady Arabella. She really is a toff. He must be one too. He acts like it.

'Are you frightened of me?' he suddenly said, pulling me face to look up at him.

'Eh, yeah, eh, no,' I said, feeling very shy, not knowing what to say.

'You poor thing,' he said, grabbing me to him again. 'You have never had love and affection in your life. Isn't that so?'

I didn't know what to say. I never thought about it. Love? Affection? Oh, yeah! That's what I must have been looking for all them years when I used to tear around the convent looking and waiting for Sister Eleanor. But I never struck lucky. Too many people after her all wanting the same thing, I suppose, now I come to think about it. But I never put a word to it before. Suddenly I felt like a little child. Yeah! That's what I want! I thought, feeling meself go warm and special all of a sudden. He likes me, and I have him all to meself. There's nobody else around fighting to get at him. No other kids demanding to be heard. But I'm not a kid any more. I'm past that. I have to find a way of making something outa me life.

'What are you thinking?' he said, putting his fingers on me chin, lifting me eyes up to him.

I looked away. Somehow I can't take in what is happening. I'm hot and cold. Me nerves are on edge.

'Why were you in the convent?' he whispered quietly. 'You can talk to me. I am a very good listener, you know.'

I felt me head empty. I couldn't open me mouth. It sounded lovely, the way he said it. But talk about what?

'Do you have any family?' he murmured, leaning his face down to get a look at me.

I shook me head. 'No,' I mumbled.

He crossed his legs, taking in big sighs, and just stared from me to the fire, watching the bars burn an orange red. They glowed around the fireplace, throwing a soft light on the pictures, making the shadows of people passing by dance up and down on the walls. I looked over at the window, seeing the day was beginning to lose the light. The early winter evening was starting to draw in the night, making the rest of the room creep into darkness.

He slowly sniffed in a deep breath, putting his hand in his pocket and pulling out the cigarette packet again. He lit one up and handed me the packet without saying a word. I took one out, holding it, waiting for a light.

'Are you going to tell me your name? Or is that top secret too?' he whispered, leaning his head into me. Then he roared, throwing back his head, giving an almighty laugh. 'Well! I shall tell you mine!' he said, lowering his head and waving his finger.

I laughed.

'Ralph! Father Ralph Fitzgerald!'

'My name is Martha,' I said quietly.

'Martha! What a beautiful name! A very ancient name. Classic. Then of course we have Saint Martha.'

'Yeah, the worker,' I muttered.

'The worker,' he repeated after me, nodding his head and smiling. 'Indeed! That is what you wish to become.'

I said nothing. Just went back to staring at the fire, enjoying sitting here in the heat, next to him for company, and feeling peaceful. I would be happy to just sit here and do nothing else.

'You know our Sacristan and his wife take out a little boy from an orphanage. Actually, it is a convent in the country,' he said quietly, looking at me then looking at the fire, breathing in the smoke, drawing it deeply down into his lungs and holding it there, then breathing out through his nose, making a loud sound, keeping his mouth closed. 'Do you know! He, the little boy, once said to me, "My daddy could be a film star. I think he is. Imagine! I could go to the pictures and sit watching the film not knowing that I'm watching my daddy!"'

I listened, watching him imitating the little boy.

Then he shook his head, saying, 'Poor little chap. He has no idea who his father is. Do you know your parents?'

'My mother,' I murmured.

'Oh! Where is she now? Do you know?'

I said nothing.

'So, you have no family. Is that it?' he said.

I said nothing, just took another puff of me cigarette, wanting to keep me business to meself.

'Hmm. Sixteen and all alone in the world. My, life has dealt you rather a blow. Bloody awful, really. I play bridge. It's a card game!' he said, giving me a big grin, showing me his snow-white teeth, with dimples on his white, creamy-looking face. 'I should think the cards are stacked against you, my little one. Now! Tell me about this convent. When did you leave?'

'A few months ago,' I muttered.

'And what have you been doing since?'

'Working,' I said.

'Yes, you little sausage! I know that! But doing what?'

'Housework. Minding children.'

'Hmm. Perhaps the nuns can sort you out. They should be able to organise that without too much trouble.'

'They did,' I said. 'But every time I lost the job. They have had enough of me.'

'Nonsense! They will of course help you. Now, give me the address. We must get moving. The traffic is starting to get heavy,' he said, flicking his head and looking out the window, seeing all of the cars with their lights on, sitting back to back.

'It's getting late! Come on! Let us go. Give me the phone number. Do you have it handy or shall I look in the phone book?'

'I have it. I can give you the number,' I said, giving up, not wanting to argue with him. Then I said, 'But you are wasting your time. Sister Eleanor won't take me back. We have to leave at sixteen.'

He ignored me, intent on getting himself moving. 'Hang on! I shall go and get my coat. Meet me outside the door. The car is parked across the road.'

I picked up me suitcase and started to walk out the door and down the passage. He bent down and switched off the heat, then galloped out behind me, switching the light off in the room and flicking the sign back to 'Available'. Somehow I had a feeling of being empty. For a while there it was lovely. It felt like I was not on me own. Now it was over. Even if Sister Eleanor decides to give me another chance and help me get a job, I won't have that feeling again, of being special. He will go off about his business and I will go about mine! I sighed, thinking happy times definitely only last a very short time. I suppose that's to keep us going – hoping it may be around the next corner again.

The car swung around and in through the big black gates, taking us up the long dark avenue. I looked up at the big old oak trees standing guard along the drive, protecting the convent and the nuns and children from the bad winter storms that blew in. The wind and rain would come howling down from the wide-open spaces of the fields and screech through the trees, shaking and lifting, mad in its fury to tear down anything in its path. The green fields where I once played and laughed and cried but mostly fought are all covered in snow now. I shivered, getting a sense of meself here. It wasn't a happy time. I pined for a hug, wanting Sister Eleanor to think me special. Jaysus! Was that not a bloody waste a time!

The priest slowed down as we reached the front entrance of the convent. His eyes took in the huge house, following the buildings attached, going for miles, with the big stone steps leading up to the front door. He spun the car around to face it back down the avenue, making a loud crunching noise on the gravel, sending the pebbles on the ground flying in all directions. He turned off the engine, leaving everything in silence.

'Looks rather a bleak place in winter,' he muttered with his head swinging around, taking in the length and breadth of the place, then letting his eyes peel over in the direction of the farm as we heard an animal roar, then the sound of buckets slamming and a man's voice, his shout, roaring over the fields, reaching us in the distance, loud and clear, the only sound to break the stillness of the quiet of the night, with the white fields shining against the clear dark sky and the stars twinkling down. I held me breath; the priest was very still. It felt like we were the only two people alive. Then he turned, looking at me, and said quietly, almost in a whisper, as he rested his hand on me shoulder, 'Martha, we really must move. Come on. Let's go.' Then he was out of the car, taking the steps two at a time.

I humped me case outa the back seat and trailed up the steps, and stood meself behind him, not wanting to show me nose back here.

The door opened and an aul nun peeped around, hanging on to the door not wanting to open it too wide. 'Oh! Goodnight, Father!' she crooned, seeing it was a priest with the dog collar wrapped around his neck.

He smiled down at her, showing his dazzling white teeth. 'Good evening, Sister. May I see Sister Eleanor?'

'Oh, indeed you may,' she clucked, opening the door wide and waving the priest in. She nearly closed it on me, she was that wrapped up in looking after the priest.

'Sorry, Sister,' I said, giving the door a little push to get meself in.

'Oh! Eh, yes. Come on in,' she said, looking around to see if any one else was coming.

'Take a seat in here,' she said, opening the door into the best parlour and waving him in. I trailed in behind. 'Would you like me to get you something, Father, while you are waiting?'

'No! No, thank you, Sister. I really must not delay.'

'Oh! Have you come far, Father? The weather is shocking! Shocking altogether! Maybe a nice pot of tea would go down well. Something to warm you up while you are waiting for Sister?'

'Eh, yeah,' I mumbled, standing behind him, giving him a poke in the back. He spun his head around to look at me. 'We could have something to eat, Father,' I whispered, looking up at him, desperate for a bit of grub. I hadn't eaten anything in days.

'No, no! Thank you, Sister,' he said, shaking his head. 'I really would like a quick word with Sister, then I must rush. Bother!' he said, whipping up the sleeve of his coat and pulling down his black leather glove, looking at his wristwatch. 'I'm running late for a meeting!'

'Oh, I understand,' she said slowly, looking up at him with her mouth open and her eyes shining, waiting to do his bidding. 'Right so! I will run out and tell Sister you are here. Is she expecting you? Who will I say?'

'Father Ralph Fitzgerald.'

'Oh! Lovely,' she puffed, crossing her arms under her cloak, letting out a big sigh of contentment. Then she rushed over to pull out a chair from under the long, beautiful mahogany table that glowed red in the light. 'Take a seat, Father! You might as well take the weight off your feet.'

'Thank you,' he said, snorting in air, letting the nun hear it, beginning to lose his patience. He pulled off his gloves and stuck them in his coat pocket. Then he planked himself down, letting his arse drop into the high-back chair, and spread his arms across the table, rubbing the shine off with his hands, looking fed up and snorting out more of his annoyance.

'Isn't that a beautiful finish on that table, Father?' she said, eying the marks he made. She waited, then when he said nothing, she muttered to the silence, 'Sister? Where would she be this time of the night? Maybe I will try the chapel. She could be in there getting in a few prayers. Poor creature never gets a moment to herself.'

Then she was gone out the door, closing it slowly behind her, still smiling. The priest lifted his eyes slowly to the ceiling, taking in big breaths. 'Oh, nuns! Nuns! Nuns!'

'Do you not like nuns?' I said, grinning up at him.

'Did I say that?' Then he muttered to himself, looking around the walls, taking in all the holy pictures, 'Poor old thing is in her dotage. Probably thinks she is doing something marvellous!' he said, opening his coat and putting his hand inside his jacket. He pulled out a pen and little black notebook from the inside pocket. Then he wrote something down and tore out the page, handing it to me. 'Here! This is my name and telephone number.'

I stared at it.

'You may like to contact me sometime in the future. Perhaps you might like to let me know how you are getting on,' he said, nodding at the piece of paper.

'OK! Thanks, Father,' I said, jumping up to put it safely at the bottom of me suitcase. I don't suppose I'll bother ever seeing him again, I thought. But you never know! There's no harm in keeping it anyway.

I sat back down at the table, feeling out of place. This is the first time I have ever sat here, I thought to myself. I looked over at the fireplace, remembering the first time I arrived here. It was just like tonight – dark and in the middle of the winter. I was waiting for the Reverend Mother to come. Gawd! I was afraid of me life! Not knowing what was going to happen. Now that's all behind me. I'm free! Gone from this place. Yet here I am, back again and still feeling the same. Nothing has really changed, except I'm not a child now. But I still feel like one.

6

The door opened and Sister Eleanor came in, stopping for a second to take me in. I watched her face as she narrowed her eyes, closing them down. Then she blinked, looking away from me, and hurried herself in, making straight for the priest.

'Oh, good evening, Father! You are very welcome,' she said, putting out her hand to shake the priest's, then sat herself down.

'Good evening, Sister! I wanted to talk to you about this young lady here, Martha. I found her wandering the streets in some distress. She has nowhere to go, Sister!' He waited for her to say something.

She just nodded slightly, listening, not taking her eyes off him, waiting for him to finish what he had to say.

He breathed in hard then held it and said, letting his breath out, 'Martha needs to stay here in the convent with you for a short while. She has nowhere to stay and she needs to find a job.'

'No, Father! I'm afraid that's not possible,' she said, shaking her head, giving me a look that said I had no right to be here. 'The girls leave here when they reach sixteen. That is the end of it, I'm afraid, Father.'

'But what will she do? I mean, where is she to go?' he said, holding out his hands then folding them again.

'I'm afraid, Father, that is not our business. I mean, if there was a problem,' she said, looking at me, thinking, 'there are places. If it proves too much or they are finding it difficult to cope. We do have places,' she said slowly letting her eyes rest on me like she was examining me.

I felt me heart race with the fear. I know the fucking places she's thinking!

'No, thank you, Sister!' I snorted. 'I know the places you are talking about. But I don't need that, thank you very much! I am well capable of looking after myself and finding me own way in the world. In fact, I can do it better then most of them.'

'Really?' she said, with a smirk on her face. 'Well, then! There is nothing further to talk about.'

'Yeah!' I snorted, the rage boiling up inside me because she has no use for me now. But that's not what she used to say when I worked myself to the bone, down on me hands and knees fucking scrubbing floors. Oh, I was a grand girl then! 'So what about all the other lazy lumps?' I roared. 'Some of them are older than me and you took them back for a while. Some of them are even staying here right now!'

'Who?' she said, with her face turning bright red.

'Miller for one! She never did a day's work in her life!' Then I stopped and took in a big breath, saying quietly, 'Sister Eleanor,' I said, barely above a whisper, because the pain of not being wanted was ripping through me on seeing clearly now she never even really liked me. 'You were always the same! You nuns had your special pets. Them that were out in the cold got sent away to a reformatory if they didn't toe the line! I will never be good enough for you! I see that now!'

'Please! This is doing no good! May we please just discuss the matter?' the priest said, looking upset and holding out his hands again.

'Look, Father! What she is saying . . . Well, there are special circumstances. Martha, would you please get up and wait outside,' she said, waving her finger at me and lowering her head, not wanting to look at me.

I got up feeling I had lost the one thing keeping me going. I had worshipped the ground Sister Eleanor walked on. She was the first person I ever thought cared about me. Now I know she never really cared at all! She just wanted to get the work outa me. Just like me ma. I lifted me suitcase and walked out the door, feeling cold and empty inside myself. Jaysus! Will I ever learn? What an eejit I am.

I opened the front door and stepped out, closing it behind me. That priest was wasting his time. I've just been getting me hopes up all day for nothing. Ah, to hell with them! I shoulda listened to myself in the first place. Anyway! Don't let her pain you! You always knew deep down, Martha, that she had no time for you. It was just better to pretend, because where do you go to when you want someone to care? It was easier to keep her face in your mind, seeing her smile because she was happy to see you. But it wasn't really true. You had to give her something. Bring her a present. Work hard for her. But thinking you might be special was better than facing the world with no one in it. Well, fuck them all! That's the end of me and this place. I will never set foot here again as long as I live. Ohhh! Was I bloody right! Treacherous bastards, them nuns. Right! So the next time you warn yerself about something, listen!

I walked through the village, passing the little sweet and grocery shop. It was all lit up and looked warm and comfortable with mountains of stuff for eating. Nelly Ryan, one of the spinster sisters who own the shop, was sitting behind the counter, reading the newspaper with her little half glasses sitting on the end of her nose. Me eyes lit on the packets of biscuits and boxes of cakes and bars of Cadbury's chocolate. They're all stacked high under the glass counter. I stared, with the hunger making me fall off me feet. No! I can't help meself! They're all in there, waiting for me to come in and get them! How? I could mosey in and ask her for something sitting high up on the top shelf. She would have to get out the stepladder. Then all I would have to do is stand looking up at her with me belly pressed against the counter, then lift the glass up gently with me two hands, letting the bars of chocolates fall down into me arms. Hmm! What else could I get? Me head whipped up and down, seeing the loaves of bread at the other end, sitting on the counter with boxes of cheese waiting for me on the shelves next to them. Right! Here goes! I picked up me suitcase and was about to make me way in the door when a car pulled up beside me.

'So! There you are!' the priest grinned, whipping the window down and looking out. 'Why did you run off like that, you silly girl? Get in! Quickly! I don't have much time.'

Me heart leapt! Oh, maybe me luck is turning at last! I rushed around the front of the car while he stretched across and opened the door. I lifted me case into the back seat and sat in the front. He took off, driving us back towards the city. I said nothing. Wonder what's happening? I was afraid to ask. Just sitting here was better than nothing. Anyway, I will find out soon enough. I sat back happy and contented, hoping I was getting in somewhere at last. Gawd! He really is a nice man. Imagine taking all that trouble to try and help me! I sighed, enjoying the lovely heat blasting out, and closed me eyes, feeling meself dozing off.

I woke, stretching me tired eyeballs, rubbing them with me fists. They felt like two lumps of hot coal burning in me skull. I lifted me head, looking out the window to see where we were. We're just heading up the quays. Maybe we're going back to his house! Lovely! I kept me eyes peeled, waiting to see where he stopped. I watched with interest as he turned right, up towards Capel Street. We turned right again, leaving the Cole's Lane and Smithfield markets on the left, and continued on down through Mary Street. No! We passed his street way back, so I know now we're not stopping there. Pity! I might have gotten something to eat while he tries to sort me out a bed for the night, or even a couple of nights. I thought maybe he's taking me back to that mad aul one who runs the B&B. But he could still do that later on! Better keep quiet. Anything is better than nothing. No, we're driving well away from her! We passed over Binn's Bridge and turned left heading up the Whitworth Road.

'Eh, so the nuns wouldn't take me back?' I croaked, hearing me voice rattle because I hadn't used it for a while. 'Would they?' I said, wanting to draw him out and find out where we're heading.

He gave a little nod of his head, turning down the corners of his mouth, and just stared ahead, saying nothing.

'I told you she wouldn't,' I sighed, wanting to hear the sound of me own voice.

Then we were passing Glasnevin Cemetery. 'Eh, where are we going?' I said slowly, with me heart giving a sudden leap in me chest, knowing this was the direction to Finglas. 'Do you know someone out here?'

'No, but you do,' he said quietly, keeping his head straight ahead. 'I am taking you to your parents.'

'PARENTS! WHAT PARENTS? I HAVE NO PARENTS!' I roared, getting the fright of me life and feeling a terrible dread snaking itself around me body. 'I have no parents,' I moaned, leaning me head down onta me chest with the shock.

'Yes, you do! Sister Eleanor gave me the address. She told me you have a family living there.'

'My mother does. But I don't have a family.'

'Yes, you do. You have brothers and sisters,' he said, still staring straight ahead at the road.

'No! I don't belong there! I'm not one of them,' I said, not able to believe Sister Eleanor told him about them, even gave him the address. Telling him I have a family when she knows full well I was sent to that convent for shoplifting! She knows exactly what was going on. I never told her anything. But nuns are not fools! She knew that aul fella was not my father. He told her and the rest of the world often enough. So she could easily have worked out what was really going on, including the rest. The bloody bastard! Trying to send me back to that hell on earth!

I felt meself close down, going stone cold. All the hope in me of him wanting to bother himself about me had just disappeared clean outa me. 'You can stop the car,' I said, twisting meself around to grab me suitcase out of the back seat.

'You must be sensible. I can't possibly let you out in the middle of nowhere,' he said, looking around at the narrow country road with all the dark fields and ditches and barely a footpath to walk on.

'You are not taking me back to that hellhole! I don't belong there! I am not one of them. That aul fella is not my father. He hates me that much it nearly suffocates him! Now let me out!' I grabbed hold of the door handle, getting ready to open it and jump out if I had to.

'No you don't!' he said, reaching over and grabbing me arm, pulling me hand away from the door. He had a powerful grip and held me jammed back against the seat with his arm thrown across me, and drove with the other hand. 'Now! Relax, please,' he said quietly, flicking his eyes at me, lifting his arm away, then turning back to keep his eyes on the long, winding, dark country road with not a soul in sight. 'You cannot continue to walk the streets, Martha. You are a young girl of sixteen in grave danger. Sooner or later the police will pick you up. Then you may find yourself being sent somewhere, well . . . you would not find suitable, if you like.'

'You mean get locked up?' I roared.

'Yes! It could happen! You are in need of care and protection. That is the state's responsibility if you are unable to fend for yourself or you have no one to take care of you.'

I suddenly felt all the life going out of me and slumped back in the seat. I can't go back and I can't go forward. No matter how hard I try or how hard I work. Sooner or later it all goes wrong and I'm out on me arse, back on the streets. I could go back to robbing me butter. Just do it long enough until I can get enough money together to get meself the boat fare across to London. I'm sure I would get a job there quick enough. God knows I made enough money when I was only a little kid! I could do it as a little kid! For Jaysus' sake! This is fucking madness! I snorted to meself. Get a move on! Do something! Work something out! I could feel meself raging with meself at being such a gobshite. Then it hit me. No, it's not that easy, and not just the worry, either, of getting caught! But once I go down that road, well, there's no turning back. There's no stopping meself. Fuck! That's not the answer.

'Martha?'

I came to me senses.

'Which way do we turn?'

'Right, then left . . . Stop here,' I said, looking in at the house with the downstairs light on. Me heart started banging in me chest. I could hear it throbbing in me ears, taking away me hearing. I could hardly breathe with the feeling of suffocation. I reached over to take me suitcase out of the back seat as he reached across me and opened the door. I hiked meself outa the car, dragging me suitcase after me, and closed the car door shut. He went up the road and turned, then came back, slowly passing me, and leaned over, giving me a wave. Then he took off, driving down the road. Soon he disappeared, vanishing out of sight, going back to where he came from. I stood staring after him, wondering why he didn't hear me. I tried to tell him me ma was no good, but he didn't want to know, because he didn't really care. Just like Sister Eleanor. I don't belong anywhere. Me heart felt like it could break if I let it. Ah, well! No harm in trying, Martha. You could have been lucky and he might have heard you, really listened. Yeah, but I think people only hear things that they want to hear. I was too much trouble for him. 'Ah, well! Better luck next time,' I muttered, trying to lift meself and get rid of that terrible feeling of being on me own.

7

I turned and looked up at the house. So, this is the house they swapped the other one for. It's not much different. It's the exact same as their old one up the road. The only difference here is the houses are a lot more run-down. Jaysus! The old road they lived on was more respectable looking. Except for Jackser giving it a bad name. The neighbours must have thought all their birthdays came on the one day when he moved out. They would have gone mad with the excitement, with parties going on for weeks.

Here, Missus! Have a drop a tha drink! We can't get over our good fortune! Did you not hear the news? Tha lot! Tha mad Jackser fella. What's he only gone and done but moved himself off down the road. Not realisin what he was walkin himself into! Ha, ha! Be Jaysus! Tha lot down there will put manners on him! He won't be goin aroun there throwin shapes up te anyone! If he does, then he better be prepared to barricade himself in, because he'll be kilt stone dead. Dug outa him, they will be! An proper order too! We were too good for the like a him!

Me heart sank, taking in the state of the houses – the holes in the garden, with hardly any grass, and some of them are even using it as a rubbish tip, with old bicycle wheels and broken chairs and all the rubbish that should be thrown into the dustbin. Fuck! Even the walls are knocked down, with the bricks thrown around the road and some left lying where the wall collapsed. Jaysus! Jackser's a right fucking eejit! He got robbed. Whatever the few bob the people paid him to swap for this place was in no way worth it. They must be still laughing.

I pushed open the gate and walked up the little path. I got a sudden feeling like I was sleepwalking. I stared at the letterbox, then gave it a bang. Not too hard. And held me breath.

'Who is it?' I heard me ma say in a loud whisper.

I said nothing, then the curtains moved back. I saw Dinah's little head appear, peeping out, not wanting to be seen. She stared at me with her mouth open and her eyes bulging outa her head. I pointed at the door, wanting her to open it. I heard her getting all excited, whispering, 'Ma, Ma! It's Martha. She's at the door!'

'Who?' me ma said, sounding just as shocked.

'Let me in!' I whispered, loud enough for her to hear but not wanting that bandy aul bastard fella to hear me voice.

The door opened and me ma stood staring at me, not able to take me in. She gripped hold of a dirty aul cardigan, making a fist of her hand, and pulled it tight across her chest. The buttons were all gone.

'Hello, Ma!' I said, standing, waiting, not wanting to go in. Yet I was ready to move in the door.

'He's up in bed,' she said, half opening the door, pointing up at the ceiling, not looking too sure if she wanted me to come in or not.

I pushed past her when I heard that. I went into the little sitting room, seeing Dinah standing in front of the fireplace, with a few lumps of coal smouldering in the grate. I looked around at the bare room with the battered little wooden table and two odd kitchen chairs, one sitting each side of the fireplace. The room felt cold and the smell hit me like a ton of bricks.

It felt like I was falling down a black hole – only to end up back where I started. I suddenly felt dizzy and leant meself back against the table, letting it take me weight. I looked down at the floor; it was manky dirty. Some of the smell was pouring up from the rotten dirty floorboards because the babies always shit on the bare floor, because they have to crawl around naked, wearing only a vest. Jaysus! Them two! They brought their dirty habits with them. The room is filthy, I thought, looking around slowly. Nothing has changed. It's even worse now, with years of dirt and decay. I tried not to breathe it in. Oh, bloody hell, no! I have to get out!

Me eyes landed on Dinah, standing looking up at me, twisting her

finger around her mouth and smiling shyly at me. 'Hello, little one!'
I whispered, going over and grabbing her into meself.

'Have you come back to stay?' she whispered, pointing at me
suitcase, looking into me face, her eyes afraid I would say no.

I didn't want to get her hopes up, so I just shook me head. 'No,
Dinah. I'm all grown up now,' I whispered. 'I have to go and look
for a job. Sure, you're going to be doing the same as me. Wait and
see! It won't really be that long.'

'So, why are you here then?' me ma said, listening and getting
annoyed.

'I don't know, Ma,' I said, looking at her, wanting her to be different,
with more life in her somehow. Be able to manage a bit better and
look after the kids. To even say something that would make me feel
I belonged. That she was glad to see me. But she can see I have
nothing in me hand. I have nothing to give her.

She turned away muttering, shaking her head, chewing the inside
of her mouth like mad. Her eyes kept flying around the room, looking
and blinking, searching from one spot to the next like she might
find an answer if she looked hard enough. Except she wasn't seeing
anything. She was gone back to the torment going on inside her head.
Then she whipped her eyes on me again, but not really looking.

'I don't know,' she moaned, keening. 'Ye'd be better off dead. I hate
this place. I wish I was six foot under.'

Ah, fuck! Here we go! Same old ma. She will moider me until I go
out and bring her back money. Then I will get to see her face light
up, happy we have a few bob and a bit of grub on the table. Until
it's time to eat again or pay the rent. Because the bandy aul fella has
spent all the money on drink. No, I can't make the ma happy! She
will have to get on without me.

'Where's everybody, Ma? Where's all the kids?'

'Where do ye think? They're all up in the bed!'

'So why are you and Dinah not up in the bed, Ma?'

'I'm keepin me ma company, Martha,' Dinah whispered, looking
up at me smiling.

'Ah, leave me alone,' me ma snorted. 'Tha aul bastard was off on the drink again. He's left me nothin, not even a penny te get a bottle a milk to make a drop a tea for the kids!'

'Oh, fuck, Ma!' I breathed, dropping me head in me hands, tired of hearing the same aul thing.

'Eh.' Cough.

I looked up.

'Have ye any money, Martha?' she asked, looking at me, seeing me and softening her voice, trying to smile. 'Just to get a bit a bread an a drop a milk for the mornin,' she said, sounding desperate.

Me heart broke seeing her in this state and knowing there was nothing I could do about it. 'No, Ma,' I said quietly, putting out me hands. 'I haven't got a penny. You know I would give it to you, Ma, if I had it. You know full well I would give you the last penny outa me pocket. But I've no job, Ma.'

'Have ye not,' she said, sounding disappointed. 'Jaysus! Tha's terrible! So wha am I goin to do for the mornin, Martha? Tha aul bastard will go mad if I can't give him a sup a tea. Not wit there bein no milk te put in it. Isn't there any way ye can get yer hands on a few bob, Martha? Look a tha!' she snorted, pointing her finger at the fire like it had done something wrong. 'The fuckin fire is nearly gone out on me! Tha's the last a the coal!' she roared, nearly crying.

Yeah! So why don't you push that aul bastard under a bus? Or fucking leave him? I thought, feeling a rage flying up me. But it was a waste of time telling her this. 'Ah, Ma! Stop! I have a pain in me head. I'm fuckin fallin off me feet! No, Ma, I have nothin, there's nothing I can do for you. I can hardly bleedin help meself this minute!'

'So wha are ye goin te do, then? Ye have te get money somewhere!' she complained, shaking her head at me. 'He won't let ye stay here, Martha. Anyway! He's goin to want you bringin in money!'

I said nothing. I felt like I was cemented to the floor, with me head gone all funny, like it's decided to stop working. Jaysus! I can't work anything out. I'm in too much of a daze. Like someone planted me here in this spot and I can't think or move.

'Wha work were ye doin? Did you get good money, Martha?'

'Minding children, Ma, and cleaning,' I heard meself say, like me voice was coming from a distance.

'Oh! How much money does tha pay, Martha?'

I just stared, not really seeing her. The light was hurting me eyes. 'I have to go, Ma,' I said, making to pick up me suitcase without even knowing I was thinking. Then it hit me. 'Ma, where's Charlie? Is he upstairs?'

'Ah, him! Don't talk te me about tha young fella. I have no time for tha bastard!' she said, turning up her face, looking like she got a bad smell.

'Why, Ma? What's he done on you?'

'Nothin! That's the problem! Lazy bastard suits himself! Well, he can fuck off for himself now! He needn't think he can come back here, near tha door! I'm havin nothin more te do wit him!'

'Ma! You never did!' I snapped. 'So where is he, Ma?'

'I told ye! I don't know! Now don't be moiderin me any more about him! Listen! Go on if ye're goin!' she suddenly said, waving her hands at me. 'I'm goin te bed! I want te lock tha front door.

'Oh, Jaysus!' she suddenly moaned, wrapping her face in her hands, sounding like she was crying. 'I don't know how much more a this I can take. Tha aul fella is goin te come down them stairs any minute an rise murder if he sees you here! Look, Martha! I'm just tellin ye out straight. He'll fuckin knife you! There'll be killins! He's still goin mad because you crossed him!'

'What are you talking about, Ma? Crossed him? Anyway, I'm not afraid a him, Ma! I can tell you that, here and now!' I snorted.

'Look! Leave it!' she said, waving her hand up in her face. 'Go on! Get out, Martha! I don't want any more trouble outa him. I'm worn out,' she whispered, looking at me.

I stared into her face, seeing how tired and beaten she looked, and old before her time. Jaysus, she still is young. Thirty-two is not that old at all. But she looks twice that.

'Yeah, OK, Ma,' I sighed. 'I was going anyway,' I said quietly, turning away from her, making for the hall.

'Martha! Don't go!' Dinah whispered, rushing up behind me,

grabbing a hold of me coat. Then she raised her head, looking up the stairs, listening for any sound. Satisfied, she swung her head back to me. I let down me case and dropped to me knees, holding her. 'I don't want you to go, Martha. I want ye to stay here wit us. We miss you!' she said, leaning her face into me, whispering. I could feel her breath on me face and her huge blue eyes stared at me, looking like she was going to cry.

We both said nothing. She just stared, her eyes desperate, searching me face to ease her pain. It was as if I was her only hope. 'Jaysus!' I whispered. 'It's breaking me heart, Dinah, that I can't stay and look after you. But I can't stay here with that aul fella. Do you see what I'm saying, Dinah?'

'Yeah,' she said, lowering her head. 'We're not supposed to talk about you any more, Martha. Cos you wouldn't come back when him an me ma asked you. Tha time when ye were away in the convent. He had to put us down there too, cos you wouldn't come here an mind us when me ma had to go into the hospidal to get a new babby. Tha's when she brought home Gerry! So that's why he hates us to mention talk about you, Martha. Yeah, he always says you an Charlie are bastards, tha youse are no good! An if he gets his hands on Charlie, he's goin te do time for him! Tha he'll kill him! An you better not come near the door neither!' she said, getting carried away about what fuck-face Jackser thinks he might do to me.

'No!' I laughed. 'He's not going to get near me! Don't be minding that gobshite!'

'But he said he would, Martha!' she said, shaking her head up and down, with her eyes widening like saucers. 'He might even kill you now, if he knows ye're here,' she whispered, looking up at the stairs, barely saying the last few words as she listened, expecting him to jump out of the dark landing and go for us.

Me heart leapt. Yeah, I thought, but I'd be out that door before he could get his next breath! But then he would only take it out on me ma and the rest of the poor kids.

'Listen, Dinah. Do you know where Charlie is?'

'Yeah, I do,' she said, shaking her head. 'Charlie's up stayin wit the

Reillys. His friend Anto gets his ma te let him. I do see him playin aroun there, Martha.'

'Ah, me little Dinah. Thanks for telling me that! Look! Your hair got lovely and long. Look at the length of it!' I said, brushing it down her back with me hand. 'Aren't you lovely looking?' I said, stroking her face, seeing her lovely blue eyes light up with me talking gently to her, playing with her hair.

'Yeah, but I don't know how te do a plait. Will you show me sometime, Martha? Some a the other young ones do have their hairs in plaits. I want te be able te plait mine as well.'

'Ask me ma, Dinah. She might know.'

'No, she can't, Martha. Me an Sally asked her to do us one but she doesn't know how.'

Or won't! I thought. Lazy bloody cow.

'Here, come on, you! You better get outa this house,' me ma whispered, losing her patience. 'Me nerves are gone, expectin him to come down them stairs any minute with you still here messin aroun.'

'OK, Dinah! Give me a big kiss.' I grabbed hold of her, squeezing her skinny little body with her ribs sticking out, and kissed her cheeks and the top of her head. Then I turned, grabbing up me suitcase, and made for the hall door, saying, 'Goodbye, Ma. I'm going now.'

'Yeah, goodbye,' she muttered, snorting in her breath, then tightening her mouth and closing her eyes, turning her head away from me, looking at the wall. I stopped, waiting. Hoping she might say something, anything that let me think I meant something to her. She turned back to look at me and we stared at each other, she reading my mind. Then she gave me a dirty look as much as to say, *Go on! Ye're no good te me! Ye're only like tha Charlie fella. Two useless bastards tha were not worth rearin. So now ye's are not wanted in this house anyway!*

I turned away and quietly opened the front door, letting meself out into the freezing-cold night air. There was nothing I could do for her, so she didn't really want to know me. She had more than enough troubles, letting herself put up with that cowardly, bandy, good-for-nothing bastard. Thank God I didn't have to clap eyes on him.

I headed off, making up the road to the shops. I'll be able to get the bus there into town. I'll just have to give the conductor a name and address from somewhere around here. I'll make up one! I felt dead inside meself. Seeing the ma gave me the feeling that nothing had changed. The years of misery just came flying back, making me feel like I was trapped again in the iron grip of Jackser. I looked at all the houses looking cosy inside, with the curtains drawn together, showing the light on and people sitting in comfort, taking it easy before they went up to bed. Why could the ma never have been normal like other people? What ordinary woman would put up with someone like Jackser? A fucking mad man! Anyway, in a way I feel somehow more free. I know now come hell or high water I will never bother even thinking of the ma again! No! I never intend setting foot out near this place again. Me life is me own! So! No more Sister Eleanor or the ma. They are all dead! So is me old life. Pity I didn't get to see Charlie.

I walked through the church grounds with me head down, trying to keep the cold from freezing me face and getting inside me coat. The open space was letting the wind run right through me, freezing me bones to the marrow. Oh, dear God! Just let me get in somewhere out of this and get a bit of heat and something to eat.

I looked ahead, seeing all the shops were locked up and bolted, with their shutters up, and the whole place in darkness. I could see the chip shop was still open, though. The lights shone out onto the footpath, picking out the ice and snow piled around the path. What wouldn't I give to murder a bag of fish and chips now! A big ray! No, shut up! Stop tormenting yerself!

Jaysus! I hope I haven't missed the last bus into town. I couldn't see anyone waiting at the bus stop. I walked across the road and put me case down, leaning meself up against the bus stop. I dug me hands deep down into me pockets, letting me neck sink down inside me coat, hopping from one leg to the other. Jaysus! It would be lovely if the bus came now.

8

I could feel the time passing. Still no sign of the bus. I must be at least a half hour standing here, waiting and hoping a bus would come. Dear God! Please say I didn't miss the last bus. Please! Just let one come. Better still, make it soon.

I heard running feet and the sound of kids laughing. I looked over, seeing two little young fellas chasing each other. Then one flew past the other, with the pair of them having a race. A little young fella galloped ahead with the hair flying on his head, swinging around to see the other fella, a bit bigger, breathing down his neck. The bigger fella swung out his arm, grabbing hold of him, tearing him back by the collar of a dirty brown jacket ten times too big for him. Then he elbowed him outa the way and flew past, laughing his head off.

'You cheated! Come back! Ye can't do tha!' roared the little fella, tearing across the road, with the two of them heading for the chip shop.

I stared, hearing the voice, seeing the hair. That's Charlie! That's me brother!

'CHARLIE! STOP! WAIT!'

The pair of them came to a skidding stop, balancing themself on their toes. They stared at me with their mouths open, looking like two statues frozen in that shape, trying to work out who I am.

'Who's tha?' said the smaller young fella.

'Is tha you, Martha?' said Charlie, walking over to see if he was in his right mind. Not believing his own eyes.

'Yeah! It's me, Charlie!'

'Wha are you doin here, Martha? Where were ye goin?' His eyes flew in all directions, looking from me, then swinging his head, bending his back to take in me suitcase. 'Have you come back? Are you – were ye goin to see me ma?'

'Yeah, I was. What the hell are you up to this hour of the night?' I said, laughing and looking at the state of him.

'Ah! We was just goin te the chip shop te see if we can ger ourselves a few chips, wasn't we, Anto?'

'Yeah, we were,' said Anto, looking me up and down, grinning from ear to ear. 'Isn't tha Martha, yer big sister, Charlie? The one tha got sent away?'

'Yeah! She is.'

'I remember you!' said Anto. 'But I was small then. Well, not too small!'

'Well, ye're not too much bigger now,' I laughed.

'Ah, he is, Martha! He's like me! He's eleven, aren't you, Anto!'

'Gerraway, you!' Anto laughed, giving Charlie a dig in the back. 'I'm much bigger than you!'

'Come on! Don't start the pair of ye's. Charlie, what are you up to? Me ma said you weren't living there any more.'

'Ah, no, I'm not. Tha aul fella thrun me outa the house, Martha. I do stay with Anto. Isn't tha right, Anto?' Charlie said, leaning in and nudging Anto.

'Yeah! Sometimes. But ye can't always. Me ma says she doesn't need another lodger!' Anto said, snorting at Charlie and half laughing. 'Lookit, Charlie! Me ma is goin to miss me. I better get back home before she does. Are ye comin?'

'Wait! I want to see me sister first.'

'Ah, well, OK then. I'm goin. But here's wha we'll do then. When ye come back, sneak in the back door. I'll leave it open for you. Is tha all right?' Anto said, walking backwards, making to run home. 'But listen, Charlie,' he said, coming back again. 'You have to go easy when you come in. Don't wake me ma or da up! An make sure ye turn the key in the back door. We don't want anyone findin out. Yeah, an another thing! You better be awake an gone early before me ma catches ye, OK?'

'Yeah! Great!' Charlie said, nodding his head up and down, taking in everything Anto was saying.

'OK! But ye have to promise, mind! Sneak outa the house early. I don't want me ma te go mad at me if she catches ye.'

'Yeah, I do know tha! Anyway, I have it all worked out,' Charlie said. 'I'll be helpin Flashey Rooney wit his milk round.'

'Oh, yeah! Great! Then you can come back later. An you can buy me something. We mightn't spend it all on sweets. Let's buy marbles instead. Wha do you think? Is tha a deal?'

'Yeah, tha's a deal!' said Charlie, shaking his head up and down, making the mop of hair on his head fly around.

'Oh, yeah! An don't go eatin the sambidges outa the press! Them last ones ye stuffed in yer face were for me da! Did you know tha? Me ma makes them for his dinner break at work. I got the blame for tha,' Anto snorted, seein Charlie grin from ear to see. 'It's not funny, Charlie! That's why me ma barred ye from the house. An blamed me for bringin you.'

'Yeah, OK. I won't do tha again,' Charlie said. letting his head drop, staring at the ground looking very worried. 'So is it still all right for me to come back then?'

'Yeah! Course it is! See ya!' Then he was gone, flying to get home.

'Jaysus, Charlie! Have you nowhere to stay?'

'Ah, yeah! Course I do, Martha. I stay wit him,' he said, pointing his head after Anto.

I looked at the state of him. He was wearing a man's tan jacket. The kind men wear serving in shops. The pockets were in ribbons and the sleeves under his arms were ripped. I looked down, seeing the trousers. The trousers were miles too big and held around his waist with a bit of twine. Someone had cut them at the bottom. The ends were in ribbons and they hung at half mast down his legs.

'Jesus, Charlie! Where did you get them rags?'

'Wha? The trousers?' he said, holding them out.

'Yeah! And that bleedin jacket! There's no heat in that. It's hanging off you, Charlie, and you can't even fasten it. You must be freezing!

Look! Ye're shivering!' I said, shivering meself and rattling me shoulders up and down. 'Are you cold?'

'No! Only sometimes! When I'm hangin around. I got them trousers offa Anto. His ma was going to throw them out. Liamo, his big brother, used to own them. Now I'm wearin them.'

'So what happened? Why did the aul fella throw you out?'

'Ah, you know him, Martha. I wouldn't do wha he wanted.'

'Like what, Charlie?'

'Ah, anythin! Like the stuff you used to do. I wouldn't rob for him an I wouldn't go te the convents for the bread. When I did, if they gave me anythin, like a bit of meat or something, then I ate it meself an gave them nothin.'

'Why did you do that, Charlie?'

'Because I saw wha happened to you! Me ma would only complain if I brought back something then didn't bring it back the next time. So I brought back nothin! Tha way they just thought I was stupid, Martha. But I knew wha I was doin.'

'Gawd! You really are very cute, Charlie,' I said. 'You were a lot smarter than I was.'

'Yeah, you were always killin yerself! But I learnt from yure mistakes, Martha. Give them nothin. Then they don't expect you to get them somethin.'

I looked at him staring up at me with the big blue eyes and the mop of dirty blond hair. He looked like a little aul fella and even sounded like one. I could see the pain in his eyes as he stared into the distance, thinking. 'I don't like me ma, Martha,' he said, shaking his head, looking like that was the only true thing in the world he knew for definite. 'She has no nature in her! Even the aul fella, bad an all as he is, but he has some pity in him. That's more than me ma has. There's no heart in her, Martha.

'Sure, wait till I tell you, Martha. I was sleepin in the fields one time, down on the back road. An I was drinkin all the dirty water from the river cos I had nowhere else te get it. Then I got really sick. Oh, Jaysus, Martha, I kept throwin me guts up! I was rollin aroun, an all hot, an the thirst was killin me. I was like tha for days. Some of the kids I play wit sawed me like tha an ran up an told me ma. She wouldn't come down. She banged the door out on their face. Told them she didn't care, tha she wasn't interested. But the aul fella came down an brought me back. Yeah, Martha. He carried me back to the house an put me lyin on the sofa. Then he got the dispensary doctor for me! It was him, tha doctor, he was the one tha said I got poisoned from drinkin all tha dirty water, Martha! Then I got better!' Charlie laughed, looking up at me. 'An I ran away again!'

'Why did you do that, Charlie?'

'Cos he wanted me to start doin things for him. You know! Robbin an stuff. But me ma didn't want to know, Martha. Jackser had to keep shoutin at her to make sure I got me medicine. No, I hate tha aul one, Martha. She's no good.'

'Ah, I don't know, Charlie. Maybe that aul fella has her that way.'

'No! She's like tha herself, Martha. She hates me!'

'But she's the ma, Charlie!'

'No! She's not my ma. Lookit all the things she let tha aul fella do te us! No, Martha. You should know tha better than me. You sawed she had you gettin things for her. So tha kept her happy. No, she never had time for you an me,' he muttered, shaking his head, looking like an old man watching his whole world collapse. 'No, them two are a well-matched pair.'

'Yeah, I knew that, Charlie. I just kept remembering the times before me ma met Jackser. You were only a baby. She was the same then. Yeah, I suppose ye're right, Charlie,' I said slowly, thinking. Remembering times when I would come in from the pouring rain when I was little. He would have to shout at her to take the wet clothes offa me. That's if I brought him back something good. 'Yeah, you know something, Charlie. It's funny but I think I could even remind meself of how many times he showed us a bit a heart, because he very rarely ever did.'

'Yeah, but the ma never did! Fuck her! I hate her! I'm never havin anything to do wit her, Martha. So why did you come back, Martha?' he said, looking down at me suitcase. 'Have ye nowhere to go?' he said, puffing himself up, lifting his shoulders with the shock.

'No. I keep losing me jobs, Charlie. The fuckers I was working for, they think you are their very own property. No one owns me, Charlie!'

'Yeah! I'm the same meself, Martha,' he said, looking mournful.

'So! Are you keeping outa trouble, Charlie?'

'Eh, ah, yeah, Martha.'

I looked at him, seeing him give me a shifty look, shaking his foot, swinging his head around looking at nothing. 'Listen, Charlie. You really can't go getting yerself into trouble and ending up being sent away to a reformatory!'

'Oh, yeah! I know all about tha, Martha. No, not me,' he said, shaking his head, showing the fear of God with the eyes lepping outa his head.

'Are you going to school? Now tell me the truth!'

'No, but, yeah. Sometimes I do. Well, not now, cos you see, Martha, I can't go lookin like this now, can I?' he said, standing back to show me the state a him. 'An anyways, I haven't any a the books. So how can I go te school, Martha? Sure, you didn't go anyways neither. Did you, Martha?'

'No, they wouldn't send me.'

'So wha are you goin te do now, Martha? Are you waitin on a bus?' he said, with his face creasing, looking surprised and worried at the same time.

'Yeah, I'm headin back into town.'

'Well, I think you mighta missed the last one. There's no more buses comin!' he said, lookin up an down the road, seeing how empty it was.

'Oh, fuck! Now what?' I moaned, not wanting to get stuck out here.

'So where are you goin when you hit into town, Martha? Do you know someone?'

I shook me head, not really caring. 'No, Charlie. I don't know anybody. But I'll worry another time. Right now, I want to get as far away from me ma an that aul fella. As far away as I can get! Do you know, Charlie, I was just thinking I might just put meself all out to get me hands on the boat fare to England. I have had enough of this bleedin country!'

'There's a bus comin! Quick! Get yer hand out!' Charlie suddenly roared, grabbing up me suitcase for me and landing it in me hand.

I put me hand out to stop it.

'Go on, Martha! Jump on!' he roared.

'You mind yerself, Charlie,' I screamed, seeing him stand on the footpath watching me take off as I ran for the bus that slowed down but wouldn't come to a stop. I looked back, seeing him still standing there staring after me. I stood on the platform waving to him. 'He looks so little and lost,' I muttered, then the tears starting rolling down me cheeks. I felt a terrible feeling of loneliness. And me heart was ripping in two, having to run off and leave him standing there, all alone in the dead hour of the night with no one to look out for him or bother whether he lives or dies. God! Where are you? Please mind Charlie and look after him. Keep him safe and protect him from all harm. He needs you, God! Help him to stay outa trouble. That's all I ask, God. Just one more thing! Will you help me to find a good job? And somewhere nice to live? Or . . . it doesn't matter, God. Anything and anywhere will do.

9

'Wake up! Come on! What's wrong with you?'

I opened me eyes slowly, looking up into the face of the conductor. Where am I? Gawd! I can't move.

'Here! Sit up! Are you sick?'

I tried to lift meself offa the seat, but it was too much like hard work.

'Ah, here! I don't think this young one is well at all,' he muttered to himself, looking around to see what the driver was doing. 'Jaysus! Ye're the colour of a corpse.' He put his hand on me forehead. 'Holy mother a God! Ye're like a block of ice.'

He jumped up off his knees and banged on the driver's window. 'Eh, Christie! This young one is lying here. She's collapsed. We're near the hospital. I think we should run her over there. It would be quicker than waitin on the aul ambulance. Will we take her there ourself? Then we can hit back over for the depot.'

The driver stared out at me through the little window on the long seat. 'Yeah, all right. It won't take us more than a couple a minutes anyway.'

'Right! We'll do that so,' the conductor said, then slapped the driver on the arm gently, giving him a little pat, and closed the winda. Then he came back and sat on the other seat beside me.

I can take it all in, but it's like I'm paralysed, frozen solid. I'm not able to move or think. Hospital! No, not that! But I don't really care. I'm so tired. I closed me eyes, wanting to go back to sleep.

Me eyes fluttered open, feeling a breeze on me face.

'Good girl, lift your feet!'

Then I was bounced into something. I'm in a wheelchair.

'Right! We'll get you inside. Ah, she'll be all right now!'

I saw the bus conductor and the driver standing talking to a nurse while I got pushed along by another nurse, straight in off the street. We were heading in through a yard, making for the hospital. 'Thanks for your help,' I heard the nurse say, then come rushing up after us.

'Me case! Me suitcase!' I said, turning around, getting a fright me case might be gone!

'Yes! Don't worry, pet! We have your suitcase,' the nurse said. 'Look, here it is!' she said, waving it at me, smiling. Then we pushed in through the doors and rushed around by a desk, heading into a room with a row of cubicles that had curtains drawn across.

Nurses were talking to doctors sitting at desks, and some were staring up at a machine on the wall looking at black pictures showing people's insides coming up in white. X-rays, I thought to meself.

'Here we are,' the nurse said, wheeling me into a cubicle. 'Now, good girl.' They hoisted me outa the chair, one grabbing me each side of me arms. 'Can you climb up onto the bed?' they shouted, slapping the bed to show me what they wanted.

I knew I wasn't deaf. I wonder why they have to shout? I asked meself, looking up into the smiling face of a nurse blowing away shiny wisps of brown hair that fell outa her starched cap and landed in her eyes.

'Come on!' They grabbed me and lifted me offa the floor, sending me flying to land on the bed.

'What happed to you at all?' the nurse said, piling loads a soft blue wool blankets around me, right up to me neck.

I said nothing, just watched her hands moving busily, setting me up in comfort. Yeah, what did happen? I'm asking meself. I tried to think.

One minute I was standing waving to Charlie. The picture of him waving, staring after me! He looked so small and lost! Then I sat down. What next? Yeah, the conductor. I gave him a name and address. He didn't argue with me. He just shook his head and walked away, looking a bit annoyed, but didn't bother to write the address. Then I felt meself getting terrible weak all of a sudden. I didn't even feel cold any more. I'd stopped shivering. I wasn't even bothered about the hunger. I just felt meself wanting to go off to sleep. So? Oh, yeah! The next thing I remember was the conductor waking me up. But I couldn't wake meself up! I opened me eyes for a few minutes but I couldn't keep them open. So, now I'm here! In the shagging hospital. I'm not staying. Where's me suitcase? Oh! Leaning against the wall. That's all right, then. Soon as I get a bit of sleep I'm getting meself out of here. It's one thing to come in under me own steam and use the facilities, but it's another when I'm carted in, having to stay here.

I could feel me strength going again. I'm so bloody tired. I'll just have a little sleep for meself, then get moving. Maybe they might give me something to eat first. No, only if I stay. Ah, forget it for now. Worry about that later. I moved me head on the pillow, getting meself comfortable, then felt meself sinking off into a lovely deep sleep.

The cold hit me.

'I just want to examine you, dear.'

I looked up into the face of a young doctor, whipping up the back of me blouse. I groaned, wanting to go back to sleep.

'Breathe in! Now again! And again!'

I gasped. Not able to get a breath. Listening to meself sound like a rusty bicycle wheel straining to get itself moving. Ohh! Would they ever let me alone? I'm too exhausted. And he has woken me up. I'm bloody freezing with all the blankets pulled offa me!

'Here, keep that in your mouth,' he said, sticking a temperature thing in me mouth. 'Don't drop it!' he said, watching to see I kept me mouth closed. Then he lifted me wrist, hanging on to it, looking at a watch he held in his hand. Then he lifted the skin on me hand, seeing it stand up by itself. Then he whipped the temperature thing outa me mouth. 'Hypothermia,' he muttered, staring at it. 'OK, you can lie down now.' He dropped the stethoscope around his neck, writing something down on a chart, then looked back at me, pulling the blankets up around me. Then he whipped himself back out through the curtain, leaving me to collapse back into me sleep. I gave a big sigh, feeling meself sink back into a lovely sleep again.

'Hello! Wake up! Can you hear me?'

I looked up into the face of the brown-haired nurse again.

'Sorry, pet, to keep disturbing you like this,' she mewled, letting it sound like a cat crying. 'But I just need your address. We need to contact your mammy and daddy. Is that all right, pet? Then we will get you upstairs to a nice ward. You will be able to sleep then without us fussing around you down here. Oh, don't pull out that tube!' she said, watching me yank me hand down under the bedclothes.

I looked to see her eyes wander from me hand to a pole standing beside me and two clear bags dripping stuff through a tube into me hand.

'Let me see if that has come loose,' she said, examining it.

I stared as well, not knowing I had that in.

'That's fine! Now, how old are you?'

'Sixteen.'

'Sweet sixteen and never been kissed,' she smiled, saying, 'that's a lovely age. Now! What's your name?'

'Martha, Martha Long.'

'Oh, I have an Aunt Martha. I love that name. When I ever get married, I will call my first child that name. If it's a girl, of course!' she laughed. 'Now, Martha, where do you live?'

I tried to think. Not the convent. No! I've seen the last of them. 'Nurse, I'm tired!' I said, pulling myself onta me other side away from her, not wanting to answer any more questions, just go back to sleep.

'Come on, pet! Just bear with me, dear,' she said, grabbing hold of me, trying to swing me around to her.

'No! I'm tired,' I moaned, not wanting the trouble of trying to work out what to say. 'I'm too bloody exhausted.'

'Martha, pet! We need to contact your parents. Tell them where you are. Where were you off to with the suitcase?' she said, whipping around to look at it, thinking.

I just closed me eyes, wanting me sleep back. I'm too weak to bother.

I heard her sigh, then jump up off the chair, bending down for something. Then make off out through the curtain.

I woke up, staring around me. I turned me head slightly, seeing the locker next to me bed with the jug of water standing on top and a drinking glass next to it. I'm in the ward!

I stared around, seeing an old woman sitting up in the bed taking out papers and letters and putting them down beside her. She lifted up a piece of paper, squinting at it, holding it close to her face, trying to read it. Another old woman was lying quiet in her bed, staring. Just watching over at the old woman trying to sort out her stuff. I felt meself nice and warm and rested. I was able to keep me eyes open. But I still feel tired and weak.

The door opened suddenly at the end of the ward. I watched as a woman came in, walking slowly on her tippy toes, looking like she was creeping. She had a big shopping bag on her arm, bursting with stuff, and a big bottle of Lucozade under her other arm. I could see oranges and a lovely box of purple Cadbury's milk chocolate sticking out of a brown paper bag. She stopped just as she got herself inside the door and stood staring, her head whipping up and down the ward, searching for someone. Then her eyes lit up, and she smiled, moving herself quietly over to an old woman dozing in the end bed just behind the door. The woman had a big white bandage wrapped across her face, covering her left eye.

'Mammy! Ma! Are ye awake?' she whispered, leaning over and putting down the bag. She left the Lucozade on top of the locker and pulled the chair over closer to the bed and sat down. 'Mammy!' she whispered, taking the old woman's hand inside hers and rubbing it gently, trying to wake the woman but not give her a fright.

The old woman moved her head, opening her one good eye. 'Ah, Hannah love! It's yerself,' she smiled, looking at the daughter.

'How are ye feelin, Mammy?' the daughter said quietly, smiling all over her face. 'What did the doctor say? You got the operation!' she said, looking at the mammy's bandages. 'It's all over!'

'Yeah, thank God, Hannah love. I have tha now behind me. The doctors said I just have te have this on!' she said, feeling for the bandage, barely touching it, but wanting to make sure it really was there. 'Tha will come offa me in a few days. Then I won't know meself. At least now I'll be able to see out wit one good eye!'

'Yeah, Mammy! I'm delighted. Then ye'll be able to get the other one done. Just think, Ma! You'll be able te see yer own way around again!'

'Oh, yeah, Hannah love. Them doctors are a power of wonders! The things they can do fer ye nowadays. Them cataracts were a blindin curse!'

'Yeah, blindin, Ma!' the daughter laughed. 'Did you hear yerself? Wha ye just said, Ma?'

'No, wha? Oh, yeah! Blindin! Jaysus! God forgive me fer cursin! I was blind all right!' the ma laughed. Then she said, 'Listen, Hannah, I hope ye didn't throw out me aul mattress?'

'No, why, Ma?' she said, looking worried at the ma, who looked even more worried.

'Well, ye see, because now I'll be able te count all me money I have hidden under it. I'll be able to see the colour a me green pound notes!'

The two of them roared laughing together. The daughter giving the mammy a little nudge with her elbow, and the ma slapped her back in the hand. The pair of them enjoying themself no end! I sighed with contentment, then realised I was smiling too.

A nurse came in carrying a tray and made straight for the old woman. She slipped a temperature thing out of her top pocket, saying, 'Do you mind if I just take your temperature, Mrs Gaffney?', but she was really looking at the daughter, asking her permission to disturb them.

'Certainly, Nurse,' the old woman said, trying to haul herself up in the bed.

'No! Don't move, dear!' the nurse roared.

The daughter stood up and busied herself emptying the bag. 'I brought ye a few things to keep ye goin, Mammy,' she said, showing her the oranges and biscuits and a load of other stuff. Then she packed them all in the locker. 'Oh, Mammy, look! I brought ye a couple of clean nightgowns, an socks for yer feet. They'll keep ye nice an warm. Especially at night when yer poor feet does feel the cold.

'It's does be her circulation,' she whispered, mouthing the news to the nurse. Not wanting to upset the mammy by reminding her about her other ailments. 'Do ye know wha I mean, Nurse? They do pain her somethin terrible,' she said, nearly shouting now.

'Yes! Oh, yes, indeed! We can't have our favourite patient getting cold now, can we, Mrs G?'

The old woman shook her head, agreeing, because her mouth was still stuffed with the temperature thing. Then it hit her. She dropped her face, looking mortified, and rolled her one good eye, looking up at the ceiling. She had just agreed she was the favourite patient.

'That's fine,' said the nurse, after taking it out of her mouth to examine it, then shaking it up and down like mad. 'You must stay nice and quiet. Get plenty of rest and let the doctor's work do its job!' said the nurse, shouting at the woman in case she might be deaf as well, then bending down and tucking in the bedclothes.

'Here's a new washbag I got you, Mammy. I got tha in Roches Stores. I put a few tilet things in as well for you. Soap and a new washcloth. Is there anythin else ye want? Will I ask the nurse te change ye into this clean one?' she said, holding up a lovely pink heavy cotton nightgown with white little flowers.

'Ah, I don't want te bother the nurse,' the ma complained. 'They have more than enough te be doin.'

'No, it's no trouble at all,' said the nurse, swinging the curtain around and taking the nightdress offa the daughter.

'Thanks very much, Nurse. Ye're very good. I think Mammy will enjoy havin the bit of comfort of somethin clean after havin tha aul operation. It takes a lot outa ye. Especially at her age.'

'All done!' said the nurse, tearing back the curtain, then heading herself off down the ward, with her eyes peeling on me.

'How are you?' she roared at me, swinging the curtain in after her as more visitors swarmed into the ward. She looked up at the bags hanging on the pole. 'I think we can take that one down now,' she said, reaching up for the empty one, then taking it outa me hand. Then she checked to make sure the other one was still dripping away.

'That's your antibiotic for your chest infection. How are you feeling, chicken? You can have something to eat now. We had to get the fluids into you. But you can take fluids by mouth now. Poor creature! What happened to you at all at all? Tsk, tsk!' she said, feeling me head, then sticking the temperature thing into me mouth and holding me wrist. 'Hmm,' she said. 'We want you to keep nice and warm.' Then she was off, rushing out the door, then flying back in just as quick, carrying more blankets.

'We can't have you getting cold on us. That wouldn't do at all at all,' she said, piling blanket after blanket on top a me, then slamming them in under the mattress.

I can't move. Jaysus! I'm suffocating! I can hardly breathe with the weight a them. She has me buried. But the comfort is great!

'Now, you are to drink plenty of liquids!' she shouted, bending down and looking into me face, holding her hands on her big wide hips.

I nodded, looking into her freckled face with the mop of ginger frizzy hair standing up over her cap, and her eyes crossed a bit, waiting for me to agree.

I nodded again, not saying anything. Everything was a bit too much effort.

'Would you like something to eat? What about a nice pot of tea and a couple of slices of nice hot toast?' She lifted her eyebrows, holding them, waiting for me answer. 'Hmm?' she said.

I nodded, giving a few extra nods in case she mistook me answer for no.

'How about if I make you a nice bit of scrambled egg as well? I think that will be all right,' she asked herself, thinking about it. 'We can't have you throwing it back up! So something light to begin with. Is that OK, chicken?' she said, rubbing me head.

'Yeah!' I managed to get out, thinking me mouth feels like sawdust now. I'm not that bothered about eating. But a few days ago I would have eaten a scabby babby, I was that hungry.

She took off, with her black soft-leather shoes squeaking on the floorboards. And her legs wobbled, because she's well fed. It must be all the hospital feeding, because you get well fed in the hospital, and she looks like she shifts a lot. It would cost a quare few bob to feed her. It's mostly only well-off people can afford to look like that! Most of the people I knew were all skinny because they are all poor and have to ration the grub. Still an all, them fat ones are never happy. They want to be skinny like the poor ones! Think I'll go back to sleep. I'm really tired again. What about me grub? I have to stay awake! Ah, I'll just have a little doze. The nurse will wake me.

I sat up yawning, scratching me head, looking around the ward. Wonder if it's dinner time yet? I thought, smacking me lips, getting the picture of a lovely steaming dinner sitting on a plate. I sat back to wait. Me eyes slid along the beds, seeing all the aul ones clapped out. Jaysus! This is like a dead house. There's nothing to look at.

'Soup!' a young one roared, slamming down mugs of soup on the lockers.

I shot up, banging me head against the iron bedhead. Fuck! Me head hurt! I gave it a rub, keeping me eyes on the young one making her way to me.

'Soup,' she said, lifting her eyebrows, holding it in the air.

I started me fit of coughing, waving at her, but she just passed me taking it with her! I couldn't speak. Me face went red trying to stop me coughing and roar after her I wanted it. Jaysus! Mammy! I can't stop. Me bleedin soup is going back out the door.

Me head whipped around, grabbing the mug for spitting into. I coughed and spit, with me head down trying to get air, and tried to croak after her.

'Me!'

She looked around! I waved at her, swinging the mug, then stopped to spit into it.

'Do you want it?'

I shook me head up and down, me face turning purple.

'Ah, you shoulda said,' she moaned, slamming the soup down on me locker.

'Fucking cow!' I gasped, grabbing hold of me soup as I finished me coughing.

IO

Oh, you definitely can't beat the grub in this place, I thought, still getting the taste a roast beef and gravy with the lovely mashed potatoes and cabbage, then jelly and ice cream for afters! Lovely! The only pity is they don't give you a big chunk a bread to mop up the gravy. I had to use me finger! I wriggled down in the bed, looking for more comfort, then mooched me head on the pillow. Ah, this is the life! I sniffed, rubbing the tickle on me nose from all the feathers in the pillow. What more could a body want? Ohh! Ahh! Sigh, I'm ready for another sleep. I closed me eyes, getting ready to doze off, when I heard stamping feet and the sound of voices. The door flew open and I whipped me eyes open. I didn't want to miss anything.

A little fat man came marching in wearing a navy-blue suit and a snow-white shirt with a matching blue tie. He had an army of people all rushing behind him, wanting to keep up. 'Ah, here she is!' he said, waving his head down at me and turning to the little nun in charge of the ward, running beside him.

'Yes, she's in with us,' muttered the little nun, not looking too happy about this plan.

I leapt up in the bed.

'Well! So this is where you are!' he said, smiling down at me and looking around at all the aul ones snoring their heads off. 'Lovely quiet ward,' he said, shaking his head at the nun, who was busy grabbing a chart from the little fat nurse, who was holding it out ready.

'Oh, indeed it is! We like it that way!' snorted the little nun. Then she smiled up at him, rattling her false teeth, and handed him the chart.

He stood flicking open the pages, while her head flew around the room, looking up and down the ward, making sure all the patients were well tucked in and the covers weren't creased, and nothing was thrown around to make the place untidy. Then she peeled her eyes on the floorboards, making sure there wasn't a speck of dust to be seen.

'Yes, plenty of rest,' he roared, snapping shut the chart and handing it to the little nun, who muttered, 'Staff Nurse!'

She leapt to attention, taking her hands from behind her back, and rushed to take the chart. Then she slipped it to another nurse, who put it at the end of me bed. A load of student doctors took a quick step after him as he moved in a bit closer to me. They all had notebooks out, with their pencils raised in the air ready to write down whatever he said as soon as he opened his mouth.

'Martha! How are you feeling?' he roared, smiling down at me.

'Grand, Doctor,' I croaked. Then it hit me! 'Eh, maybe just a bit better,' I said, looking up at him. Not in any hurry to get meself thrown out.

'Fine! Not to worry! We'll have you fit as a fiddle in no time. What was your last job?'

'Eh, a mother's help. Minding six children.'

'Ah, no, that's too much,' he said, shaking his head. 'It's a lot to expect from a young girl of sixteen,' he said, looking around at everyone. The nun and her nurses all shook their heads agreeing. Then the student doctors stopped their writing and looked around, seeing the shaking heads, and shook theirs, wondering what they were agreeing to. The doctor gave his head one more shake, satisfied he was on the right track, then he turned back to me, saying, 'What would you like to do?'

I hesitated, trying to think. Everyone waited. The students lifted their heads, waiting to write down what I said.

'If you had a wish,' he said.

'A wish!' I muttered, me head flying thinking about it. 'I would like to be a secretary! Learn to do shorthand and typing!'

'Yes, I am sure we can work something out!' he said, looking down at the nun.

She nodded her head up and down. 'Yes, Doctor. That can be arranged.'

'Good! I am Doctor O'Hara. I run the children's clinic. Don't worry, Martha. I will look after you. Six children! Can't imagine it!' he said, thinking about it and shaking his head. 'My daughter, Cliona, she is the same age. My wife complains she can't even get her to clean her own room!' Then he laughed, looking around at everyone.

They all screamed their heads with the laughing! The students laughed the loudest, stopping for a minute to give each other a sly dig, then take in huge breaths and roar even louder, making sure the doctor heard them. He gave them a dirty look and snorted, 'Come along, you lot, behave! It wasn't that funny!' Then he was gone, marching out the door with the lot of them falling over each other, everyone wanting to be first behind him, no one wanted to be last. The students used their elbows to get past each other.

I moseyed back along the passages making for me own ward. I sighed, looking in at the wards, seeing the same old faces with their heads springing up, thinking I might be something of a bit of interest coming their way, then turning away in disgust, looking even more fed up than meself. I'm sick listening to aul ones talking night and day about their ailments. I can still hear them. Jaysus! They're still at it! I could hear them talking as I wandered back into me bed and leapt up, sitting meself in the middle, pulling at me toes, with nothing else to look at. I'm just in time to hear the bandage woman telling a new patient next to her, 'Oh, yeah! It's the same wit me, Missus! Now say, after eatin onions for example. Oh, Jesus, Missus! I do be crucified! Rollin around the bed, I am! They give me terrible wind! It blows me up somethin terrible. No, Missus! I couldn't eat anythin like tha!'

'No, no! Shockin! You have to be very careful wha you put into yer mouth!' the new patient agreed, shaking her head and squinting over at bandage woman. Not able to see much of her, because she hasn't got her eyes done yet. 'But you know wha else runs the life outa me, Missus?'

'No! Wha? Tell us!' the bandage woman said, shaking her head up and down, and fixing herself in for more comfort. I held me breath, turning me head from one to the other, resting me eyes on them while we all waited to hear.

'Liver!' the new woman said, leaning forward and pointing her finger at the air, sucking in her breath, letting it out in a big snort, then dropping herself back into the pillows, completely disgusted at having to even mention the name a liver! 'Oh, I do get a terrible doze a the scutters after eatin tha stuff!' she moaned, twisting her face in agony at even the memory.

We all whipped our eyes to the door at the sound of the trolley. 'Dinner!' I shouted, me heart lifting like mad at the sound a the dinner covers getting lifted off the plates, then watching the steam pour out, making me mouth water.

'Where did you wander off to?' the nice nurse with the fat legs said, coming into the ward to dust the lockers and make sure nothing was outa place. She threw her eye at me empty plate sitting squeaky clean on the tray at the end of me bed. 'I see you managed to make it back for your dinner! Of course, I should have known! The mere rattle of a dinner plate is enough to send you running back here like a tornado is hitting the place!' she moaned, twisting her face, half laughing. 'Martha, I'm telling you this now!' she said, waving her duster up and down. 'Sister Munchin threatened she's going to put a lead on you and tie you to that bed! That nun will crack up if you don't stay put,' the nurse said, pointing to the bed. 'We must have order! Everything should be in its place! And there is a place for everything!' the nurse said, stretching her head in the air, making her voice squeak, sounding just like the little nun. Then she gave me a little dig in the ribs and we screamed laughing, sounding like a pack of hyenas.

'So where were you this time?' she said, getting on with her dusting while I followed her around, hanging onta her arm.

'I went up to see me friend on the other floor.'

'Which one is this? Sure, you know more people in this hospital than I've met in a lifetime!'

'Babs! Barbara Caulfield. She has a big iron bolt hammered through her leg. And it's stuck up on a pulley!'

'Tsk, tsk! That sounds very nasty,' the nurse said, swinging her head at me then back to her dusting.

'Yeah, she broke it falling off a bus!'

'The mercy she wasn't killed!' puffed the nurse.

'Yeah, anyway! Oh, Nurse! You should see her! She's the most gorgeous-looking one I ever saw in me life!'

'Really? What does she look like?'

'Ohh, she has this lovely silky, wavy, curly blonde hair that she put up today in two pigtails with two brown ribbons, one on each side a her face.'

'Tsk! She sounds lovely,' the nurse said in a moany voice, rubbing the back of her own hair, wishing she looked like that too.

'Yeah, and her skin is creamy white with shiny big blue eyes that glow in the dark!'

'Glow?' the nurse said.

'Yeah, well you know what I mean, Nurse!'

'Yeah, luminous,' the nurse said, listening and carrying on with her work.

'Yeah, that's right!' I shouted. 'Just like that! Lumlynus!' Even though I didn't know what the word meant. But it sounded right.

'Martha?'

I looked around at the sound of me name being called. I stared at the priest, Father Fitzgerald, walking into the ward slowly, staring at me. 'Well, hello again!' he said, smiling at me. Taking me in from head to toe like he was examining me to see if I was the same person he met before.

I leapt with the fright, not taking in how he was here. 'Are you coming to see me?'

'Who else might I be seeing?' he laughed, waving his arms, looking around the ward.

'But how? Who told you I was here? How does people know I met you?' I said, not being able to take it in, how he found out about me.

'The hospital telephoned me to say you were here,' he said, looking a bit confused himself now.

'We found the telephone number in among your things, Martha,' the nurse said, watching and listening. 'The hospital put it in your records.'

'Yes, that's right! A Sister Munchin telephoned,' the priest said.

'Yes, that's the sister in charge of this end,' the nurse said.

'Oh, right,' I said, trying to take in the priest was here. I felt meself tightening up inside. Not really sure if I wanted to have anything to say to him. The last time I'd seen him makes me feel sick to even think about it. I would be up one minute, feeling content in meself that he might be able to help me. Then nothing! In the end I was even worse off. Finally the fucker drove me straight into the lion's mouth! That bastard Jackser!

The nurse left and the priest took me arm, saying, 'Which bed is yours, Martha?'

I pointed and wandered over to sit on the side of me bed.

'So,' he said, taking in a breath and smiling down at me.

I flicked me eyes up, letting them drop, seeing him staring down at me with his hands in his pockets. I said nothing, because I'm not really interested in talking to him. He said nothing, just stared, letting his eyes wander around me, taking in me bed and locker.

'You are looking a lot better,' he said in a quiet voice. 'The rest has done you good. But you are still looking a bit peaky, rather pale and thin in the face. We shall have to build you up!' he laughed, tapping me on the arm.

I blinked, giving him a half look, then dropped me head down again. We, me arse! He's making himself sound again like he really cared, I snorted to meself.

'I believe you are going to come under the guidance of the children's clinic. They are going to fix you up with some training!' he said, sounding delighted.

'Yeah,' I muttered, wondering when that was going to happen. I hadn't heard anything since.

'Listen, Martha. I shall go and have a few words with someone. Perhaps that sister, or maybe even the doctor, OK?'

'If you want,' I muttered, watching his black shoes and black suit moving away from me. I didn't want to lift me head and look up at him. He causes more trouble than he's worth. I climbed into the bed and lay down staring at the window, seeing the light was beginning to turn into the dark evening. It will soon be time for the tea! I thought, feeling meself lifting with that idea.

I picked up me washbag, grabbing hold of me pyjamas, and shuffled out. Jaysus! I'm going to ask the nurse for something better than these. I looked down at them. They're miles too big for me around the waist and I keep walking on the legs. Surely she has something better than an aul man's pair that they shoulda buried him in. They're not worth keeping! Half the bleedin buttons are missing an the collar's ripped. But I'm not wearing either, them aul grannies' nightdresses that she offered me! Jaysus! I look a holy show!

I bent down and put me washbag into me locker.
    'There you are!'
    I heard a roar next to me ear and leapt with the fright.
    'Good girl! You had your bath!'
    'Yes, Sister,' I said, looking up at the little nun.
    'I am glad to see that, because I was going to get very cross when I saw you were missing again!'
    'Yes, Sister. No, Sister. I didn't go missing.'
    'Very good! Now listen to me, Martha,' she said, wanting to tell me something and get back quick to the business of chasing the nurses, getting them to pick up specks a dust, then rush around shouting at everyone, making sure they are keeping order and the patients are not messing up her wards. 'You are being discharged today!'
    'I am?' I said, feeling me face going white as a sheet.
    'Yes!' she said, shaking her head up and down slowly. 'It is marvellous news!'
    I held me breath, waiting to hear what else she had to tell me.
    'Now! In two week's time to the day, you will come back to the children's clinic. That is run by our Consultant, Doctor O'Hara. You met him!'

I shook me head, agreeing, still holding me breath.

'Now! Here is a letter for you to take back. You will see Sister Bonyventure Aloysius! She is one of our nuns. She runs one of the departments there. Now! You will be under her charge. She will be responsible for you. Now! Take this letter and mind it carefully. Don't lose it. You hand that to her when you meet her. Now have you got all that?' she said, looking at me, making sure she didn't have to repeat herself.

'No, I won't lose it, Sister,' I said, with me nerves shaking like mad. Jesus! Where will I stay? I'm afraid to ask in case everything collapses. They might not think I'm worth the trouble. Nuns are very peculiar about paupers! They only help you when you have plenty! Say nothing, Martha.

'Yes, right! Thanks, Sister,' I said, wanting to get rid of her in case she starts asking awkward questions.

'Now! One other thing. Father Fitzgerald has been informed. He will be arriving to collect you sometime after 2 p.m. Now! You be ready. I expect you sitting on that chair waiting and ready when he comes! Do you hear me?' she said, waving her finger at me.

'Yes, Sister!' I said, getting another shock. What the hell is that fella up to now? He needn't think he is taking me back to any convent or fucking Jackser!

II

I put on me good frock and the good black patent shoes the nuns bought me when I left the convent. Then I folded the trench coat neatly and left it down gently, sitting on the bed, not wanting to crease it. The nuns bought me that too, and the matching soft wool French beret. They got me a whole new rigout when I was leaving. It seems like years ago now, I sighed. But it was only a few months ago. I put me old set of clothes back into the near-empty suitcase and folded me washbag on top, making sure the letter was still sitting safe at the bottom, then clasped it shut and put it sitting down on the floor next to the chair and sat down to wait on the priest. I sat with me hands in me lap, with me head down thinking.

I wonder where that priest is going to take me? One way or the other, I can get along without his idea of helping me. I will ask him out straight, then walk off if he is messing me around. The eejit thinks he knows everything. He didn't listen when I told him the nuns wouldn't have anything to do with me. Then he had the fucking almighty cheek to take me back to Jackser's! What was I thinking going along with that? OK! So where to, Martha? I can go down and ask around in the buildings where I used to live. See if anyone will put me up for a week or two. I can always sleep on the floor. Then I can look for a bit of work. Anything will do. I just need a few bob to keep me going, pay me way. Until I get to see that nun in the clinic. The job should be easier, because I'm not looking for anything living-in. Then if it doesn't work out with the clinic – maybe that was all codology about doing shorthand and typing – they might just want me to do cleaning in their bleedin

103

convent! Anyway! If they're messing, I will save up the fare and get meself off to London! That's the place for opportunities. And there's no bleedin nuns or priests! Or fucking Jackser! Good! That's settled. I let out a big breath, feeling easier in meself now I knew what I was doing.

'Good afternoon, ladies!'

'Ah, hello, Father!' I heard, as I lifted me eyes seeing the priest waving and smiling at all the aul ones, showing a mouthful of white teeth as he squeaked his way down to me in a soft leather black pair a shoes.

'Well! Don't you look nice?' he shouted, letting the whole ward hear him, making everyone look over.

They sat gaping at me, shaking their heads, murmuring, 'Ah, yeah, Father! She looks lovely in them clothes. They really suit her, so they do!' Then watch him letting his head drop sideways, taking me in from head to toe.

He moved himself closer and bent down with his hands on his hips, pretending he wanted a better look. He watched me, staring into me face with his bright-green eyes that leapt and danced in his head, looking like he could get up to plenty a mischief. 'Hm! You polish up well!' he grinned, nodding his head at me. 'Now! What about a smile?'

I ignored him and turned to look at me case. Then stood up to put on me hat and coat. Jaysus! He acts more like a kid than a man, I thought, watching him sweep back the lock a shiny brown hair that flopped over his eye, then make a grab for me suitcase.

'Are we ready, shall we go then?' he said, looking at me then taking off outa the ward, giving the women another big wave.

I took me time and he put his head back in, saying, 'Come along! Or have you decided to wait for supper?'

'I'm coming,' I muttered, still taking me time.

'OK! Follow me then, please! My car is parked outside,' he said, making it sound like we were marching off on an expedition.

'Bye now! You look after yerself, love!' the new woman shouted after me.

'Thanks, Missus Grey,' I said, walking back to her. 'Sure, you will be next out the door now that your operation is over and you even have the bandages off.'

'Ah, yeah! Please God I should be goin home soon enough meself. Do ye know something?' she whispered, leaning over to me. 'I'm delighted at seein ye lookin so well. Ah, Gawd almighty, me heart often went out to you. Because in all the time I'm here I never once saw a soul come up to see you. I hope ye don't mind me sayin? But ye see,' then she lowered her voice, leaning into me, and I bent down to listen, 'I often heard the nurses talkin about you! Oh, nothin bad. Just tha they were sayin ye were all on yer own. An you just a young one, an all tha! Have ye got no one belongin to you, love?'

'No, not really anybody, Missus Grey.'

'Ah, sure, I thought tha too, meself, love! Even without them sayin. Ah, sure, isn't there many more like you,' she said, shaking her head, thinking. 'An there's been many more before you. Ah, God is good! He'll mind you! Tha priest there seems nice enough. Wit the help a God, ye'll land on yer feet. Whatever you do, don't be worryin yerself. Tha does ye no good. That's wha I always told mine! Now I'm tellin you! Worry only puts ye in an early grave! I managed to get through some very hard times. An I'm still here, an I'll have plenty a more years left to me, please God, if he spares me!' she laughed, shaking her head like she meant it.

'Course you will!' I said, smiling at her.

'That's right, love! You keep smilin an the world will smile wit you!'

'Thanks, Missus Grey!' I said, giving her a big smile, seeing the years of suffering in her poor eyes. The good one was all red and bloodshot, and the other one stared at me, trying to see. I looked at the mass of wrinkles on her tired old face, seeing the years of hardship had left their mark.

Yeah, she could tell I was a bit worried and even lonely in meself be times, because she's lived a long and hard life. 'Thanks, Missus Grey,' I said quietly, leaning into her and putting me hand on her hand. 'You take care of yerself. And I hope your eyesight will be better than ever!'

'Oh, indeed it will, daughter! Sure, don't I see you, here now, clear as day, wit me new eye! Thanks be to God!'

'Yeah! And won't it be great when they do the other one?' I said, laughing.

'Oh, the sooner the better! Now go on! Run! You better catch up wit that priest. He's gone runnin wit yer suitcase. I hope that's not loaded wit money!' she laughed.

'Yeah! I better get moving before he leaves the country!'

'Where in blazes has that girl gone to? Martha!' the priest snorted, putting his head back in the door. 'Come along quickly! Heavens! I was halfway out of the hospital when I discovered I was talking to myself!'

'Yes, Father. Here I am. I'm coming,' I laughed, racing to catch up with him as he belted himself off down the passage again, making himself in an awful hurry.

The light made me squint and the wind caught me breath as I walked out through the front door and into the open air. It felt strange having the feel of fresh air on my face after being inside the hospital for over a month. I could see and hear the traffic flying past. Me legs felt a bit wobbly after taking it easy for so long. I followed the priest over to the car and he opened the door and shoved my suitcase into the back seat.

'Hang on, Martha. I want to dash across the road to the shops and get a packet of cigarettes,' he said, taking off out the gates. 'I won't be a minute, wait here for me.'

I walked over to the gates and stood outside, watching him fly across the road. His hair flopped behind him in the wind and he ran with ease, lifting his long legs, hopping on to the footpath. He rushed in the door of the shop, straight into the arms of a young one coming out. They danced around each other, him holding on to her waist and she laughing up at him. Then they broke away and he jumped back, holding his hands down in fists by his sides. 'Terribly sorry!' he said, standing back and waving her out the door with a big grin on his face as his eyes followed the length and breadth of her. She sauntered past, wearing a long black midi coat with a matching long scarf wrapped around her neck. The coat was wide open and streeled out behind her showing her flowery mini frock hugging the top of her legs, nearly showing her knickers. She had on lovely white tight boots that hugged her calves.

'That's all right, Father!' she laughed, noticing his shiny brown floppy hair and the green eyes flashing on her in admiration.

'My! A pretty girl to brighten up my day!' he said, bowing at her.

'What?' I snorted.

I watched yer woman flapping her long black false eyelashes up at him, with the eyeliner curling out at the end. She flipped back her thick, long, straight brown hair, throwing it swinging through the air to land on her shoulders. It was cut straight with a long thick fringe that just tipped above her eyes, making her the image of Cleopatra. I watched as she sashayed off, wriggling her arse, giving him a look back with a smile on her face much as to say, 'Yeah! I wouldn't mind gettin to know you!' He stood like a statue, taking her in, still staring after her with a dirty big grin on his face, enjoying himself no end. I watched, feeling meself raging. Huh! He's not supposed to be doing that! He's a priest.

I then peeled me eyes on the young one. She turned and walked on with a look that said, *Pity, though, he's a priest.* He whipped his head back and flew inta the shop, remembering he has something to do. I looked after the young one. Gawd! She's smashing looking! Wish I could wriggle meself off looking like that! Huh! No one's going to look at me like that, I thought, looking down at meself in me nearly new outfit. I thought I looked lovely until I saw her. Now I look, compared to her anyway, like one a them aul ones in the Legion of Mary! Haunted and hunted looking. I can't see the police having trouble with crowd control because all the fellas are after me. But that young one would. Huh! She fancied herself too much anyway!

I looked out the window, seeing all the shops open and cars and buses honking at cyclists, and horses dragging carts full of coal behind them, moseying along in front of all the traffic, going over O'Connell Bridge. The other drivers went mad.

'Oh, bother!' muttered the priest, trying to pull out from behind a man pedalling his bicycle in front of him. Another car shot past, not letting him out. 'Damned bloody awful drivers!' he muttered under his breath.

I looked up at him cursing, then went back to me sightseeing. Everyone was going somewhere. In and out of the shops, rushing to get across the road, ducking in and out of the traffic, then hopping back when they didn't make it. Some were standing at bus stops, waiting for a bus, reading the newspaper. Everyone seemed to have a purpose. I felt somehow like I wasn't a part of it. I still feel weak from the hospital. But still and all, I don't like being stuck with this fella. It's like he has taken charge of me. I can't do what I want. Well, I don't like that! I'm not getting meself taken anywhere it suits him, like he did with the bleedin convent, then worse! That bastard who should be dead and buried, fucking Jackser! Right! He's not taking me away from the city until I know where I'm going!

'Eh, excuse me, Father Fitzgerald, but where are we going?'

'What?' he said, spinning his head at me, looking annoyed at me interrupting his flying in and out of the traffic, trying to get himself moving. 'Oh! Wait! We shall talk later!' he snapped, throwing his head back to stand on the brakes as a bus pulled out in front of him. 'Bloody awful people, bus drivers!' he muttered, snorting out his breath, looking like he wanted to kill someone.

I stayed quiet, watching as we flew past Trinity College, heading towards Merrion Square. Jaysus! I'm getting further away from the city centre! Better keep quiet for a while, though, seeing the mood he's in. I can always get the bus back. Fuck him, though! He doesn't own me!

'Father!' I said, as we raced along Sandymount, with the waves from the sea trying to lash over the wall. 'You better tell me where I'm going, because I'm getting out of this car as soon as it stops unless you tell me now!'

'My!' he said, looking over at me, giving me a grin. 'You are a fiery little thing!'

'Tell me!' I said, feeling meself go cold, not interested in his silly childish ways.

'Wait and see!' he said.

'NO! Stop this bleedin car! I have had enough of yer messing!'

'Oh, dear. She is a little spitfire,' he muttered to the road ahead. 'Tsk, tsk! You should develop a vocabulary, young lady,' he said, looking over at me with a disgusted face.

'I'm warning you!' I snorted, really beginning to lose me rag.

'Oh, dear! Should I be terribly frightened?' he said, looking at me with his eyebrows creased. Then he shook himself, making it look like a shiver, then settled his face down to concentrate on the road.

I could feel me face going red with the rage. And I was holding me breath. Then me head flew around, wanting to land on something to rip or throw and show him I meant business!

'Ah, ah! Temper, temper!' he said, shaking his finger at me, warning me.

'I am serious! I will do something to hurt you if you don't stop yer messing! NOW TELL ME! Where the fucking hell are you taking me to?'

'To my mother,' he said quietly.

I listened, hearing it again in me head. 'Your mother?'

'Yes. You can stay with her for a few days. She lives alone. You will be company for her.'

I said nothing, just collapsed back in me seat, letting out a breath I didn't want him to hear. I don't want him thinking, or knowing, I am depending on him. Because no one is in charge of me.

12

We drove in through big gates with a high wall around it, and up an avenue surrounded by trees. Then we turned onto a wide area covered in pebble stones to park the car. I looked up at the big old house with windows down to the ground, nearly, and a glasshouse at the side for growing things in.

'Does your mother live in this big house all on her own?' I said, not able to get me breath at how well off his family was.

'Yes. But she has a housekeeper who looks after her. Does a bit of cooking and that sort of thing. Her husband takes care of the gardening work and will sometimes act as driver, to collect guests from the station, or whatever is needed when she has friends to stay. They have their own living quarters. Look,' he said, pointing back down the avenue through the trees. 'Down at the gate lodge.'

'It's a bit like a convent,' I muttered, looking around at all the windows that even went to the side of the house and loads more at the back. I could see a red-brick wall surrounding another area, with big apples trees hanging over the wall.

'Eh, is your mother very rich?' I said, staring up at him as he hiked me suitcase out of the car and slammed it shut with a bang.

He didn't answer me. He just stopped to look around, staring at the trees blowing in the cold March wind, letting his eyes peel up to the stone steep steps, with a small heavy old black gate that led into another garden. His eyes had a very faraway look. 'Our family dogs are buried up there,' he muttered. 'Our dear old faithful companions,' he said, sounding a bit lost in himself. Then he half smiled, seeing me watching him, but it was a sad smile.

'Really? How many are buried up there?' I asked quietly.

'A few. Mine, for one. Toby! A Scottish Highland terrier. He used to follow me around as a boy. He was my little shadow!'

I listened as his eyes stared, going back in time, remembering.

'He was a wonderful companion,' he whispered. 'My best friend. He died when I was away at school.'

'What age were you?' I said, listening and wondering about him as a boy.

'I was, oh, perhaps about eleven. Something like that.'

'Did you miss him something terrible?' I said, getting the picture of him as a little boy losing his poor dog.

'Yes, something terrible,' he said, shaking his head then marching off, heading for the front door.

I followed, feeling a bit nervous. I hope his mother doesn't mind him landing me in on top of her. 'So, is she rich?' I said, watching him pull out a big key on a leather string.

'Who?' he said, looking at me with his eyebrows raised.

'Your mother. Is she rich? I asked you.' Dying to know all about him.

He stopped what he was doing and stared, trying to think what to say. Then he turned his mouth down, thinking hard about it. 'She has a private income. I suppose you could say she is comfortable,' he said, making for the big heavy door, holding out the key to open it.

The door swung open into a big hallway. I followed him in, seeing doors on each side, and looked up at a high ceiling with a long chandelier hanging down. Me eyes looked up at the lovely polished dark wood staircase, with bars curling up around a big knob. The staircase went up to a landing with more doors, and I leaned around, seeing it go up to another long passage on a higher floor with even more doors.

He dropped me suitcase in the hall, next to a big press with a mirror and drawers at the sides and places for hanging your coats, and black boxes for holding umbrellas. I looked in, seeing fancy canes with silver tips and sticks for sitting on when you go walking, and ladies' umbrellas with silver in the middle of the handles. And men's big black umbrellas with thick wooden handles and gold stamps on them showing who made them. The hall tiles were reddish brown and a big rug was thrown in the middle. Me head swung on me shoulders trying to take in the size of the place, never mind the style.

The priest wandered down around the staircase and vanished in through a door. Then he put his head back. 'Martha? What are you doing? Come along! Don't stand there gaping!'

'Right! I'm coming.' I rushed after him, dying to see more. Jaysus! Imagine living in a place like this! Comfortable, me arse! They must be rich as . . . Maybe they own a bank!

I went in through the door, following him down a passage with more doors on each side. It was a bit dark with a window trying to throw in light at the end of the passage. We walked into a sitting room with a big fireplace and a window at the end of the room showing the same view as the end passage one. I looked out, seeing big old trees and a high stone wall with ivy growing up it. Me head swung around to take in the two sofas, one each side of the fireplace, facing each other. A long wooden table sat behind each sofa. The wood glowed a lovely burnished red from years of polishing. On top of the table sat big matching lamps with painted glass that glowed different colours when the light hit them. The priest leaned over and switched on the lamps, bringing a gorgeous orange glow into the dark room.

It really looks very cosy, I thought, not being able to take in the comfort. Then he picked up a big box of matches sitting on the mantelpiece and struck one, lighting the paper and sticks sitting under the logs. I sat down on the sofa as he took off his priest's black jacket and threw it across the room, landing it on a big armchair with a high back to get yerself lost in. Then he reached up and unfastened the collar around his neck and ripped it off, sending it flying to land on the jacket. 'What about some television?' he said, walking over to a wooden cabinet and opening the door and switching on the box.

'Gawd! I never saw a television as fancy as that before,' I said, staring at it, waiting for it to come on.

'How many televisions have you seen?' he said, smiling at me.

'Not many! I don't watch television. We had one in the convent but it was rationed. Only once a week to watch *The Virginian*! A bloody cowboy show!' I said, snorting out me disgust. 'But everyone loved it.'

'Perhaps they were desperate,' he laughed, throwing his head in the air. 'I mean, what choice did they have?'

'Yeah, suppose that was it,' I said, watching him take off his shoes and wander over to take a packet of cigarettes out of his jacket pocket. He lit one up and handed me the packet. I took it, trying to take out a handful.

'Only one!' he barked, taking the packet back. Then he held the packet out to me again. I took only one this time and he held the match, lighting me cigarette. Then he took in a big drag, letting his head drop back, and wriggled his shoulders, letting himself fall back on the sofa opposite me and swing his feet up, making himself the picture of comfort and contentment.

I sucked on me cigarette, taking in big drags like him, and tried to blow smoke rings around me head after watching him do it. 'No! I can't make them!' I coughed, getting a mouthful of smoke land down the wrong way in me chest.

'You are too young! Takes years of practice,' he muttered, looking at his smoke rings circling around his head then wafting into the air.

'How old are you, Father Ralph?'

'Hmm!' he murmured, not taking any notice of me. He was too busy lying on his back watching himself blow smoke rings.

'How old are you?'

'What?' he said, lifting his head to look over at me like I had said something shocking. Then he let his head plop back into the soft cushions and murmured, 'M.Y.O.D.B.'

'What's that mean?' I said.

'Mind your own damned business!'

'Jaysus! There's no need to be bloody touchy,' I snorted, feeling he was giving out to me. I turned away from him and peeled me eyes on the television. I sat in silence watching the blank screen with only a round card showing the photograph of a little young one in the circle. It was too early for the television to start showing anything.

Then suddenly the jingle of music came on. I sang along. 'Nah nah nah NEH NEH!'

'Good God! What is that?' he squeaked, leaping his head up to get a look. 'Oh, bloody balderdash! Switch that awful stuff off.'

'No! I like it,' I said, wanting to torment him after he insulting me.

He dropped back down, letting out a big sigh, shaking his head, knowing he can't win with me.

'Father Ralph, where's your mother?'

'I have no idea,' he murmured, reading a book he took out of a bookcase that stands against the back wall.

'What are you reading?'

'A book,' he muttered, throwing his head at me slowly and smiling.

'Jaysus! You really are very childish!' I snorted, getting fed up he was taking no notice of me.

I got up and wandered over to look at photographs spread out all over the place, sitting on tables and hanging up on the walls. 'Oh, look! There's you when you were younger,' I said, lifting it up to get a better look. He was sitting in a boat with a load of other fellas all holding oars in their hands and rowing together at the same time. They were even dressed the same. All wearing white trousers and white jumpers with a stripe in the neck.

'Oh, this is a nice one of you, Father Ralph! Where was that taken?'

He lifted his head to look over, then dropped his head into his book again, saying, 'Cambridge. My old Alma Mater.'

'Yer what?'

'School! That was my university. I went to Cambridge!'

'In England?' I said.

'Yes, of course, you old sausage!'

'Did you go to school in England as well?'

'Yes, we all did. It is a family tradition. We all attended fine old public schools in England. Now, any more questions, sweetheart?' he asked, looking at me like he was waiting to hear. But not really! He wanted to get back to his book.

'Did you always want to be a priest?' I said.

He lifted his head, saying, 'No. I practised medicine for a while.'

'You were a doctor?'

'I am a doctor!' he said, making sure I understood that.

'Where did you work? Did you work in a hospital?' I said, looking at him.

'No, a clinic. Harley Street,' he said, dropping his head back to read his book.

'What were you doing?' I said, thinking he really is important.

He lifted his head, raising his eyebrow then took in a deep breath, thinking about it. Then he said, 'Mainly looking after neurotic, wealthy, middle-aged matrons.'

'Matrons in a hospital?' I said, trying to figure that out.

'No, you silly goose!' he roared, laughing his head off. 'Married ladies!'

'Oh,' I said, thinking about that. 'What does neurotic mean?'

'Oh,' he said, breathing in heavy, 'they were bored from the constant round of trying to entertain each other and themselves.'

'Ah, so they weren't sick!' I said, smiling.

'No!' he said, still looking at his book.

'So they all came to see you! I bet I know why!' I said, laughing.

'Why?' he said, looking up at me.

'Because they all thought you were gorgeous!' I said.

'Perhaps, there may be a grain of truth in what you say,' he said, smiling, without opening his mouth. But just stared at me, thinking. Then he said, staring straight into me eyes, really taking me in, 'You are very astute for one so young.'

'I bet they missed you,' I said, smiling.

'Oh, I am sure they will get along without me,' he said, looking at me with a big grin on his face.

'So why did you give up being a doctor?' I said, trying to figure him out.

'I simply thought I would do better as a priest. Be more useful.'

'Why?' I said, thinking it would be a whole lot better being a doctor than an aul crabby priest.

'Why what?' he said, staring at me.

'What's so special about being a priest?' I said. 'Everyone has to keep their distance from you.'

'Nonsense! Look at you! My goodness! You would be sitting on my lap with a pen and notebook taking down my history if I let you! Distance! Oh, you are funny!' he said, making a face at me.

'Jaysus! I can't figure you out at all!' I snorted, getting fed up with not being able to get a straight answer outa him.

'When's yer ma comin back?' I said, getting really fed up.

'Oh, Martha! Don't speak like that, darling!' he said, putting down his book and looking at me like he was in pain.

'Why? What's wrong with the way I speak?'

'You speak beautifully when you wish. But you sound much better when you open your mouth.'

'The bloody cheek a you. Insulting me! There's nothing wrong with the way I speak.'

'Of course not, Martha. But I just think you sound so much better when you speak clearly and open your mouth. That is all, my sweet,' he said, looking at me like he really cared and speaking so quiet and gentle I felt meself melting inside and even wanted to cry. It feels lovely to have someone like him look at me like I am really special. That has never happened in me life. I desperately wanted Sister Eleanor to notice me. But it never happened. Now I have someone all to meself. I wanted to go over and sit next to him. Have him put his arms around me, like he did the first time. I stared at him lying there reading his book. But, no! I would never be able to do that. That only happens to family. If I was his sister, or even if he was my father . . . But I'm not related. And he is a priest! So, I couldn't even be his girlfriend in a couple of years, because I would have to wait to catch up with him. But that will never happen.

'How old are you, Father Ralph?' I heard meself saying again, wanting to know.

'I am thirty-six. Almost! Or I shall be soon.'

'Oh! That's not very young,' I said. 'You will be heading for forty very soon!'

'Thank you! I look forward to impending old age! When did you say?' he asked the wall, looking very serious. 'Ah, yes! Soon, very soon!'

I roared laughing, delighted I had gotten a rise outa him.

'Listen! One more derogatory word out of you, young lady! And I shall . . .'

'What did I say wrong?' I moaned.

'Old age indeed!' he muttered, sounding like he was really worried about that idea.

The fire crackled and a log slipped because the fire was dying down. He stood up and reached down and loaded up more logs, stacking them in the fire, making it blaze and send sparks flying.

'Take care! The sparks are landing in your hair!' I shouted.

He brushed himself down, running his hands through his hair, then sat down on the sofa, putting his shoes back on. 'Yes! That was a nice and relaxing rest,' he sighed, standing up and rubbing his hands slowly together. 'But enough of that!' Then he stared at me for a few seconds, looking like he was thinking. Then he put out his hand, still staring at me. I looked at him, then looked at his hand stretched out for me to take. I stood up, wondering where we were going.

'Come along, Martha. Let us go and see if we can find ourselves something to eat in the kitchen. It looks like we are being left to fend for ourselves.' Then he leaned his hand closer, waiting for me to take it.

I hesitated, feeling very shy. Then I let me hand drop into his. I felt his hand curl around mine and then tighten, and he pulled me close to him and took off out the door, walking quickly down the passage dragging me behind him. 'We must feed you, you poor thing,' he said, sounding very serious. 'We don't want you fading away on us again, now do we?' he said, stopping to look at me, then wrapping his arm around me shoulder and pulling me into him, letting me rest against him with my head on his chest. 'You are very precious, you know,' he said, lifting his hand and stroking me cheek. 'You really do need lots of love and tender care,' he murmured, speaking so quietly I could barely hear. Then he let me go and grabbed me hand again, making for the kitchen.

I felt like me whole world has suddenly changed. Like I'm a little child again, not sixteen, but six. All my life I have waited for someone to tell me they care about me. Now it has suddenly happened out of the blue! How can that be? I looked at his hand holding mine as he pulled me along. It feels so strong and warm and soft. He's holding my hand! He gave me a hug. He's thinks I'm special. Well, I sort of think he does. The best bit is I don't have to fight off any other young ones to try and get his attention! Not like in the convent! Gawd! He's like the daddy I always wanted, and even a mammy, all rolled into one. Because he fusses over me like a mammy would. The only pity is I am sixteen. A bit too old for a daddy and mammy. I don't want to look foolish, letting him see me act like a kid. Even though I feel like one suddenly. Pity, though! The hug didn't last long. I would love to sit and be hugged by him, with nothing else to do. Just hugs and more hugs! And I'd never get fed up with it! This is definitely the best thing that has ever happened to me in me whole life! Imagine me! Special! I let out a big sigh, getting a lovely feeling of peace melt all over me insides, and me head stopped thinking. I feel like me face is smiling, because I'm warm all over and content. It gives me a feeling of being still inside meself and at peace with the world. Never did I ever think I could be so happy.

'Here we are!' he said, as he opened a door down at the far end of the passage into a big kitchen. It had a long wooden table with high-back wooden chairs that looked very old. A huge old Aga sat in a big wide alcove with a mantelpiece overhead. I looked at the big kitchen dresser that was built into the wall. Every inch of it held dishes and big carving plates for serving meat. I could recognise what a lot of this stuff was for from working in the kitchen when I was in the convent.

'Ah! We have cheese,' he said, lifting the lid off a dish sitting in the middle of the table. 'Celery?' he said, pointing to a tall dish. I looked at it, then pressed me nose close to smell it.

'No! I'm not eating that stuff! I don't like the smell of it!'

'Nonsense! It is delicious! Here, try some!' he said, picking up one and taking a bite out of it.

Suddenly we heard dogs barking. He stopped munching to listen. 'Ah! Mother is home,' he said, dropping the celery onto a plate sitting on the table and wiping his hands in a teacloth that was hanging up next to towels and aprons.

'Darling? Ralphie? Where are you?' I heard a woman in a very grand voice shout out like she was singing.

'In here! Kitchen!' shouted the priest, throwing open the door.

Two little dogs came rushing in, barking and tearing around the kitchen all excited, then came steaming back to run around me, barking their heads off.

'Ah! No! Nice doggies! Don't bite me!' I'm afraid of me life of dogs. Even little ones! I took little steps away from them, holding me feet together, watching them snapping at me ankles. 'Eh, help, Father! Get them away from me.'

'Oh, really, Martha! Surely you are not afraid of those tiny mutts?' he said, looking back and laughing his head off.

'Get the fucking things away from me!' I moaned.

He let out a roar. 'Eddie! Simps! Come! Heel!' he growled. They came rushing over, dragging their bellies on the ground. 'Stay!' he muttered, when they sat looking up at him waiting for more instructions.

'Now, Martha, please! This kind of foul language is quiet unbecoming. You must develop a vocabulary,' he said quietly, pointing his finger, then marching out the door.

Fuck! Now he's annoyed with me! Well, fuck him and his dogs! I don't want to get meself bitten! Fucking eejit, laughing when I was afraid of me life.

I3

'**M**am'ma! How are you?' I heard him say.

'Oh, Ralphie darling! It is so lovely to see you! My poor darling boy! You must be ravenous! Have you had anything to eat yet? Oh, I was so cross with myself when I could not be here to meet you after you telephoned. But Julia Simmons phoned during the morning. She is up in town. A flying visit, she said! Tom, Jeremiah's friend! Well, she wanted to meet him while he is home. Catch him before he starts gadding about. So what could I say? – What was I saying? Oh, yes! She asked if I was free for lunch. So of course I couldn't refuse. Especially after she said Livonia Moleswent had pencilled me in for her salon this afternoon. Oh, everyone will be there, she said. So I could not but say yes. Then I heard that awful woman Fay Melbing-Forth would be coming along too! Oh, what a dreadful bore that woman is!'

'Mam'ma!' I listened, hearing her voice carrying down from another room.

Jaysus! Me heart is in me mouth! Supposing she throws me out? Maybe she won't like the look of me. Or think her son has an awful cheek bringing a stranger into her home. Anything can happen. I wonder if he even told her? Jaysus! I think he takes an awful lot of things for granted. Like he thought Sister Eleanor would take me back! I could feel me heart sinking. Ah, well! Nothing lasts. I still have time to get meself back into the city centre and rush down to the buildings before it gets too dark. I looked at the kitchen window. It was very dark already! But maybe the trees are blocking out the light. I went over to try and get a look up at the sky. Yeah, it is dark.

120

I wonder what time it is? I looked around, seeing a clock over beside the window, high up in the wall. Ten to six! No! I still have time. Maybe the priest will give me a lift back into town. I'm not staying here if I'm under compliment. Even if she agrees, it would be only half-hearted, because he's putting her under the pressure. No! That would only make trouble for meself and her.

Right! Dear God, please let his mother not mind me staying here. Please! I would be so grateful. Especially as I really like Father Ralph. It would be a really good thing for me to be able to have someone like him that cares for me. Will you do that for me, God? Please! I will do everything in me power to be good! Work hard, stay out of trouble, not get into fights with people. No more bad language, cursing. I will give that up. OK? Thanks, God. I love you with all my heart! Just let me stay here! Right! I could feel meself all hot and bothered with the nerves. OK! Sit down, Martha. Sit still. Just wait and see what will happen.

I sat waiting, holding me hands together, folding them on the kitchen table. It's very quiet! I listened to the big clock sitting up on the wall, ticking away the time. I looked up at it. This reminds me a bit of the convent somehow. The clock is the same one they have there. The one I broke. Or yer woman, she broke! That mad young one that worked in the kitchen. Mad cow! Throwing that big knife at me when we had that fight. Oh, fuck! I hate this waiting. Me nerves are gone. OK! If the worst comes to the worst, I can always go me own way. And there is always the nun to look forward to. Maybe I really will end up getting to do that shorthand and typing. Jaysus! That would be a miracle! Then I would really be on me way up! Yeah! Nothing to worry about. I let out me breath, feeling a bit better. Nothing is going to kill me, so what if she doesn't want me? Wonder where they're gone?

'Martha?'

I held me breath. He's calling me! Me heart leapt with the fright. I jumped up. 'Yeah, Father Ralph! I'm coming.'

'Where are you, Martha?' he said, rushing into the kitchen. 'Come along! Come and meet my mother. She is waiting to meet you.'

I hesitated. Feeling afraid. Not wanting to hear her say, sorry, but she can't let me stay.

'Come on! Don't be shy! I promise she won't eat you!' he laughed, grabbing me hand, pulling me out the door. Then he walked on and I stopped.

'Where are the dogs?' I moaned, afraid of me life of getting the ankles bitten offa meself.

'What? Oh, don't worry about them. They are outside chasing goodness knows what. Martha,' he said, stopping and coming back to me. 'Are you really frightened of dogs?' he said quietly, bending his head down and looking into me face.

'Yeah, I really am, Father. Until I get to know they won't bite me. I'm always getting chased by dogs. Well, I try not to run,' I said, looking up at him trying to get him to understand.

'Oh, I promise you they won't bite you,' he said, speaking very softly and putting his arm around me shoulders, giving me a tight hug.

'OK, I believe you,' I said. 'Even if millions of dog owners all say the same thing, just before the bleedin—'

'No! Try saying something like awful,' he said, grinning at me.

'Right! Bleedin awful things,' I said, laughing me head off when he chased me back down the passage.

'You are incorrigible,' he said, grabbing a hold of me and swinging me through the air like I was made out of a bag of feathers!

I screamed, 'Lemme down!'

He landed me on me feet.

'I can't believe how strong you are, Father Ralph!'

'Of course,' he said, stretching out his arms. 'All down to games as a boy. The public schools are famous for it! Now come on. Come and meet my mother!'

We headed down the passage and ended up back in the hall and around by the stairs and down another passage. 'Gawd! You would get lost in this place,' I said, not able to get over the size of it for just one family.

'It's not really that big,' he said, stopping to open a door into an even bigger sitting room.

I crept in behind him with me heart in me mouth.

'Come on! In you come!' he said, waving me in.

I took me time and appeared around the door with him waiting patiently to close it.

'Oh, come on, slow coach! Go on! Go and sit down, relax.'

I wandered over to a long sofa and sat down, sliding off it. I ended up sitting on the edge, digging me heels in to try and stay sitting. It's too silky. I looked around, not feeling very comfortable with me seat, seeing all the sofas and armchairs I could have sat in.

Me eyes peeled around, taking in the style of the place. The big cabinets with the lovely ornate carvings on them were standing against the walls, with statues of a man holding a book under his arm. And another one of a young fella standing on a ship, holding a wheel in his hand, and the other arm raised in the air. That one looked like some kind of metal. Some of them were in marble. There were small tables everywhere – behind sofas with lamps on them and books and silver photographs. And a big painting hung on the wall of the mother when she was young. I would say around seventeen or eighteen. She had on a long white frock, with a fur band on her head and a big white furry-looking feather sticking up. She was wearing a long, lovely white cloak hanging around her shoulders. It had white fur lined all around the edges. The whole lot was topped off with her wearing silver slip-on shoes. She really looked very beautiful.

I looked down at me feet resting on a big Persian carpet. They have two that nearly run the length of the room. Well, they look Persian! I saw pictures of them in books on the convent table, in the big parlour for the important visitors. I looked up at the big crystal chandelier swinging out of the ceiling. Holy God! This place is just out of this world. I have never met the like of any people so rich in all me born days! They must own two banks! One wouldn't buy you all this!

'Mam'ma! Would you like a drink?' the priest said, looking at a tall thin woman standing with her arm resting on a big white marble fireplace. She was watching a fat little grey-haired woman suffocating in black smoke that was belching outa the fire she was trying to light.

'How is Mattie? Any improvement in the lumbago?' the Mam'ma said to the old woman, leaning herself across the mantelpiece with her arm stretched across it.

'Oh, he's mighty better, M'am,' the little woman said, lifting her head outa the grate, and looking up at the mother, showing her face smothered in black soot. Then she said, 'Thank you for asking, M'am! That stuff you gave me did him a power a good! I gave it to him as you said. Three times a day and one before he went to sleep. Mind, he wasn't too fond a the taste a that stuff! Whatever was in it! I had to—'

'Taste?' the Mam'ma shouted, grabbing hold of her neck and hanging on to it. 'Did you? Did he drink it, Maeve?'

'Of course he did, M'am! Sure, what else was he supposed te do with it?'

'Oh, dear! Oh, goodness, NO!' shouted the mammy, holding her chest, with her eyeballs hanging outa her head. 'Maeve! You were supposed to rub it into his back,' she whispered, letting her eyeballs burn a hole through the aul one. Then she said, 'Not have him DRINK the bloody stuff! Oh, really!' she snorted, turning her head away. Then she whipped her head back. 'Is he all right? Was he ill, poor man? Ralphie dear! Would you please get me a drink, darling?' she said, turning to the priest, holding her forehead like she had a pain in her head.

The woman sat on her hunkers, staring up at the priest's mother, trying to take in what she had done wrong. Her lips kept moving but nothing came out. Then she got fed up and said, snarling up her face, 'Ah, sure, isn't it true what they say – if it doesn't kill yeh, it'll cure yeh! Sure, it did him no harm at all. An if it was coddin me he was, well, it worked just as well! Because he certainly did not like the taste a that stuff. An it sure got him up an moving fast enough! Now he tells me he's hale an hearty! Ails him? What about me poor self? There's no one to ask me what ails me. Isn't he grand now? He's grand now,' she repeated, muttering to herself and going back to putting more coal and logs on the fire, building it up.

I sat listening, drinking in everything that was being said and done. I couldn't get over the mother's way of speaking. Or even the priest! He talks just like his mother. I never heard anyone speak so grand in me life. They really are toffs! But I don't like the way she shouted at the woman. I hope she doesn't shout at me like that. I stared at her, thinking she looks like something out of a film. But, somehow, I don't know what's missing. She has all the glamour all right. But it's not really stylish.

Me attention settled on the style of her. She has no style. It's very plain, the kind of stuff she wears. I wouldn't be seen dead in a get-up like that if I was her. Yeah! Them clothes she's wearing is very old fashioned. She's wearing a dark-green Donegal tweed suit with a crisp snow-white blouse and a wine silk cravat tucked inside the neck of the blouse. An them brogues! That's what they're called. Them shoes cost pounds in money. I saw them up in the Brown Thomas shop in Grafton Street. Jaysus! They're very old fashioned. Imagine paying loads a money to wear shoes like a man! Still, she is a bit old, I thought, staring at her. She must be in her sixties. But she still looks grand for that. Some people her age can go around looking a bit bent! But you would think she was starved for the want of a good feeding, to look at her. She looks like a skeleton, because she is very bony. Her cheekbones stand up! They are very bony looking. No! She is really too thin for my liking. I always thought the rich should be more fat than that. But I love her hair. She has gorgeous hair. It's silky gold and wavy, with a lick hanging over her forehead. I see now where the priest gets his eyes from. His mother! She has beautiful green laughing eyes with that same mischief look in them. Like you have just told her something funny and it's supposed to be a secret but you know she's going to tell!

'Did you say you would like a drink, Mam'ma?'

'Oh, yes, darling! Thank you. I will have a gin. And just a little tonic, sweetie,' she said, swinging herself around to stand with her heel lifted off the floor and her ankle crossed, resting it behind her other ankle. I watched, admiring the way she acted. Then she lifted a cigarette to her mouth, taking a long deep drag. Then she slowly lowered the cigarette away from her mouth, letting her hand dangle in the air, with the cigarette held between two pointed fingers, and crossed her arm, resting it on her elbow. Then she slowly pushed out her bottom lip, letting the smoke hiss out, leaving herself buried in a fog of smoke. Then she let herself drop back against the fireplace, watching Father Ralph make for the end of the room and stop at a long mahogany table.

He lifted out a fancy crystal bottle standing beside two others. They were all sitting in a wooden box with a lock on it. I watched as he poured the drinks. 'Would you like a drink, Martha?' he said, looking back at me.

'Eh, eh . . .' I tried to think. What kind of drink does he mean? Is he offering me a gin too? 'Eh, what kind of drink have ye got, Father?'

'What would you like?' he grinned, seeing me thinking about it. 'No, not booze, silly!' he laughed.

'I think there is some lemonade left from the children, Ralphie,' the mother said, lifting her head to point over at the press next to the table. He looked around. 'Try underneath, in the press.'

'Got it.' He held the bottle up like he had just won first prize and held it out. 'You are in luck! Otherwise it would perhaps have been the gin after all!' he said, laughing his head off.

'Oh, really, Ralphie! You mustn't say those things,' she said, smiling over at me, shaking her head saying, 'Tsk, tsk. He can be very naughty!'

Jaysus! Yeah! Very naughty! An he is only heading for forty! I was dying to say. Well, thirty-six. Gawd! These very grand people can be very childish. I suppose they have nothing to worry them.

'Mam'ma! Your drink!'

'Oh, thank you, darling!'

'Martha, come and take your drink.'

I took it out of his hand and he wandered over to sit down in an armchair in the centre of the room with a table beside it and a lovely lamp sitting on top. He picked up a book sitting beside it and switched on the lamp. The Mam'ma picked up a silver lighter from a side table sitting against the wall next to the fireplace and lit up another cigarette. 'Would you like one, darling?'

'No, thank you, Mam'ma.'

I looked over, wishing he would light one up so I could have a smoke. But nobody offered me one.

I contented meself watching her smoke. I wanted to learn how she makes it look so glamorous. A bit like a film star. Because I want to look like that too. I watched as she did the same thing again. She took a big drag of the cigarette, sucking it down into her lungs, and held it. I watched as she let it come pouring out through her nose, holding her head back. Then she slowly moved the cigarette away from her, holding it between two fingers, and held her hand up in the air, letting her elbow rest on the other hand. Right! I think I know how to do that! All I need now is practice! People might even start mistaking me for someone important. Then she dropped her head and went back to watching the old woman managing to get a blaze coming outa the fire.

'Oh, you really are a wonder with that fire, Maeve! I don't know how you get it to work.'

'No trouble, M'am!' said the woman, slapping her hand on the rug and hauling herself onto her feet. 'I'll get the supper started now, M'am!' she said, making it sound like she was under sufferance, after working day and night. Then she took off, taking herself out of the room in an awful hurry, not looking at anyone, just keeping her eyes down sideways, but still managing to take everyone in. Then she lifted her head, throwing an eye over at the priest, saying, 'Supper won't be long, Father.'

'Thank you, Maeve. No hurry,' he said, lighting himself up a cigarette. Then he looked at his watch, making a face.

When the door closed and the woman left, I moved meself away. Moving up a bit closer to him. Sitting in the chair next to him.

'OK, we may speak,' he said, looking back to make sure the door was closed and the woman had really left. 'Come here!' he said to me, smiling, standing up and gently putting his hand on my shoulder.

'You have not spoken since we came into the room. You really are a shy little thing. Mam'ma, I want you to meet a friend of mine, Martha.'

'Oh, how lovely to meet you,' she said, smiling and coming over to take my hand. 'Father Ralph has told me so much about you!'

'Mam'ma, Martha will be staying for a short while. She will be good company for you.'

'Oh, how marvellous! How old are you, dear?'

'Sixteen, Missus Fitzgerald.'

'Oh, how sweet! Yes, Ralphie has mentioned that. Oh, I am delighted to have you stay.'

'Thanks very much!' I said, me heart flying with the delight, knowing she really means it.

'Another drink, Mam'ma!'

She took the drink, giving him a big smile, saying, 'Oh, thank you, darling, that is kind! Oh, darling! Did I tell you? Amelia is arriving next week. She is bringing the children with her. They will be staying at Bertram's. Then Maud is arriving on Thursday! She, too, is bringing the children. I must speak to Maeve. We will need to organise the house and food.' Then she landed her head on me again. 'Goodness! You poor things! You must be absolutely famished! Oh, yes, it will be wonderful having a young girl around the house,' she said, patting me arm and smiling at me. Then she rambled off over to the fire and threw the half-smoked cigarette in, making the fire sizzle up and burn with yellow flames licking up the chimney.

Oh, Gawd, Mammy! This is the life! I thought to meself. She really is a lovely woman. And I'm going to be living in the height of luxury for the next . . . did he say few days? Hope it's a bit longer! Jaysus! I'm not walking on the sunny side a the street! I'm over on the other side where it's raining down pennies! Ohhh! Never could I ask for more!

14

'Thank you, Mam'ma, that was lovely. But I really must go now,' the priest said, looking at his watch and throwing down his linen napkin.

'Oh, really? Must you go so soon, darling?'

'Yes, I am afraid I must, darling Mam'ma, duty calls.'

'Oh, really, Ralphie! You could stay on a little while longer, I am sure. For goodness' sake, we have hardly finished supper!'

'Oh, Mam'ma!' he laughed. 'You know I am not a man of leisure. I have work to do!'

'Bah!' the mother said, slapping down her napkin in disgust.

I looked down at me empty plate. Them lamb chops were lovely. But we didn't get enough of them. Only two, and they were tiny! You could hardly see them sitting on the plate next to the ten green peas keeping them company and the two little potatoes. They cut all the skins off, cutting the potato into a little round ball shape, leaving hardly any of the potato left by the time they were finished. Jaysus! No wonder the mother is so skinny. They hardly eat anything. And it all sits in the middle of a huge big white plate.

Then we all come in here, to sit at this huge long dining table surrounded by big sideboards and cabinets with silver, and paintings of people in old times carrying baskets of fruit and picking stuff off trees. I looked at the dining table with the big silver ornament for holding little glass dishes sitting inside little silver dishes, holding everything from salt to sauces. It was about a foot off the table and made in the shape of people, and little babies flying with their arms out all carved into it. Or however they do it. The dining room is outa this world. With the big heavy carved dining chairs and the long narrow window going down nearly to the floor showing a big field with huge trees sitting well back. And the silver dishes for holding hot food. With big silver carving dishes all sitting along the sideboard that went nearly the length of the wall.

I looked over at the big white marble fireplace with blue veins going through it, and the huge heavy gold mirror that covered the chimney breast over the fireplace. Yeah! The height of luxury. And all looking like this. So you could come in and sit down and eat to your heart's content. A banquet, with no money spared. Except they don't do that. They eat nothing! I thought, staring down at me empty plate. It was snow-white clean with not a scrap of food left. Or nothing else even coming. Jaysus! What a big fuss about nothing.

'Come along then! Shall we have a nightcap before you go, darling?' the mother said, looking at the priest. She had changed herself into a lovely silk frock before we had the dinner. It looks lovely on her, I thought, staring over at her as she got up from the dinner and walked over to a table against the wall and helped herself to a whiskey. She stood with her back to us, wearing the lovely wine frock with long sleeves and a belt going around her waist. It clung to her and settled itself into the shape of her, making her look like a real lady who is very delicate and fragile. And you want to mind her, because she might break.

I looked down at her soft wine suede shoes with the low heel and a little silver buckle in the middle that looked like a little brooch. It gleamed and flashed when the light hit it. The priest stood up, saying, 'I must go and dress, Mam'ma. Where did I leave my things?'

'In the first sitting room we went into, Father.'

His eyes straightened, coming out of his doze, and looked at me. Then he winked at me, giving me a big grin, and jumped up making out the door. 'Won't be long, Mam'ma. Then I must say take my leave.'

'Oh, really? Won't you have a drink before you go?'

But he was gone, flying out the door. I watched the door half shutting behind him as he flew. Then I was on me feet pushing back the chair and tearing out after him. I wanted to be with him. 'Father Ralph!' I shouted, flying down the passages after him.

'Go back and wait for me,' he said, waving me back. 'Darling, I must go!' he said, seeing me after I trailed him into the sitting room. 'You be good for Mother! Look after her,' he said, slipping the collar around his neck and pulling on his jacket.

I felt me heart sinking, watching him get ready to go. I wanted to say something. Me heart was flying! But I didn't know what to say.

'Now, darling,' he said, grabbing me and hugging me into him. 'You enjoy yourself with Mother. She is very pleased you are here.'

'But I don't want you to go!' I heard meself whining into his jacket, knowing I sound like a little six-year-old kid. But I don't care! It's how I am feeling right this minute.

'Yes, I do understand that, sweetheart. But I shall see you again quite soon,' he whispered, leaning his face around me head and breathing hot air into me face. I could smell wine and the faint smell of soap, and get that smell of mothballs again on his jacket. Then he let me go, gently pushing me away, and made to move off out the door.

'Wait!' I shouted, grabbing hold of his jacket.

He whipped his head down, looking a bit confused and annoyed and half laughing all at the same time. 'What is it, darling? I must go. You are delaying me.'

'I want a cigarette, Father Ralphie!' I grinned, using the name his mammy calls him.

'Oh! Of course,' he said, whipping out his packet and handing me a handful. I counted five.

'Ta!' I said.

Then he said, 'You may ask my mother. She has plenty of cigarettes floating around the place.'

'What! Ask her? She won't like me smoking!'

'Why not?' he said, looking confused. 'Of course she will not mind. She smokes herself.'

'But people don't like ye smoking when ye're young,' I said. 'They're always giving out.'

'Nonsense! If you make a decision to smoke, then this is your decision. You are old enough to make up your own mind about these things. Ask her.'

'OK! Thanks, Father,' I said, feeling delighted with meself as I tore after him, running down the passage making for the dining room again.

'Goodbye, Mam'ma,' he said, rushing to take the mother into his arms and hold her very gently, kissing her on the cheeks while she lifted her head, saying, 'Darling, we shall expect to see you during the week when Maud and Amelia arrive with the children. Do come for dinner!'

'Mam'ma, I am not sure about that. I shall contact you. Telephone! How long do they intend staying in town?'

'Oh, I'm not sure yet. I think perhaps they intend travelling down with Maud. They may be staying with her in the country.'

'I shall try to make time, Mam'ma,' he said, twisting around and stopping to look at me, saying, 'Goodbye, Martha,' as he leaned back, getting ready to turn and make for the front door.

Me face dropped as I watched him with a worried look on me face. Then he rushed over, grabbing me, and gave me a little peck on me cheek, saying, 'Now behave yourself. I want you to act as a young lady! Not a vagabond!' Then he grinned as he opened the door and took off out, slamming it shut behind him.

We listened for a minute then the Mam'ma said, 'Oh! Where are the dogs?'

We could hear them barking. She rushed out and opened the door. Father Ralph stood looking down at the dogs, giving out to them. Then he walked over to us, saying to his mother, with his lips pressed together and a laugh lightening up his eyes, 'Mam'ma, you really must teach those little rascals to behave. The brutes tried to chew the tyres off my car! Mam'ma, really! You do tend to indulge them far too much. They are positively savage.' Then he watched them flying in behind each other, wagging their tails, bringing the cold with them and mud on their paws. They flew into the hall, barking and flying around her feet.

'Oh, you are funny, my darling!' the Mam'ma tittered, watching him march to the black car and launch himself in, pulling in his leg, and slam the door shut. Then he started up the engine and pulled off, making the gravel on the ground fly up and the tyres make a crunching sound. Then he was off, shining his headlamps down the dark drive of the avenue, taking himself back to the big priests' house next to the church, leaving me feeling very lonely without him.

The mother watched for a few minutes. Then, when the lights from the car disappeared around a bend and were hidden by the trees, she slammed the big heavy door closed, shutting out the world with a big loud bang. Then she looked down at the dogs. 'Oh, you naughty pair. What have you been getting up to?' she said, bending down and rubbing them. They rolled on their backs, looking like two little rugs wriggling. She gave them a quick rub, running her two hands up and down their bellies. Then she stood up quickly, saying, 'Now! Away with you!'

Maeve came shuffling along in her slippers that looked like they were probably blue once but now they turned a dirty grey. 'I'm going te clean away now, M'am,' she said, making it sound like an order more than asking.

'Oh, yes, Maeve dear! Do! I must say the supper was delicious! Those lamb chops were exceptionally nice. Thank you so much.'

The little fat woman just nodded and headed herself off into the dining room to clear up all the dishes we had. And all for just the look of a bit of lamb chop! Sure, there was no eating in them at all. I would say that butcher, whoever he is, robs them blind. Yeah, he's sure making money hand over fist robbing this house! It's true what the old people say: only a fool an his money is parted! Still, I thought, looking at her, seeing the soft gentle look in her lovely green eyes that are a bit faded now. They're not as clear as Father Ralph's. His would blind you! They shine like emeralds. But she is very kind, and a bit lost too! Rambling around in this huge big house all on her own. Except for Maeve! I don't suppose she's much company. She seems like a real, definite grumpy aul one to me.

'Martha,' she suddenly said, bringing me outa me doze. 'What would you like to do?'

'Eh?' I looked at her, wondering what she meant.

'Would you like to go and watch some television? I am sure there may be something interesting you would like. Oh, no! Perhaps we should get you settled in first. Where would you like to sleep?'

I looked at her, wondering does she mean I am going to have to sleep in one of the sitting rooms or something. 'Eh, would it be all right if I could sleep in maybe a spare bed?' I said, feeling a bit forward about asking her.

'What? What do you mean?'

'A bed?' I said.

'But of course that is what I meant! Oh, goodness me! You really are a funny little girl! Come along! There are plenty of beds to choose from. Where is your luggage?' she said, looking up around towards the hall.

'Me suitcase is up there,' I pointed, 'in the hall.'

'Oh, good. Go and get it. Then come along and we shall choose you a room. Oh! I know where would be just ideal for you. You youngsters always love the top rooms. It has a marvellous view! They always like to romp about the top floor. My grandchildren, when they come to stay, always have those rooms. They can romp about and leave the adults in peace. I think you will like it. They have the most marvellous views. You can look down on the sea and even to the city beyond!'

I rushed to get me suitcase and hurried back, making me way up the stairs behind her. We passed a landing, then up more flights of stairs onto a corridor with a line of doors and an alcove in the middle. It has a lovely big long window in the centre going from nearly the ceiling to the floor. The glass is like church glass, with lead around the panes. Then we went up more flights of stairs, holding on to a lovely old black wooden banister with heavy ornate knobs at the landing parts. We came onto another floor with more doors along the corridor and a big window at the end showing the fields and trees outside. I looked at a big black old chest sitting against the wall. It has lovely carvings of people's heads on it.

'Do you know what that is?' she said, stopping next to me and smiling at me, seeing I was staring at it.

'No,' I said, thinking you could hide a couple of bodies in that.

'Oh, well! That is called a marriage chest.'

'Yeah?' I said, bending down to get a better look after wondering what that was.

'You see, in olden times when the young girl was preparing to marry, she would start to receive presents. Things that she would set away in her marriage chest. They could be linen tablecloths and silverware for her table. All sorts of things, really, she would need for her own household when she married. It was in preparation to help her start up her own household. So she would keep all these things in here, you see!'

'Oh, yeah,' I said, getting the picture of a young girl wearing a lovely long frock and living in a house like this. Getting presents of lovely lace tablecloths and boxes of silver knives and stuff. Then putting it all away, ready for when she moves into her own home. 'That was a great idea,' I said, smiling at the mother.

'Yes, it was,' she said, lighting up a cigarette.

I still had my five in me hand. 'Eh, could I have a light for me cigarette, please? I said, showing her me cigarette.

'Oh! Do you smoke? Yes, of course you may. Here! Would you like one of mine, dear?'

'Eh, yes, please,' I said, taking one out of the box and holding it in me mouth while she lit it for me with a lovely little lady's silver lighter.

'OK! We are almost there,' she said, walking off and turning up more stairs and up another landing. Then finally we stopped outside two doors. 'In here! I'm sure you would like this one better,' she said, pushing open a door into a huge room with big black beams running across the ceiling. I looked around, seeing two beds against a far wall, with two big stout wardrobes in each of the corners. The beds were far away from each other, with big mahogany lockers next to them and a table lamp sitting on the top.

The wall behind the door had two more beds with the same – a locker standing each side of them. Then, under the windows, one each end of the room facing the door, was a bed with a locker, and a table lamp. The windows came slantways from the ceiling to the floor. A big press took up the whole wall just inside the door. I looked around, seeing all the beds had the same dark-green covers with a tassel around the edges. And they covered the whole bed, going down to just inches from the floorboards. I looked down, feeling the softness of the lovely dark-blue rug under me feet. It covered the whole of the middle of the floor. 'This is just lovely,' I sighed, feeling really contented in meself at being so lucky to have landed meself here.

I walked over to the window and lifted me leg, resting me knee on the cushioned seat that wrapped around the window, and leaned over to get a look out. I couldn't believe me eyes. 'Oh, my God! Look at that view. It's just beautiful,' I whispered, holding me breath looking down, seeing the sight of all the lights just underneath us, then spreading out, way into the distance. Me eyes followed the light, then there was a big gap. I was looking at all the darkness in the middle. A big beam of long light was rolling from the lighthouse, sweeping its light across the sea, warning ships about the rocks. Letting them know, beware! I watched, seeing the beam of light go dull then fade away into darkness. I waited, staring, seeing it come to life again, the light getting stronger until it lit up the whole bay. Beyond that are more lights. A long line in the shape of a half moon, looking like how a diamond necklace would sparkle. It lit up all along the bay. It's the city lights, stretching for miles and miles.

Then I could see lights closer, moving slowly. Blinking on and off, as the headlights of cars, looking like little dots of light, disappear, leaving only the black night. Then more light would appear, pushing out the dark.

'You see!' the mother pointed, leaning in beside me and sitting down. 'It is so beautiful,' she breathed, holding her hand on her chest, staring into the distance, her eyes moving, taking in everything. 'Really, one could never tire of this sight,' she whispered, half to herself and half to me.

I shook me head, barely moving, hardly breathing.

'Look! Do you see the lights all along the bay? Oh, look, out to sea. It is the ship sailing over to Holyhead.'

I stared, seeing the ship all lit up, making its way in the dark lonely sea. Everyone on that ship knowing they were in safe hands. The ship though small and the sea mighty. It could be tossed up on waves and rolled from side to side. But the sea would not win. The little ship would get there. Yeah! Because it was made by people, and we know how to fight what life throws at us, I thought to meself.

We stared for a long time, leaning our heads close, the pair of us lost in the sight of such beauty. Sitting together, not saying a word. Never in all me born days have I had such contentment.

She sighed and turned, then stood up. 'I think you should be very comfortable up here. What do you think?' she smiled, looking at me and looking around the room.

'Oh, yes, Mrs Fitzgerald! Thanks very much for everything. Definitely, I really love this room,' I said, smiling and nodding looking around the room, feeling all delighted with meself.

'Yes,' she said, looking around the room. 'These rooms once served as the servants' quarters. The servant girls would have slept here.'

'Did you have servants living here, Missus Fitzgerald?'

'Well, we did have girls when the children were young. We would have had a nanny and a nursery maid. And the cook, of course! And other help. But the house was once closed up for many years. It was when my husband died. I was terribly young. All the children were still in nursery, so we upped and left and went to live in my parents' house in England. They had a much bigger house, of course. So needed a larger staff. We then had plenty of help with the children. Naturally, I took along some of my own staff. Nanny and the children's nurse. We did, of course, return for the summer season. By then, the children were a little older. They were away at school. So this was a nice change for all of us. I suppose you could say this was our summer home.

'Yes, the servant girls! They did indeed live up here!' she said, swinging herself around, looking and remembering back to them times.

I didn't ask her how many children she has. Or what her husband died from. Because I didn't want to be nosy and get meself into trouble with her. I could imagine she might get insulted by me asking her business. It's not like talking to ordinary people. She doesn't live like other people. Her concerns are about what? Maybe just being lonely? Not really having anyone living with her any more, after living all her life in a big house with servants and family around, and children to keep her occupied. Yeah! But still and all. I'll keep me distance until I know her better. But I might ask the priest when I see him. Wonder when that will be? I could feel meself sinking a little, feeling a bit lonely without him. It makes me feel a bit cold and empty somehow. Like the lovely warm feeling of having someone around me, it made me feel I mattered. Now he's gone, taking the warm feeling I had inside meself. Leaving me with a strange feeling. Like I'm more on me own now than I ever was before.

'Choose whatever bed you like,' I heard her say. I whipped me head around the room, seeing the table with the marble top just behind the door. I looked across, seeing the lovely basin for washing yerself in, and a matching big jug sitting inside it. I suppose you put the water in the jug and carry it up when you want to wash yourself. I'm not doing that. I'll take meself off down to the bathroom. Me eyes peeled on all the beds. The one at the end in the right-hand corner – 'I'll take that one!' I said, pointing down to it.

'Oh, but of course, dear! Whatever may suit you. Yes, they are all made up. I like to have everything in readiness. People, you see, are always popping in. Then they invariably end up staying over. Or I have invited people, weekend guests, that sort of thing. Or friends and family who have guests spilling over. These, they shunt onto me. The unfortunates are offloaded here!' she laughed, making a tinkly sound. 'Then of course there is the family. They will be arriving shortly. They are bringing their children. My grandchildren. So they will be storming the house. Goodness! That should be fun. Of course that will play merry hell with poor Maeve! She hates the chaos!' Then she threw back her head and roared laughing.

I watched her, being reminded in an instant of Father Ralph.

'Poor woman is getting on,' she muttered. 'Yes, I am sure you will enjoy them. There are some of the children who would be around your age. Of course some are younger. But they entertain themselves. Now! Do you have everything you need?' she said, looking at me.

'Yes! What about toiletries? Towels? Come along with me and I'll get you some. Oh, yes! I had forgotten. I must show you the bathroom; it is just the next floor down. Perhaps, dear, you might like to take a hot bath before bed? Poor thing! You must be exhausted.'

'Eh, yeah, I would, thanks,' I whispered. Not wanting her to think me a bother.

'Now if you want anything, just ask Maeve. Help yourself to whatever you need. Try the kitchen if you are feeling peckish. You youngsters are always grazing. I'm sure if you rummage around there, you should find something to eat. Maeve looks after the larder. She orders all the food. If you need me, my room is on the first floor. I don't like beetling up and down all those stairs. Not at my age, thank you!'

15

I woke up and for a minute I wondered where I was. The place sounded different. There is no sound and the bed feels different too, softer. Oh! I'm with the priest's mother. In her house!

I swung over and lay on me back, looking around at the room, seeing all the beds and getting the smell of polish from the floorboards and the furniture. I could even smell a bit of must in the room. That must be because everything is very old. I lifted me eyes over to the window, seeing the trees blowing in the wind. Ohh! I don't have to work! I can live here in great style for a little while and do what I like. Me time's me own. I snuggled down in the bed, feeling the heat from the lovely white sheets and the blankets and heavy eiderdown weighing me down. Yeah! I've died and gone to heaven! My Gawd! I can go from nothing, living on the streets, to this! How did I ever do that? How did this ever happen to me? God! It was you! I have you to thank for looking after me. I knew you wouldn't let me down in me hour a need.

Think I'll get up. Yeah! I'm starving with the hunger! It's not early anyway. Must be after nine o clock. I dived into me clothes and made out the door, taking the stairs two at a time. Where's the kitchen? I turned left and ended up in the big sitting room. Nobody here! Where the hell is the kitchen? I rambled back down the passage and heard pots banging. Ah, yeah! Here we go. I remember now.

I opened the door and made me way in. The little woman was lifting a pot off the kitchen table. At the same time the two little dogs were growling in their bellies, having a tug o' war with a little rag doll. I watched as they tore each other up and down the kitchen right under the feet of the woman. Suddenly, as she lifted the pot, heading over to the Aga, the dogs landed themselves sitting on her feet. Her hands flew in the air as she went back, losing hold of the pot. It flew through the air and landed all over the kitchen floor. Meat and carrots and onions went one way and the cold water ended up mostly landing on her, drowning the front of her apron and big woolly skirt. 'The curse a Jaysus on ye's!' she screamed, turning the colour a beetroot. 'Get out! Get out!' she roared, lifting her slipper feet and giving them a kick up the arse. They skidded sideways, only getting a bang of the slipper that flew off her foot. Then they tore back and grabbed their doll, and the pair of them flew past me, making for the door. One of them came flying back to bark at me ankles and look up at me, then look at her flying down at them waving the sweeping brush.

'Them bloody dogs are the bane of my life!' she screamed, raging she couldn't get her hands on them, then throwing back a lump of grey hair that found its way out of the hair clips and landed over the side of her face. 'Well! What are you standing there for, looking like an ornament? Do yeh want something?' she snapped at me.

'Eh, would it be OK if I got meself a bit of breakfast?' I croaked, looking up at her staring at me, wondering to herself if she could give me a bang of the brush as well. I moved meself well out of her way and edged over to the other side of the table.

'Help yourself? Well, yeh don't think I'm going te wait on yeh hand an foot? Go on! Go over te that press there and take out the cornflakes. Then get yerself out of my way! I have more than enough to be doing!' she snorted, going back to pick up the meat and stuff that landed splattered all over the place.

'Eh, would you like me to give you a hand?' I said, bending down to pick up a lump of meat that ended up on my side.

'Go on if ye're doing it!' she said, still raging.

Ah, Jaysus! She really is a cantankerous aul biddy if ever there was one, I snorted to meself, rushing around and picking up the stuff, landing them back in the pot. I'm sorry I didn't leave her to get on with it herself!

'That's the lot,' I huffed, after flying and bending and looking to make sure there was nothing left lying on the floor.

She said nothing, just carried the full pot over to the sink and dumped the lot out, washing them under the tap. I stepped over the puddles a water, deciding not to wipe it up. To hell with her! I made me way over to the press, seeing only cans of beans and all sorts of stuff. You can't eat that for breakfast, I told meself, looking disgusted. I looked around, wanting to tell her. But her back was to me and she worked away, intent on her business. Right! I'll have a root around.

I closed the press and opened another one. No! Bottles of wine and boxes of fancy cheese, and sauces and all sorts of rubbish ye can't eat. 'Where's the cornflakes, Missus?' I said, beginning to lose me own rag.

'Didn't I tell yeh? In that press!' she snorted, stubbing her finger in the direction of thin air.

'What? This one?' I pointed.

'Yes! Are yeh capable of doing anything for yerself?' she moaned, flattening her nostrils and squeezing her mouth shut tight as she rushed herself over to swing open a press well away from the one she pointed out to me. She lifted up an empty box and shook it. 'I declare te God the larder is empty. Where is that delivery young fella with me groceries?' she asked the window, looking over to see if anyone might appear. 'I specifically told them in that shop I wanted them groceries by ten o clock at the latest!' she snorted to the window, waving her finger at it. I waited to see if she might have another idea for getting me something to eat. But she just took off, rambling back to her pot and ignoring me.

'Eh, ah!' Me voice wouldn't come out! 'Excuse me!' I shouted, not meaning to do that. 'A bit of bread will do me,' I said, hopping from one foot to the other, not wanting to get into a row but feeling I could if she starts me off.

'Didn't I just tell yeh? There is nothing in the larder until that useless article of a young fella gets himself here with my groceries! Now, go on out an wait for yerself. I'm busy enough without all these interruptions.'

'OK. Thanks anyway,' I muttered, making me way out the door. Bloody aul cow! Acting like she has the whole fucking world on her shoulders! Wonder where the mother is?

I made me way back up the stairs and stopped, wondering which door was hers. There's three of them on this floor. I knocked quietly on one of them and stood back waiting, holding me breath. I'll just say good morning. Then if she asks me did I get me breakfast, I'll say no!

I listened, hearing only the quiet. Then I knocked on another door, harder! Nothing. 'Eh, hello?' I heard meself croak. I coughed and cleared me throat and shouted louder. No, she's not in her room. Wonder if I should open a door and see what the rooms are like? No! She might think I am robbing the place.

I heard the dogs barking and the sound of tyres rushing on the pebble stones. Someone is coming. I raced down the stairs, seeing the front door open.

'Good morning, Martha! Did you sleep well?' she beamed at me.

'Yes, thanks very much, I did.'

'Yes! You do look rested. Have you been up long?' she said, slamming the door shut and whipping off her long fawn cashmere coat with a cloak attached that comes down over the shoulders. 'Are you planning on going outside?' she said, rubbing her hands. 'Goodness! It is the weather for wrapping up warm. It is quite cold! I can't wait for this awful weather to end. The March winds and April showers! Brrr! Oh, but I do love Paris in April,' she said. 'I have no idea why I still spend winters in this awful climate. Now! Have you eaten?' she said, rubbing her bony shoulders. 'I have been out getting early Mass. I do like to go during the week. It is more intimate. Less people. You tend to see the same faces. I suppose we are the early-morning hearty brigade! Now! Did Maeve feed you?' she said, looking at me.

'Eh, she wanted to, but the messages haven't come from the shop yet,' I said, not wanting to start any rows.

'Oh, I see,' she said, not seeing anything at all, because her eyes were beginning to stare as she walked off, muttering something to herself.

The doorbell rang. 'The door is ringing!' I shouted, getting all excited it might be someone interesting.

She swung herself around on her heels. Then she lowered her head and marched to the door, opening it. A young fella stood there wearing a check apron nearly tipping the ground. 'Morning, M'am!' he said, pulling a lock of his hair. 'Got yer delivery here. Wha do yeh want me to do wit them?'

She stood looking down at them, not really thinking. 'Oh! Good boy!'

'I'll tell her! Maeve!' I shouted, running for the kitchen. 'Missus! The messages are here!' I shouted again, still only halfway in the door.

'Is that right now?' she said, putting the last of the stuff back into the pot. She didn't move herself. 'Tell that young fella te come around to the back door! He's no right te be knocking at the front door. He knows where I am.'

I rushed back and opened the door. He was already gone! So was the mother!

I raced back to the kitchen just in time to hear the aul one taking the face off him.

'If that aul fella Mickey Ryan does not give yeh the boot soon enough, then yeh can tell him for me I'm taking me custom elsewhere!'

'Ah, go on outa tha, Missus Doherty! Sure, where would yeh be without me?' the young fella said, taking me in with one eye, while the other one was going back to buttering up the aul one.

'I don't want any of yer aul guff outa yeh!' she muttered, letting him collapse all the messages onto the table. She eyed the long string a sausages, holding them up in the air, running her eyes down the length of them. 'Did he put seasoning on them the way I always like?' she said, dropping them onto a plate and standing with her hands on her hips, lifting her bushy eyebrows at him.

'Oh, I did tha all right meself! Special! And I hand picked the best leg a lamb, special, only for the likes a you! Cos I know yeh would throw anythin else back at me!'

'Yes,' she said. 'After I picked you up first an threw yeh out the door!' she sniffed, checking the meat, then making sure the packets of tea were the ones she ordered.

'Sure, I know yeh know all about quality, Missus D. Some, now, wouldn't know their arse—'

'None a that filthy language in my kitchen!' she roared, snorting into his face.

'Eh, sorry about that, Missus! But you know I always see yeh right! Wouldn't yeh agree wit me now?' he said, trying to lightly land his hand on her back.

'Don't be getting too familiar with me now! You're beginning to lose the run of yerself wit yer smart talk!'

He rolled his eyes, letting his nose looked pinched, and dropped his mouth, getting fed up at not being able to get around her.

'Here! Take yer tip!' she said, giving him sixpence. 'Next time yeh won't be getting a penny outa me if yeh come rambling up here when the whole morning is gone! Ye've just cost me the better part of a whole day's work with yer rambling in here when it just suits yeh!' she moaned, flapping her hands and chasing him outa the kitchen.

He was out the door and fixing the rest of his deliveries down into the big basket sitting on the front of his bike.

'Close that door behind that young fella. He never closes that bloody door after him!'

'Right, Missus,' I said, rushing over to close the door.

I stood for a minute, seeing him throw his leg over the bike and turn around heading off to make the rest of his deliveries. He saw me looking and stopped for a minute, letting his foot drop on the ground. 'How're yeh, doll?' he said, winking at me. 'Haven't seen you here before?'

'No,' I said, looking at the size of him. The bike was bigger than himself. 'Ye better keep goin, sonny,' I said, thinking, the cheek at him, tryin to chat me up! An he only a sprat of a young fella.

'I come here all the time,' he said. 'Maybe the next time I might get teh know yeh! Wouldn't tha be nice? Will yeh be stayin in this place long?'

'No, definitely not long after meetin you!' I said, watching him scratch the big boils on his neck and rub his hands through his long, thin mousey-brown hair. I felt a bit sorry for him, though. Because his eyes were crossed, and I couldn't figure out if he was looking at me or looking at the wall.

'What age are ye?' I said, thinking he's definitely younger than me. But he has an awful cheek! Thinking I would be interested in a string a misery like him!

'I'm sixteen and three-quarters!' he said, wriggling his neck, trying to stretch himself.

'Fucking liar! Ye're no more than around fourteen,' I screamed.

'Sixteen!' he shouted. 'Nearly! I will be when me next birthday comes around!' he roared.

'Well, ye can have sixteen more birthdays for all I care! I wouldn't be seen dead walking out with the likes a you!' I snorted, giving him a dirty look.

'Who said I'm asking yeh out? I'm not tha bleedin desperate!' he roared, lepping up and down on the bike with the rage on him.

I lost me rag altogether at the idea he was not asking me out! 'An don't go callin me doll! I'm not yer bleedin doll! I'm a guest in this house! You're not even supposed te be talkin te the likes a me!' I screamed.

'Ye're as common as muck!' he screamed back! 'Ye're only the hired help!'

I nearly suffocated with the rage. 'Fuck off, ye four-eyed little squirt!' I roared. 'If ye really are sixteen an three-quarters like ye say ye are, then ye're only a fuckin little midget! An ye have no business—'

The aul one came flying out the back door, grabbing hold of me and pushing me outa the way to get at the young fella. 'Tommy Price!' she roared, standing with her hands on her hips. 'If you don't get yerself going this very minute, I'll take the back of me hand te yeh!

You should be attending to yer own business! It's no wonder I'm left standing here with one arm longer than the other, waiting all this time on me groceries. Now get going!' she roared. 'The pair of yeh! Before I do something I regret!' waving me in one direction and him off in the other with a slap of her dishcloth. Then she turned on me. 'Tut, tut! That's no way for any decent young girl to be talking,' she sniffed, turning herself all the way around to stick her face close into me.

I stared at the broken veins in her face, seeing her big round cheeks and the thick bushy eyebrows, with some of them standing up. I wanted to get a little brush and comb them down.

'Eh, yeah, sorry,' I said, after not really listening to what she said.

'Now! Are yeh coming in or do I close the door an leave yeh standing out here?' she ordered, waving her hand at me then at the open air.

'I'm coming in,' I said. 'To get me breakfast!' I snorted. Not knowing what to get for meself. I clapped eyes on the eggs and the rashers and black and white pudding! To hell with her! I snorted to meself. She doesn't own the bloody house!

'I would like to have a nice fry-up,' I said, standing me ground.

'Ye're not looking for much,' she said, looking at me like I had the cheek a the devil. 'Are you sure yeh wouldn't like me te cook it for yeh while ye're asking?'

'Oh, I can do that for meself. Or, it's your kitchen! If you want to cook it, I don't mind!' I said, letting on I didn't know she was jeering me.

Then I said, thinking I might know a way to get her to do it for me, 'But I can't cook. I might burn the place down! Missus Fitzgerald said I am to have a good breakfast. She was the one wanting me to eat a fry,' I said, looking at how her face was dropping at the mention of the mother.

'Oh, did she now?' the aul one muttered, picking up the sausages and rashers and getting out the frying pan. 'Go on then. Out! I don't want yeh getting under me feet, as well as them bloody dogs. Don't go far. I'll call yeh when it's ready.'

'Right! Thanks very much, Missus D.,' I said happily, all delighted with meself now at getting a lovely big breakfast.

'And don't call me Missus D. I only let tha young fella get away with tha because he's too thick to learn!'

'Right so! Sorry, and thanks again.' I think I'll go and find the dogs. They should be good for a laugh. I don't think they will bite me, not really. Not now that they know me.

'Thanks, Missus!' I said, chewing on the last bit of rasher and lathering on the good butter to the last bit of black crusty bread, then eyeing me plate and mopping up the grease and the egg yolk all mixed together. 'That was lovely!' I sighed, standing up and bringing over the plate to the sink.

'Hmph!' she muttered, beating the hell out of a cake or something she was mixing in a bowl and giving me the eye as much as to say, *Are you sure now you wouldn't like to eat any more?* Sure enough, she says, 'Is there anything else I can get yeh! Would yeh like te start on eating the plate?'

I looked at me plate, wondering at what she was talking about? I didn't eat that much. Except maybe she's annoyed I ate nearly the whole loaf a bread.

'I thought yeh were going te eat me out of house an home, the way yeh went at it. Where did yeh get that appetite? I never saw anyone in me whole life shift as much food as you just did! I wouldn't mind, but I don't know where yeh put it! There isn't a scrap a meat te be seen on yeh. Ye're as skinny as a rake.'

I laughed. 'Yeah! I can eat what I like, but the old people say it's a sign you have worms! Do you want me to wash up these few things for you, Missus?' I said, rolling up me sleeves.

'No! Don't touch them things!' she roared, looking at me in shock. 'Have yeh got worms, then?' she said, moving herself down the kitchen, taking her bowl of dough with her.

'No! Of course not! What gave you that idea?' I snorted.

'Are yeh sure? Because I can get yeh a doze of something in the chemist te shift them quick enough.'

'No! I haven't got worms! I only said . . . Because you said . . . I said that the old people . . .'

'Yes, OK! Don't go on about it!' she said, waving her hand up and down at me.

'So, do you want me to wash up these things, Missus?' I said, holding me hands over the sink with me sleeves rolled up.

'Go on if yeh want te,' she said. 'But don't go telling people I asked yeh.'

'No! Why would I do that, Missus? Sure, haven't you been very good to me! Going to all that trouble to cook me enough grub to feed the whole Salvation Army!'

'Well, I'm glad yeh appreciate it,' she sniffed.

I poured the washing-up liquid into the sink and got cracking with the washing up. Ah, she's gruff. But that's only her manner. She has the old ways of going on. Get people before they get you! I met many people like her in me lifetime. They have a heart of gold underneath. She probably gets fed up running after people, judging by what the mother said about having loads of people coming and going. All moidering her with their demands.

'Anything else I can do, Missus?' I said, watching her roll out dough and slap down round silver cutting things, making the dough into shapes, then lift them out and put them sitting in a black baking tin.

'No, ye've done enough! Why don't you take yerself off out an get a bit of fresh air for yerself? It's windy out, mind! But that won't kill yeh. Just wrap up. Wear a warm coat,' she said, looking at me with a half smile on her face and her brown eyes looking at me like she cared.

'Yeah! Ye're right, Missus. I'll do that. Thanks very much!' Then I was off up the stairs to grab me coat and rush out the front door to see what the outside was like. I rambled down around the side of the house and up the gravel path with the high wall on me left and ivy growing over it. I passed the kitchen, seeing Missus bending down to the Aga. Maybe we're going to have lovely home-baked cakes for tea tonight! Jaysus! Imagine living like this all the time.

Not having a worry in the world about money. I never in all me life knew people lived like this. I saw them from a distance. But I never knew how they lived their life. Now I know!

16

I turned in under a big stone arch and landed in a courtyard. The ground was made of cobblestones. There were four doors on each side of the yard, with the top half doors opening out. They looked very run down now. Some of the doors were open. I wandered in, seeing stalls for the horses, with wooden walls dividing them. They only came up halfway, with a black iron railing on the top to stop the horses jumping over I suppose.

I could see someone had carved their names on the doors and walls. 'Helena and Georgina! Best friends xx July, 1867.' Me heart melted. Aah, Gawd! All them years ago. Nearly going on for a hundred years now. There they were! They stood here in this very spot where I'm standing right now. Two girls! I wonder what they were like? What were they wearing? Probably long frocks. I wonder who they were? They must have lived in this house. They probably went off for rides on their horses that would have been munching away on the hay over there. The horses probably lifting their heads in between the munching and looking up to see if there was anything happening, thinking would the girls take them out for a run!

Gawd! Imagine! They all had a life going on before I was even heard of. They're all dead now. To make room for the like a me! So, here I am, standing in the same spot thinking about them. Right! I'm going to do the same thing! I want to leave a bit of meself behind in this house. What would I do it with? Carve me name?

I rambled around the stables, looking at old rusty wheels of horse carts. I picked up a black metal lamp that would have been sitting on the side of a carriage. Gawd! They left things behind, all them people long ago. I stared at it, then gently put it back down on the wooden shelf in the corner. I picked up a rusty old horseshoe. That's supposed to be for good luck. I read that in the *Beano* comic. You throw it behind your back, over your shoulder. Hah! They did that in the *Beano* and it clobbered someone on their noodle – the head! No! Can't find nothing to carve me name with. I wonder what they used? Something sharp. A knife? No! Missus wouldn't let me near her kitchen knives. She might think I want to commit murder!

I wandered up the old path leading up the steps that the priest said was where his dog and the rest of them was buried. I pushed open the gate and walked along a path made out of stone and stood on the path overlooking the mountain down below. When I turned around, I was looking at five tombstones all in a row. The rest of the area was covered in trees. 'King! A dear and loyal friend. You had a good innings, old boy. We shall often think on you.' 'TOBY! A loyal and faithful companion to Ralph Fitzgerald! You are dearly missed, my friend. A little boy weeps at your passing. Farewell, faithful friend.'

I stared, me eyes moving up and down the tombstones. All dogs. Not people. I never saw that before. Only the rich could think of something like that. Yet I stared at the one for Father Ralph's dog. TOBY! He really loved that dog. It meant the whole world to him. Imagine how lonely he must have been, rambling around here with no dog running up beside him. No more sticks to pick up and throw, then watch while the dog ran and brought it back, wagging its tail all delighted with himself. All that gone. He couldn't run his hand over Toby's warm back and feel the soft fur and the heat of his skin underneath. No, poor Ralph! He was left without his little Toby!

I wonder why he became a priest, though? I would love to have him all for meself for the rest of me life! Imagine meself if he was me daddy! I could stamp me feet, making all me demands. Get away with murder! Just like the kids who are well off – toffs. I used to watch them at that caper. I would come across them when I was running around the city centre looking to get something, robbing for me ma and that bleedin Jackser.

Me belly suddenly turned to fire, remembering that. No! Let that go! I got the picture of the priest back in me mind's eye. Going on with me happy thoughts. Yeah! Or I could run to him and put me arms around his neck. Strangling him with me hugs! He would probably just laugh. But he could have been me father. What age would he have been? Twenty years old. Yeah, that's definitely old enough.

But what's the point? I felt me heart sinking. That is just wasting time even thinking about what might have been. Forget that idea. Still, I have never in all me born days met anyone who seems to treat me like I'm special. All I want when I'm around him is to sit next to him and have him hug me. But then when he does, I feel meself tightening up inside, holding meself like a statue. It's as if I'm afraid to believe him, because he's just being nice. Then soon enough he'll get fed up with me. Then he will be gone. Because why would I be special to him anyway? He knows nothing about me. I'm a stranger to him. No, he's nice to me because he's a priest. He thinks he's supposed to love the whole world. Growing up in a place like this would make anyone think the world is a bowl of cherries all the time.

I have an awful feeling of being empty inside meself. But now it's worse. It's like a sickening hunger beginning to gnaw away at me insides. Like getting the smell of lovely food cooking, and you're starving with the hunger, then clapping eyes on the table full of good food, but you know you're not going to get any. Except it's not food this time. It's the terrible want of having Father Ralph wrap his arms around me and snuggle me in, making me feel warm and safe. Now that I know what I'm missing, that's all I want.

Will I ever get someone for me very own, I wonder? Suddenly I've changed completely. I don't feel meself any more. I've gone from just wanting a roof over me head, a job and a bed to sleep in – well, I have that at the minute – but now I want to belong. Like them two girls who wrote on that wall in the stable. They must have belonged here. God! If only I belonged somewhere – here! But I don't belong here. Yesterday I didn't care. Now today I feel like crying me heart out. Like I found something I didn't even know I had been searching for all me life. But it's lost from me before I even got it. Father Ralph has become me whole world. Yet I hardly know him! Sure, yesterday – was it only then? – I could barely stand the sight of him. But today it's as if I have always known him. In the same way that, somehow, I feel like I belong here. Like I have wandered around this place and known it for ever. It doesn't feel strange to me. It's like I have arrived home. Yet, as I know, I can never belong here. I'm going to have to keep searching.

This new hunger has taken something away from me. I feel like I'm not in charge of meself any more. I'm like a leaf getting blown in the wind. Because I'm at the mercy of depending on someone like the priest to make me feel safe and warm. Even today with that young fella. The poor fella was only wanting to have himself a girlfriend. He was not as cocky as he looked. I could see the desperate look in his eyes, even when they kept crossing. No! A young one wouldn't look twice at him, he knew that. But he was still chancing his arm with me. Maybe I should have kept me mouth shut. It wouldn't have cost me anything to let him think I thought he wasn't bad looking. So what did I do instead? I demolished him for having the cheek to think I would be even interested in talking to him. Jaysus! People can be very vicious. Like meself! Acting like I was too good for the likes of him. No, I'm sorry for pulling him down. I have to watch meself. I know only how easy it is to belittle people. It hurts you in the guts. But I think I'm losing the run of meself because I'm hobnobbing with the gentry!

The thought hit me. Me! With the gentry! And already thinking I'm one a them! I started to roar me head laughing at the idea. Jaysus! That's a good one! Who would believe it? That one day I would be turning me nose down at someone else because I thought I was too good for them? Don't ever do that, Martha, I whispered to meself. Yesterday I was nobody. I had nothing. But I had a heart. Today I'm staying in a big house. For a minute today I thought I was somebody. But I had no heart. Don't be a gobshite! Ahh! I'll make it up to him. Yeah! I'll have a laugh with him the next time I see him. We won't start fighting again. He's really a gas character! Especially the way he got around the aul one! Buttering her up like mad so he could get his hands on the sixpence. Hmm! That was good money! I wonder how much that job pays?

The wind started blowing me coat around me, slapping the back of me legs. Gawd, it's beginning to get much colder. Wonder if I should go back to the house? I think I will, I thought, rubbing me hands together to warm them up. But maybe I will just have one last look around before I do. Right! I'll go round this way and see what else there is to see. I turned left and walked past the front of the big house, admiring all the ivy growing up the walls and framing the windows. Gawd! It looks so lovely. The big old house with the rich people living inside. Well, the mother is on her own now. But still and all, imagine, I'm living here now too. Yeah, well, even if it is only for a little while. But I still got to live with very rich people and I'm not just working for them either. No! I'm in there living in the middle of them. I'm nearly sort of living like one of the family.

I turned left, passing the big glasshouse for growing stuff in. I could see pots all along benches and sitting on a big wooden table that sat in the middle. There was green stalks creeping up the glass and lots of plants and things. But I don't know anything about garden things. I won't bother going in there. There's nothing to see.

I walked on, looking straight ahead, seeing a big barn sitting to the right, in against the high wall. I wonder what's in there? I headed over, seeing the doors wide open. Oh! That's very nice.

I walked in, getting a look at a big black old-fashioned car with huge headlamps sticking out the front. I walked around the side, standing up on the running board under the door, and looked in the window. Me eyes took in the long brown soft-leather seats, with all the lovely red-brown wood going underneath the steering wheel. The shine on it would let you see your face in it. Gawd! That's something like the Queen of England would get herself driven around in. Talk about fancy! That really does tell everyone straight away: *Look at me! I'm a very important person with loads of money! So you can get outa me way!*

Jaysus! I can imagine what it would be like to sit up in the back of that and have everyone staring at you. Hmm! I wonder if I could get the mother to take me for a spin in that? Better still! Get her to go past Jackser's house, with him standing outside with his eyeballs sitting on his cheeks at the sight of me drawing up in the car. I could open the window and shout, 'Bandy aul bastard! Watch out! You're on me hit list! I'm living with the Mafia.' Yeah, someone like Al Capone that chased Tony Curtis and Jack Lemmon with Marilyn Monroe in the film *Some Like It Hot*. They were all running for their lives with the gangsters chasing them with big machine guns! I loved that film when I went to see it! Oh, I would give me eye teeth just to see Jackser flying down the road with the coat flapping out behind him. But instead of chasing me, he would be running for his life, shitting himself like mad and screaming for mercy. Yeah, the gangsters, they even had cars that looked something like this one in the film.

I turned away, giving out a long sigh. I had a big smile on me face and a feeling of contentment, thinking, nothing is impossible. You can do anything you like in this world. Lots of people must have started off poor to begin with. I bet this family even had a few paupers if you go back far enough. Yeah! Life is definitely a bowl of cherries!

I spotted an old man working further down along the wall, hunched over a shovel, digging at the bushes. Right, I'll make me way down and see what he's doing. He had a wheelbarrow next to him and he was busy throwing big clumps of earth with weeds, sending them flying to land in the barrow.

'Hello, Mister! How're you?' I said, coming up behind him.

'Gawd almighty! Where did you come out of?' he said, whipping his head around, showing the whites of his eyes.

'Oh, sorry! I didn't mean to give you a fright. I'm just on a ramble. What are you doing?' I said, looking at his big wellington boots, with the tops turned down, digging into the shovel making a big hole in the earth.

'Oh, I'm transferring a few aul bushes. I'm hoping they may do better with the bit of shelter here,' he said, pointing at the bushes lying beside him, waiting to get buried again. He stopped, with his foot still on the shovel, then wiped the snots hanging down his nose with the back of his hand.

I stared at him, taking in the red weather-beaten face from years of working out in the open, with the bit of purple around his nose and mouth. He had a greasy flat cap on his head, and he pulled it down tighter, settling it well down on his head, and went back to work.

I stood and stared, enjoying the sight of what he was doing, saying, 'How long did it take you to learn all about doing this, Mister? Telling the difference between all the different bushes and flowers and things?'

'Well,' he said, lifting the cap and wiping the sweat off his forehead with the sleeve of his aul jacket that was as old as himself. 'Sure, what is there te know? Yeh just stick them in the earth an away they grow! Then, if ye've done the wrong thing, ye'll know soon enough. Then yeh learn! Sure, isn't that the way of everything? Yeh just get on with something an learn as yeh go.'

'Yeah!' I said, thinking he's right, and watching as he slapped the greasy aul cap back down over his nearly bald aul grey head. Then he landed his head back to the shovel and carried on digging. The two of us watching the hole get bigger.

'Right!' he muttered, dropping the shovel and reaching down to lift up a little bush lying on the ground.

'Have you worked here long, Mister?'

'Long enough,' he said, keeping his eye on his work.

'Do you like working here?'

'It's a way of life,' he said, landing the bush in the hole.

'Did you work here when the woman's family were all young?'

'I did,' he said, shaking his head slowly.

I waited to hear more. But he was quiet again. I stared at him filling in the hole around the bush. Ah, he's not bothered much about talking. Maybe I'll move on and leave him in peace. But I hung on, watching him quietly for a while, saying nothing.

'I worked for the young Justice Fitzgerald, the present lady's husband,' he said quietly, out of the blue, nodding his head over to the house. 'An his father before him. All gentlemen!' he said, as he nodded again, going back to slapping the back of the shovel on the earth and stamping his boot down, making sure the bush was well stuck down in the ground.

'A Justice? Does that mean her husband was a judge?'

He nodded. 'Yes. He sat on the High Court bench. He was indeed a judge in the High Court. As was his father before him. He was a judge in the Supreme Court. The highest court in the land.'

'So this was where the mother's husband grew up?' I said.

'Yes, that's right.'

'Didn't he die?' I said, wanting to hear the whole story.

'He did!'

'Was he young? Because the woman told me she was young when her husband died.'

'Well, she was a lot younger than him! But he was young enough. I would say he was turning for the forty-year side of life.'

'That's not too old!' I said, looking up into his face, trying to catch his eye. 'Sure it's not?'

'No! He dropped down dead of a heart attack one Sunday evening as they were about to start dinner.'

'Was he eating his dinner at the time?' I asked, shocked at the thought of his head landing in the dinner plate, straight into the food.

'I can't say. But it was the beginning of the end for this house. Things were never the same after that! End of an era, it was. They all went back to her relations in England, the whole family. Only came back te open up the house for the summers. A lot of people who had worked for years an years were let go. Lost their jobs.'

'Gawd! What did they do?'

'I don't rightly know,' he said, shaking his head slowly, thinking about it. 'Me an the Missus, we were fortunate. We had the cottage down below. She grew up there. Her family had lived in it for years. They had the tied cottage, yeh see. It goes with the job. Her mother an father before her had worked here. They met an married here. The mother was the cook an the father looked after the grounds, just like me. Did all the repairs needed doing, keeping the place up to shape.'

'Oh, are you Mattie?'

'I am,' he nodded, lifting the handles of the barrow and starting to push off.

'Oh, yeah! Your wife is called Missus Doherty!'

'So ye've met the missus!'

'Yeah, she's a great cook.'

'She is, right enough. But she, eh, has a terrible temper!' he smiled, lifting his head sideways to me. 'Did yeh cross her?'

'Eh, only sort of!'

'Dogs an kids are not her cup of tea,' he said quietly, muttering to himself but wanting me to hear.

'So, do you not have any dogs or kids?' I said, wondering why I didn't see any around, seeing as they lived here.

'No.'

'What! You have no kids?'

'No,' he said.

'Not even a dog?'

'No.'

'Oh, that's terrible! Because I don't think your missus hates kids all that much! I think she likes them underneath all that giving out!'

He dropped his mouth, thinking, and nodded his head. 'Could be you are right,' he said, nodding at me again and looking at me, giving me a smile.

'Right!' I said, looking around seeing the sky beginning to get darker, and rubbed me hands feeling the chill March winds going through me. 'I think I will head off back into the house. It's getting a bit too cold out here for my liking.'

'Aye! It could be rain coming,' he said, eyeing the sky. 'Go on in an tell the missus Mattie said te give yeh a nice mug a hot cocoa for keeping me company out here. That should warm yeh up.'

'Right, Mattie! I'll say you told me to,' I said, laughing, thinking she will eat the head off me.

'You do that,' he said, nodding his head at me and laughing back. His eyes lit up and the skin went all crinkly. I enjoyed seeing him laughing. It made him look like a real happy granddad. 'I'll keep moving, before the rain hits. I want to get down to the orchard an do a few bits an pieces in the vegetable garden.'

'Right, Mattie! Thanks for talking to me.'

'I can return the compliment,' he said, nodding his head and waving his hand at me without looking back.

Then he was gone. I stood staring after him, seeing him slowly pushing the wheelbarrow with his back bent and his head lowered, trying to lift the big wellington boots. But instead, he was only managing to drag his feet along the ground, like the boots were too heavy for him, as he headed himself off, making his way down towards the orchard, hidden inside a big, long, red-brick wall with two tall black gates standing in the middle under an arch. Ah, he's such a nice poor man. But he's getting too old for this heavy aul kind of a job. He should be taking life more easy at his time of life. It's a pity he has no children to take care of him. Then they could bring him in a few bob and he could take life more easy. Gawd! It's terrible being old.

Right! I better get meself moving too. I whirled around, digging me hands deep inside me old green coat and set me sights on getting back to the house. I sighed happily at the thought I had somewhere to get in out of the cold. Bloody hell! I really am steeped in luck. It's just so great having somewhere to go, and not just any aul place either! I still can't believe I landed on me feet! I took off, running through the trees and shouting into the wind, 'Yeah! Life's a bowl of cherries!'

I flew through bushes, sending birds screaming out of trees, making room for a squirrel that was running for its life straight up the tree. I shot around a big long hedge, galloping for all I was worth. Then I was around the corner and nearly ended up head first in a pond. Fuck! 'Aaahh! Ohh!'

I came to a skidding halt, balancing meself over the water with me feet still skidding and me arms waving. I flapped like mad trying to get meself back, then landed on me arse, right on the edge with me feet dangling in the dirty water. 'THE CURSE A JAYSUS on whoever was thick enough to put a bleedin waterhole right where no one could see it!' I screamed, getting meself back on me feet and brushing the mud and wet off me one and only good coat. 'I need this for wearing every day,' I moaned, nearly crying with the rage at seeing the state of it. I snorted me breath, heaving in and out through me nose, raging there was no one around I could let fly at. Fucking eejits! Rich people are so thick when it comes to wasting their money! They have no bleedin sense! I sighed, looking down in disgust at the dirty rotten leaves and dead plants floating in the filthy green water.

Then me eyes peeled over to a big grey statue of a woman standing over in the corner. They had her up on a big block of cement or something. She had nothing on but a woolly hat on her head and a scarf wrapped around her neck. Her hand was pointed in the air and the other one holding her hip. Someone thought, because she was stark naked, she might like the hat and scarf to keep her warm. I had an idea. I rushed over to get a look. Yeah! There's nothing wrong with the hat, and the scarf is in good condition. Right! They're just what the doctor ordered. I'll wear these meself.

'Thanks, Missus!' I peeled the scarf off the statue's neck and grabbed the hat. It fitted me grand. The scarf even smelled of lovely perfume. I put the hat on me head and wrapped the scarf around me neck. Lovely! But they're a bit damp. That's from being out in all the elements.

Right! I'll wash these and I won't know meself with all the comfort when I go out in the cold. Then me eyes landed on the two ducks scraping themself out of the water, squawking like mad, telling each other, *Hurry! Run for your life!* They tripped over each other, then rolled back on their feet, screaming in rage and fright. They took off again, heading for the bushes, dragging their back legs behind them and their arses held in tight, thinking I was going to give them a good kick up the arse with all me shouting and roaring. 'Sorry, ducks!' I laughed, waving me scarf over at them hiding in the bushes. Right! I'm feeling better now with me new stuff. Anyway! It was me own stupid fault. I should have gone more easy. Then me coat would be OK. Jaysus! I came too fast around that big bleedin hedge.

OK! Which way? I could see more statues and white benches for
sitting down resting yourself. No! I'm not interested in that. It's too
damp and cold and miserable out. Where's the way into the house?
I don't want to go all the way around to the kitchen entrance then
have the aul one giving out to me. Or worse still, in by the front
door! The mother, or the aul one, if she has to answer the door,
might think I am just a bloody nuisance and the sooner I'm gone
the better for everyone. Oh, no! I can't be having that. The longer I
stay, the better for me. But I have a fear of being in the way. I don't
like going where I'm not wanted. So, I'm going to make sure I don't
become in people's way. Then they might forget I'm even here! I
could ramble around here for years, nipping in and out for me grub
and a lovely warm bed to sleep in! I thought about that, getting the
picture of people forgetting all about me. Yeah! It could work if I
keep me head down. The place is bloody big enough! Ah, stop yer
kidding, Martha. It's a lovely dream.

17

I walked back the way I came, looking for a way in. Me eyes peeled over to the side of the house, spotting a side door. Ah ha! Maybe I can get in that way! I rushed over to see if it's open. The handle turned and I put me head in the door, seeing a dark passage with a door on the right and one in front of me. I shut the door behind me and looked around. There was a long line of wooden pegs on the wall, with raincoats and jackets hanging on them. Down on the cracked and worn out aul red tiles on the floor was a line of wellington boots and old shoes. A big black box sat in the corner with walking sticks and umbrellas sitting in it. Ah! This must be for when you're going outside. I lifted up a black walking stick made out of a tree. This could come in handy, I thought, swinging it around. I could use it for hitting the bushes when they're thorny, and other things that get in your way. I had a look at a long cream-rubber raincoat. This could suit me grand when I'm going out for walks, I thought, trying it on and twirling around to get a look at meself. Might as well try on the wellingtons while I'm at it. This coat and the boots would save me own coat. And the wellingtons would keep me feet nice and dry.

I put me new hat on me head and wrapped the scarf around me neck. I was so busy checking meself out, wondering if I looked all right, that when the door suddenly opened and a figure appeared I let out a scream with the fright!

'Ahhh! Oh, my goodness!' roared the mother, grabbing her chest with her hand. 'Where on earth did you come out of?'

'Oh, you gave me a fright!' I said, standing in me new get-up, with her eyes flying up and down me, taking me in wearing her raincoat and wellingtons!

'Goodness! You startled me!' she puffed, with her eyes staring out of her head and the colour drained out of her face.

'Sorry. I was trying not to disturb anyone,' I muttered, feeling like I got caught like a robber.

'Well! You have certainly managed to do quite the opposite!' she snorted. 'What are you doing wearing those things?' she said, pointing at me, sweeping her finger up the length of me, trying to make out what I was up to.

'Eh, I thought, eh, maybe you didn't want them,' I said, me face going all colours with the shame in me at she thinking I'm getting up to no good.

'Why did you not come in through the kitchen? Surely you are more familiar with that way?' she whispered, looking very annoyed with me.

'Sorry, I didn't mean to do any harm,' I muttered, grabbing all the stuff off me and even putting the hat and scarf I got off the statue back up on the wooden pegs for holding the stuff.

'Come along, dear. Go inside,' she said, waving me through the door she just appeared out of. Then she turned the big key in the lock in the back door and made to come in after me. I held the door for a minute, then left it open and walked around the passage, then started running, looking for the stairs to get to me own room.

Jaysus! Ah, help, Mammy! Now she thinks I'm a robber! And on top of that, now I've gone and lost me red matching hat and scarf. I rounded passages and eventually found the front hall and took the stairs two at a time. Me heart was sitting down in me belly with worry. Maybe now she won't trust me. She might make an excuse and tell me I can't stay here, I have to go! What will I do? There's no point in telling her I wouldn't touch anything. She's not going to believe me. She definitely thinks I was sneaking around the place looking to see what I could get me hands on! Oh, sweet divine Jesus! Why can't I ever stay out of trouble?

I made it to me room and charged in, closing the door. Me heart is going like the clappers! Right! I'm not moving out of here until I see which way the wind is blowing. Keep quiet. Say nothing. Do nothing. Or maybe I could ask Missus Doherty if she wants me to give her a hand in the kitchen! I could make meself useful. Earn me keep. The missus might then start to sing me praises to the mother. Yeah! That way I could get back in her good books! Right! I'll try that!

I flew out the door then thought a bit more. No! Keep well out of the way for the minute. She's probably down there right now waiting for me to show me nose. Then she will show me the door. No! I'm getting meself into the bed. I won't even bother going down looking for something to eat. Right! That sudden thought really hit me. Without warning, I could hear me belly rumbling. Jaysus! I'm starved with the hunger! I could get the picture of roast meat and gravy and lovely roast potatoes. I bet that's what they're going to have. They're bound to have something really lovely like that for the dinner. Ah, Jaysus no! I'm going to miss that, and on top of everything, to make matters worse, I won't even get to taste them cakes she made this morning!

I dropped meself down on the bed feeling like I have really put a noose around me neck. No! I want me dinner! Even if I have to sneak down later when the mother's in bed and the aul one's gone for the night. Right! I'll do that. Better not to chance going down now. That's only looking for trouble. I'll get into the bed. Ah! Fuck meself anyway! I'm pure stupid. If only I had more sense, like I used to.

I woke up seeing it was nearly dark. I held me breath for a minute. Then it hit me. Ah, bloody hell! I upset the mother. Right! Enough is enough. I'm going down to see if I can get something to eat. If she doesn't want me here, well, it is going to happen anyway. Better to find out what is happening.

I was out the door and taking me time down the stairs, not in any hurry, then I heard her voice. I stopped to listen.

'YES!' she screamed, then roared laughing. 'It was priceless, my dear. Oh, if you had seen the face! But of course I was so cross! YES!' she screamed again. 'One can't possibly keep up at my age!'

I moved down the stairs, trying to see if she was talking to someone. Me head peeled around the corner looking down into the hall. Ah! She's talking on the phone! I better wait until she finishes then come back down when she's gone.

'Yes! One of Ralph's strays!'

Me ears pricked up. The priest! Strays! I hope she bleedin isn't talking about me! I'm no stray. Who does she think she's talking about! I'm not a fucking dog! Then I listened, moving meself down the stairs to get a better listen.

'Yes! A waif! Oh, you are dreadful!' she screeched, laughing her head off.

Wonder who the fucker is she's talking to? I'm no waif! That word means I'm a tramp! The cheek a her!

I could feel meself getting all hot in me belly, and the fire was running up to me chest and nearly choking me with the rage. First a dog! Now a tramp! Right! That's it! I'm going straight back up these stairs to get me suitcase. Then I'm walking out that front door. But before I do, I'm going to tell her to shove her charity right up her skinny arse!

'Oh, but she really is very charming. She is so sweet! I was highly entertained this afternoon by the whole thing, my dear. The sight of her standing in that ridiculous hat and that bloody awful scarf! My dear, do you remember? Bertie Winter-Fellows had tied it around one of the statues out in the grounds! YES! Exactly! Our little waif!'

Then she stopped talking to start screaming like a banshee with the laughing coming out of her.

'She decided to claim it for herself! YES! It was a screech! Oh, you have no idea, Antonia! Oh, yes, but then the best bit was . . . Yes! Yes! Ha, ha! Do let me tell you! It was a hoot when she said—' I leaned me ear over the banisters, not wanting to miss anything '—"I didn't want to disturb anyone!"' she screamed, copying my voice! '"You have jolly well done a good job of doing just that," I bellowed!' Then she screamed her lungs again, sounding like a horse gasping for breath with her so-called laughing.

Oh, so she's stopped being annoyed with me! But now she's

laughing at me! Well! Who cares? But thank God I don't have to worry now. I let me breath out, feeling the terrible weight lift outa me belly. Now I can go about me business. I turned on the stairs, slapping me way down so she would know I can hear her. She looked up at me and gave me a big cheery wave with a row of yellow smile teeth plastered on her face. Then she crossed her legs and turned away from me, carrying on her conversation.

'Oh, yes! Do tell! No, indeed not! I am simply dying, my dear, to hear all the dreadful details!' she breathed into the phone, with the eyes collapsing out of her head and the mouth hanging down on her chest looking that excited. 'Is it true, do you think? Was it a little interlude? Or! NO!' she gasped. 'How awful! And poor Monty had no idea! Oh, yes. He is rather a fool, my dear. Such an awful bore. But then we did say it would end in tears. I mean taking a floozy! Then to marry! Yes, of course! She was much too young for the old goat. But nonetheless, one does have standards! One shouldn't on one's own doorstep! But where did she find this old boy? A Count, you say? Italian? Well, do you mean? Hmm. Probably hasn't got one sou to his name. Monty had better watch out. Keep the arsenic under lock and key! Ha, ha! Yes, yes! Exactly, my dear. They are both wanting the same thing. The young trollop will realise her mistake too late. Yes, gold-diggers and ageing gigolos, they are all the same! Ohhh! They met in St Moritz? Oh, please! Do not spare me the juicy details. I want to know all! Listen! Do come for lunch. No? What about dinner? I am thinking of giving a dinner party. Just a small select few. Say twelve, sitting for table.'

I wandered off, getting fed up listening. I couldn't make out what they were saying, because I couldn't get to hear the other one talking. I crept into the kitchen, not wanting to annoy anyone else. Especially the missus. I put me head around the corner, seeing she was sitting on a high wooden stool cleaning silver – knives and forks and stuff that sits on the dining room table. The radio was on and some aul culchie was screaming about a hurling match.

'Eh, is it all right to come in?' I whispered, afraid to bring the rest of meself into the room.

'What? Come in out of that! What has yer nerves scalded?'

'Eh, hello. Is there . . . could I, eh, get something to eat?'

'Of course yeh can! What do yeh think I'm doing with meself all day? But it's not for the good a me health I'm slaving an cooking an cleaning!' she roared. 'Sit down there an I'll get something hot into you. Yeh must be starved with the hunger! I haven't set sight, nor heard sound or foot of yeh all day long.'

She threw down the polishing cloth and washed her dirty black hands from the silver-cleaning stuff under the tap, then picked up a big silver spoon with a long handle that twisted at the end, and filled up a big white bowl with lovely hot stew. 'Now! Get that down yeh!' she said, landing the bowl down on top of a big white soup plate.

I stared at it, seeing the steam coming out, and lovely big chunks of meat and carrots and onions and big roundy white things that looked like potatoes but weren't, floating around in brown gravy. I grabbed up a big silver spoon she put down beside me and started to make short work of it. Then I stopped with me mouth full to examine me spoon. It was big and heavy and silver. I looked at the back and it had a mark to let you know it was silver. Gawd! This is better than Bewley's! And I don't even have to pay for it. Or, I mean, run for me life after eating it because I don't have the money to pay for it.

'Here! Would yeh like some of these scones? They're lovely with a bit of butter an jam, or maybe I might have some clotted cream left. Herself had them for afternoon tea today. We were looking for yeh, but yeh went missing. Where did yeh get yerself to?'

'Eh, in me room,' I croaked, trying not to talk with me mouth full but spraying dinner everywhere. 'Eh, sorry,' I said, holding me mouth to hide it with the back of me hand.

'I left yeh out some nice fairy cakes! I put a few cherries in them. Do yeh like the cherries? I buy them dry. For baking me cakes!'

'Yeah! I love cherries,' I croaked, feeling shy at her being so nice to me, and enjoying all the fussing I was getting.

'There you are!' the mother screamed, walking slowly into the kitchen and looking from me to the missus. 'We were hunting for you! Where on earth did you disappear to?'

'Eh, I was out taking an airing for meself.'

'Oh, no you were not!' she said, looking at me sideways and laughing.

'Eh, up in me room,' I squealed, not meaning to. Wanting all the fuss, but it was getting a bit much for me. I couldn't enjoy me dinner in peace because they might think I was a savage if I ate it too fast! So I put down me spoon and watched it sitting there waiting for me. But the hunger was killing me. Me belly was rumbling and I was tormented letting meself sit here and stare at it.

'Mattie told us when he was in this evening. You were last seen this afternoon, terrorising the wildlife! He also said you were great company for him. He enjoyed you immensely. He did, did he not, Maeve?' the mother roared.

She doesn't talk but shouts like she is giving out. But she's not really. Because she keeps getting a twinkle in her eye and her mouth twists like she's trying to stop herself laughing.

'Eat up tha dinner!' shouted the missus, going back to her polishing. 'Mattie is right!' she moaned. 'Isn't it grand for him he has nothing better to do than stand idling his time, wittering away like the village fool, instead of taking himself off down an do a bit of work for himself. When it would suit him better te be down seeing to my vegetables for the table,' she snorted, slamming down a silver jug with a vengeance, nearly battering it. Then picking up a silver candlestick and examining it, before rubbing on the silver-cleaning stuff, nearly making a hole in it.

'Oh, Maeve! You are terrible! Don't be cruel!' shouted the mother. 'The poor man hardly ever stops working!' she laughed, looking like she was giving out to the missus. 'Where are my cigarettes?' she said, whipping her head around the kitchen. 'Did I leave a packet in here, Maeve?'

Missus lifted her eyes to the ceiling and went back to polishing hell out of the silver.

'Perhaps I have left a packet in the study!' she said, making for the door. 'I am trying to muddle through those awful bloody accounts for that dreadful little man, my accountant,' she said, stopping and looking at us. 'He is coming next week. Really! I have no idea what it is I am supposed to do,' she breathed, whipping her eyes at the ceiling and snorting air out through her nose, then giving her head a quick shake. 'But I do know,' she said, waving her finger at the air and thinking about this, 'as soon as he sets foot inside the door, he will immediately start scolding me for not having these silly papers in order. He is such a bloody awful boorish little man,' she muttered, dropping her head and looking like her whole world had just ended, then headed herself off out the door.

I watched it close, then looked down at me dinner and started to make short work of it again. Then I grabbed for the cakes, lathering on lumps of good butter, then nearly half the pot of raspberry jam, and piling a big gob of cream on top and trying to get the lot of it into me mouth with one go. It wouldn't fit. I lost half the jam down the front of me one and only blouse. 'Ah, fuck!' I muttered, holding me mouth open staring at it.

'Now, now! I heard that!' muttered the missus, waving her finger at me. 'We'll have none of that kind of language in my kitchen!'

'Sorry,' I muttered, trying to wipe it with me hand and making an even bigger mess.

'Give it over te me when you are finished your dinner. I'll give it a wash for yeh,' she said, dropping her head back to polishing her silver again.

'Ah, no! I can't let you do that, Missus Doherty. That really is very good of you. But sure, I'm more than capable of washing it for meself. But this is me one and only . . .' I said, staring at me clothes, wondering what I would wear without it. I suppose I can go around in me cardigan and vest until it dries.

'Have yeh nothing else to wear?' she said, lifting her head to look at me.

'No, not yet. I have the one good set of clothes. But I need them for good wear.'

She shook her head, agreeing with me. 'Never mind! Leave it down to me when yeh put on yer nightclothes. I'll give it a quick wash out an hang it over the Aga,' she said, throwing her eye up to a clothesline pinned back against the wall on a pulley. 'It will dry overnight. If yeh have anything else needs washing, I can throw it in the washing machine.'

'Ah, Gawd, no! Thanks very much, Missus. But I prefer to wash me things by hand. Them machines eat the clothes,' I said, thinking back to the time I lost me last job because I made mincemeat out of all the stuff. Everything got shrunk!

'No! Ah, that's a load of nonsense, child! Not if you know what you are doing. Some people are very queer when it comes to these modern machines. They expect the clothes to get up and walk themself into the machine, then complain when things go wrong. No, don't you fret yerself! Bring down anything that needs doing. I'll take care of the rest.'

'Could it wash a coat? I have a lovely French coat. It was an off-white colour when it was new. Now it's gone very grubby and dirty.' I was thinking of all the times I slept out in it, covering meself at night.

'Bring it down. I'll take a look at it first. Herself likes to get everything sent out to the laundry. All the bed linen an that kind of thing. The good stuff, her own clothes, gets sent to the cleaners. I use the machine for her smalls an tea towels an that kind a thing.'

'Right! Thanks, Missus!' I said, delighted at getting me clothes clean at last. 'That is very good of you altogether, Missus Doherty! I'll bring down me stuff as soon as I've finished me dinner. Maybe we could wash what I'm wearing? These are the only one set I have for going around in. Do you think this wool skirt would dry for the morning for me?'

She squinted over. 'I could run that with the blouse. That would have to be hand washed as well. As I said, leave everything out yeh want washed an I will have it ready for yeh. Now! Have yeh had enough to eat?' she said, seeing I had cleaned the plate of all the cakes and left the stew bowl looking nice and shiny!

'Yeah! Thanks! That was really lovely. I haven't enjoyed meself as much as this for a long time. Gawd! Ye're a marvellous cook!'

'Yes, well! My mother before me, God rest her, I learned me trade at her knee,' she said, shaking her head and dropping her eyes back to her polishing, looking like she regretted something that is long lost now.

I stood up and took the dishes over to the sink and started to run the hot water, putting in the washing liquid, then started to wash the dishes. I dried them and looked in the presses to see where they went. Then I wiped down the wooden table that was a goldie colour from all the scrubbing then oiling it got.

'Can I give you a hand with the silver? I'd love to polish them! Or I can put on the polish and you can shine them.'

'You shine and I'll polish,' she said.

I grabbed up a teapot from the worktop and started to polish with a yellow polishing cloth.

'Here! Grab that stool,' she said, pointing to a corner beside a little alcove. We sat down beside each other and she rubbed in the stuff and I polished it off, getting up a massive shine. We sat quietly, intent on our work, and listening to the radio. I kept at it until I could see me face in it.

'What do ye think of that?' I said, holding up the teapot that would blind you with the shine.

She lowered her head at me and winked. 'Yeh have a job for life,' she muttered, laughing. It was the first time I really saw her smile.

I sighed with contentment as I put it on the table with the other stuff all ready and waiting to be put away. Then reached up, taking down a big fancy jug. 'I would never know what any of this stuff is used for, Missus!'

'Ah, yeh get used to it,' she said, eyeing the mountain of silver sitting piled on the worktop, still waiting for a good clean. 'There was a time when they had a kitchen girl for doing this kind of thing,' she said, shaking her head and putting a big serving spoon next to me for polishing.

'Did you work here then, Missus?'

'Oh, when I was a girl, I did my bit here. My mother was alive then, God rest her! She was the cook. That's how I learned my trade. Sitting up there next to her at that table. Watching an helping. I was knee-high to a grasshopper. I would sit quietly, rolling my bit of dough, keeping one eye on my mother, watching as she baked the bread, scones, an all class of cooking.

'It was lovely here at Christmas for the family. Not us, mind! We did the donkey work. But all the same, it was a great air about the place. The hunt would start off from here on St Stephen's Day. I would help the older staff te hand out the mince pies an mulled wine.'

'What's that?'

'Mulled wine? Oh, that's wine heated slowly with all sorts of spices thrown in. It was served in silver mugs an handed out on silver trays,' she said, with a smile on her face and a dreamy look in her eyes. 'They would host the hunt ball here, up in the drawing room. That's on the first floor. My Gawd, the amount of fussing and cleaning. It was all hands on deck, I may tell yeh.

'Come December the first, then it would all hit off! Rugs would be pulled up and you would have to be able to see your face in the wooden floors before satisfaction was given. The housekeeper then – what was her name? Oh, Miss Latchbelt – she was a holy terror! The poor young girls who worked under her spent more time in tears! Well, it was no wonder half of them got themself into trouble. Oh, it happened te at least three or four of them in my time. Poor girls! Foolishly hoping the fella would make a decent woman of them an they could set up home together. It never worked that way. The bowzie would be gone. Leaving a clean pair of heels, with the dust flying up behind him an the girl left to fend for herself. The ones who did manage to trap a fella. Well! They skidaddled off together. It was down te some slum tenement in the city. She would be no better off than the other poor unfortunates. Left with one poor hapless little child after another while the work-shy, no-good of a husband got his comfort in the public house. Frittering away any pennies he could get his hands on. Leaving her an her little ones to sink or swim! I don't know who was worse off! The poor girl left abandoned te her fate, or the unfortunate who was lucky he married her. With her children half starving te death. Of course that was OK. The poor will always be with us, so the powers-that-be tell us.'

I listened, watching her shake her head, looking very miserable. Then she dropped her head and stared at the silver spoon in her hand, not seeing it. Because she was thinking back to a picture in her head of things that she saw happen long ago. I felt like saying, 'You are right, Missus! I know all about that. It happened to me ma.' But I kept me mouth shut. That is something I will never tell another soul as long as I live. People don't want to know you! Even if they are kind. Somehow it belittles you in their eyes. They can't help thinking that way. A bastard is a bastard! A person can't be lower than that!

'Did you never have children of your own?' I said quietly, thinking she was the one person who would have made a great mammy. Yet, people who don't want them get to have them. It would make you laugh. Otherwise you would only cry!

'No, we never had any of our own. But we did rear two children. Two girls. We got them as babies. Both of the mothers had worked in this house. I had been married for a few years. But nothing happened. We couldn't manage one of our own for some reason. I kept losing them. I would only carry for a few months, then that was it. Seven I lost! Never managed to carry it more than five an a half months. That was a boy,' she said, looking terribly mournful, with the pain showing in her eyes, looking like she still hurt from all that time ago.

'I went down te see a girl who had worked here. She was in a convent down in the heart of the country. My mother was alive then. The girl had managed te get a letter written te my mother te ask for her help. My mother, God rest her, was a very good woman. She would do anything for anyone. She always said, "If you can't do good, then don't do bad!"

'Anyway, the long and the short of it was me an my husband Mattie, we went down an signed the girl out. Otherwise, they would have kept her there. She would have stayed locked up an her baby would have been sent on te a home. Eventually the children end up getting reared in one of them industrial schools, that's what she told me she had found out. Well, that's no life for anyone,' the missus said, snorting and shaking her head quickly with the disgust of that thought.

I said nothing. Just listened and shook me head quietly.

'She wanted to get herself an the baby out. So it was agreed we would take the baby an rear it as our own. The mother left the baby with us te rear. Then she took off te England. We never heard from her again. The last we saw of her was when we parted at Heuston Station, just after we stepped off the train. We were after making that terrible journey back from that convent, hidden away in the middle of nowhere. We were all exhausted but happy too. I was holding the baby, wrapped up in a little pink blanket. My mother had given me that along with a new set of baby clothes she had bought for me to put on the baby that day I was taking her home.

'She had said she wanted te leave Ireland an get as far away as she possibly could. Mattie handed her an envelope with the boat ticket te London and a few shillings. We managed te put in two guineas. That was two pound an two shillings. The poor girl had nothing. That was my mother's savings. But being her, she insisted it would do more good giving a helping start te that poor young girl than sitting under her mattress waiting for a rainy day. Kathleen was her name. Poor creature. She looked into the little pink bundle in me arms an laid her hand gently on the baby's head. Then she bent down an kissed her. "Goodbye," she said to me an Mattie. "God bless you! I won't ever forget you for what you have done for me. I know I'm leaving my baby in good hands. I want you te call her Maeve, after yourself, and Catherine for her second name, after my own mother." Then she was gone. We stood watching her go off, hurrying to get the mail-boat train from Westland Row that would take her all the way te London, where she could get lost an no one would ever find her again! Yes,' she muttered, staring back to that time. 'We never did hear from her again.'

After a minute, she started rubbing the silver again, still lost in herself. I said nothing. Not wanting to disturb her in her memories. Then she started talking again.

'It was about seven months after that. A young girl by the name of Angela. Ohh! She was no more than about seventeen years old, or there about. Anyway, she had worked here in the kitchen as a kitchen maid. I remember my mother complaining when she didn't turn up in the kitchen for work after having her Sunday off. It was then they noticed she had left. Up an taken all her bits and pieces, without a by-your-leave. Then one night. God! It was very late. It must have been in the middle of the night! Oh, about nearly one o'clock in the morning. We heard this banging on the door. It woke up little Maeve sleeping beside me in the bed. I always had her little body wrapped in me lap to keep her warm,' she said, with a smile lighting up her eyes.

I nodded, smiling and listening.

'God almighty, child! In them days it used te get very cold,' she said, giving a shiver, remembering. 'You see, we only had the turf then. Not like nowadays! We have the coal. An there's nothing like the heat that comes out of that. Then when she woke up, Little Maeve,' she nodded at me, making sure I knew who she was talking about.

'Yeah, the baby!' I said.

'I would reach up to this little table I had then that stood handy next te me, beside the bed. I could take the bottle sitting in boiled water, keeping it warm, then feed her without the pair of us having to stir ourselves much. I would just shove it in her mouth an let her guzzle away, then take the bottle out of her mouth when she dozed off. Before we knew where we were, the pair of us would be out like a light again, fast asleep.

'So this night anyway! Between her roaring in me arms an the mother shouting in the next room for Mattie te get up an see who was making the row outside! He lifted down the storm lamp left sitting on a shelf in the hall an lit it with the box of matches left for that purpose. That was used for lighting our way when we travelled up an down between the big house an here at night. I sat up on the side of the bed feeding the baby, not able to rest until I knew what was happening. I knew it was no good news coming that hour of the night. He went out an shut the bedroom door behind him. But I could feel the breeze coming in through the open front door. It was a very bad night out. Cold an windy. I always remember that night.

'It was the year Nineteen-fifteen. The twenty-second of November, Nineteen-fifteen. Yes!' she said, shaking her head, looking very shocked.

'Straight away I could hear crying. It was the sound of a young girl wailing an I could hear the crying of a newborn baby! It sounded just like a little kitten. I could hear Mattie talking to someone, voices, but I couldn't make out what they were saying. The black smoke and the smell from the fumes of the oil in the storm lamp poured in under the door. It was from the force of the wind blowing all around our little cottage. These mountains can be very treacherous in dark stormy winter nights. The trees may give shelter. But they can kill as well if one happens to come down in the wrong place. I looked down at Maeve, feeding on her bottle in me arms. I wanted te lift her up an take her out te see what the matter was. But I didn't want her te catch cold. "Who is it?" said my mother, appearing in the bedroom from her room beyond, wearing nothing but a long shift with a shawl thrown over her shoulders. "I don't know, Mammy! Go back te bed before you catch your death of cold. Mattie will see te it. Don't go out there this hour of the night," I said, seeing her making for the door.

'She whipped it open, pulling it out behind her. "What is it, Mattie? Who's there?" I heard her say through the open door.

'"Oh, please don't turn me away, Missus! I'm sorry te bother yeh! But I'm in terrible trouble." I clearly heard the sound of a young girl crying, pleading an sobbing her heart out. Before I could give a name te the voice I recognised, I heard my mother say, "Angela! Is that you? Come into the light! In the name of all that is good an holy! What brings you back here? Come in! Come in!" The door was pushed open and little Angela appeared wearing nothing but a light summer shift with a shawl thrown over her head. Oh, God almighty, she was in a terrible state! She was the colour of a corpse an looked like a walking skeleton.

'My mother was the first to act. "Quick, Mattie! Throw a few sods of turf on the fire an get it up and going. This poor child is half frozen to death," she said, moving Angela back into the hall an taking her into the warm kitchen with something crying under the shawl. I put little Maeve down in the big empty bed an covered her up after she fell asleep with only half the bottle drunk. Then I threw a shawl over my shoulders an whipped up the candlestick that was always left sitting on the little night table. I lit the candle by the dying fire in the room an crept out te see what the matter was. I brought in the lighted candle an stopped dead in me tracks. It was at the sight of seeing Angela sitting in the fireside chair. My mother was pulling back the shawl te see what she had hidden there. A little scrap of a bundle was clinging te her naked breast, fighting for the milk, little an all as it was that the poor child had to offer.

"'Holy mother of God!" my mother said, going into the shock at seeing the poor mite wearing nothing but a dirty white bonnet an a filthy rag of a blanket wrapped around her. "Here! Give the child over te me," my mother said, taking the baby out of her arms. It was blue with the cold an weak from hunger an exhaustion.

"'Maeve, love! Make up a bottle. This child won't last much longer if we don't get nourishment an heat into it fast."

"'Mattie! Bank up that fire!" I said to himself standing in the middle of the room with his mouth open, still hanging on to the storm lamp an gaping like a fool. Not able to make head nor tail of what was going on.

"'Oh, dear God!" my mother moaned, sitting in the opposite chair an opening out the blanket with the baby laid out on her lap. "The poor creature is naked."

'I looked over, seeing the baby had nothing on but a filthy nightgown covered in diarrhoea an sopping with the wet. The poor child was nearly half dead. It was weak an shivering. Oh, I will never forget the sight of it, or the terrible condition of the young mother.

'I made up a bottle an rushed over te the hot press, grabbing out some of Maeve's newborn clothes. She was too big for them now. By that time my little one was eight an a half months. We washed her as best we could. Her little bottom was in an awful state. Red raw from the neglect. Then dressed her in warm, dry clothes an wrapped her up in a heated flannel sheet, then the little blankets belonging te Maeve.

"'Listen, Maeve, love. You feed the baby while I heat up that drop of soup sitting in the pot. Mattie! Listen, son! Would you ever put more turf in that stove an get it burning fast. This child looks like she is on her last legs. How in God's name did yeh get here, Angela, love?"

"'I got a lift on a hay cart into the city. The countryman took me as far as Sackville Street. Then I walked the rest of the way here," Angela muttered weakly.

"'Say no more! Just rest yerself," my mother said, buttering chunks of bread an cutting slices off the baked ham we had for our supper. "Here, love! Take that mug of soup while it's hot. An eat up that bit of bread an meat," my mother said, feeding the poor girl crouched in the armchair over by the fireside, shivering from shock an exposure. "After that yeh can get your head down. Mattie, love! Give me a hand te pull out the settle bed here an we'll make it up." That bed went along the wall just beyond the window an into an alcove. They pulled out the long wide seat an opened the lid. It was very deep, with a mattress and blankets inside. When it's not in use, we use it for sitting.

'Well, anyway,' the missus said, lifting her head to me, pausing for a breath.

I listened, with me mouth open, forgetting to polish me jug. I looked down at it and went on polishing. Then she started talking again.

'We settled them down for the night in the bed tucked into the alcove, with the baby clinging to her chest. It needed what nourishment it could get out of the poor exhausted child. But at least they had the bit of comfort of a warm room an a little hot nourishment in their bellies. Next morning we went about our business up to the big house. I had a bassinette sitting by the stove there, next to the heat. My little Maeve slept in that during the day an amused herself playing with her toes an soaking up any attention going her way from the staff coming and going in an out of the kitchen. As I said, my mother was the cook, an I helped her an did the running after Mrs Fitzgerald. Not this one, mind! She wasn't even heard of then. But she would make her appearance soon enough when she married into the family. We said nothing to anyone. We thought it best to let the poor child stop where she was an have time enough to get back her strength, before taking any further steps.

'The story came out gradually. My mother asked her who the father was. She hung her head at the mention of that an wouldn't say. "Was it someone in the big house?" my mother asked.

'She looked up and showed her face, shaking her head saying, "No."

'"Are yeh sure about that?"

'"No one here laid a hand on me," she said quietly, shaking her head like she meant it.

'We were satisfied she was telling the truth an at least spared the misery of knowing someone up there had done the poor child harm. "Will yeh not tell us who the blackguard was?" said my mother, pleading with her. "We could make him do his duty! Get him te stand by yeh."

'"Please! I can't say. It would do no good anyway!"

'"But, sure, were yeh even walking out with someone when yeh got your monthly Sunday off? I never heard tell of yeh mentioning a fella."

'"No!" the girl said, sitting like a little mouse, barely breathing out the word.

'We stared at her, trying to figure out when an how this had all happened.

'"It was on one of my visits down te the city te see me married sister. A man attacked me. He had his way," she muttered, barely above a whisper.

'"Attacked yeh! How? When? Did yeh know the man?"

'She nodded her head, muttering, "Yes."

'"Be Gawd! He'll answer to Mister Fitzgerald. He is not a chief justice for nothing!" roared Mattie, listening an going red in the face with the rage on him.

'"No! I don't want any trouble! Say nothing! Please!" the poor creature roared, crying an nearly losing her mind with the fright.

'"Where did you stay when yeh ran away from here? Yeh took all your stuff, so yeh must have had a plan," my mother said, trying to make sense of it all.

'She nodded her head. "I made me way back home te me family in the Curragh. We live just outside the army camp. Me father was labouring for a farmer. It was his cottage on the land we all lived in. But things were not right when I got there. Me father had died just that few months before. I didn't know that. I found me mother lying sick in the bed in the corner. The news was bad. The army sent a message, one telegram after another, saying three of me brothers were missing an two were known to be dead. They had all joined up with the intention of getting the King's shilling te help me mammy out. The two youngest were only fifteen an sixteen. They went looking for adventure, me mammy said. They should never have been allowed. Me mammy didn't even know till it happened. Them two were missing just a few days after they set foot in a place called Flanders. I don't rightly know where that is, Missus."

'More like blown to smithereens!' the missus said, looking at me.

I nodded, shaking me head, not able to get over the terrible things happening to the poor girl and her family.

'That was what was said by them that seen it first hand,' said the missus. 'They never talked about it. Poor devils. But they did say "missing in action" meant they were blown to the high heavens. They couldn't find the bits of them.

'"Me father's brother had moved in to help out, he called it, but he wouldn't do a job of work, an came home fleutered every night an beat me mammy an the rest of us senseless.

'"Then when he discovered," she said, breaking off an pointing at her baby. "He wanted me te go over te the army barracks an entertain the soldiers! It was then I made me way back te Dublin and knocked on me sister's door. By then her husband had joined up with the Dublin Fusiliers an gone off to fight in Flanders, where all five of me brothers were kilt! Me sister had a houseful of childre! Five of them. The biggest was only five. She had two rooms – a scullery an one room for eating an sleeping. When me time came, I made me way around to the Rotunda. I said I was married. But when it came te marking me babby's name for the birth, I didn't have a name for the father. Then they knew. There was talk of sending me up te the

Union. The workhouse! I left in a hurry, taking me babby wearing the stuff the Lady Almoner in the hospital gave me.

"'I went back an knocked on me sister's door again. She opened the door a crack an I could see the husband stretched out in the bed. "He's back! For the love of God! Don't let him catch yeh here with that!" she said, pointing at the babby under me shawl.

"'How, Mary?" I asked. Not able te take it in! "I thought he was off in the war?"

"'He was! But he made his way back! Now get going!" I was afraid of me life of tha fella, Missus! So I turned away from the door an made me way back onto the street again, not knowing which way te turn. Without knowing where I was walking, I made me way outa the city. I slept in a hollow under a tree in the Phoenix Park that first night. I begged, knocking on doors asking for food an something warm to wrap the babby. Mostly people turned me away. Especially in the better off-houses. I managed to get tuppence once an bought a loaf of bread. It kept me going on the roads. I was making me way back home to me mammy. Then one day I was sitting on the side of the road. A man driving a horse and cart with a load of hay thrown on the back was coming in the other direction. He pulled over te give the horse a rest an a drop a water an throw a sack over its back because it was raining. I was soaked through te me skin. He saw me shivering on the side of the road an asked me where I was heading for. I told him I was just a few miles down the road from home. He saw me plight with the babby an asked me was I doing the right thing? Maybe I could think of somewhere better te go! He didn't think it would go down too well with me family an the locals nearby. It was then I thought of you, Missus! I mentioned I had worked in a big house. He said that was probably my best bet. It would be wise te take me chances wit you. He would take me as far as the city, then I could make me own way! He was a grand kind man. He shared his bread an cheese an can of buttermilk with me. It took me two days an nights of walking te get here. I was hopin te throw meself on yer mercy an goodness, Missus! After this, I didn't know what else te do! I think I would have drownded meself an the poor little babby. All that kept me going night an day was the hope you would show me mercy. I'm grateful to yeh, M'am! God led me te your door."

'So that was her story,' the missus said, turning to me with her eyes watering.

'That was shocking!' I said, coming back to me senses and looking at her. Seeing the lovely warm kitchen and hearing the man on the radio saying, 'Now we bring you the voice of Nat King Cole.' I listened, letting the sweet tones melt into me as he sang, 'When I fall in love, it will be for ever'. I shivered with contentment inside meself, knowing I was all snug and warm inside. Having the idea I knew only too well what that poor girl must have gone though. No! Not many people will help you when you are down and out. You really have to be very lucky. Just like me and her was. To be able to find someone that won't look down on you, or have enough to spare they will share it with you. Most people still have very little. I think the only difference is we now have motorcars and buses to get around in. But I suppose they had them then too. Yeah! You just have to have the money.

The missus said nothing. Just got lost in her thoughts and went on scrubbing the stuff onto the silver. I wanted to ask her what happened after that. But I was afraid to disturb her thinking.

'Did you get to keep her little baby?' I asked her quietly.

She nodded without saying anything. I kept cleaning and polishing, trying to work up a glittering shine. But I could feel the air heavy with me wanting to know and her holding it in. After a while, she said, like she was talking to nobody but herself, 'We did our best for her! The poor thing lay in the bed, resting with the baby in her arms. I would run down an make up a bottle for the baby an bring her down something hot te eat. But she didn't pick up. One day, oh, it was probably about four days after she arrived at our door, I found her slumped on the floor. God! She was very poorly. I managed te get her back into the bed after taking the baby away from her. The poor thing was lying alone in the bed, crying for the comfort of its mother. I wrapped the baby in blankets an took her off with me, rushing back to the big house. I was afraid te leave the little mite alone.

'I rushed into the kitchen an handed the baby over to my mother. She was covered in flour. "Quick, Mammy! Angela has taken bad! We need te send for a doctor!"

'"What? But, sure, nobody knows about Angela! We'll have the whole house talking!"

'"No, Mammy! It's too late te worry about that. I'm going up right this minute an telling herself we need the doctor right away. She can make it happen fast."

'"Go on then!" my mother said, sitting herself down in the chair by the stove an taking the baby from me.'

Then missus stopped talking. I stopped me polishing, waiting for her to keep talking. But she just sat and stared, seeing nothing.

'Was she all right?' I whispered.

'No, she was too far gone. The doctor, when he came, said she wouldn't last. Sure enough. I sat with her as the day turned into night. She was collapsed out of this world. The poor thing sweated an her breathing was terrible. She had no notion of what was going on around her. All day long people had come an knocked quietly on the door an stepped in holding their caps in their hands. The women came an whispered prayers over her. Later on in the evening the Missus Fitzgerald came down to check on her. By then it was just the waiting. We watched as she fought for every breath. Her little thin body was just a bag of bones lying in the bed.

'At exactly twenty-one minutes on the hour a one o'clock in the morning, she drew her last breath. Exactly four days almost te the hour when she had used the last of her strength to get her baby to safety. It was the twenty-sixth of November Nineteen-fifteen when she died. Only seventeen years old. People who were there keeping the vigil started the praying for the sorrowful mysteries of the rosary. She lays buried now, down in Mount Jerome Cemetery. That's where all her mother's family came from. She was a Dubliner. She had married a countryman. I took the little baby. We had her christened before the burial. While the mother's body lay in one part of the church, we were all in another, over at the christening font having the baby christened. Then we set off across the city te bury her mother. The family couldn't afford the burial, but there was no question anyway! None of them turned up for the burial. The only instructions given was where she was te be buried.

'Angela had named her little baby Emily. So we had gone from having no children to having two little baby girls all in the same year, with only a little over eight months between them. Emily was slow to thrive. She was very delicate for a long time. But we managed to bring her along between my mother and meself. Everyone in the big house doted on the two of them. Especially Emily. She was a real little smiler! We called her "Smiley"!

'Well! That's that lot!' she said, throwing down the cleaning cloth and giving out a big sigh and shaking her head with a terrible regret. Looking like she wanted to get rid of something terrible. 'Come on! Finish up the last one there an we'll call it a day,' she said, looking up at the clock on the wall telling us it was ten past eleven at night.

'Where are your girls now?' I whispered, without even realising I was asking that. But it was strange she didn't say any more about them.

She stopped and leant her hands on the table and dropped her head. Then snapped up her hand again and stared out at her reflection showing in the window from the dark night outside. 'They died. Both of them,' she said quietly. 'I lost them te the Spanish Influenza. Just after Christmas. January the seventh, Nineteen-nineteen! In the morning, they were fine, the two of them. By evening, they were sick, very sick. They died the same night within hours of each other.

'I lost my mother the next day. All told, four fine solid people had died up in the big house. Seven, if you include my mother an my babies! My lovely, precious babies,' she murmured, seeing them in her mind's eye. 'Only three years old. Just swept away from me. It was so fast. So sudden! I could never understand it. For years I would wake up thinking it had te be a bad dream. Things like that can't happen so fast. Nowadays, I would have gotten them photographed. But not back then. It was too big an occasion. Yeh had te plan it for months ahead. Get yourselves all dressed up, put on yer best Sunday clothes an take the day out te go off to the shop in the city.

'Oh, but they were terrible times after the war ended. I can tell yeh that now. Everyone experienced heartbreak then in some form, shape or other. No one seemed te escape trouble. Everyone we knew had lost someone. Whether through the war or from the sickness.

'Now! Enough talk for one night! Why don't we put the kettle on an have ourselves a bit te eat before we hit the bed?' she said, grabbing the big kettle and holding it under the tap, not filling it. 'Gawd almighty!' she said, looking over at the clock. 'Mattie is going te come crashing in that door any minute now, wondering what the hell happened te me. Then on the other hand,' she said, thinking about it, 'he's probably still stuck in his newspaper. Enjoying the bit of peace he's getting without me moidering him.' Then she looked over at me, half snorting, with her mouth clamped shut. But she had a smile in her eyes.

'Yeah! Men are worse than little kids, sometimes!' I said. Not knowing if they really were! But repeating what I hear all the women saying when they are giving out about the men.

'But of course! Ye'd know that now, with all yer experience!' she said, dropping her eyes and mouth to me, making me laugh.

'Yeah! I would! Didn't I give that messenger young fella a run for his money! He was raging I didn't throw meself at his feet.'

'Oh, now! Don't start on that one,' she laughed. 'There was a pair of yeh in it! Do yeh want a sandwich? With pickles and roast beef?'

I hesitated, not wanting to put her to any trouble.

'Go on! Yeh might as well! I'm going te make one for meself!'

'OK! Grand! Thanks, Missus,' I said, laughing happily at getting a bit of grub.

'We might as well finish off the buns while we're at it. Here, I'll stick them in the Aga to heat up while I'm making the sandwiches. Then the kettle should be boiled.'

The door opened just as we were milling into the grub. 'Oh! What's this? A girls' midnight feast?' said the mother, putting her head in the kitchen. 'Is it a private party?' she laughed, pulling out a chair and sitting herself down.

'Oh, help yourself, M'am!' the missus said, taking a big bite of her sandwich and pushing over a plateful to the mother.

'No, Maeve, dear! I won't bother! But I will tell you what I shall have. A nice hot whiskey toddy! With cloves! What do you think?' she asked, leaning herself forward with a big smile on her face and the eyes staring, waiting to hear what the missus says. 'Awfully good idea! Don't you think?'

Maeve said nothing, just sat trying to work out something of an excuse. I could tell by the way she was throwing the eye at me then creasing her forehead, trying to think.

'Perhaps you would like to join me? Help you sleep! Always gets me off. Do hang on and I shall run and fetch a bottle.' Then she stood up, making for the door. 'Do we have some in the kitchen?'

'Hang on an I'll check,' said the missus, standing up and wiping her hands in her apron. She opened a press on the top of the wall and brought down a bottle of brandy. 'Will this do? I think I opened this for making me brandy butter last Christmas.'

'Oh, gosh, no! That stuff is lethal! Gives me a bloody awful headache. I won't be a moment!' Then she was gone.

'Oh, Gawd!' said the missus. 'We're for it now. Hurry up an finish eating! Otherwise we won't see our beds this side of Tuesday.' She shoved another half-eaten sandwich into her mouth and stood up, grabbing the dishes and running to the sink.

I roared laughing, seeing the hurry on her with half the sandwich gripped in her mouth.

'You won't be laughing when she gets going. Herself only comes wide awake when the rest of us are falling off our feet. You mark my words! She thrives on talking, arguing, gossiping. By the time she is finished with yeh, yeh will need the fire brigade to come and hose yeh down with the smoke pouring off yeh from all the blowing she does on top of yeh with them cigarettes. Mind you! Her aul cigarillos are worse! Them awful aul brown long things she goes around puffin on. Sticking outa one of them long gold cigarette holders. They stink the place up!'

'I'm back!' the mother sang, rushing into the kitchen with two new packets of cigarettes and a bottle of whiskey.

'Oh! You just missed Mattie!' the missus suddenly said. 'He's not well! I'm te go home!'

'Oh! When did that happen?' the mother said, with her eyes standing out of her head, looking disappointed and whipping her head around looking for Mattie. 'Where is he? Do tell him to come in and join us. Just for one little nightcap! Go on, Maeve! Do go and tell him to join us.'

I looked at the missus as she curled her face up to the ceiling, showing the whites of her eyes, then made for the back door. 'No! He's gone!' she said, looking right then left and whipping the door shut again.

'Oh, well! Never mind,' said the mother, happily pouring out a full glass for herself and getting ready to pour out Maeve one. 'Say when!' she said, holding the bottle over an empty tumbler.

'Never!' said Maeve.

The mother dropped her mouth open looking shocked.

'What I mean is, never would I think a leaving poor Mattie down in the house on his own. An he under the weather an all tha! Don't yeh see, M'am?'

'Oh, yes, dear! Of course. How selfish of me! Of course you must go home. Goodness! Is that the time? I had no idea,' she said, looking up at the clock and seeing it was five to twelve. 'I must take myself off to bed and get my beauty sleep! Goodnight everyone!'

'Goodnight, M'am,' Missus muttered, lifting her eyes and watching to make sure she really was going. 'Ohh! Thank God for small mercies!' she sighed, letting out a big breath. 'Joking aside, she really would keep yeh going all night if yeh let her. Then again, why wouldn't she? Traipsing outa the bed at all hours of the day! While the rest of us have to be up at the crack of dawn ready for a day's work. Now you should get te yer bed an get a good night's sleep. Yeh still have a bit of growing te do. Yeh need your sleep for that. Now, goodnight, love, an God bless!' she said, whooshing me out the door with the tea towel and looking around to make sure everything was in its place and nothing was left burning by the stove. Then she made to switch off the lights. 'Go on! Up the stairs before she catches yeh!' the missus said, making sure I did the right thing and went to me bed.

18

I sat in the waiting room watching mothers sitting with their children waiting to be seen. I had me letter in me coat pocket for the nun and felt me hand on it to make sure it was still there. It's hard to believe they are going to get me a course in the shorthand and typing just for nothing. But the doctor said they would. Jaysus! It just dawned on me this minute! Where will I live when I'm doing that? You don't get paid for something like that. You have to pay them! And what will I live on? What am I going to do for money? Oh, Jaysus! Me nerves are gone with this worrying.

I looked around me trying to take me mind off all the worries. A little young fella of about six or seven was roaring his head off, trying to escape out the door. 'No, Miley! Enough now or I'm going to take me hand to the back of yer arse and give ye a good slap!' the mammy said, getting all red in the face and losing the rag. She dragged him by the two arms and carted him across the yellow tiled floor. He streeled his feet along the floor and screamed his head off, knowing she couldn't really hit him because too many people were watching. He suddenly stopped, dropping his mouth open to stare at a young one coming in with her mother. They stood just inside the door wondering where to sit. Without warning, the little fella suddenly sprang at the young one's legs and gave her a slap. 'Get out!' he shouted. The mother was suddenly galvanised into action and grabbed her daughter by the shoulder and steered her over in our direction, well away from the little young fella. We all slid up in the seat and the two of them squeezed in at the end of me, leaving the little fella and his mother plenty of room for themself.

'That's it!' shouted the mammy, grabbing hold of him and slapping the hand of him. He leapt up and down, trying to get himself free, and clouted the ma with his other hand.

'Ah, ah! None a tha!' said a mammy sitting beside me. She pointed her finger at him, leaning towards him, warning him. He stopped to give her an unmerciful dirty look, snorting and heaving his chest, trying to get the measure of her. 'No! None a tha now, not at yure age! Ye can't be hittin yer mammy!'

His mammy laughed, half in mortification and half delighted he was being put in his place. 'I'm tellin ye, Missus! Yew have no idea wha tha young fella is after puttin me through these last few years!'

'Jaysus! The size a him!' the mammy beside me laughed, looking him up and down.

'Four girls and three boys, I have. I reared them easier, the whole lot put together. Then it is tryin teh rear this one!' the mammy said, pointing at the young fella.

'Wha ails him? Do yeh mind me askin? I mean, why have yeh to bring him here?'

'Don't ask me!' his mother snorted, fixing the scarf on her chin. 'I have teh drag meself all the way in here from Crumlin! Leaving the rest a them teh fend for themself! I hope the house is not burnt down when I get back! The eldest young fella, he's nearly fifteen, an he still hasn't a blade a sense on him. No! It was the school. They can't control him! He keeps leggin it out the door when they take their eye offa him. The kids spend their time shoutin up at the teacher, "Lookit, Teacher! He's gone! Miley O'Flynn is high tailin it outa the door!" That poor aul one, the teacher, is blind bothered an bewildered tryin teh control him.

'An he's killin the other young fellas. I've had more mothers comin to me door mornin noon an night! Complainin about him knockin the shite outa their kids!'

'Jaysus! That's terrible carry on!' the mammy beside me puffed. 'How old is he?'

'Nearly seven! Another two months an he'll be makin the Communion! I don't know whether teh get his clothes or not! They keep threatenin not teh let him make it. He told the priest to fuck off outa tha when he went wit his class to make the first confession. Stood up in the box, Missus! The priest leapt outa the box an chased him down the chapel! I was scarlet wit the shame when tha priest turned up on me doorstep teh complain!'

'SHRRUP!' the young fella suddenly shouted. 'Stop talkin about me! Or I give ye's all a kick up ye's are arses!'

'You won't kick me!' shouted the mammy beside me.

'No! Nor me neither!' shouted another mother sitting beside her.

'Jaysus! I wonder wha has him like tha?' his mother muttered to herself, shaking her head trying to understand. 'Yeh know! It could be worrums! They can do terrible things teh childre! Did yeh ever see kids throwin themself around the bed at night an grindin their teeth? Wit the poor things tryin teh get a bit a sleep!'

'Yeah, yeah! That's true, right enough. It can put them in very bad form when they're riddled wit the aul worrums.'

'An if tha doesn't work,' snorted the mammy beside me, 'maybe a good clatterin around the ear every time he back answers yeh, Missus! That's what I would give him!'

'No! It does no good. I should know! The hands are nearly fallin offa me from all the killins I do give him. Imagine at his age! The school are goin teh bar him! Can yeh believe it, Missus?' she roared, with the eyes bulging out of her head, flying it around the room, landing from one mammy to the next.

The mammy beside me snorted, giving her head a quick shake. Then giving the young fella a dirty look. 'I still say a good kick up the arse is wha tha young fella wants!'

'If only it was tha easy!' his mammy said, collapsing her shoulders and drawing in her arms to wrap them. 'Do yeh know wha the head nun said about him?'

'No, wha?' they all said, leaning in for a good listen.

'She said he might be sufferin from somethin called – wha was it now?' She lifted her eyes to the ceiling trying to think of the word. 'Oh, yeah! I wonder if any of youse ever heard a this! She said he was sufferin wit "motion nally upset"! What's tha? Do any of ye's know about tha one?'

'No! Never heard tha one,' they all said, shaking their heads.

'Did you?' the mammy beside me asked the mammy beside her.

'No! Is it a brain thing?' the one beside her asked.

'I don't know, it could be!' the mammy beside me said.

'Yeah! Yew could be right!' the young fella's mammy said. 'Only thing is, they were wrong about the original idea they had. At one time the head nun says teh me, "I think your son is retarded! Maybe you should see about getting him into a handicapped school!"'

'Wha?' they all shouted.

'Exactly! My words exactly, Missus! I lit into tha nun! I can tell youse all tha here an now! Him?' she pointed, snorting at her son. 'Sure any fuckin flies on him is payin rent! Tha fella would buy an sell youse!' she roared. 'The whole lot of us put together! I'm tellin ye's all, Missus!' she moaned, shaking her head, looking very sorrowful. 'He has me heart broken!' she groaned, smacking her fist to her chest, then rolling her eyes to the ceiling, imploring, 'Jesus! What did I ever do . . . te deserve such a crucifixion,' she sniffed, then roared, 'AS HIM?!" She snorted, losing the rag and whipping the head over to give the young fella a dirty look.

'Oh! I would agree wit ye there, Missus!' they all said, giving the young fella a sideways look, shaking their heads and snorting out their disgust as he stood with his feet wide apart and his mouth hanging open, listening and taking everything in, with the eyes peeling from one mammy to the next.

Then everyone went silent, watching as a man in a brown suit wearing a snow-white shirt and a brown tie suddenly appeared in the door and looked around smiling. I caught me breath staring up at him. Gawd! He's just gorgeous! He had a mop of jet-black curly hair and bright blue eyes that shone outa his head, and a lovely set of white teeth that he flashed around the room looking at everyone. All the mammies gaped up at him.

'Miley O'Flynn?' he said, looking at the two boys sitting on their mammies' knees, then over at the young fella kicking the bench and the woman sitting on it. She kept moving up closer to me.

'That's him, Doctor! Come on, Miley!' the mammy said, grabbing her shopping bag and trying to catch hold of him.

He flew out the door, shouting, 'Gerraway from me! I'll fuckin kill ye's.'

'Got you!' said the doctor, sliding himself around and picking up Miley, all in one sweep. He held him under his arm, with his hand held gently down on his head, and dangled him well away from himself, so he wouldn't get a kicking. 'Off we go! Follow me, Mammy!' said the doctor, laughing.

'You fucker! Lemme go!' roared Miley.

The doctor twirled him around and gave him a slap on the arse! 'Keep talking like that, Miley, and your bottom will be red hot!' the doctor said, taking him off down the passage and into a room, with the mammy rushing behind to keep up on her high heels!

There was silence for a minute. Then the mammies roared laughing. 'Just what the doctor ordered! Didn't I tell youse all! A good clatter on the arse,' the mammy beside me shouted, sounding like she had just won the pools.

'Oh, but my God! Did yeh ever see in all yer born days anyone as gorgeous looking as the like a tha doctor? I'm gone weak in the knees just lookin at him!' the mammy beside her moaned, sounding like someone had told her she only had one hour left to live!

'Oh, will yeh stop!' the one beside me sniffed. 'The man a me dreams! Jesus!' she breathed out slowly. 'Wouldn't I just love a dip a the wick from him?'

'Yeah! Or he can bless me wit his relic any time!' laughed the other one.

We all looked up when a nun covered from head to toe in a white habit appeared in the door. Even her shoes were white. The snow-white veil wrapped around her head nearly covered her face. The veil stood up on top of her head and looked like two horns sticking out. She had a big heavy gold cross on her chest. I stared, holding me breath. Wondering if she was going to call me. She leaned in with a smile on her face; it was covered in freckles.

'Mary Ann Murphy?' she said, looking at me.

I shook me head.

'That's us, Sister!' the little fat woman gasped, standing up and dragging the young one with her.

'Hello! How are you?' the nun said to the young one, who stared at her with her mouth hanging open. 'Now! What age are you again, dear?'

'She's just gone sixteen, Sister! She had her birthday on the twenty-third a February gone past!'

'Yes! That's fine, Mrs Murphy. But would you mind if I asked you to hang on for just another minute? I want to get my keys from the desk. I'm locked out of my room! Will you wait there?' she said, smiling at the two of them.

'Oh, take your time, Sister! Sure, there's no hurry on us. Come on! We'll sit back down,' she said to the young one, dragging hold of her and walking backwards, collapsing herself on to the bench again.

'Oh, by the way. Did you ever have an EEG before?' the nun said, whirling back and walking over to bend down and whisper the question.

The young one shook her head, looking like someone had asked her was it her that murdered someone! She looked in fear for her life.

'No, Sister. This is the first one,' the mammy said, all smiles and false teeth, then fixing her shaggy wool hat on her head, shoving the tight-permed grey curls underneath and pulling the hat tighter down on her head.

'Don't worry about it,' the nun smiled, showing a row of buck teeth, then resting them on her bottom lip. 'It's electrodes. We put them on your head, then strap you up to a machine. You won't feel a thing,' the nun said happily, then turned herself, making her habit swish around her, and took off, flying out the door, leaving the young one in an even worse state.

They're just up for the day from the country, I thought, looking them up and down. I stared at the young one, wearing a brown-leather pair of strap shoes, with white knee socks covering her fat legs. She had a mop of curly ginger hair standing up on her head and a green flowery frock hanging down under a bawneen grey and white flecked wool coat. Jaysus! She's a holy show! The state a her! Imagine letting yer ma dress you like that? I kept staring at her, thinking she's definitely very childish looking. There's no way the ma is going to let her out of her sight for long. I shivered, glad I was meself and not her, thinking it must be terrible to be like her and nearly need your ma's permission to just go for a piss!

'Mammy!' the young one suddenly moaned, managing to work her voice. 'I don't want them electric things getting put on me head!'

'Why not, dotey? Sure, they can't harm you!'

'Yeah, they can, Mammy. Did yeh not hear yure one say, that nun, it was electric stuff they are going to be using on me head? Then I'm to get strapped up on a machine! I'll get electrocuted, Mammy!' she puffed, staring up at the mammy with the eyes rolling in the back of her head at the shock of what she just heard.

'Ah, will yeh stop outa that! Of course they know what they are doing, sure! They wouldn't be doing it otherwise, would they?' said the ma, not looking too sure now, and staring at the young one, hoping she would come up with the answer.

'No! Be easy in yureself! They know what they are doing!' said the ma, slapping her big handbag on her lap, gripping a tight hold of it. Then she let her chest sink down on the bag and started rocking like mad with a terrible worried look on her face. Then she said, getting a thought in her head, but she looked like she was hoping against hope, 'Ahh, they know what they're about, dotey! Sure, wouldn't they have told us if someone had been killed already?'

The young one stared at the ma with her mouth open, taking this in. Then she suddenly jumped up, saying, 'I'm going home, Mammy! Quick! I want to get out of here. That nun's a bit queer looking to me!'

Just at that minute the nun swooped her head in the door with a big smile plastered on her face and waved at them to follow her. She didn't look back to see the mammy dragging the young one behind her, with the two of them muttering, trying not to let the nun see them. The mammy was red in the face and trying to keep a grip on the young one, who was pulling away like mad and getting ready to roar her head off with the crying.

'What was all tha about?' said the two mammies to each other.

'Gawd! Tha poor young one is gone off thinkin they are goin teh put her in the electric chair!' Then they stared at each other and turned their heads back to the door to make sure they weren't hearing things. Suddenly the pair of them started roaring their heads with the laughing.

'Ah, God love them! Sure, they're only up from the country! Wha would they know?' said the mammy beside me, wiping her nose with the back of her hand.

'Yeah!' said the other one. 'They must be just a bit simple in the head, God love them!' Then they collapsed their necks to the floor with the sudden burst of more laughing.

'Stop, stop! Jesus, Missus! I'm wettin meself!' roared the mammy beside me.

I looked and she was red in the face and trying to cross her legs without being able to lift her head. The mammy beside her gave her a push with the laughing roaring out of her, and the mammy beside me screamed, 'Help! I've pissed meself! Now I won't be able to move!'

The pair of them were roaring like hyenas when another nun appeared and said, 'Christopher Hannigan?'

The woman beside me put out her hand, not able to say it was her child. She stood up, holding her legs crossed, and tried to grab up a little fella of about four, sitting playing with another little fella on the floor beside them. I kept thinking I could get the smell of piss!

'What's happened?' the nun said, staring and smiling at the two women.

'That woman needs the tilet, Sister!' said her friend.

'Are you desperate?' asked the nun, not looking too sure.

The two of them went into hysterics again, seeing the nun looking and waiting for your woman to start pissing on the floor as soon as she moved her legs.

'Come on! Quickly!' said the nun, rushing and stopping to get the woman moving.

'Hang on!' said her friend, grabbing up her son by the hand and rushing after them. 'I need to go too!' she said, jiggling her legs.

'Martha Long?'

I looked up, seeing another nun pushing past, trying to see her way around the door that was now blocked with everyone trying to fit themself out at the same time.

'Sorry! Excuse me,' said a tall nun with a snow-white face to match her habit and big grey eyes that looked very gentle.

I leapt up and made me way over saying, 'Yes, Sister! That's me! I'm Martha Long.'

'Hello, dear!' she said, smiling down at me and looking with her head turned sideways on her shoulders, examining me from head to toe.

'Oh, you are so pretty,' she said, admiring me lovely clean French coat and black soft wool beret to match. Because they're both French! I look like a spy out of a film in these clothes. They're me one and only good set! So I wear them only on special occasions. Like now!

'How old are you?' she said, looking like she was admiring a lovely baby girl in its pram.

'Sixteen, Sister!' I said happily, feeling me neck stretch with all the praise I was getting.

'Come on down to my office,' she said, still looking at me sideways and walking beside me. 'I'm Sister Bonyventure Aloysius,' she said, opening a door into an office, waiting for me to follow her in. Then she closed the door and went behind a big wide desk. 'Sit down,' she said, pointing to a chair in front of her, still smiling and looking at me like I was a really sweet baby. Then she said, folding her hands in the air with her elbows joined on the table, 'So, you would like to do a secretarial course?'

'Oh, yeah, please! I would really like that!' I said, shaking me head at her and holding me breath.

'What kind of job do you think you would do?' she said, looking at me hands waving in the air while I tried to drag in me breath and get started on the reasons I would do grand if she let me do the course.

'Well,' I said, suddenly having everything fly outa me head. I couldn't think what I could do. 'Eh, eh!' Jaysus! Think quick! But I just sat looking at her, giving her a really stupid smile. Now she's going to think I'm retarded! Fuck! Why does this always have to happen to me when I'm desperate to learn something or explain?

'Don't worry! Take it easy. Let me explain a few things to you,' she said, sitting up straight and stretching her hands together on the table. 'I will be in charge of you. Now, the first thing we have to do is organise you into the system. You are going to have to have a good reason, a medical reason, for us to claim the allowance you are going to need for your upkeep. Especially to get you on the secretarial course. Now, you will be living in a girls' hostel. That can be very expensive. So we will need to get that sorted.'

'A hostel?' I said, thinking of the homeless hostels me and me ma used to live in. They were run by the Legion of Mary. A load of aul biddies who were religious maniacs! But they had no problem robbing most of the few pennies me ma got to keep me and me baby brother! Robbing aul fuckers! I snorted to meself. Me face was falling at the thought of ending up in something like that.

'Oh, you will like it!' she said, smiling. 'There are quite a lot of them around the city. They are run by different orders of nuns. Oh, they do a marvellous job of helping young girls who come up from the country for the first time. Yes,' she said, thinking. 'They're very handy for the girls after finishing school and leaving home. When they arrive in the city, the poor things are lost.'

Yeah! I thought, getting the picture of them coming down O'Connell Street with the suitcase in one hand and hanging on to a piece of paper in the other, showing an address. You can spot them a mile away. Creeping along with their shoulders hunched and their mop of red hair sticking up with their heads swinging on their shoulders and their necks leaning forward, dragging their arses behind them. I suppose they get that way from leaning down to avoid the big winds they must get in all that open space they have. Poor, me arse! It doesn't take them long to get their hands on our jobs and leave us to make do with the leftovers. They end up running the country. All the politicians are culchies, and the teachers and priests and nuns. They run everything and own the lot. They even have the cheek to arrest us! Because they're the coppers, too! We even get run out of the country! That's why the Dubliners have to take the boat to England! The fuckers! It's no wonder we have no time for them! I snorted to meself, getting very annoyed at all these thoughts.

Then I shook meself and blinked, trying to tune in again to what she was saying.

'Most of the girls get jobs in the Civil Service. A lot of them would have been at boarding school. Because in the country there are very few secondary schools in the villages. So they have to be sent away from home to the larger towns. Poor things!' she said, tut-tutting and shaking her head at the sorrow of it all. I sniffed and turned down me mouth, looking at her in disgust. Ready to tell her what I thought if she asked me. 'Of course,' she continued, 'these girls are all from good homes. Most of them would be the daughters of publicans and shopkeepers and well-to-do farmers,' she said, looking at me like I needn't worry, I would be mixing in good company!

'Now you have lived with nuns in a convent, is that not true?'

'Yeah,' I muttered, shaking me head thinking about this. Does she think I was in a boarding school? I wondered. But then she rambled on before I could get a question in.

'The girls' mothers naturally would prefer them to stay in the safety of a controlled environment. Just to start them off until they find their own feet. They can make friends there and after some time they can usually join up and get a flat together. I'm sure you will do the same when you finish your course!' she said, smiling at me like I'm the sweetest thing she ever clapped eyes on. 'OK! Is that clear?' she said, staring at me because I didn't answer, just stared back wondering was this all good or bad.

I could see she was now expecting me to say I'm delighted. I love nothing better than nuns and culchies. I was afraid to say it mightn't work out! What about a Protestant hostel? Surely they had some? But I better keep me mouth shut. I nodded me head, looking doubtful. Ah, Jaysus! More bleedin nuns! Worse! A whole shower a bleedin culchies! There's going to be killings! They hate us as much as we hate them.

Come to think about it, not all of them are like that. The best time I ever had in me life was that Christmas I had with them really nice people. The ones that took me out of the convent and brought me to their own home. They were all culchies! Yeah, and they treated me like I was one of their own. Yeah! I still remember every detail of the great time I had staying with them. No! I won't ever forget them for as long as I live. I feel bad now! Thinking all them things about the culchies, it's like I'm turning me back on them good people. Sorry, God! I should think before I start putting people down. You know I don't mean it! Well, only a bit. Some of them are still hungry fuckers! They would live in yer ear! But not all of them, God! Ah, you know what I'm trying to say. I am grateful for all you've done for me. So please don't land me back where I started. Down and out without a prayer's chance of getting anywhere. An all because I stuck me nose in the air at the idea of living with a load of culchies! So I will be good!

'Now!' she said, taking in a deep breath, getting ready to start talking again. 'Meanwhile that is a long way off,' she said, moving on and leaving that behind her. 'First you will have to see a doctor, he is on the panel. You will have to get past him in the first step for us getting our hands on the funds,' she laughed. 'But I wouldn't worry yourself about that,' she said, shutting her eyes and dropping her mouth, looking like she had a bad smell under her nose, then waving it away with her hand in the air. 'That is just a formality. But I will write to you in due course, when we have things moving. You are still staying at this address?' she said, showing me a form sitting in a file.

I looked. 'Yeah! I am!'

'Good. But it is all going to take some time. So just be patient,' she said, standing up and walking me over to the door. 'Goodbye now! I will see you again.' Then she slammed the door shut. I stood looking at the white door for a minute, wondering if that was it. Then I was gone! Out the door and into the sunshine!

So, that's it! I really am going to become a secretary one day, or work in an office anyway! No more scrubbing for me! I'm going to be respectable! I could hear them in the shops! 'Anything else, Miss?' 'Excuse me, Miss! You dropped your files!' Men smiling and saying, 'Ladies first!' I had a big smile plastered on me face at getting the picture of me hurrying in the door of Switzer's wearing a long cashmere coat with me shiny hair swinging around me shoulders, wearing black high-heel shoes and holding a big leather handbag on me arm, with a fat big purse inside, bursting with money.

A gentleman wearing a mohair coat with his shiny hair slicked back with Brylcreem was smiling and holding the door open for me. I rushed past him, nodding me thanks with a little smile on me face. Then he bowed, getting a whiff of me perfume, and hurried in after me, trying to think of something to say that would give him an excuse to ask me to meet him for dinner. He would pick me up in his new Rolls-Royce!

I blinked, seeing a young fella fixing onions in a box outside the vegetable shop. He stopped what he was doing and fixed his dirty mousey-brown hair, running his fingers through it to get it back off his forehead.

'How're yeh, chick! Do yeh want some of these onions?' he said, resting one hand on his hip and the other on the box of onions.

'What?' I said, coming to me senses and looking at him.

'They're lovely an hard,' he said, holding up two of them and squeezing them. He was trying to make himself sound like Elvis Presley and look like him by lifting his left eyebrow. His jaw was hanging open, showing dirty rotten teeth. I stared at the boils on his neck.

'Wha makes ye think I want onions?' I said, snorting at him, thinking he really has got a cheek thinking I would be interested in him or his onions!

'Well, if it wasn't the sight of me onions tha made yeh smile, it must be the sight a me that brought a smile to them lovely rosy-red lips!'

I stared at him, trying to make out what the hell he was on about.

'Yeah, go on! Take me in, baby! I have tha effect on women all right!'

'Ah, would ye ever go an take a runnin jump for yerself, ye dirty-lookin eejit!' I snapped, going on me way.

'Listen! Me da owns the shop! I can get yeh anythin yeh want for yer ma! All yeh have teh do is come out wit me!' he roared after me.

'Nah! Thanks anyway! But we have all the onions we want, thanks!' I said, grinning back at him, seeing him searching the boxes for something that might make me change me mind.

'What about a bunch a bananas?' he said, holding them up. 'Come on! Come back! I want teh talk to yeh!'

Jaysus! He's mad! I thought, hurrying off, trying to put distance between me and him.

'So why were yeh fuckin givin me the come-on by smilin at me in the first place?' he roared, throwing an onion after me!

I ducked and it flew past me head. I crossed me eyes and stuck me arms under me armpits, saying, 'Ugh, ugh! Ye hairy fuckin gorilla! Ye can't even throw straight!'

I saw his head whip up and down the boxes sitting on the table. He was getting ready to start throwing more onions. I flew! Then looked back. An aul fella wearing a long brown apron was clapping him around the head! I roared laughing, seeing him have to pick up all the stuff rolling along the ground. Fuckin eejit! Serves him right! I wouldn't be seen dead going out with the likes a him!

Right! Where will I head off to now? I could have a look around the shops. Nah! I would be only tormenting meself with all the lovely stuff I can't get me hands on. No point in that when I haven't two halfpennies to rub together. OK! Time I was thinking of getting the bus back anyway. I'm dying to tell the mother and the missus all me news! I love the way they drop everything and give all their attention to anything I have to tell them. Even when I'm talking a load of rubbish most of the time! They still make it look like I'm the most interesting person they ever met in their whole life! Yeah! Life is definitely a bowl of cherries! What more could a body want?

I sure was born under a lucky star! No matter how bad things get, something always turns up for the good! Yeah! I'm lucky to be alive! Imagine if I was never born! I would never get to feel so happy!

I took in a deep sigh of contentment, looking around at all the noise and people. My eyes peeled on a mother hurrying across the street pushing a high pram with a baby trying to see around the hood. Two little fellas were trailing behind. They had stopped and collapsed on their hunkers, trying to dig up a toffee that was stuck into the ground. They had to fight off a mangy dog that was licking at it, trying to beat them to it!

'Come on, will ye's!' screamed the ma, stopping to look back at them. 'Fuck ye's, then! Stay there! This is the last time I'm warnin youse two!' she said, losing the rag and fixing the coat hanging off her shoulders, then she took off, turning right off O'Connell Street, heading down to Gloucester Street.

'Wait, Ma! No! Don't go!' screamed the little fellas, they were only about three and four years old. Their eyes peeled to the toffee sticking up in the ground, tormenting them, then seeing the torment of their ma having the nerve to keep her promise and run off without them. They jumped up and ran after her, screaming with the rage and the terrible loss at letting go of the toffee. I watched them run on their skinny, dirty little legs. Me heart went out to them, seeing the black faces streaked with tears and snots and dirt from playing on the streets. Pity I haven't got a couple of pennies! It would make a world of difference to them. But I bought meself a big bar of Cadbury's chocolate when I got off the bus. I only have enough for the bus fare back. They remind me of meself and me little brothers and sisters! Ah, Gawd love them. Right! I better get moseying to catch the bus. I can't wait to get back. I wonder what we'll be getting for the tea?

19

I sat up straight, making sure everyone could see me sitting in the front seat of the big black car as we made our way down Baggot Street. The mother sat behind the steering wheel having a running conversation with herself. 'Did I phone Petunia to make my excuses? I do hate that awful gaggle of women she hangs about with! The poker twins. Oh, yes! Particularly those two old hags. They would rob you blind. Well, they most certainly have had their last shakedown of me!' she snorted, slamming the gears and hammering the pedals, making the car jump and take off like a scalded cat!

'Mind the old woman!' I screamed, seeing her heading to run down an old woman trying to make her way across the road on a walking stick.

'What?' she snorted out her annoyance, staring over at me. 'Why are you yelling?'

'Look out!' I shouted, pointing me finger at the old woman now stopped in the middle of the road with her eyes staring at the car in shock. I could see the whites of her eyes, and her chest heaved up and down with her trying to take her last gasp just before the car mashed her to kingdom come. She knew she was going to be killed stone dead. I could feel me face turning all colours, and I couldn't let meself take a breath as I watched her turn herself away, thinking maybe she could make it back towards the footpath before her end came. The mother turned back to the road then stared, blinking and looking surprised, trying to figure out where the old woman suddenly appeared out of. Then she slammed on the brakes and pulled the steering wheel, swinging the car to the left, and kept on going, barely missing the woman by a hair's breath.

'Really! You must not do that sort of thing when I am driving!' she huffed, looking over at me, not minding the road again. 'You could quite easily have caused me to run down that poor unfortunate woman. Nevertheless, what did that silly woman think she was doing, gadding about in the middle of the road? Really, I have no idea why they let that sort of person loose. It nearly gave me a heart attack, I can tell you!' she said, not looking one bit shocked but only annoyed because she couldn't keep driving straight ahead. 'I have no idea what makes such people so irresponsible. Especially at her age! The idea of it! Really, these things make me so vexed! Luckily for her I am an excellent and highly experienced driver! I have been driving since I was a girl,' she puffed, lifting her face and sniffing, then fixing her fur coat, dragging it up from her shoulders and patting her hair in the driving mirror.

I felt meself nearly collapsing from the shock and stuck me nose out the window, heaving in and out, trying to get fresh air, thinking next time I'm taking the bus!

We whirred over to a stop and parked the car under the trees, with their branches hanging over the railings of St Stephen's Green. 'Oh! We are here!' she said, looking over in surprise at the Shelbourne Hotel. 'Goodness! I drive almost on instinct! It comes from having been driving for most of my life,' she said, giving me a huge smile, showing a mouthful of near-yellow teeth, then switching off the engine and whipping around and swinging her big maroon leather handbag from the back seat and landing it on her lap. 'How is my face?' she said, making faces at herself in the car mirror.

She opened the bag and dipped in, pulling out a red lipstick and spreading it along her lips, then patted her lovely wavy goldie hair and slammed the big silver catch shut on her handbag. 'Hmm! OK, dear! You run along and we shall meet some time this evening. Maeve will hold dinner for you. I shall be out to bridge tonight. But I am sure our paths will cross sometime before then. I shall not be leaving until nine-ish! Do you have money? Wait!' she said, tearing open her handbag again and grabbing at notes loose all over the bag. 'Here!

Do take that! Will that be enough for you?' she said, handing me a ten-shilling note.

Me breath caught, staring at the red ten-shilling note. 'Oh, yeah, thanks!'

'Take this,' she said, handing me another note.

I looked. It was a pound. 'Oh, this is too much!' I said, feeling like I was grabbing all her money.

'Nonsense! Take it, child! Do have a little treat! Take yourself in for some lunch. Now! Be gone with you. I must hurry! The ladies are waiting. I don't want to miss out on anything. They will have started the fun, the gossip, without me!' she laughed, swinging her legs out of the car with the shiny black leather boots that she bought in Harrods in London, she told me, when I admired them.

She locked the car and made for the Shelbourne Hotel across the road. I watched her walk across the road not hesitating for the traffic, knowing the cars would slow down and wait, letting her get across the road with their eyes following her every move, staring in admiration, even if she was an old woman. You could easily tell she was a fine lady. Everything about the way she looked and held herself – it was not just the clothes that told you that. I could see the doorman in his top hat and white gloves, wearing a swanky uniform, already getting himself set to swing the door open for her with a little bow of his head. She gave him a big smile, then disappeared in the door. I headed off, making for Fitzwilliam Square to see the doctor for me test to get into the secretarial college.

Where the hell is number sixty-two? I walked up and down and all around the square, seeing the numbers not making any sense. Seventy-one – where's seventy? Ah, Jaysus! I'm going to be late. At last! Sixty-nine. Now! Which way are they going? This way! I walked past, seeing eight, seven . . . here we are. Number two! Last one on the corner. I walked up to the door and pushed it open. It led into a dark hall with the stairs around the corner on the left of the hall. The banisters creaked and moved as I grabbed hold and walked up the old stairs with the wood splitting and heaving under me, making me think I was going to go crashing any minute to land on the bleeding hall.

I stopped on a landing with two doors and squinted in at the brass nameplate on the wall. Jaysus! I can barely see the name! They are very mean with the electricity. That bulb hanging out of the ceiling barely shows a foot in front of you. 'S. Simms. Orthodontist.' No, that's not him, whatever that is. I can't even say the word. 'Messrs. Heinemann. Importers.' No, Jaysus! I'm going to be late. Half twelve, the letter said. Me eyes lifted up to the next landing. I grabbed hold of the banisters and swung me way up, taking two stairs at a time. The banister rail moved and creaked. Ah! It's going to give! I let go and walked up, then heaved meself up, taking two at a time again. A long corridor this time. I stopped at the first door. 'Dr Douglas W. Matthews' with a load of letters after his name. Yeah! That's him.

I took in a deep breath and lifted me shoulders, straightening meself. Then looked down at me new white canvas leather boots and me pink skirt with the light-pink bars running down it. I pulled down the zip a little on me new multicoloured hairy fun fur jacket with a hood. Then I made sure me new white polo neck jumper with the yellow bars around the neck was fixed properly. Right! This is the best I can look. I'm wearing all me new stuff that I bought with the money the mother keeps giving me when I'm having to go into town on all me appointments. That nun keeps bringing me in and out to see her. Oh, I have to see her as well today! Quarter past three, she said.

OK! Here goes! I knocked on the door and a voice said, 'Come in!'

I pushed open the door and walked in slowly, getting a look around me first. A handsome man sat behind a big desk under a big window smiling at me. Oh, he's lovely looking altogether. He watched me walking across the rug thrown in the middle of the huge big room. I saw his eyes peeling from me boots to me face, still smiling.

'Martha! You are she!' he said, standing up showing the height of himself. He must be well over six feet. He rushed around from his desk and grabbed me hand. 'Good girl! You made it then.'

'Yeah!' I squeaked, not meaning to but I was trying to get me breath working properly. Suddenly me heart was flying. Not knowing what he was going to do or what kind of questions he would ask me.

'You sit here!' he said, pulling out a big old chair with a black-leather scratched seat and a round back. I sat down and pulled me new red shoulder bag around to the front of me, letting it sit on me lap.

'OK! Here we go!' he said, rushing around to his side of the desk and sitting down pulling open a big file with loads of documents. 'Now! I just want to ask you a few questions,' he said, looking up at me and smiling, showing a row of white teeth, letting his bluey-grey eyes dance up and down in his head, looking like he was all excited. 'They are only fun things, really! Teasers! See how many you get! Shall we begin?'

'Yeah!' I croaked, clearing me throat, then saying, 'Yeah' again. It came out worse, making it sound like someone had pinched me. I decided to shut up.

'OK, Martha. Suppose you were about to step out the door and you saw it was raining. What would you do?' he said, looking at me in earnest, waiting for me answer.

I thought about this, getting the picture of spilling rain outside, then wondered what the answer should be.

'What would you do?' he said, trying to help me.

'I, eh, I would run back inside and wait for it to stop raining!' I said, thinking that's what I would do.

'OK,' he said slowly, not really sure about me answer. 'But suppose you had an urgent appointment, like you have with me today?' he said, looking more hopeful I would come up with the right answer.

'Well, eh, in that case I would make a run for it, hoping the bus won't be too long in coming,' I said slowly, not sure if this was the right answer.

'OK!' he laughed. 'Do you know what you were supposed to say?' he said, grinning at me.

'No, what?' I said, dying to hear the right answer.

'Bring an umbrella!' he laughed.

'But I don't have an umbrella!' I said. 'So how can I bring one?'

'Well, that's true!' he said, shaking his mop of dirty blond hair and writing something down. 'I'll give you points for logic on that one,' he grinned, looking up at me quick, then looking down at his papers again.

I waited for more. Hoping to get the next one right.

'Now! I will give you a list of numbers. You listen carefully to what I say then tell me the next number in the sequence.'

Sequence? What does that mean? I wonder.

'Eleven. Thirteen. Sixteen. Twenty. Give me the next four numbers in the sequence,' he said, speaking slowly.

I listened to the missing gaps. 'Twenty-five. Thirty-one. Thirty-eight. Forty-six.'

'Excellent!' he shouted, laughing. 'Now! Next one. What is fifty per cent of ten pounds?' he said, looking at me.

'Five pounds,' I said, quick as a flash.

'Good,' he said quietly. 'Twenty-five per cent.'

That's a quarter, I thought. 'Two pounds ten shillings,' I said, without too much thinking.

'Well done! Now! What is forty per cent?'

I went blank, thinking, I can't figure that one out. 'No!' I shook me head. 'I can only do halfs and quarters. That's all I ever managed to figure out!'

'Did you go on to secondary school?' he asked me.

'No.' I shook me head, not saying I didn't even barely make it to baby school. I only got a few months at school in the convent before the nuns took me out to work for them.

'OK,' he said slowly, dropping his head down to his papers, looking like he was trying to figure me out or something.

Me heart dropped, seeing him not looking too happy. Oh, please, God! Don't let me fail his tests. I will be grateful to you, God, for the rest of me life if I get past him and into the secretarial college.

'Let's try this one!' he said, lifting up a sheaf of papers and settling them together. 'Every evening a man returns home from work. Each evening he takes the lift to the fourth floor. He lives on the sixth floor but he gets out and walks up the other two flights, taking the stairs. But,' the doctor said, pausing and waving his finger at me, 'every morning when he starts out to work he takes the lift to the ground floor. Why does he do that! Hmm! What do you think, Martha?' Then he let the papers drop against his chest and leaned over the desk, smiling at me, waiting for me answer.

'Ah, because he wanted the exercise! Because he works in an office sitting on his ars . . . behind all day long.'

'Nope!' the doctor grinned, shaking his head and closing his eyes, then looking at me again.

I lowered me head to the desk, not seeing it. I pictured getting into a lift and staring up at the buttons. One floor, two . . . seeing the row of buttons all in a line going up the wall. Not because he wants the exercise, but he comes all the way down in the morning . . . I pictured the buttons again. Then me mind's eye flew to the buttons coming down in the morning. Ground would be the first button.

'Because he was a midget! He couldn't reach the top button for the number six. He could only reach as far as four! But coming down was easy. It was the first button!'

'Brilliant piece of deduction, Watson!' he shouted, slamming down the papers.

'I got it right!' I said, lifting me head sideways to get a look at his head hanging down to fix his papers.

'Indeed you did! Well done! You have above-average IQ,' he said, grinning at me and putting his papers back into his file.

'So did that mean I passed?' I asked him, holding me breath in case I was jumping the gun.

'With flying colours!' he said, standing up and coming around to lead me to the door.

'Eh, what is an IQ?' I asked, wondering what I was good at. Above average, he said!

'You are above average intelligence!' he said, smiling down at me. 'In other words, a very intelligent young lady who will go far!'

'Yeah!' I said, smiling up at him with me heart lepping with excitement.

'Yep! You should have no problem coming to grips with your course!'

'Ohh! I really have passed, so, then?!'

'Take it from me you have!' he said, slapping me back and laughing. Then he opened the door and held it wide. 'Bye, bye!' he said, getting another look at me boots and looking me up and down, seeing me wearing all the colours of the rainbow in me new outfit.

'Bye, bye, Doctor!' I shouted happily, waving as he watched me then slowly shut the door.

I'm finished! That's it! I'm going to be going to the secretarial college. Yeah! I leapt into the air with me heart flying with happiness! 'Oh, I do like to be beside the seaside!' I sang as I hopped down the stairs, taking them two at a time. Then I was out onto the street again. OK! What now? I wonder what time it is? I could feel the thirty bob burning a hole in me pocket. Then me belly rumbled and suddenly I was starving with the hunger. So! What's the first thing I'm going to do now? I think I will find somewhere to eat. Then mosey on over to see the nun.

I bounced along the road, hearing the birds nattering to each other while some of them were busy getting on with the business of building themself a nest. I could see two flying across the little park with long bits of twigs gripped between their beaks. They looked like they were working together. The sun was trying to get through the white thick clouds but was only managing to give a watery bit of sunlight. It wasn't very warm. I pulled up the hood on the back of me jacket, making meself look like an all-coloured teddy bear. I felt snug as a bug in a rug as I walked on, not seeing too many people or cars. Me chest was buzzing with contentment. Gawd! It's great to be alive on a day like today. Nothing to bother me and not a care in the world. Who could ask for more? Ah, thanks, God, for looking after me. I always knew you wouldn't let me down, not even in me darkest hour of need! I knew, even then, you were still looking out for me. How lucky can a body get? Ending up where I am now! I thought to meself as I headed back down to Baggot Street.

I stopped on the corner and looked around, seeing the line of shops and the street busy with people running back to work after getting their dinner. Right! Din-dins! Where will I go? I thought, looking up and down and all round the length and breadth of Baggot Street. Then I looked to the side of me. 'Maggie's Eating House' the sign said. I looked up at the green building, seeing people sitting and eating and looking down on the street through a big window. Wonder what they're offering here?

I stepped into a long hall and made me way up the stairs. On a little landing a door was open showing a toilet. Think I will hop in there first. I rushed in and closed the door then sat down. But not putting me arse on the toilet seat. I don't want to catch anything. Me ma always said you would catch disease from using public toilets. You never know where people have been! Or what they were up to! Someone had written on the back of the door, using a lipstick, 'The definition of contraception is what Hitler's mother should have used sixty years ago!' I thought about that. Oh, yeah! Then he wouldn't have been born! Someone else had written underneath, 'If no such thing available – as in this poxy backward country – then an aspirin can come in just as handy. Simply stick it between your knees!' How would that work? I wondered. Ah, yeah! Then you can't open your knees! Very good! I like that one. But you wouldn't be able to hold it for long! It would fall after a few minutes!

I flushed the chain and looked at the little sink for washing me hands. No towel! I dipped me fingers under the cold tap and hurried out, making me way up the rest of the stairs, and stepped onto a landing. I could smell grub and hear the voices of people speaking very loud.

I pushed in the door, seeing a load of people sitting around a long, wide wooden counter. They were all sitting up on high wooden stools talking to a really fat, stout woman sitting behind the counter. The room was thick with smoke. And along with the smell of cabbage I could get a very heavy, sickly-sweet smell of something. It smelled like smoke. And it wafted outa the big, long, thick cigarette a fella sitting in front of the bar was holding between his two fingers. He took long sucking drags on it, then held it in his lungs and eventually let it out, blowing it into the faces of everyone sitting around him. 'Oh! Manna from heaven,' he croaked, closing his eyes, looking the world of contentment. Then he dropped his neck inside a big hairy fur coat and slowly waved it from side to side, getting the wrinkles out of his muscles. Then he passed the cigarette to a tall, skinny young fella sitting on the seat next to him with long, thin fair hair that nearly tipped the collar of his shirt.

'We need to be radical, man! It's the only way to bring down the establishment, I tell you!' gasped another fella with a big thick mop of curly hair that looked like a bush growing on his head. 'We need to get the fascist stinkers to sit up and take notice of us,' he snorted, slamming his fist down on the counter and flicking his granny glasses back up off his nose.

'Yes! Hear, hear!' shouted another little weasel, tearing the college scarf off his neck and throwing it down on the counter in disgust. Then lifting his arse, not realising he knocked his sheepskin coat off the seat, landing it on the floor, while he had a good fart! Sending a wave of blue poison smelling like rotten eggs floating in my direction to land under me nose.

Fuck! The smell! I moved away, then stood, wanting to get the attention of the fat woman to see what they were serving and how much it costs.

'*Saturday Night and Sunday Morning*! That's the book to set you on the right road!' said the hairy coat, looking around at everyone and shaking his head, dropping his mouth. 'Radical is the name of the game!'

'Oh! Blow that! You need to read Jean-Paul Sartre!' puffed the long hair, picking at his long pointy sharp nose, then examining his finger to see what he had. He flicked what he got in the direction of the fat woman. '*The Roads to Freedom*! And *Iron in the Soul*! That will set you straight! We are all existentialists!' he moaned, looking like he had just lost a pound and found a penny!

Aw, fuck! This place is only for Beatniks! And yer woman is not taking a blind bit a notice of me, I muttered to meself, feeling about to lose me rag.

'We have to raise awareness among the masses!' she huffed, leaning into them and resting her six chins on her big fat hands that are joined together like she is praying. 'We have to have a revolution for women!' she hissed, getting annoyed when no one took any notice.

'I say we have a protest!' squeaked the weasel. 'Get everyone up in arms!'

'Hear, hear!' shouted hairy coat. Then he said, 'What's this one about?'

'Well, women's rights! Freedom for women! We need to be liberated. We have been shackled to the men LONG ENOUGH!' snorted the fat aul one, slamming her fist down on the counter.

'Oh, but come on, Maggie! You women already have the vote!' said a little wizened fella with greasy black hair and a rash all over his hands and face. He sounded like he had a woman's voice. Then he started laughing, making it sound like he was gasping for breath.

'Listen! How dare you, Joe O'Brien? The biggest revolution of all time is yet to come. It will shake the whole world. We women were meant to rule the world. You fellas have had it too good for long enough! This is no laughing matter, I will have you know!' she screamed, banging both her fists down on the counter. 'You little pipsqueak!' she gasped, getting all purple in the face and boring holes in him with her big red goitre eyes.

He stared and snuffled, making snotty sounds, then blinked. Shocked at the idea his joke only landed flat on its arse.

'Excuse me, Missus!' I roared, getting weak from the hunger and dizzy from the sweet smell. I wanted me dinner.

The woman lifted her head to me. 'Take a seat over there,' she said, pointing in the direction of all the near empty chairs and tables. 'Do you want the three-course?'

'Yeah! What are you serving?'

'Soup – vegetable, mince, potato and cabbage followed by a cup of tea.'

'Eh, how much is that, Missus?'

'Three shillings and sixpence.'

'Right! Thanks! I'll have that.'

'One customer! Three-course, Fanny, dear!' shouted the fat woman into an open door beside her where the grub was going to come out through.

I made me way over to a round corner table next to the big window where I could sit and look down watching the people going by. The only other customers sitting at the tables were next to me. I stared at a woman wearing a coloured shirt with a man's tie. She had on a pair of black trousers and a man's jacket. Maybe she's not a woman, I thought, staring at her stone-grey hair that was cut short like a man's. I looked down at her men's black laced-up shoes. Yeah! Must be a man. But he has a big chest! Can't figure that out!

'Oh, Poppy! Did you hear the latest?' a woman with a green scarf tied around her neck, wearing black eyeliner curling out at the edges, leaned over and said to the man. 'No! What latest?' he said, sounding like a half-man with the voice of a woman who has been up all night smoking and drinking herself to death.

Poppy? That's a woman's name. I stared over with me mouth hanging open trying to work out was she really a she or a he, while Poppy sat forward, resting her chest on the table, ready to drink in every word yer woman was saying.

'It's a scream,' the woman said, holding a smelly cigarette in her mouth and squinting with the smoke. Then she started coughing but wouldn't let go of the cigarette, even with the amount of smoke pouring itself into her face and smothering her in a fog. She patted her huge mass of curly, fuzzy red hair, trying to flatten it down in the front with the palms of her two hands.

'Aw, really! It's a corker!' she mumbled, squinting with one eye shut. Shaking the cigarette up an down, trying not to let it slip outa her mouth while she fixed a long thick black velvet band, letting it cover a bit of her forehead and sliding it underneath the nest of hair, letting the rest of it blow in the air, making it look like she carried a big gollop of red candy floss on top of her head. 'Tipsy Lawler, you know him?'

Poppy nodded her head, sliding her eyes down on the packet of cigarettes sitting on the table. 'Before you start, Mamie! Throw over that packet of Gauloises!' she said, pointing to the fat little blue packet of cigarettes belonging to Mamie.

'Oh, get on with the story!' said another woman sitting next to Mamie, giving her an elbow in the chest.

'Patience, Willie darling!' Mamie laughed, taking the cigarette outa her mouth and spilling the long ash down the front of her wine jumper that didn't match with her hair.

'Oh! Do you mean that defrocked priest who is on the run from Maynooth?' Willie said, rolling herself a big cigarette, then puffing out more sweet sickly smoke. Letting it come over in my direction. With me having no way out but to breathe the bleedin smoke in.

'Yaw! He was caught smooching one of the girls.'

'She was in his theology class or something,' said the Willie woman with the big lips plastered in pink lipstick and her mousey-brown hair tied up in a brown ribbon. I stared at her, seeing she had a hatchet face. It was too long and plain, with a long pointy chin.

'Absolute rubbish and nonsense!' roared Mamie. 'He was only a clerical student! They kicked him out when they rumbled to his shenanigans! His parents were too mean to pay for university fees, so they hatched up a plot. Wait for it, girls! They sent him on for the priesthood. Telling him he could leave before his ordination, providing he got his degree first!' They all screamed laughing.

'Now! He told me,' and they all leaned in with their heads pressed together, not wanting to miss a word, 'the bishop denounced us from the pulpit! Said we were a disgrace to womanhood, he called it. Then really started throwing brickbats. He called us harlots!'

'Who, us?' they roared! 'We are all still pure as the driven snow! Absolute virgins, one and all!' they roared, with their eyeballs hanging out and their hands on their chests. Then they roared their heads with the laughing, slapping each other.

'Stop! Wait! I'm not finished. It doesn't end there,' screamed Mamie, laughing and getting annoyed because her story kept getting interrupted. 'He said we were Communists!'

They all stared for a minute, flying their eyes from one to the other, then started roaring like a pack of hyenas, landing their heads in each other's laps. Poppy rocked back on her chair and went flying, lying plastered on the turned-up chair with her legs stuck in the air. Everyone looked around to see what was happening. The other two sent the table moving on top of her with their grabbing and holding, trying to get themself a breath with the laugh on them.

'He did! He did!' Mamie squeaked, shaking her head up and down at them, getting herself all red in the face.

I spotted me dinner coming. A little fat woman wearing a long white apron appeared carrying a tray with me soup and dinner. She landed it down on the table and took away the tray. 'Come on, girls! Share the joke!' she said, turning to the three women upending the place beside me.

I got on with digging into me dinner while Fanny busied herself sorting out the women, picking them up off the floor and putting the table and chairs standing again. Then she sat down to listen to the story. I took no notice. The soup was gorgeous. Fanny sure can cook! I thought to meself, making short work of it and starting on me dinner.

'But what brought all this on?' I heard Fanny say.

'Oh! That must have been the little fracas we had,' Mamie said. 'A few of us got together and descended en masse down to the meeting of the Countrywomen's Association. The branch held in West Meath.'

'Yaw!' said Hatchet-face. 'We got there ahead of them, persuading the caretaker to let us in. When the farmers' wives arrived, expecting a cosy meeting over home-baked buns, they couldn't get in! We were having a sit-in! We commandeered the place, barricading ourselves in by stacking the tables and chairs blocking the doors. Oh, it was a scream. They were demented. The local sergeant arrived and started trying to talk to us through the window. We drew the curtains, making his sorry face vanish. They sent for reinforcements! Two more police cars arrived from further on up the country. One of them had a megaphone! He kept shouting, "Come on outa dat, ladies! We know you come from good homes! Now you don't want to be shaming your poor families! Think of your poor unfortunate mothers!" Naturally we got a great innings out of that one! It was on the early radio news the next morning: "Women's rights anarchists bring chaos to Meath Countrywomen's Association!" the morning newspaper headlines screamed!' Then they started again. Neighing like a pack of donkeys! Even Fanny threw herself around with the laughing. Slapping hell outa the lot of them with her big massive man's arms.

I had me belly full. The dinner was lovely. Well worth the three bob and sixpence. I stood up, making me way over awkwardly, feeling dizzy from all the smoke. The money seemed to be swimming in me hand even though I was trying to keep meself steady. 'Here's ten bob, Missus!' I sighed, feeling very tired, not understanding what the hell is come over me, but I wanted to make sure she knew how much I was giving her just in case she gave me the wrong change.

'Here you are, dear,' she said, handing me the change. A half crown and two two shilling pieces. I counted it.

'That's right! Six shillings and sixpence!' she said, seeing me count the money. Then she settled herself in for more talk with her pals. She lifted her massive chest, getting it more comfortable sitting on top of her arms, and went back to listening to the conversation.

That's a peculiar place, I thought, staggering off out the door, trying to make me way down the stairs without falling head first and breaking me neck.

'Goodness! What's happened to you?' the nun said when she brought me through to her office. 'Have you been getting enough sleep?' she said, leaning across the desk to get a better look at me.

'Yeah!' I said, putting me hand over me mouth trying to hide a yawn.

'You have dark circles under your eyes and you look a bit peaky! You better get to bed early! I'm not sure I believe you are getting enough sleep,' she said, looking sideways at me then looking away.

'I am,' I said, giving another yawn. Not caring any more if she thought I was being well behaved. Jaysus! Me head hurts and I feel banjacksed, I thought, wanting to take me eyeballs out and put them in a cup of cold water to cool them down.

'How did you get on with the doctor today?' she said smiling, waiting for me to give her all the information.

'Oh, grand!' I said, feeling too tired to talk.

'Listen, Martha. There is something I want to ask you,' she said, getting a shifty look in her eye and moving her arse on the chair trying to get comfortable. 'I am doing a little project,' she said, folding her hands in the air and resting her elbows on the desk. 'I want to do one on you!' she gushed, giving me all smiles and gums. 'What do you think about that? It would be a little booklet. All about you! You are going to be my little success story! Oh, I will write a few details about your background. Then how you came to us. What do you think about that?' she said, leaning into me and smiling into me face.

I shook me head. 'No! I wouldn't like that at all, Sister. Thanks very much,' I said, thinking come hell or high water! If she thinks I am going to let the world know my business then she has another think coming. I keep meself to meself!

'Oh! That is a great pity,' she moaned, lowering her head, staring at the desk.

I said nothing.

Then after a minute she said, 'Well, look! I have the photographer here. Would you agree to have your photograph taken? If you still don't want to go ahead then I will leave it at that. You can at least have the photographs taken of yourself. You may keep them! Wouldn't it be nice to get it done with a professional photographer? I have to pay him for his time, so we might as well get something out of it!'

'Yeah, OK,' I said. 'Only the photographs. Then I get to keep them, Sister. But nothing is to be written about me. Or else I can tell you straight away I am getting up and walking away. I'm not prepared to give my business away for anything or anyone. I'm entitled to me privacy!'

'Yes, of course you are, dear! I couldn't possibly do anything without your permission. OK! Let that be the end of it. I will say no more. We won't mention the subject again. Especially now you are so dead set against it,' she said, standing up and making her way around the desk to me.

'Yeah! Nothing on this earth is going to change my mind,' I said, looking up into her pale-blue eyes, making sure she got the message.

'OK! Come on with me and I'll introduce you to him. He should be here any minute. I said we would meet at three-forty!' she said, pulling out a watch from a pocket in the side of her white habit.

I followed her out the door and down the passage, seeing a man standing at the reception desk with a big camera hanging over his shoulder. This should be great, I thought, getting me photograph taken for nearly the first time in me life. I don't remember ever having that done. I saw some of the other kids talking about it when I was little. They used to get theirs done in school. But I never got lucky with that. I would have missed it because I barely ever set foot inside a school.

'Mr Clarke, this is Martha, the girl I was talking to you about. I want you to photograph her. The before and after shots.'

'OK, Martha! Are you ready to give me your best pose?' he said, smiling at me with brown mouldy teeth stained from years of hard work. He probably got that from chewing gobs of tobacco, I thought, staring at him with me nose curling in the air.

'Yeah!' I said, nodding me head at him.

'Let's go. I think the grounds are our best bet. I had a look around first. There are some nice trees and shrubbery outside. Hurry while we can still catch the light.'

I rushed out after him, then he lined me up against a mouldy dripping drainpipe. I wonder why he bothered talking about trees? A bleedin green mouldy drainpipe! I'm not going to look much standing beside this bleedin thing.

'Good girl! Keep that look!' he said, grabbing his huge camera and looking through it. 'Perfect!' he said, after me blinking at a flash coming outa the camera. 'Now! Throw your bag over your shoulder. I want you to look like you are even more fed up with the world than you do now!'

I snarled at him, dropping me mouth and staring like me eyes could turn him into a ball of hot cinders. Thinking he really is a gobshite.

Not only has me planted here against this metal thing. But he thinks he is doing wonders with his bleedin camera.

'Great! Lovely!' he gushed. 'Come on! Let's go around the corner. OK! Now stand in front of that bush and think you are the luckiest girl in the world. Give us a big smile! Come on! You are a very pretty girl! Young and have the world at your feet. Dance for me, baby!' he shouted. 'Give us a smile,' he said, stamping his feet.

Suddenly I broke me face laughing, seeing him dance and nearly slip in the muddy grass. Then trying to grip hold of the camera, holding it out in front of him, shocked at the idea he might drop it when he landed on his arse. The camera kept flashing and I kept trying to smile until I had a pain in me face.

'OK! Lovely! Thanks. That's it!' he said, putting the camera away in a big brown canvas shoulder bag.

I went back to the nun. 'Finished?' she said, waiting for me at the reception with her arms folded under the top half of her habit.

'Yeah, Sister. When can I get the photographs?'

'They should be ready about two weeks from now. Next time you are here I will have them for you,' she said. 'They are no good to me. I wanted them for my little booklet. It was really an academic thing. The ordinary people wouldn't even get to know about it!' she said, looking hopeful at me.

I shook me head. 'No, Sister! I want nothing written or said about me.'

'OK,' she sighed. 'Let that be the end of it. I have others willing to do it but, well, you would have been perfect!' she said, smiling at me, saying, 'You know you are very pretty!'

'Am I?' I said, giving her a suspicious look, knowing full well she was trying to butter me up. 'I meant what I said, Sister. My business is my own business.'

'Of course!' she said. 'Now! I don't want you to ever mention the subject again,' she said, losing patience with me, then making to walk off. 'Goodbye, dear! I will be in touch again!' she said, turning around and waving at me. Then she was gone back to her office and I was out the door, hurrying through the grounds and out the gate.

The bleedin cheek of that nun. All smiles when they want something. Nuns! You can't trust them. I knew it. There had to be a catch. They never do anything for nothing. Nothing is for nothing in this world. Well! She has a better chance of becoming the Holy Mother of God, the Virgin Mary, than she or anyone else has of getting information about meself outa me! I snorted, rushing meself off down the road to catch the bus back to the mother and the missus. I had enough of the city for one day! I just wanted to get back and lie down in me bed and have a good sleep. Whatever bleedin came over me after leaving that eating house? I'm not setting foot ever again in that place. The smoke would eat yer lungs alive!

20

I woke up early, thinking something great is happening today. Me heart was lepping with excitement. I held me breath, waiting to remember what it was. Then it hit me. Yeah! Oh, Mammy! I'm going to be leaving today to live in the hostel and do me secretarial course. I leapt outa the bed and dived into me clothes. First, get me breakfast. Then I can sort meself out. I was flying out the door and galloping down the stairs, taking them two at a time. I flew open the door into the kitchen, giving the missus a fright.

'Don't be doing that to me! Jesus! I thought it was a herd a elephants tearing down them stairs.'

'Oh, sorry, Missus Doherty!' I laughed, seeing the shock on her face as she held her hand over her chest.

'At my age yeh get used to the peace an quiet. What has put the skids under you anyway at this hour a the morning?' she said, getting back to sorting out her shopping list.

'I'm leaving to start living in the hostel and do me secretarial course!' I gasped, feeling outa breath.

'Well! Take yer time! Ye'll get there soon enough without all the hurry on yeh!' she muttered, opening presses to see what she needed.

'Ah, no! I can't wait to get going. Imagine, Missus Doherty! I'm going to be working in an office!'

'Yeah! I suppose we'll all be needin an appointment te see you! Ye'll be that far gone up in the world!' she said, still staring at her list.

'Ah, no. I won't be that high up. You have to work your way up first.'

'Hmm. Most people would,' she muttered. 'But they haven't met the like a you yet. Gawd help them!' she said, raising her eyes to the ceiling. 'If only the world knew what's about te hit it!'

I stood with me mouth open, staring at her. I could see she was codding me, really wanting to laugh. But still an all, I'm not that bad!

'Missus Doherty, why? What's wrong with me?' I said quietly. I didn't like her saying that, even if she thought it was only a joke.

'Ah, no, lovey! I didn't mean any harm by what I said. I just mean you are . . . very lively! The lot in that hostel won't know what hit them when you get there!' she said, roaring her head laughing at the idea of me moving in to live with loads of other people.

'Oh, right! Yeah, I see what you mean!' I said, shaking me head up and down, thinking about it, but not really seeing anything at all. Because what's in my mind is, I'm definitely going to become someone different. I will be real ladylike. Polite to everyone. And copy the other respectable young ones who don't get themself into trouble. Because even though I'm forever getting into trouble – and I still haven't figured out why that keeps happening to me – now I can make a fresh start! Nobody knows me yet. So I will keep me mouth shut and me opinions to meself. Not go passing remarks on anyone! Yeah, they'll all think I'm a lovely person altogether!

I had the picture of me sitting with the other girls, having polite chats. And I'm included in all their plans to do things and go places. Yeah, because underneath I'm really a very peaceful kind of person. I like things to be nice and quiet sometimes. Missus Doherty is right. There's nothing like a nice peaceful life.

Right! I'm starving with the hunger. 'Missus Doherty! Can I take an egg for me breakfast?'

'Help yerself!' she muttered, still writing away, making her list.

'What about cornflakes? Can I have some of them too?'

'Oh, have whatever yeh want, chicken. Why don't yeh have it poached for a change?'

'Yeah, good idea! But, eh, how do you do that?'

'Sit down!' she said with a big sigh. Then she dropped the pencil and dragged herself over to the press and took out a little pot.

'Ah, no! I can look after meself,' I said, not wanting to make work for her.

'I'll do this,' she said. 'You put on the toast an set the table.'

I grabbed a box of cornflakes outa the press then opened the refrigerator, seeing milk in a jug. But then I spotted the bottle of milk with the thick yellow cream on top. It wasn't opened yet. I love cream on me cornflakes. I looked around, seeing she wasn't looking, and grabbed the bottle, then emptied half the box into a huge big bowl used for the soup, and emptied half the bottle of milk on top. Then I plugged in the toaster and stuck two slices of white bread in. Not the brown soda bread. That's only nice when it comes outa the oven. Then it tastes horrible when it gets stale.

'Do yeh want a couple a rashers?' she said, turning around to look at me.

I looked up with half a shovel full of cornflakes in me mouth and muttered, 'Yeah!', spitting milk everywhere.

She shook her head and sighed, going to the refrigerator to take out a big pile of rashers and took a few from the top. 'I don't know where yeh put all the grub,' she said. 'God knows, yeh never stop eating! God bless yer appetite! I'm going to miss feeding yeh! Heaven help us! But if I never cooked another meal in this house it wouldn't even be noticed. Herself wouldn't eat enough to keep a bird alive!'

She took the toast out before it started to go on fire. 'I'm always doing that! I keep forgetting.' Then landed the egg on top of it sitting in the middle of a big white plate. And she put four rashers beside it, with the fat burned crisp the way I love it, and put the lot sitting in front of me.

I emptied half a bottle of tomato sauce on top and dived into the egg, taking half the toast with it. 'Oh, I'm going to miss all the lovely cooking you do, Missus Doherty!' I said, making short work of the rashers. 'I bet the grub in the hostel won't be anything like this,' I said, reaching across the table to grab a piece of bread from the basket and mop up all the sauce and grease and bits of egg.

'Oh, well! Yeh have te take the bad with the good,' she said, sounding mournful. But she wasn't really grumpy. It's just her way.

People have to get to know her first. Then they would find out quick enough she has a heart of gold. But she mainly keeps to herself. Then everyone thinks she's a terrible cranky aul one altogether! Like the window cleaners and the girls from the village when they come up to give her a hand with the cooking and cleaning. That's when the mother has people coming for one of her dinner parties, as she calls them.

I'm never around for that. I keep outa the way! Especially after getting into a row with one aul one. She found out I came out of a convent. It happened when the mother and all the guests went marching up to the drawing room after the dinner was over. We all sat around in a circle on little gold French chairs looking at each other. One of the women started asking me questions about the convent. Before I could get in an answer, she started: 'Oh, really! One has to say the nuns do marvellous work with these girls, giving them a first-class training. Otherwise, my dears, what would become of the poor creatures?'

'Eh, excuse me, Missus!' I said, interrupting her load a bullshit. 'They get paid for it, ye know!'

'Oh, of course!' she said, leaning her baldy blue and grey and white head over to me sitting at the end of the circle. 'But nonetheless,' she moaned, looking slowly around at everyone. 'It has to be very little! They do so much for so many on such a small pittance. I mean, imagine if there was no place to take all these unfortunate women and children! We would be living once again in the Dark Ages!'

'Nnnhh, yes,' they all agreed, shaking their heads and murmuring quietly, with their eyes in shock and holding their chests to steady their hearts at the thought of us all running loose and maybe murdering them in their beds. They looked over at me from under their eyes, afraid to lift their heads and speak to me like I was a normal person!

I stared at them, thinking, what do they know about anything? The almighty bleedin cheek a them pack of aul hags thinking they are better than me! The rage blew straight up through me and out through me mouth. Then, before I knew where I was, I heard meself saying, 'Well, I suppose every night you lot get down on yer bended knees, thankin God ye were all born with a silver spoon in your gobs. Otherwise, if ye didn't have the money and the big houses to keep ye's all safe, well, it wouldn't be the nuns keepin themself busy in their convents makin ye get down on yer hands and knees and scrub their floors! Oh, no! You lot would be mistaken for being retarded. They would shove you in the madhouse and leave you to rot! Because all youse are good for is eatin and drinkin and back bitin behind each other's backs! Imagine you lot born homeless or something!' I said, looking at them with me fists clamped on me sides.

They all stared back, trying to work out what I was talking about, looking crucified with the shock of it all.

'Not one of you lot has ever had enough sense to wipe yer own arses! You have had it handed to ye all yer lives! You were born rich! You know what you are? Morons with more money than sense. So don't look down on me! Stick yer pity and yer charity up yer arses! I feel sorry for youse! Because ye're never happy! You always have to be wanting something new! To amuse yerselves, as you say!'

I was roaring. Forgetting all me diction after losing the run of meself. Not caring if I was thrown straight out the door to land on me arse. Huh! Nobody is going to think they are better than me! Then I shot up, knocking over the little gold chair that was too light anyway, and flew out the door, slamming it shut behind me, making the floorboards rattle. I hauled meself up the stairs, trying to take them three at a time, hanging on to the banisters. I could hear me breath heaving with me gasping for air, and the mother squealing at the bottom of the stairs, trying to tear after me to come back and apologise at once! No! I didn't and wouldn't. I even packed me bags and took meself off back to that Father Ralph fella. He leathered the arse offa me with them big shovel hands of his. Acting like I was a very bold little child! He swung me with one hand and belted me on the arse with the other after he listened to me story about them aul ones. It was only before he grabbed me that I saw when it was too late the colour drain outa his face. It was the thought of me insulting all his mother's friends that did it! Oh, no! Not the very fact that they were insulting me! Then he took me straight back to the mother! He got his work cut out for himself, trying to bring the peace between the two of us! But Missus Doherty didn't agree with them acting like that when I got to tell her me story. But she didn't disagree neither. All she did was sigh and shake her head, saying, 'Come on! Let's bake a few cakes for the tea.'

That cheered me up no end. I felt better in meself after that. But I'm still not speaking to him! No, never! Because he said I was impossible. I made all sorts of difficulties for people. That, coming from him, hurt me feelings. So I told him to go and fuck himself! I got another leathering in the arse for that one! Fucker! Treating me like a little kid.

I could still feel the rage flying up around me, thinking back to that time. I came back to me senses hearing the missus saying something. I blinked, trying to tune in.

'Eh, what did you say?' I said.

She sighed, trying to keep her patience. 'You better make sure yeh get all your things gathered up. You don't want te be leaving anything yeh might need behind. So get ready early an I will have a nice bit of dinner cooked for yeh. Then yeh can catch the bus early an make sure yeh get there well in good time.'

'Yeah, you're right, Missus Doherty! I'll do that. I better get moving and sort meself out. I want to have a good wash first. That always makes a good impression on people, doesn't it?'

'Oh, yeh can't be wrong there, love! Always look yer best! That's what I say.'

'OK! I'm off as soon as I get these few things washed and put away,' I said, gathering up the dishes and heading over to the sink.

I looked back, seeing the mother and the missus still looking after me. They smiled and waved, and I waved back, then set me sights on taking off for the bus. I carried me shoulder bag swinging around me back with the strap thrown across me, and me suitcase gripped in me right hand, remembering the other times I had to carry it. Gawd! That was only months ago! But it feels like years! I shivered, getting a feel of how empty, cold and hungry I had been, with me head going round and round trying to work out where I was going to sleep and what I was going to eat that night, and the terrible fear I might never get back on me feet again. But then again, without that happening to me I may never have met that doctor in the hospital and end up getting me secretarial course. Or better still, meeting Father Ralph and getting to live with his mother.

I have had the best time I ever had in me whole life living with her. She really is a true lady and very, very kind. But the best bit is I now have Father Ralph to go to. Since I met him and get all them hugs he gives me, well, now I can't do without him. I live for the minutes when I get to see him and he grabs me up in a big bear hug. But it feels like it is never enough. The more times he tells me he cares about me, the more I want him to just stay with me and let me feel warm and safe inside. But it's over too fast. Then he has to go about his business and I wander off feeling even more lonely at the loss of him going than I ever felt in me whole life. Still, I have to be really, really lucky. God must be certainly looking out for me because I got all that in the last few months. Now, here I am, back on me feet and going on me way to make something good out of me life.

I turned right down Tara Street, passing the lovely old Victorian red-brick bathhouses where all the women and children used to go and wash their clothes. They would bring all the dirty washing, dragging it sky high in an old baby's pram. They buried the baby in the back, if that was going for a wash too, and the soap and scrubbing board for washing the clothes was left balanced on top of the mountain in the pram. You could hear them coming before you even clapped sight of them, with the wheels screaming and squealing, rumbling along the old cobblestones on the road because the tyres on the wheels was long gone. Then you would see the mammy putting all her strength into trying to steer it because the wheels were so bokety they all wanted to go in different directions. That came about from all the child rearing it had to do. The poor aul ma's used to be blind bothered and bewildered with the thought of all the washing and scrubbing that lay ahead of them. Then, on top of that, having to drag a load of scruffy kids behind her, shivering and whinging at the thought of getting themselves a good wash, and worried the ma might even carry out her threat to drown them if they didn't get a hurry on and keep up with her and stop all that no-good whinging.

If it was a good pram, then you knew the baby was left stuck back in the house with a young one left to mind it, and the pair of them were now stranded because there was no way to get the baby outa the house. Yeah, a new pram could carry any amount a stuff, so every stitch in the house, curtains and blankets, just pile the lot in. Leave the babby at home. I used to see them hurrying here every week. Years ago, one of the kids told me it cost money. A whole shilling or sixpence or something. But you got all the steaming hot water you wanted for that money and the kids got a good scrubbing as well. They were good mammies, I thought, smiling to meself. Not like the bleedin ma! She was far too lazy and stupid to even think like that, I thought, curling up me mouth with annoyance at the picture of her appearing in me mind's eye.

I turned left onto Townsend Street and crossed the road at the big shop with the huge sign over it saying, 'Mônsell Mitchell'. They must be French! I suppose you need money to go in there! I carried on, trying to keep me mind off mooching around the shops. I don't want to get carried away and turn up to the hostel late. Or, worse still, get me bag or case robbed! Me heart gladdened, remembering the money the mother shoved into me hand when I was leaving. A whole five-pound note! Even the missus made me take the pound note she sneaked into me hand. I didn't want to take that from her because she works too hard for her money, and her and Mattie are getting old. They will need a few bob behind them when the times comes and they can't work any more.

I rounded the corner and headed under the bridge at Westland Row. I crossed over and passed the train station. That's where you get the train to take you for the boat to England. I might take that meself some day! I would love to go over there and get a good job.

The wages are much better paid as well. That's what everyone has always said.

I turned left and walked on, then stopped to look. It's somewhere here! I walked on for a bit, seeing a big building with a statue of Our Lady sitting on top of a concrete shelf on the wall hanging way up over the front hall door. A big old black-iron railings with spikes on top wrapped itself around the basement, going each side of the stone steps that went up to the heavy front door. The hostel went all the way around a corner and down into a laneway. I stood staring for a minute, then fixed the belt on me coat and straightened me shoulders. Then I gripped me suitcase and made for the steps. I rang the big roundy bell built into the wall and waited, stepping back a bit.

The door swung open and a girl with a massive head of bright-red hair appeared. I stared at it. Gaping with me mouth open. It was the colour of a pumpkin and she had a black lace mantilla sitting on top of her head. I knew straight away she was a postulant. She was going to become a nun!

'Hello!' she said, smiling at me, showing a big mouthful of horse's teeth.

'Eh, hello! I'm starting here! Eh, I mean I'm going to be staying here!' I said, thinking I was saying it all wrong. Me nerves were suddenly getting the better of me. I wanted to make a good impression. 'I'm Martha!' I said, looking up at her, still getting it wrong.

'Oh, hello, Martha! Come in! You are very welcome!' she said, moving back and swinging the door open wide, then standing up straight like she was a ballerina.

Oh, to hell with it! I thought, getting annoyed with meself and grabbing me suitcase, making me mind up to have another go.

I marched in, deciding I would be like the mother. I grabbed her hand, saying, 'How do you do? It's lovely to meet you.'

She stared at me, looking down at me gripping hold of her hand. I let go and she smiled, half laughing, saying, 'Great to meet you, Martha. I'm Anna. Will you sit down in that chair over there and I'll just knock on Reverend Mother's door and let her know you are here.'

I sat down on a priest's chair. You can tell what it is because it has a cross on the back. I let me hands fall into me lap and thought about what I was going to say. Right, Martha. Just keep your mouth shut! Say nothing. Just keep listening and smiling, the way Anna did to you just now. OK! Fine! I'm grand.

I heard a voice say, 'Come in!' Anna went into the office and shut the door, then she was back out. 'Mother won't keep you,' she whispered, leaning down to me. 'She'll be out in a minute. Bye! See you later!'

'Bye, bye!' I said, watching her disappear around a corner.

The door opened and a little fat nun with big red rosy cheeks and chocolate-brown eyes came smiling over to me with her hand held out to shake mine. 'Martha, is it?' she said, looking at me with the kindest pair of eyes I ever saw in me life. 'Oh, you are so very welcome here in the hostel, Martha,' she said, grabbing me hand in both of hers, then letting go to put her arm around me shoulder. 'I have heard so much about you from Sister Aloysius,' she said, smiling and speaking very gently.

Jaysus! I wonder what Allie told her?

'You are going to start a secretarial course!' she said. 'My, you will get a marvellous job when you finish your training. Jobs for secretaries are so plentiful. What a clever choice you made!'

'Yes, Mother! That's what I thought meself. I'm even thinking of travelling!'

'Oh, how wonderful,' she said, with her eyes widening. 'Where would you like to go?'

'Eh, London! Maybe even America!' I just thought of that right this minute, but, yeah, I could go to America, thinking that was the best idea I ever came up with.

'Oh, it is so well to be young and have your whole life ahead of you,' she sighed, sounding like she was jealous! But I knew she wasn't, maybe just a little sad, I suppose, because she was now getting on a bit. She had to be at least forty!

'Well!' she said, taking me hand and holding it in both of hers very gently, then looking around. 'Where is Anna? Now, Martha. You can share a room with Anna. It is a four-bed room. But there is only herself in that for the moment. I will get her to take you up. Anna is a lovely girl. You should get on fine with her. I will tell her to keep an eye on you, poor little lamb! What age is it you are? Only sixteen! Isn't that right?'

'Yeah, but I will be seventeen in a few months' time, Mother!' I said, letting her know I'm not just sixteen.

'Yes, of course! Oh, you young girls are always in a hurry to grow up! What is it Oscar Wilde was supposed to have said?'

'Eh, I never heard a him, Mother,' I said, seeing her waiting for me to come up with the answer.

'"Youth is wasted on the young." Oh, if only we could bottle it!' she said, wandering off to look for Anna with her hands joined under the cloak of her habit.

I laughed, thinking to meself, I definitely like her! She really is a very nice and kind nun. No, this is better than I thought. It's not like being back in the convent. Here it looks like you can come and go about your business. I'm still free to come in and out when I like.

I looked around seeing the big door opposite where the Reverend Mother just came out of. That must be her office. Me eyes peeled around the big hall, taking in the high ceiling, then landed over in the corner by the hall door. A big red statue of the Sacred Heart stood high up on a wooden platform. He looked very sad, with his arms held out wide showing his hands dripping with blood from the nails the Romans stuck in him. I stared over at it, thinking that reminds me of when I was very small. Me ma used to take me around to St Augustine's Church to light a penny candle when she had the spare penny. She would kneel down in front of the statue of the Sacred Heart and pray like mad with her face looking up at it, hoping he would hear her prayer and grant her intention. Yeah! In a way that statue makes me feel safe, just sitting here and being beside it. It reminds me of times gone past when I had a lot to fear. But I managed to get this far without any harm coming to me. So I know our Lord is always looking out for me.

I sighed, feeling easy in meself, then let me eyes peel to the double front doors. They only open the one door, I suppose. Then I saw a big notice plastered on top of the other door they keep locked. I got up and went over to have a look:

IMPORTANT NOTICE. PLEASE ENSURE THIS DOOR REMAINS SHUT AT ALL TIMES. PLEASE TAKE NOTE: THIS DOOR IS LOCKED AT NINE P.M. SHARP. PERSONS NOT RETURNED BY THEN WILL BE LOCKED OUT. YOU MAY RETURN IN THE MORNING TO COLLECT YOUR BAGS, AS YOUR PRESENCE IS NO LONGER WELCOME IN THIS HOSTEL. BY ORDER. MOTHER PAULA THERESE.

Jaysus! In by a certain hour! Get locked out and they kick you out on yer arse! Oh, I better not let that ever happen to me! I shivered, thinking about the idea I could end up in tatters with nowhere to go! OK, I won't be making that mistake.

'Martha?'

I looked up, seeing Anna appear behind me.

'Come on!' she said, tipping me arm and pulling me behind her. 'You are in with me, I'll take you upstairs.'

'OK!' I said, rushing over to grab me suitcase and race after her up the stairs.

We came on to a corridor and she went right and I continued up the stairs. 'Down here!' she laughed. 'We are on the first floor.'

'Oh, right!' I said, following her down a long passage with doors on each side and more further down the other end.

'In here!' she said, opening a door into a room.

I followed her in, seeing a long narrow room with four beds lined against one wall and a locker beside every bed. Two big wardrobes stood against the wall facing the beds and a big window at the end of the room threw in loads of light.

'This is my bed,' she said, pointing to the first one and sitting down on it. 'Take your pick, they're all empty,' she said, smiling and pointing at the other beds.

'Oh, great! So I can take any of them?'

'Sure,' she said, shaking her head.

'Right! I'll take the one at the end next to the window,' I said happily, rushing down and landing me suitcase on it. I pulled down the grey quilt that looked very thin in the middle. It was well worn out. I lifted the blankets, seeing the bed wasn't made. Two orange blankets covered the battered mattress, sagging in the middle. The bed was nice and low, though, what they call a divan. That is the modern beds most people buy now. But this must have been one of the first ones that came out! Wonder when that was?

'Anna, I have no sheets for me bed. What will I do?'

'Oh, right,' she said, sitting up off her elbow and looking over at me bed. 'Hang on. I'll get you some.' She flew out the door and I wandered over to have a look in the wardrobes.

The first one had her stuff in it. I had a look. A long grey skirt that a granny would kick up murder if you told her you were going to bury her in it! That must have been handed down from her great-grandmother. A grey wool cardigan with red hickey buttons. A long black coat that went out with the American Indians! It was flared at the waist and full of hairs and white fluff. Jaysus! No wonder she wants to be a nun. No man would give her a second look in that get-up! I lifted up the stuff sitting on the shelves that come all the way down on the inside of the wardrobe. Long navy-blue bloomers – knickers! You would break your neck if you went out in them. They would be hanging around your ankles. Two long grey vests and a brassiere that you could carry two melons in!

'Here we are!' she said, flying in the door.

I got such a fright, the heart went crossways in me, and I slammed the wardrobe door shut, making it rattle against the wall.

'That one is empty,' she said, pointing at the next one.

'Yeah, right. OK, thanks. Sorry about making it look like I was going through your stuff, Anna,' I muttered, trying to keep me face that was turned red as a tomato away from her sight. 'I wasn't really being nosy! I was, eh, looking to see what one was free.'

'Don't worry about it! Sure, I haven't much to look at anyhow,' she said, sounding like she wasn't bothered about clothes. 'Do you want a hand making your bed?' she said, bending down to take off me blankets.

'Ah, no, not really . . . But only if you like!' I said, seeing she was already getting started.

'Here we go!' she said, putting me suitcase down on the floor and grabbing the blankets through the air, landing them on the next bed.

'Ah, you're very nice to want to help me, Anna. I think you're going to make a lovely nun. You have a very kind and gentle nature,' I said, seeing her looking at me with her eyes sparkling, like she was already on her way to being a saint. She had a look in her eyes that would make you think she was mad about some fella, or her mind was in another world, or she had some secret that kept her mind on it and she wasn't really here, present in the room with me.

'Thanks for helping me, Anna. That was very good of you.'

'No trouble,' she said, wandering over to rest her elbows on the window and looking at the passing sights.

I lifted me suitcase and started taking me stuff out. I lined everything up in the shelves, putting in me two pair of knickers. The elastic was gone out of one of them. Jaysus! I better go into Dunnes Stores and buy two new pair. I need a few things. Nylons and a pair of new shoes so I can wear the black patent ones the nuns bought me when I left the convent. I hung up me two coats on hangers: me green wool one for everyday and me good French one for good wear. Then last, me new multicoloured jacket. I love that! It's so warm and snug and soft, I thought, running me hands over the woolly jacket when everything was put away nice and neat, and everything in its place.

I lifted the empty suitcase and stuck it on the bottom of the wardrobe, putting it standing up on its side. 'Ready!' I said, slamming shut the wardrobe.

'Oh, good! Come on! I'll show you where everything is,' she said, putting her hand on me back.

Gawd! I'm very lucky to have her sharing me room, and she couldn't be nicer, I thought, following her out the door.

'The bathrooms are all on the ground floor,' she said, with the two of us walking side by side down the stairs.

We turned right at the bottom of the stairs and went into a huge big room. 'This is the sitting room,' she said, standing in the middle of the room. I looked around, seeing blue shiny paint walls, a load of grey plastic chairs in a line and more down behind each other all facing a shelf high up in the wall with a television sitting on it. There was a window high in the wall but you couldn't see out anyway because it was toilet glass. A big table was pushed against the wall with a record player on top. In the corner beside the window was a shelf holding a statue of St Martin De Porres.

'That's it. This is the recreation room,' she said, smiling at me and looking at the room like it was something the Queen of England would sit herself in.

'Grand!' I said, not meaning a word of it. I was now used to better. It didn't take me long to get used to the comfort of living in the height of luxury when I was staying with the mother. I sighed, thinking, Jaysus! It doesn't take long to ruin a body. A few months ago I would have been down on me knees thanking God for all the comfort of this place if I hadn't just come from living with the aristocracy, as they call themselves! Still, this is all mine. I'm not under compliment. Freedom is worth more than money. Yeah, oh I do love to be beside the seaside! I smiled, then laughed, rushing over and throwing me arm around Anna, saying, 'Come on, Anna, baby! Show me the rest of the place.'

She laughed, wrapping her arm around me waist, and the two of us went flying out the door, getting caught in the frame because we wouldn't fit.

21

I followed the crowd down the stairs to the basement, then into a big room with long wooden tables and benches along three walls, and another table with two benches went nearly the length of the room and sat in the middle of the floor. A little hatch opened and a girl started pushing plates of food through. I looked around for Anna, seeing no sign of her. Ah, yeah! She must be over in the convent with the nuns. Yeah, that must be right. Because she's one of them now. She told me she entered the convent a few months ago. Before that she lived here with the girls. Wonder why she's still sleeping in the girls' rooms? Hmm! Doesn't matter.

Right! Where will I sit? I saw a spot at the head of a table near to the hatch and made straight for that, sitting meself down, and waited for the grub. A young one with thin black hair and a grey face full of blackheads, wearing eyeglasses, slammed down a white plate in front of me then slid another plate to a girl sitting on me right.

'Ah, Josie! Could you get me a few beans to go with this?' the girl said, looking down at her plate like she would die of the hunger if that was all she was going to get.

'Can't!' said Josie, narrowing her nose and turning away, curling her mouth. Looking like she would love to poison the lot of us with the dirty looks she was giving everyone.

'Young one!' I said, calling her and looking down at me plate with the dry bit of hard toast in the middle and a lump of yellow rubber planted on top. Jaysus! That looks like it would poison you. I'm definitely going to starve to death if that's all they feed you. I could feel me heart sinking. I really was looking forward to get something nice to eat.

'Wha do yeh want?' she said, passing me on her way back to the hatch.

'What's this called?' I said, pointing me finger and lifting the plate to show her.

'It's whatever yeh think it is!' she snapped.

'Well, do you have some tomato sauce?'

'No!' she said, and kept going.

'Well, at least would you give us a bit of bread and butter? Or maybe a few beans? I'm starved with the hunger,' I said, trying to keep me patience but ready to erupt if she didn't act civil to me.

'Yeh can waeat fur dat!' she snorted at me.

'I can what?' I said, not understanding a word she just said.

'Josie just said you can wait for that!' a blonde curly-haired young one said, sitting on the left of me.

'Why?' I said. 'Can she not give it to me now?'

'She'll give it to you all right!' the young one laughed, nearly choking on her bit of rubber with the sudden laugh at her own joke. 'Best not to upset any of the kitchen girls,' she said, leaning into me and chomping on her hard toast and yellow rubber.

'That doesn't bother me!' I snorted. 'Not if they're going to be serving me up slops!'

'Oh, Jesus!' she laughed, nearly choking at a sudden thought. 'Wait! That's nothing. Rub them up the wrong way and you'll get a special plate all reserved for your little own self. Isn't that right, Joyce?' she said to a young one with a big mop of frizzy ginger hair and a white face plastered in freckles, sitting next to her.

'Yeah, say nothing!' the girl said, looking at her and nodding at me.

'Ah, Jaysus! This place is not worth the money they're getting,' I moaned, lifting the rock-hard toast with the bit of egg on top and trying to chew it.

A big fat woman moved in between us, slamming her elbows into me to make room for herself. 'Tea!' she said, slopping it into the cups without waiting for an answer. It spilled on the table and I jumped back, not wanting to get me good frock ruined.

'Yeah, give us a cup!' I snapped, shoving the cup and saucer at her. She only half filled it, then leaned on top of the girl beside me to serve the one next to her. I could see the girl was nearly suffocating with the fat aul one's chest stuck in her mouth. I looked, seeing her going red in the face at having to lean all the way back on her chair, nearly toppling over and making suffocating noises with the laugh trying to squeeze out of her.

'Thanks, Madge!' she puffed, getting herself a bit of breath to squeak out after the fat aul one's back, as yer one moved off to try and scald someone else.

'Jaysus! This is an awful place,' I snorted to the blonde young one who was laughing again and making faces behind the Madge one's back.

'Ah, you take no notice,' she said, looking at me. 'When did you get here?'

'Today,' I said.

'Oh! Where are you from?'

'Dublin,' I said.

'Lucky you! I'm from the back of beyond. The bog!' she laughed. 'Dingle in Kerry. What are you doing?' she said to me.

'I'm going to be starting a secretarial course on Monday,' I said. 'What are you doing?'

'Law, God help us. At Trinity!'

'Oh! You are going to become a solicitor!' I said, looking at her admiringly.

'Yeah, that's the general idea. But the mother wants me to go for the bar.'

'What's that?'

'A barrister! She loves the idea of me strutting my stuff, lording it around the law library in a wig and gown!'

'So are you going to do that?'

'Not bloody likely! What? And have to sit through all those dinners at the King's Inns with all those dried-up old fogeys? Never! The district court will do me.

'I have a brutal mother,' she said, making a face, thinking about it. 'Me poor father is at home grieving for me. I bet he's even planning a funeral for me right this minute, with a huge monument to my memory. He's convinced something terrible is going to happen to me up here in the wicked city, if I don't die from natural causes first! He's a doctor. And when I was young I got rheumatic fever. Since then he's been trying to wrap me up in cotton wool. He wouldn't even hear of me coming to Dublin. He wanted me to go to Cork or somewhere close to home. But the mother said I was strong as a horse and he could stop his nonsense! She packed me in the back seat of Father's car with all me new luggage. Jesus! I'm going to need a freight train to move me by the time I leave here with all the stuff she keeps sending me up. Then she settled poor Father in the driving seat and ordered him to drive me to Dublin. They don't call her Attila the Hen for nothing! But thank God she got that right! I play the two of them off each other like a violin!' she laughed. 'Daddy says yes, giving me a wink. Our secret! She says no. He uses reverse psychology on her, telling me loudly to listen to my mother. He agrees with her. She gets suspicious. Then she goes against him, thinking she has worked it out. My mother is daft as a brush! But you would have to love her!' she roared, laughing her head off.

'God!' I said, getting the picture of her father fussing and gnashing his teeth with the worry over her. Imagine! He must be a lovely soft man, really kind, that cares about his family more than anything else on this earth. That cheered me up no end, thinking I might get someone like that for meself some day.

'So!' she sighed, letting out a big breath then peeling her eyes away from me to land on the gingery-haired girl sitting on me right. 'Are you going home this weekend, Joyce?'

'Yes, I have to hurry! I want to get out of the city and on the road before it gets too late. I don't want to get stuck in the middle of nowhere and end up trying to hitch a lift in the dark.'

'Ah, Joyce! Give it a miss. Come out to a dance with me on Sunday!'

'I don't know, Odette,' Joyce said, creasing her face, wanting that but not too sure. 'I told Mammy I would be home this weekend.'

'Ah, for Christ's sake, Joycie! Give the mother a miss for once.

Come on! Come out with me. Sure, the crack will be great! You never know, we might even meet a couple of fine things!'

'Where are you thinking of going, is it the National Ballroom?' Joyce said.

'Jesus, no! The one across the road from that. They have a better class of fella there. They buy you a mineral first before they leap on you with their big paws and start trying to drag the knickers off you!' puffed Odette.

'Are youse going to a dance?' I said, thinking that was a great idea. I never set foot inside a dance hall in me life.

'Yeah, why? Would you like to come?'

'Yeah, I would! When are you going?'

'Sunday after lunch. It starts at three in the afternoon and ends at eight. That gives us plenty of time to get all dolled up and put plenty of war paint on! Are you interested? Come with us! Joycie is coming, aren't you, petal?' she said, digging your woman in the side.

'Oh, I don't know! Mammy worries when I don't come home.'

'Ah, for Jesus' sake, Joycie! Come on with us out of that! You need to cut the umbilical cord! If you keep this up, she'll have you out of that nice spot you're in with the Department of Agriculture and back home taking care of her. She's a civil servant,' Odette said, flying her head around to me.

'The mammy made her get a nice safe job. Joycie, the daft cow, had other ideas. She wanted to be an artist. Go to the Sorbonne! Paris, if you wouldn't mind! The idea of it!' snorted Odette. 'The poor mammy would lose the mind! That would have definitely turned her into a full-time invalid. She only gets a touch of the vapours when Joyce is due home!'

'Ah, stop, Dottie! That's my mother you are making fun of!'

'No, it's true, Joyce. Didn't you tell me yourself the neighbours say there's not a bother on her. She's to be seen from dusk till dawn, out in the pinstripe wellies, digging and smothering her vegetable garden in horses' manure! That's all going on behind your back, you know, while you're up here in the bright lights of Dublin, leading a shocking, decadent life! Wrestling with all them big hefty farmers coming up to whinge they can't get a living out of their twenty acres of land and complain they can't understand all them forms you are sending them.'

'Most of them can't even read the bloody things,' moaned Joyce, sipping on her tea and looking very woebegone, probably at the thought of all she was missing out on.

'They even offer to take her out and ply her with all the lemonade she can handle, with a drop of poteen slipped in to help the romance along!' Odette whispered, making sure Joyce could hear.

I roared laughing. 'Gawd, ye're gas!' I said, enjoying her no end.

'By the way, what's your name?'

'Martha!'

'OK, Mart! It looks like it's going to be just you and me hitting the town on Sunday! Are you game?'

'Yeah, definitely! I can't wait,' I said happily, shaking me head up and down with the excitement waiting ahead for me.

'Right, be ready around two o'clock.' Then she lifted herself up and stood stretching. 'I better start getting the head down to the books,' she yawned. 'See you later, Mart! Don't do anything I wouldn't do, Joycie, darling! Make sure to wear your chastity belt or the mother will have you certified! The first time I met her,' Odette whispered to me, 'she asked me for the lend of a hacksaw!'

'Why! What for?' I said, wondering what she was talking about.

'She's desperate! That's why!' Odette said, leaning into me and laughing, looking sideways at Joyce. Then she was gone, making it out the door with Joyce's shoe flying after her.

'Jesus! You're an awful scourge, Odette Clarke!' Joyce roared, hopping over to the door to pick up her shoe. Then she rushed back laughing, saying, as she sat back down, 'That one is mad as a hatter.

'God, I'll never hitch a lift home at this rate!' she moaned, throwing her head back and giving a big yawn.

'Why do you have to hitch?' I said.

'Because the train is too expensive. It would set you back a fortune! Nearly a full week's wages!' Joyce said, stirring herself and making a move for the door. 'Bye!' she waved at me.

'Bye, bye!' I said, standing up meself and making for me room.

That was great, I thought. I have new friends. Well, one good one. Odette is very easy to get along with. I really like her. Gawd! I'm doing great – meeting nice people and starting me new life! What more could I want?

22

'We're here!' Odette said, eyeing the long queue waiting to get into the dance hall. 'Jesus! I look like an Amazonian woman in these shoes!' she said, looking down at her black-patent high heels. 'I'm going to be towering over these little shrimps,' she said, eyeing the fellas all mooching up the queue slowly and checking the change out of their pockets to get the right money. 'I can see it now! They'll have their heads pressed to me bosom, sucking on me mammary glands!' she snorted, pulling the front of her lovely lemon silk frock down and tightening the lace around her chest.

'That frock is gorgeous, Odette! Where did you get it?'

'In a little shop not far from home, believe it or not,' she said, fixing the gold chain that hung around her waist then dropped down the front.

I had one too. But not as good as hers. Mine was cheap! You can tell the difference. But I'm delighted with the new clothes I bought meself yesterday, specially for the dance. I looked down at me new white skirt with the chain hanging down, and me gold sandals. Then up at me lovely red shirt with the white stripes. I'd even done up me hair in curls. I put in hair rollers last night after washing it. I bought the rollers in Arnotts Stores in Henry Street. Me hair came out looking lovely.

'Do you like me hair, Odette? Does it look OK?'

'Oh, yeah! It really suits you! I love the way it flicks in a wave over your right eye. Very chic!' she said. 'You look like a 1940s film star!'

'Ah, will ye stop outa that, Odette!' I said, delighted with meself.

'No, honestly! You should get it permed like that. Your hair has a fabulous texture. It's silky and the coppery highlight tones come through really lovely in the sun!'

'Ah, you look even better, Odette! The fellas will be going mad to get a dance with you. You are gorgeous looking, with your lovely creamy white skin, and your hair is out of this world.'

'Jaysus! Would you listen to the pair of us?' she laughed. 'We have a mutual admiration society going together! Who needs a man?'

'Three shillings and sixpence!' said the skinny man with the warts on his face and the bald head with a few strips of greasy hair plastered across the top. He snuffled like mad, then started wringing his hands, getting all worked up with impatience at the sight of the load of money landing down on the counter.

'One shilling and seven pence,' I muttered, counting out all the pennies.

He watched me, breathing himself heavy on the air, trying not to lose his patience. Then he had had enough. 'Ah! For the luv a Jaysus!' he screamed, losing the head. 'Were you out all night singing for tha? Wha am I expected te do wit tha lot? I can't carry tha home on me bike! The weight will burst me tyres! Could ye not have done better than bring me in a bag of bleedin coppers?' he roared, flaring out his nostrils, with his one good eye burning holes in me. The other one was marble.

'I'm gettin there, Mister! Three shillings and fourpence ha'penny!' I droned . . . 'There ye go, three shillings and sixpence to the last ha'penny,' I gasped, slapping the last penny down and pushing the lot over to land in a big mound in front of him.

'Holy Jaysus!' he muttered, shaking his head, looking around the walls of his little box. 'Give it here te me. The bleedin band will be gone before I have a chance te make any money!' he growled, whipping up the lot, sending half of it flying in all directions before he had a chance to drop it into his cardboard Oxo box sitting under the counter. 'NEXT!' he roared, snapping his head at Odette laughing the head off herself. 'I've a good mind to bar youse!' he snapped, waving his finger and narrowing his good eye at the pair of us.

'You can't! We have a contract! You accepted our money!' snapped Odette back at him, then dismissed him with a wave of her hand. 'Come on, Mart! Let's go,' she said, grabbing me arm and making for the inside.

We walked out into a yard and through a shed into a big hall with shiny floorboards and benches lined all along the walls. A platform was at the top, with five fellas getting all the music sorted out. One fella was tuning up his banjo and another fella was pulling an accordion in and out, pressing buttons on the side of it, with his hands jammed in a leather strap. Then they started the music, while another fella, with a big curl on top of his head – it went two feet into the air and was kept in place with Brylcreem – started singing down a microphone, 'Schtep it out, Mary! My fine daughter! Schtep it out, Mary, if you can! Schtep it out, Mary! My fine daughter! Show yer legs to the countryman!'

Everyone leapt up and started dancing. The fellas that were holding up the wall on one side galloped across the room and grabbed the women all standing on the other side. Fuck! I got caught in the melee!

'What's happening?' I roared. Me head was spinning around trying to get me bearings. A big countryman landed his size ten boot on me new sandals and dragged a dozy-looking fat woman after him, swinging her around and slapping her straight into me.

I went mad! 'Ye dirty-looking culchie eejit!' I screamed, pushing him outa the way as he swung himself and her around, slamming into me again. I was the only one left without a man! I'm suffocated. Jaysus!

'Odette! Where are ye?' I screamed, trying to fight me way out. I made it to the side of the room and stood next to three women all looking desperately for a man. I could see why! They looked like they belonged in a convent. I stared at the woman next to me. She had her cardigan hanging over her handbag, lying on her right arm, and her eyes searched desperately up and down the hall, hoping someone would ask her for a dance. I looked down at her brown missionary sandals, the kind priests wear out in Africa. She had long hairs coming out of a big black mole on her chin and another one on her cheek.

'Will we get up ourselves, Bridie, and have a twirl on our own?' her friend asked, shuffling in beside her, sounding desperate. Then she dropped her head, looking down at herself and fixing the red, blue, white and orange nylon frock that kept riding up to her arse. 'There's nothing happening,' she moaned when Bridie said nothing – she was too busy keeping her eyes peeled, looking for a loose man. 'I don't see any sign a them fellas from last week, Bridie,' she moaned, pulling the skinny matching belt tight around the frock, making her chest stick out. Then she felt her arse to make sure the frock was still covering it. Her arse was too big for the tight frock; it wouldn't stay down.

The woman on the right of me moved in closer. I could get the smell of talcum powder and mothballs. 'They're a lovely band!' she muttered in me ear, spitting down me earhole. 'I like them: "The Fast Cowboys"!'

'Yeah, they're smashing!' I said, beginning to feel weak from the heat and the noise and the smell. The four of us stood watching every man flying past, twirling and grabbing the women. We were hoping one of them would grab us. The men were dripping in sweat and letting their shirt tails stick out. One fella flew past us with a woman twirling through the air. He suddenly clapped his arms and stamped his feet, giving a loud screech like a mad Indian. But then he couldn't get his hands back in time to catch the woman and she went flying past him, still sailing through the air.

She landed, taking a pile a bodies with her. The rest all flying in that direction ended up under a heap of bodies. Frocks blew up and knickers of all colours, shapes and sizes were there for the looking. A big country-looking fella with a cannonball head on him and a mop of dirty brown straw hair crawled out first. He looked at the pile of bodies sprawled under each other then grabbed a woman by the leg and started pulling, trying to untangle the lot of them. 'Come on, Monica!' he shouted. 'Get up and stop exposing yureself!'

She was showing a big pink pair of knickers with a safety pin in the waist to hold them up, and pink garters to hold up the stockings. 'Yeh stupid gombeen!' she screamed. 'Let go a meh leg!'

'Shockin! Tis mayhem! Not dancin at all, at all, tis they are at!' muttered the women beside me.

'Isn't that shocking carry-on in pure broad daylight?' shouted the talcum-powder woman straight into me face, getting all excited, with her eyes dancing in her head at the sight of them all rolling on top of each other with the excuse they couldn't get up. Some of the fellas were managing to grab the wrong places in the women. Then handbags were flying.

'Ah, it's disgraceful carry-on,' I said, thinking this is better than the pictures!

'True for you! Tis fierce! This place is like one a them houses for loose people!' she snorted. 'Bridie! Let's see if we can get ourselves a mineral. There's no use of us standing here! Come on!'

'You could be right,' Bridie said. 'We might do better, right enough, around the minerals.'

I watched them go, then suddenly started roaring me head laughing when I saw Odette cracking her white handbag over the head of a blond fella wearing white bell-bottom trousers. She was trying to get away from him but he kept pulling her back, trying to say something. She gave him an unmerciful blow of the handbag again, making his nose spurt with blood, then she made straight for the front door, looking around for me.

I stared at your man, seeing blood gushing down, pumping out of his nose like a fountain, turning his get-up from blue shirt and white trousers to red shirt and red trousers. Then I whipped me head around and chased after her.

'Wait, Odette!' I flew, squeezing and shouting me way through the crowd. I caught up with her trying to make her way back in again.

'There you are! Come on, quick!' she said, grabbing hold of me. 'Let's get out of here!'

'What happened, Odette?'

'Ask me outside,' she mouthed, looking to see if the fella was after her. Then the band stopped playing to take a break and suddenly there was an unmerciful rumble. I looked back, seeing a herd of men and women making a terrible stampede straight in my direction. They were rushing for the mineral place. 'Fuck! Help! MAMMY!' I screamed, getting the fright of me life as I got sent flying out the door and nearly ended up under a ton of bodies herding down on top of me.

Odette grabbed me hand and yanked me out the door after her. 'Come on! Don't lose your footing!' she roared, tearing me behind her out the door.

We flew past the empty box; Baldy was gone. Then she yanked open the front door and we were out into the street.

The fresh air was like honey in me lungs. 'Jaysus! Jaysus! I never want to go through the like of that again!' I said, waiting for the blood to rush back into me face.

She shook her head. 'Yeah! You and me both, kiddo! Never again! From now on I'm sticking to the National,' she puffed, with her face red as a beetroot.

'To think we paid for that!' I snorted.

'Yep!' she laughed. 'I thought it was a clodhoppers' dance, but it turned out to be the wild men of Borneo!'

'Yeah, but do you know what was even worse?' I said, pulling her arm to get her to look at me. 'Do you know what?' I said, making sure she was looking at me.

'No! What?' she said, staring into me face.

'Not only did I pay good money, three shillings and sixpence, then nearly collapse from the lack of air, but after all that them fuckers didn't even ask me up for a dance! Can you believe that, Odette? Can you?' I muttered, feeling disgusted thinking about all that hardship I went through and all for nothing. 'Imagine, Odette!' I roared, holding me head. 'I was rolling around in me bed all night in them bleedin spiky rollers. And all in the hopes of getting meself a lovely mass of curly hair. Now look at it!' I screamed. 'It's all collapsed! Gone dead straight from all the sweating I went through!' I said, feeling me hot damp hair. I was nearly crying at all me loss.

Odette stared at me then suddenly collapsed herself back against a black iron railings and started roaring her head laughing.

'What's funny?' I said, half smiling at seeing her getting hysterical.

She kept waving her hand up at me, trying to talk. 'Oh, God! Don't say any more,' she said, wiping the tears and snots rolling down her face. 'Whatever about the dance! We sure got a run for our money.' Then she started wheezing, with her mouth wide open trying to get the laughing out again. When she did, you could hear her screams all the way back to the hostel. I looked at her sprawled at the railings, grabbing at the bars to stop herself slipping. Then I suddenly saw the picture she had and let out a roar, falling beside her with the laughing screaming outa me. We kept trying to grab onta each other, because I was falling, knocking her down. Then we went quiet; we had no more strength left. We just sat on the little wall with our backs against the railings, looking around and watching people milling past, running to catch the last film showing for the evening on the Adelphi picture house around the corner.

'Odette,' I suddenly said. 'Why did you have to give your man a slap of your handbag? What did he do to you?'

'Oh, that creep!' she said, dropping her mouth and turning to look at me with a sour look on her face. 'He grabbed the cheeks of me arse with his big dirty paws and jammed me against him, rocking himself up and down, giving himself a cheap quick thrill. That's when I lashed out with my bag, letting him have it.'

'Dirty swine!' I said.

'Yeah, but that wasn't enough for him. He then came after me, bleating with a filthy sneer on his ugly conceited mug, "I was only trying to service you! You were dying for it!" That's when I gave him the full force of the Odette knockout! I won that match!' she said, giving a little laugh.

'Ah, the dirty, filthy, pig, swine toerag,' I said.

'Pity I didn't wrap his balls around his neck while I was at it!' she muttered.

'Yeah! But, ah, no! I mean – come to think about it, you did do one better! Did you see the new white trousers he was wearing?'

She shook her head, listening to me.

'He must love them, Odette! Because, well, I certainly noticed the crease down the middle as the blood was splattering all over them! And down his electric-blue nylon shirt! So, if it's any consolation to ye, I saw all the lot, because you were too busy scarpering trying to make your getaway. But take it from me, Odette! You left him destroyed!' I said, wagging me finger at her, getting again the satisfying picture of him being splattered all over himself. That eased the fire flying around me belly with the rage at the filthy cheek of that no-good bastard.

'Yeah! It's going to make him nervous around women for a while,' she laughed. Then she staggered to her feet, pulling me up with her. 'Come on, Martha! It's getting late. We better start making our way back to the hostel before we get locked out or locked up!' she said, giving a look around to see who was watching us.

'Yeah, but let's stop first for fish and chips,' I said. 'I'm starving with the hunger.'

'Gawd, Martha. Not only have you beauty but brains too!' she said, letting her huge blue eyes widen in shock. 'Come on! Brilliant idea! Let's go!' she said, wrapping her arm around me shoulders.

I roared laughing, thinking she says the funniest things, then grabbed me arm around her back, and the two of us started heading off down onto O'Connell Street, with me thinking this is the first time in my whole life I ever had a friend. I feel so warm and cosy inside meself. People are getting to like me!

23

I came rushing down the stairs, trying to be patient and not push ahead at the crowds of girls all going in the same direction. Gawd! I don't want to be late.

'What time is it, please?' I said to the crowd, looking to catch someone's eye. They all ignored me, intent on getting themselves out the door and off to work as quick as they could.

'What time is it, please?' I said to the young one with the black mantilla wrapped on her head standing holding the door wide open, taking in who was going out and who was trying to get back in. She was busy telling two shifty-looking young ones they had to wait outside until the Reverend Mother got her hands on them.

'But, Eileen! We spent the whole night in the hospital, didn't we, Lola? Tell her!' said the one with the matted black hair streeling around her head, digging Lola in the ribs with her elbow. Lola just stared, with her big brown eyes hanging out of her head looking shocked.

I stopped to listen, looking from one to the other, wanting to hear what was going on. 'Move out of the way!' the ones coming up behind me shouted, pushing me out the door and onto the step.

'What time is it, Eileen?' I hadn't met her before. But now I knew her name.

She shook her head at me, muttering with a sour look on her pasty pimply face, 'How would I know that? I don't have a watch!'

'Thanks! Jaysus! Don't smile whatever you do. Your face might crack,' I muttered under me breath, then moved off, hearing her say to the two still begging to be let in, 'No! The pair of you were out prowling the streets all night, getting up to no good when you should have been in your beds like decent Christians! Now you can expect to bring the full wrath of Mother down on your heads!'

Brown-eyes started to roar her head crying. I looked back, seeing Eileen leaning her head out the door, saying with a big happy smirk on her face, 'Mother will be writing to your parents! Don't forget that!' she said, enjoying herself no end.

Fuck! I ran on. Not wanting to hear any more. Oh, God almighty! I hope I never get meself into trouble like that!

I started to hurry, worrying about the time. I don't want to be late for me first day at the secretarial school. I turned left onto Fitzwilliam Square and rushed on.

'Excuse me!' I said to a man in a pinstripe suit carrying a big leather briefcase. 'What time is it, please?'

He pulled up the sleeve of his jacket, showing lovely gold cufflinks in a snow-white shirt, and looked at his big man's watch. 'Eight-fifteen!' he said.

'Is that a quarter past eight?' I said, looking at him with the worry on me.

'Yes!' he grinned, smiling at me and staring. Then we turned: he going on his way and me hurrying ahead on mine.

Jaysus! I'm never sure of the time on hearing it said that way. Not since that Jackser aul fella taught me the clock when I was little. He banged it into me, making me learn it in a flash! But I missed out a few bits. Anyway, I'm grand for time. It shouldn't take me more than half an hour, maybe less, to get there. I am to be there at a quarter to nine, the nun, Sister Allie, told me. For the first day anyway. Then after that I won't start until nine o'clock.

I turned right before I got to Mount Street, crossing the road and continuing to head on up Fitzwilliam Square. Girls were hurrying past in all directions wearing lovely short mini frocks in all colours with lovely high heels. One stopped in front of me and went up the steps heading in to one of the offices. Oh, she's lovely, I thought, staring at her black miniskirt with the baby-blue tight jumper showing her pointy chest sticking out. She took her time getting up the steps on her red stiletto slingback high heels, wagging her arse as she moved each leg. Her hair is lovely too. She has straight black hair swinging around in a ponytail with a long thick fringe, and black eyeliner, with long black eyelashes caked with mascara. Her face is lovely and pink and brown from the make-up, with red rouge to make her cheeks red and blue eyeshadow on her eyelids.

A fella in a black suit, wine tie and snow-white shirt, wearing shiny black lace-up shoes, with his thick black silvery hair slicked down with hair oil at the back and sides, came flying up behind her, waving a briefcase, then slowed down to walk beside her with a big smile on his face. 'Good morning, Miss Dowling!' he said, sounding very grand. 'Did you have a nice weekend?' he said, putting out his arm and letting the briefcase wave in the air, then pushing the door open with his other arm to let her go in the door first.

'Oh, good morning, Mister Wilson!' she said, wagging her arse in the door and giving him a big toothpaste advertisement smile, then lifting her nose, pretending she wasn't really interested in the way he was fussing around her.

I looked at the shiny brass plate on the door: 'Messrs H.W. Wilson and partners. Solicitors'. Oh, that is definitely going to be me in next to no time at all, I gasped to meself, shutting me mouth and taking in a deep breath, hearing me breath sob outa me chest. That is exactly how I see meself. I'm even getting meself a pair of them stiletto high heels to wear when I'm working in an office job. I better practise me diction! Very important! And me walk!

Right! Keep moving. I turned left, passing by the 'Pepper Canister' Protestant Church, and came out onto the canal. I crossed the road, wanting to walk beside the water. I walked on right to the top of the canal and turned left again. Jaysus! This is taking longer than I thought!

At last! Here we are. I rounded the corner after leaving the traffic behind and stood looking the length of a long road with big houses on each side. It's nice and quiet here. These houses are very well-off looking, I thought as I crossed the road looking for number four. These are all the big-wig people living along these parts. Right! Number four should be at the start. Me heart lifted, then I started to rattle a bit with me nerves. Here it is! I walked up a long passage and up the three big stone steps and hesitated. Do I press the bell? I tried the doorknob and the door pushed straight in. OK! I breathed, closing the door behind me and trying to steady me breath. I went through the hall and up the stairs, and turned on a little landing. Then up another flight of stairs and stopped on a landing with two doors. Which one? I knocked gently on the one facing me and stood back waiting.

'Yes?' said a woman with ginger curly grey hair, wearing a red frock with yellow flowers and a matching belt, opening the door and staring at me, wondering who I was.

'I, eh, I'm Martha Long. I've come to start me – my secretarial course. Is this the right place?'

'Yes! Come in,' she said, standing back and holding the door open for me.

I looked around a small room with a big desk weighed down with books and papers. It was sitting in front of a big window looking out onto a back garden. A bookcase stood piled with books on one wall, and the other wall was stacked high with books on shelves. A big picture on the wall showed a cartoon of two aul fellas in old-fashioned clothes. One said to the other fella, holding a sack, 'Shush! Don't let the cat out of the bag!' putting his finger to his mouth. It was called 'Dublin Castle. The Crown Solicitor's Office'.

'Sit down there,' she said, pointing to a mahogany old chair with the stuffing hanging out. It was covered with black insulation tape.

I pulled out the chair from the desk and sat meself down while she went around the other side and sat in a big old-fashioned armchair padded with black leather and decorated with studs. The mahogany wood all around it was carved. She stared at me for a minute, taking in me red frock with the white little flowers and the white linen collar. I took in the smile she was holding, making her big watery grey eyes light up. They looked like they were laughing.

She leaned her big chest on the desk, folding her hands with brown freckles covering them and going up her arms, then said, 'So! Good girl! You got here in time! Now, my name is Miss Finley. I will be teaching you. Have you done shorthand before?'

'Yeah—'

'Say yes,' she said, nodding her head up and down at me.

'Sorry, Miss! Yes, I have. I did, done! Yeah, I did shorthand before.'

She gave a half smile, raising her eyes to the ceiling. I looked at her, trying to figure out all the things I said wrong.

'Go on!' she said, waiting for me to finish.

'Yes, I done it before. But only for a short while.'

'Well, when you done—' Then she lowered her head and started again.

I kept the laugh inside meself, seeing her get confused at what I was saying.

'What was it? Pitman or Gregg?'

'Pitman,' I said.

'Oh. Will you be able to switch over? We do Gregg here.'

I thought about it, getting the picture of all the lines and dots and squiggles I sweated over. 'Yes, I didn't learn too much!'

'Good! I'm sure you won't have a problem,' she said. 'Now! Do you have a typing book?' she said, eyeing the book in me hand.

'Yes, I do! Look! I bought this one brand new and never got a chance to open it because they did the typing on different times. First you did the shorthand, then the next week you might get a chance at the typing. But I never did! They didn't have many typewriters anyway, and the place wasn't cheap!' I said, getting annoyed now at the thought I didn't really get me money's worth.

Her eyes looked like she was laughing but she kept her face straight. I suppose she thought it was funny I didn't complain at the time – that it was only hitting me now!

'Good! You will be doing bookkeeping as well. Are you good at figures?'

'Do you mean counting and that kind of thing?'

'Yes, of course!'

'Oh, yes! I'm not bad at that. But I don't know anything about bookkeeping!'

'No, of course not. That's why you've come here to learn,' she smiled. 'But you will need that for keeping the books in an office. It is all part of the secretarial course.'

'OK,' I said, waiting to see what it was like.

'Now I expect you to work hard. You are lucky to get in here. I have only a very small group of students. I practically give you individual attention. So you must be here on time. Exactly nine on the dot. You are not allowed to miss a day unless you bring me a doctor's note. We break for lunch at half past twelve, so you can go back to the hostel for your dinner. I expect you back here on the dot of two o'clock. Not a minute later, mind! Then you finish classes at half past four. OK?'

'OK!' I said, seeing her stand up, so I stood up meself.

'We'll go into the class now,' she said, opening the door and letting me out, closing the door behind her. I waited, then followed her, walking into the other room, and everyone went silent, with about seven pairs of eyes all looking up at us.

'Good morning, everyone!' she said, smiling and looking down at the people all sitting around a big shiny oak table standing in the middle of the room, with a big window well away from it at the end of the room looking out onto the road.

'Good morning, Miss Finley,' they said, all smiling and staring at me.

'This is Martha. A new student.'

I looked down at the faces as they all looked at me, smiling. Two girls were nudging each other, speaking with their hands. I watched. Ah! They're doing sign language. They must be deaf. One of them had absolutely gorgeous big blue saucer eyes with eyelashes the length of a fan for cooling yourself. She has lovely blonde, wavy, long, curly hair down her back. I couldn't stop staring at her. She was making signs to her friend, watching the teacher to see if she was watching. The friend kept shaking her head and looking around Blondie's shoulder to examine me and get a good look. I stared back, seeing her black bitty hair that looked like straw. Her eyes were very small and close together and she must be nearly the plainest girl I ever saw in me life. Imagine that! I thought to meself. The good-looking one still likes her and they look like the best of friends to me. That would come in handy for getting fellas. Blondie would have all the fellas after her and her friend could get the ones left out!

'OK! You can get to know each other during your break. Meanwhile, we don't have a minute to lose. Time is precious,' she said, making for the next room with big doors between them. The doors were pushed back and slide into the wall so you could see what everyone was doing. 'Now! You sit here. I am going to start you on the typing.'

I sat down at a front-row desk with a black typewriter sitting on top.

'This is an Underwood,' she said. 'Very solid. They don't make them like this any more.'

I stared at the keys, seeing them stand up in the air with a wheel at the side for pulling the paper through a black barrel and a clamp to keep it locked with the paper standing up and then you start typing.

'Now,' she said, opening me new book, 'we will start at the beginning. Rest the four fingers of each hand on these keys. The left hand will always – always! – rest on the letters A S D F. The right hand will always rest on the letters SEMICOLON L K J. That is where you begin from when you are typing. So now, the first thing we need to learn is keep the fingers on those letters and practise! Follow the book. I want to see pages of lines beginning with A. Press the bar down with the thumb, then semicolon with the right-hand little finger and so on. So you should have a line of A SEMICOLON S L D K F J. Have you got that?' she said, looking at me. 'Now it must be smooth. You must get into a rhythm. So take it nice and slowly. Do not try to rush it. You will make haste slowly, when you have mastered the rhythm of those keys. Then, and only then, will we move on. Now! Do you understand all that?' she said, looking down at me with her eyes laughing.

'Yeah!' I said, happily, grabbing at the keys, dying to get started.

'Not so fast! First we must learn how to put in the typing paper. I'm not one to dampen down a spirit as keen as yours but make haste slowly! Now,' she said, picking up a white sheet of paper, 'we turn the wheel this way and open the bar, inserting the paper in slowly, making sure it is straight. That is very important. Otherwise your boss will throw you out of the job on your very first day when you go presenting him with a crooked page of nonsense! Now! I am very strict about waste! I do not want to see one inch of space on this page. Cover every last bit!' she said, finally letting go and shaking her finger at me.

'Right, thanks! That's great, Miss Finley,' I said, at last being let have a chance at typing meself. I put the paper in as she showed me, then twiddled the wheel to clamp the bar locked and looked down at me fingers to rest them in the right place. Then started banging.

'No, no!' she said, standing behind me back, watching. 'Don't bang the machine. You will break it! Now, you are not allowed to look down at your hands. You must follow the book. You can't go wrong if you keep your fingers always in the resting position on the keys. Now, begin again.'

I rested me hands on the right keys, keeping them there. Then looked at the book, seeing the same keys there, with a picture matching me fingers. Then I started.

She watched. 'Good! Good,' she said, sounding satisfied, then moved off to talk to the other room. People came in behind me and started battering away on the typewriters. But I took no notice. I'm too busy trying to get meself master of the resting keys.

'OK, you can all go for your break,' Miss Finley said, walking in and out of the rooms, looking at us and telling everyone to put down their books.

I finally took me eyes up from the book and looked at what I had written on me typewriter. The first page I finished was all wavy lines of nonsense. As the teacher said, I had put the paper in crooked. It's hard to get it straight. But me next paper was grand and straight. And only about every second line was wrong. I have to work on me concentration, the teacher said. I left the new page in the typewriter, because it was only barely started, and got up to follow the crowd out the door. The teacher went into her office and closed the door.

I followed them down into the hall, then turned left down a dark basement stairs.

We ended up in a big room with bars on the windows looking up to the street. But all you could see was a wall in front and the top of the grass overhead. A long old wooden table stood under the window. I looked around, seeing the walls are bare whitewashed bricks and the floor is made of old red flagstones. A huge fireplace in the middle of the room, facing the window, is blocked up with a thin wooden partition. People started congregating around the fireplace. It is freezing down here and everyone started to shiver because the sun doesn't get down this far. A big metal teapot was on the table with a jug of milk and sugar and kitchen mugs for people to help themself. I made straight for the tea. A woman with straight brown hair that is thick with clumps of grey running through it and parted at the side, held back with hair clips, was pouring tea for herself and a fella with sandy hair. He looked a bit dopey. It was the way he was trying to get a cigarette out of his box of Carrolls. It looked like it took all his concentration, because he was pulling the cigarette out very slowly.

'Here, Kevin!' the woman said, handing him a mug.

'Thanks, Betty!' he said, smiling at her, showing his yellow teeth gummed up with months of food. He needs to clean them, I thought, thinking they would be nice because they all looked very straight. The two of them walked over to the fireplace and started talking.

I waited me turn as a girl with dead-straight long white hair poured herself a mug of tea. Her face was very plain. It was too white and even looked a bit grey. Even her blue eyes was a bit dead. She looked like there was very little life left in her. No! She's not what you would call glamorous, even though from the back of her, with the hair, you would think she was.

I finally got me hands on the teapot and poured meself a cup, then opened me bag and took out me packet of ten Major cigarettes and lit one up.

'They're very strong,' said the woman with the brown-grey hair.

'Yeah!' I smiled. 'But I like them like that. I can't get a good drag any more, outa them Carrolls you are smoking.'

'You've just started?'

'Yeah,' I said.

'Well, this is Kevin and I'm Betty. How did you find your first morning?'

'Grand! It was great!'

'Yeah, we were behind you. We could see you trying to wrestle with the keys,' she laughed, looking at Kevin.

He grinned at me, shaking his head. 'Yes! They are really archaic! I think Noah brought them with him out of the Ark,' he laughed, shaking his shoulders and holding the cigarette really tight between his two fingers that look like two burnt sausages. I could see bits of scurvy skin sticking to his eyebrows, and white bits were sitting on the hair coming out of his ears. His face was red and blotchy, and there was dry spits stuck to the corners of his mouth and long strings hung on his mouth when he opened it. But the woman didn't seem to mind. She was standing very close to him and talking and laughing into his face. He liked that and moved in closer to her.

She must be well in the thirty mark. I looked at her finger. No, she's not married. Yeah, I knew she was a spinster. She looked like someone who never took much notice of how she looked. I don't think she ever wore make-up in her life. Or bothered about wearing modern clothes. Not judging by the long brown skirt down past her knees or the hickey brown shoes and the big old green cardigan that probably belonged to her mother. I would say she looks like someone who had to take care of her ailing mother. I met a lot of women like that. Some of them had to go out to work and get a neighbour to look after the mammy, then rush home to get the dinner and take care of everything that needed doing, never getting a minute to themselves. Then by the time the poor aul ma was gone they ended up looking like Betty. Too far gone to care any more, with no man to give them a second look because they were too old and didn't know where to start looking anyway, because by now all the men were married. Me heart gladdened looking at the two of them and how happy they were with each other's company. Ah, that's lovely! They must have met here, now they're probably going out together. Even though he's a bit younger looking. Yeah, there's always someone for everyone! You never know what's around the next corner. Just like me – finding all the luck in the world and now getting to come here.

'Hello,' whispered the white-haired woman, coming over quietly and standing beside us, gripping her hands around the mug to warm them.

'This is Esther,' Betty said.

'Hello, Esther! I'm Martha,' I said, nodding and smiling at her.

'The Siamese twins over there,' Betty said, pointing to the two girls sitting at the table, 'are Sonia and Stacey. The blonde girl is Sonia.'

'Why do you call them the Siamese?' I said, laughing.

'Oh, don't ask! That pair are inseparable. You see one, you see the other!'

I looked over, seeing them shouting at each other, making screeching noises. They were waving their hands and shaking their fingers like mad at each other, the pair of them slamming their fists down on the table then closing their eyes and whipping their heads away, refusing to look at each other. The blonde one, Sonia, picked up her packet of Tayto crisps and a sandwich and moved herself down the seat, sitting right on the edge. The other one did the same, grabbing up her packet of Cleeve's Toffees and a sandwich and giving a screech at her friend, who ignored her. Then she stood up and went to the edge of the bench and upended it, giving it a jerk into the air, and everyone ran just as Blondie was hitting the floor.

Betty went for the villain and looked into her face and waved her finger, saying very quietly, 'You are very bold, Stacey! That was very dangerous. You could have broken Sonia's back.'

Kevin picked up Sonia, who was trying to sit up and rub her arse. She started crying. Me heart went out to her, seeing her big blue eyes pour down with huge tears. Ah, God love her, she wasn't expecting that. Jaysus! Stacey is very vicious! I better not get on the wrong side of her! I looked down at her, seeing her shake her head and wriggle her shoulders, trying to make out she didn't care.

Betty walked over to Esther and me, saying, 'That girl has a terrible temper!' Then she mouthed, 'Are you all right, Sonia, love?' catching

Sonia's eye. Sonia dropped her mouth and sniffled, blinked and shook
her head up and down, then wiped her snots with the back of her
hand and opened her sandwich, taking a bite. She looked very lonely
without her friend. I could feel it. But the other one wouldn't give in and
apologise. She kept giving quick looks down to see if Sonia was looking,
then pushed out her mouth, looking like she was trying to stretch it,
keeping it pressed together, and lifted her nose, keeping her eyes peeled
down, staring at the floor, making out she was in the right.

'Come on, everyone! You better all go! Miss Finley just put her
head over the banisters. She wants you all to get back upstairs now!'
said a girl coming in on crutches. She looked about twelve, because
she was very small. But I could see by her face she was older. Maybe
even sixteen or seventeen. The crutches were very big and strained
under her shoulders, squashing her neck, and her little legs were like
matchsticks. They were strapped into steel callipers and she had to
wear strong leather brown boots with laces. Ah, Jaysus! How unlucky
can you get? That poor girl caught the polio! Some of us did and more
didn't. I watched her tear out the door again, making it to the stairs
before anyone could get going. Bloody hell! She moves like greased
lightning on them crutches. She doesn't walk; she flies through the
air, swinging herself like mad. I wonder if she would let me have a
go of them sometime? Just to see how fast I can go!

We all trailed out the door and back up to the classrooms. I went
back to me business of trying to become master of the keys on the
typewriter.

'Good,' said Miss Finley, appearing up behind me.

I blinked and lifted me head off the book.

'Now you can carry on following the book. Move on to the next
keys.'

'OK, Miss Finley!' I said, feeling very satisfied with me morning's
work at getting up a nice rhythm without making too many mistakes
now.

'OK! It's time to go for lunch,' Miss Finley said, coming in and
blowing her nose with a hanky. 'Make sure you are all back on time,

please. I don't want any shirking! Martha,' she said, coming over and leaning down to me, 'this afternoon, when you get back from lunch, I will be taking you into the other classroom. You will be starting shorthand. So I want you to get a shorthand notebook like this one,' she said, holding up a notebook and letting me see the one I needed to get. 'There's a stationery shop not too far from here. You should be able to pick one up there. Is that all right?' she said, smiling at me.

'Yes! I'll bring that back with me, Miss Finley.'

'OK! Run along now like a good girl and don't be late back.'

'No, I won't. Thanks, Miss Finley.'

Me heart leapt! Oh, this is great! I thought it would be weeks before I would start that. I even thought I would have to practise the typing day in and day out without any let-up. But, no, it seems you get a chance at everything in the one day.

We all stopped what we were doing and made straight for the door. Everyone went in different directions. People smiled and waved at me. 'Bye! See you later!' we all shouted to each other.

I turned me back and raced past Brenda flying along on her crutches. 'Bye! See ye later!' I shouted.

'Yeah! Will ye bring us back a parrot?' she shouted, knowing I was going down past the canal where you used to meet one of the barges from Guinness. They used to go down the River Liffey as well. We would always say to the barge men, 'Eh, Mister! Will ye bring us back a parrot?' Because it used to look like they were going off somewhere foreign.

24

'Hello, everybody!' I said, rushing in the door and sitting meself down at the big table and shouting over to everyone. They were all talking away like mad after not seeing each other for nearly six weeks.

'Did you have a good summer?' Brenda said, looking at me.

'Yeah, smashing! What about you?'

'Yeah, it was great. Nothing to do and all day to do it.'

'Not me,' I said. 'I went mad!'

'Oh! What did you do?'

'Jaysus! What didn't I do? First of all I went out all dressed up in me nightie.'

'Your nightdress?' everyone shouted, getting to hear me.

'Yeah! I bought this lovely lemon, all frilly around the edges, linen nightdress in Dunnes Stores. Then, after looking at it one night, I decided it would look lovely as a frock. So I wore it out.'

'Well. I don't believe you! You didn't?' said Esther.

'Ah, no! Tell us you didn't!' said Betty and the rest of them, all laughing.

'I did! Yeah, really!' I said, shaking me head at them.

'She would!' said Brenda, nodding her head in agreement at me then looking at them. 'She's mad enough to do anything!'

'Yeah, why not? I even put flowers in me hair. I robbed them from the park in Fitzwilliam Square just around the corner from the hostel. I wanted to look like I was a hippie! Everyone else was at it. Mind you, half of them gobshites are off their head. Going around talking about "Free Love" and "Let It All Hang Out" and "Peace,

Man". It's all happening in America. Now it's come here!'

'Yeah, so is the bloody student riots! Everyone is at it nowadays, especially the Women's Liberation Movement brigade!' said Betty, looking disgusted. 'I wouldn't mind but most of them women are all well off. They mostly come from middle-class backgrounds and went to the university. They don't know they are born, half of them. The same with the bloody students! There are riots now all over Europe. Especially France.'

'Oh, yes!' said Kevin. 'They want to bring down the establishment. Do away with the middle class and establish a society for the working man. Share the wealth!'

'Oh, yeah! I would be in favour of that!' I said, thinking that was a marvellous idea.

'Yeah, like hell they would!' laughed Kevin. 'It would be something like the Communist system they have in Russia. Except the people are still poor there. Now they are all prisoners. No one can leave from behind the Iron Curtain except the ruling classes, the party leaders. Ha, ha!' he roared, laughing his head off. 'Nothing ever changes. The ones who have the power keep it for themself. You have to be a member of the club to get in.'

'Oh, stop! Kevin! Don't go off getting carried away on your politics,' said Betty, giving him a dig and laughing.

He blew her a kiss.

'Go on, Martha. Tell us what happened.'

'What? Oh, yeah!' I said, getting back to where I left off. 'I was even thinking of going out in me bare feet, like Marianne Faithfull did. But me friends wouldn't let me. So I had to wear shoes! That meant wearing me gold sandals and tights! It didn't look the same! I didn't look—' I was trying to think of the word.

'Carefree, windblown and beautiful,' said Kevin.

'Yeah! Yeah, that's it exactly!' I said, getting all excited.

Kevin nodded, shaking his head up and down, delighted with how quick he was with the words. Betty gave him another dig, saying, 'Behave yourself, you!'

'Anyway, then I made a few bob selling raffle tickets for a charity. I flew up and down Grafton Street and all over the place. I got hundreds sold in no time at all. I made five pounds altogether in commission, then took meself off on the boat to England. I told the Reverend Mother in the hostel I was staying in the country with friends. She believed me even though me friend Odette wasn't there to back me up. She was already gone home! Anyway, she didn't phone Odette's mother to ask her. Just as well for me! Then I was gone out the door without a stitch to wear, just all me savings. I took nothing else.'

'Oh, you are a real little demon!' muttered Betty, shaking her head at me.

'But wait until you hear what I did! Jaysus! I hitched hiked all across England. Not knowing where I was going or even where I had landed up! But it was great gas. Everyone I met who gave me a lift kept telling me to be careful. I could be murdered. I knew that! But still an all, the drivers were really good to me. I never got in a car if there was more than one person. Or except if the driver had a woman with them. They all bought me food in cafés, thinking I was starving with the hunger. I was no such thing because everyone had the same idea: stop at the nearest café and bring me in and feed me. Men kept worrying about me. They would stop each other at the petrol station on the motorway when they got to be where they wanted and say, "Here! Are you heading to Coventry? Will you take this young girl, mate? Mind her! Make sure you leave her in a town!"

'I ended up getting a lift in a black Volkswagen with an old man in a heavy brown overcoat wearing a trilby hat. So there I was, flying through the night with the radio blasting out a Jewish love song sung in Polish, with this old man crying and telling me his life story. "I was hunted by the Nazis because I am a Jew," he said, sounding just like it was really still only happening to him. He had a terrible mournful way of talking. Like all the sadness in the world had collapsed down on top of his shoulders. Oh, God! You should have met him. He was really haunted. "They killed all my family. I took my revenge. I went back and I too killed the bastards," he said slowly, narrowing his eyes and thinking about it. "A hundred. No, a thousand times over.

"'I came to England from France during the war, with the Polish Air force. I flew over Dresden. Every bomb I dropped, I shouted, 'Die, bastards! Here is one more. I will drop ten for every one member of my family you have murdered. I will survive to spit on all your graves!' Yes, and I did," he said quietly, looking across at me and shaking his head with terrible regret. "We wiped out a whole city. Men women and children. Old people who had lived and survived already a war! Soldiers taking refuge. They all thought it was safe. Nobody bombs Dresden, they believed. My God! The fires that raged through that city burned everything in its path. It lit up the night sky! I could imagine the heat underneath me was licking up to devour me and avenge the innocent lives we bombers with our planes had just swept away. We could see our paths almost all the way back to England! Oy vey!" he said, throwing up his arms into the air, letting go of the steering wheel. "For why did so many people have to die? What purpose did it serve? Now I am an old man. At night I sit and think about these things. So now I know nothing! I think maybe life is not good or bad. Life is to just live! It is too short to worry. Be happy while you can, help each other. Because there is no tomorrow. It may never come. So then we die. Yesterday is gone. What more is there to say? To think, to do? Yes, just live your life.

"'I suppose you could say I have become a philosopher," he said, turning down his mouth, shaking his head, agreeing with himself. "The only thing I am sure about is I am a survivor. I have outlived most of my enemies."

'We arrived in the early morning in Coventry. I saw cars stopping and people milling their way into a church. The bells were ringing for Mass. "Listen! Would you ever let me out here, please? This will do me grand! I want to go in there and get Mass. It's Sunday, that's the day I'm supposed to go there!"

"'Yes! It is important you look after your religion. We need spiritual nourishment as much as we need food for our bellies!" he said, pulling up to a vacant spot at the footpath outside the church, then he let me out.

'"Goodbye!" I said. "Thanks very much for everything! For the fish and chips!"

'He waved me away with his hand. "Don't even think about it! I did nothing. Nothing!" he said, smiling at me then driving away.

'The priest was up on the altar speaking in a foreign language. I looked around wondering what was going on. "Excuse me, is this a Catholic Mass?" I asked an old man coming in the door behind me.

'"He is speaking Polish," the old man said, taking off his hat and holding it down on his knee while he knelt at the end of the church.

'I knelt down beside him, not understanding a word of what was going on. Then the Mass ended and the priest stood outside the door speaking and laughing with all the Mass-goers. My turn came to shuffle past him. "Thanks, Father," I muttered, not thinking he would understand me.

'"Where are you from?" he said, suddenly putting out his arm gently to stop me moving on.

'"Oh! Do you speak English?" I said, looking at him in surprise.

'"Of course! I'm from Ireland."

'"Oh, yes! So am I," I said, saying, "But you were speaking Polish."

'"Yes!" he laughed. "I look after the Polish community here. Where are you living? I haven't seen you here before."

'"No! I was just hitching me way around England. I wanted to see what it was like."

'"Where are you going now?" he said.

'"I don't know. Maybe I should think about going to London. I would love to see Carnaby Street. I heard a lot about that place."

'"Oh, in that case you are in luck. In ten minutes' time I am heading down to London to pick up my mother. I am taking her off on a holiday to Spain. Would you like a lift?"

'"Oh, yeah! That would be great. Thanks very much, Father."

'I was off again, heading to London. The priest kept handing me his box of cigarettes while he was driving, saying, "Take out a cigarette and light one up for me. Light one for yourself, too, if you want one." It was great! I flew all the way to London in just one go. The problem only started when I got there. I sat down in a park bench in the evening wondering what I was going to do next. It was nearly too late for the shops. I really wanted to get a look around Carnaby Street, especially. But then a copper came along and asked me what I was doing. Resting, I said. Before I knew what was happening I was landed down at the police station with him demanding to know my address back here. I gave him Sister Aloysius's phone number. Jaysus! I could hear her screaming at the other end of the phone. "Tell her to get back home here at once!" He lifted the phone to my ear, letting me hear the screams. "The deceitful little minx!" she was snorting!

'I said nothing and handed him back the phone. He grinned at me, saying, "You better get your story straight! I think it will be a long time before she takes her eye off you again! Now! You are on the next boat-train home!"

'So, yeah, I had a great summer!' I gasped, watching them all listen with their mouths open and their eyeballs staring, forgetting to even blink.

'Holy mother of God!' gasped Betty. 'You must have two guardian angels watching over you. One for each shoulder!'

'Oh, yeah! I have always been lucky that way,' I said, thinking of all me near misses when I nearly managed an early grave! 'But I love a bit of adventure! Life is very short, you know.'

'Really!' said Esther. 'It looks to me like yours is going to be very short if you keep on taking chances like that!'

'Ah, no, Esther! You only go when your time is up! That's what I always believe. Especially when I think about all the second chances I got! So it has to be that. Nobody goes unless their number is up!'

'Where is Miss Finley?' Betty said, suddenly looking around.

'Oh, she's in her office talking to a new girl starting this morning,' said Tommy Byrne, moving away from the end of the table next to the 'twins' and squashing himself in beside Esther. 'Talk of the devil!' he suddenly said, straightening his face and looking around.

'Yes, good morning, everybody! You are all very welcome back!' Miss Finley said, coming in the door with a new girl trailing in behind her. We all stared at the girl while Miss Finley said, 'I hope you are all well rested and ready to get started back to work. Now we must begin with how we intend to continue. I want to see lots of hard work. No half-measures this term! I want you all wide awake and bushy tailed!

'We have a new girl,' she said, bringing her closer to her. 'This is Lucy-Jane.'

'Hello, Lucy-Jane!' We all smiled up at her.

She lifted her lips, showing snow-white teeth, and flapped her fingers at us, saying, 'Hello!' but didn't make a smile. Her lovely green eyes swept the room, taking us all in one by one. Then she looked away. She didn't look too happy about being here. I love her hair. It's a golden brown colour, cut short and wavy, coming in a V around the front of her ears. And it's brushed to one side. It really suits her. But there's something missing. She's too stand-offish to be really good looking. Yeah, she looks it for an instant but then, no, I wouldn't take to her.

'You can all introduce yourselves later. We must get cracking down to some work. Come along with me, Lucy-Jane. I will get you started on the typing. Open your books, please, the rest of you! No more talking.'

'Ahh! Put out the cat! Take in the dog! Ahh! Yakety yak,' sang Tommy under his breath, drumming his knuckles on the table.

'Tommy Byrne! I will put you out if I don't see your head in a book this minute!'

'Miss Finley heard you,' we all sniggered.

'Jaysus! She has ears like a bat!' he muttered.

I came into the tearoom, seeing people looking around at me, then whispering and moving together, turning their backs on me. Me heart dropped. Gawd! No one must be talking to me! What did I do on someone?

I decided to go over to the fireplace and pulled out me packet of cigarettes, lighting one up, not wanting to go over near the tea table. I turned me back and stared at the white board covering the fireplace. No one would look at me. Then suddenly I heard a shout: 'Surprise!'

Me head flew around. They were holding a box of mixed cream cakes and Esther handed me a cup of tea, then they all started singing. 'HAPPY BIRTHDAY TO YOU! HAPPY BIRTHDAY TO YOU! HAPPY BIRTHDAY, DEAR MARTHA! HAPPY BIRTHDAY TO YOU! THREE CHEERS FOR THE BIRTHDAY GIRL!'

'HIP, HIP!' said Tommy, 'HURRAY!'

'Oh! So that's it!' I said, going from me heart in me stomach to me heart in me mouth with the shock. 'I thought I had done something to annoy you. I really thought no one was going to talk to me over something I did wrong!' I said.

'Ah, Gawd, no! We would never take anything you say to heart! Sure, you and Brenda go at it hammer and tongs! That's how we knew you are seventeen today. The pair of you were arguing like cats and dogs about it, remember? She kept telling you you were in your seventeenth year. You kept going mad saying you were sixteen.'

'But that was ages ago,' I said.

'Yeah, well! We remember these things.'

'Happy birthday, love,' Betty said, wrapping her arms around me and giving me a big hug and a kiss on me cheek. Then everyone gave me a hug.

Tommy said, 'This is your lucky day. I am going to take you for lunch across to the chipper, and spend—' Then he rooted in the pocket of his trousers and lifted out his hand, seeing what was there, saying, 'A WHOLE SIXPENCE my very generous mother gave me this morning to spend all on myself, if you wouldn't be minding!' he said, wrapping his arms around me and giving me a big hug.

'Here! A present. We all clubbed in together and bought you this,' they said, handing me a little parcel wrapped in yellow gift paper tied up with a white ribbon.

I opened it, taking me time, and everyone watched, smiling. 'What is it?' I said, opening it, seeing a box.

'Go on! Don't ask!' said Brenda, hitting me with her elbow. 'Open it! We're all dying to see it!'

I opened the box, taking out a brand-new silver Parker pen and a matching pencil. I caught me breath, knowing they cost an arm and a leg.

'You can use that when you become the managing director's secretary,' said Betty, seeing the tears roll down me cheeks.

I tried not to cry and wiped away me tears and snots quickly with the back of me hand. 'Thanks ever so much!' I whispered, not able to lift me head, knowing I could never tell them what this meant to me, having friends that thought so much about me. They even saved their money and bought me a present.

'You all mean the world to me!' I whispered.

'Ahhh! You mean the world to us!' said Betty, grabbing and hugging me again.

Everyone put their arms around me again one by one, saying quietly, 'Happy birthday!'

'We hope you have the best year of your life,' Esther whispered to me, smiling and patting me, rubbing me back.

This is one of the best days of my life! I thought. I have friends that take me as I am. What more could a body need?

'OK! Quick! Who wants what?' said Betty, lifting up the box with the mixed cream cakes. 'Martha! First choice for the birthday girl.'

I looked in, taking out a cream chocolate éclair. Then everyone dived on the box, but trying not to grab. 'There's one for everyone!' shouted Betty, slapping the hands off the twins, with the two of them trying to grab the one cream hornpipe!

Oh, I love doing this, learning Roman numerals. It makes me feel very educated. Now I will be able to read all them numbers on old tombstones in the churches and the big stone monuments around the City. III is three, IV is four, V is five, VI is six, VII is seven, X is ten. Gawd! This is easy. Doctor Foster went to Gloucester in a shower of rain. He stepped into a puddle, right up to his middle, and never went there again. Ha! I like that. I'm even learning loads of nursery rhymes. That's something most people know. I didn't but now I do! Hey diddle diddle, the cat and the fiddle. The cow jumped over the moon! I got a picture of that. Somehow it reminds me of being a child again. I used to take everything to heart. When someone said, 'Oh! You just let the cat out of the bag,' I would look for the bag, wanting to see the cat jump out.

Me typing is coming along grand. I can now type without looking at the typewriter, just copy from what the book says. Now all I have to do is build up me speed. But I hate the tabulating – having to do sums to work out the bleedin margins! But I'm getting there! When I take me time, I can work it out the right way. What I most certainly won't be doing is bookkeeping! I hate that. No matter how hard I try, I can't master it. I manage to get all the figures right. That's easy! But then I end up putting them all in the wrong place. 'No, no!' Miss Finley says, nearly wanting to lose the rag with me. 'Purchase and balance! You have them in the wrong columns!' Then I get a huge red X splattered right across me lovely pages. She does that with great gusto, using her red pen. I hold me breath, then stare while she walks off leaving me trying to work out how to get it right. Then I have to start all over again.

No! To hell with that! They can do their own books! The only thing I need to worry about is how to count me own money when I make it. Ha! That is something I have never had a problem with. Right! Keep going. Get the speed up! Learn to tabulate! That is important.

25

I looked around seeing all the new faces, thinking how it was nearly a year ago since I started here. Now here I am, nearly at the end of my course, and everyone else has moved on. They are all out in the world working at good jobs. There's only two of the old faces left – Tommy and Lucy-Jane. Soon we will be moving out and joining the workers coming out of the offices in the evening.

'Martha! Have you finished your work?' Miss Finley said, interrupting me thoughts.

I looked up at her, seeing her staring down at me over her glasses, not looking too impressed. She hates us idling.

'Yes! Just about ready, Miss Finley,' I said, getting me head back down to work.

'OK, when you are finished translating the shorthand into longhand, then back to shorthand, I want you to read it for me. Then I am going to dictate a letter to you. I want to see what speed you are up to. Then you may type it out. I will be timing your typing as well!'

'OK, Miss Finley,' I said, giving all me attention now to me work. Jaysus! Get a move on, Martha. I want to get me top speeds!

I pulled out the paper from the typewriter and handed the letter to Miss Finley. I watched her eyes flying up and down the pages and held me breath. She adds on time for mistakes. I don't think I made any, I hope!

'OK! That is fine!' she said, handing me back the paper with one red mark. I forgot to put a capital letter after a full stop. 'You have fifty words a minute on the manual typewriter and eighty words a minute in shorthand.'

'Oh, that is good, isn't it, Miss Finley?' I said, trying to think what some of the others got when they finally left to start working.

'Well, you could get your speeds up in shorthand, you know, if you work a bit harder! Now, come along. I am going to give you some practice on the electric typewriter.'

She went off to the corner of the room and lifted the dust cover off the electric typewriter sitting on a small table. She only hauls that out when we are ready to move on. I don't think I have ever seen it up this close before. Nobody is allowed near it except the masters! The ones who have learned everything there is to know about being a secretary. Yeahhh! Now it's my turn! But I don't think I know that much. Still, she must think I'm ready!

'Now!' she said, stooping down and plugging it in. 'Sit down here and I will show you what to do.'

I sat down with me hands braced over the machine like a conductor ready to conduct an orchestra.

'There's no need for that!' she said, slapping me hands down. 'Now with this machine, you must be very light fingered. It is electric. Let it do the work. Just barely tap,' she said, giving it a light tap to show me.

I watched her put in the paper. Then she put the typed letter I had already done down beside me on the table. 'Now practise!' she said, slapping the paper. 'I want you to type this letter. When you get used to the electric, your typing speeds should improve.'

I landed me fingers on the machine and the bar flew off at such a speed the typewriter nearly slid of the table.

I stared. 'Bloody hell!' I gasped.

'No, no! You did not listen to me, Martha. Tut, tut! You are not supposed to assault it! This is the modern way. Most typewriters in up-to-date offices are now electric. Here we are using the old Underwood. You did have to work hard at them. But now gentle, gentle, is the operative word.'

'OK, Miss Finley!' I said, letting out me breath through me nostrils and sighing. Getting ready to have another go and tap gently. I looked down at me letter and readied me fingers on the keys. Then I was off again, sending the electric typewriter nearly flying through the wall! Miss Finley gave up! She raised her eyes to the ceiling and went off to do something more productive.

I tapped it gently, leaning over and barely breathing. 'Now I have it,' I said to meself. I looked down at me letter and started again, reading the first line, 'Dear Sir'. The machine took off, sending the ribbon flying in all directions, getting itself all snarled up and mashed inside the machine. 'Ah, for the luv a Jaysus!' I muttered. 'No! I'll stick to the old Underwood!' I said to meself, nearly crying with the rage at these bleedin electric things!

I came into the hall, shutting the door behind me, blocking out the heat and the lovely warm golden light of the afternoon sun and breathing in the familiar dust of the old school. Everyone will be getting their summer holidays soon. But I will be starting me first office job. Me heart lifted. Oh, I can't wait to start working. No more studying, and I will be paying me own way.

'Oh! Wait for me, Martha.'

I looked around halfway up the stairs, seeing Tommy rushing up towards me.

'How're ye, Tommy? Jaysus! You're in a hurry. Don't tell me you're dying to get up and start working?' I laughed.

'No chance! Listen, Martha, I wanted to ask you,' he said, dropping his head to the stairs, trying to find the best way of saying something. 'I was wondering, what are you doing tomorrow night?'

'Why?' I said, looking at his pale face turning red and his lovely blue eyes getting hidden behind his long eyelashes because he was flapping them like mad trying to get up the nerve to say something. He has lovely eyelashes, really long. They look like they should be on a girl. Pity we can't swap!

'Would you like to go to the pictures with me tomorrow night?' he suddenly said, saying it all in one breath.

'Ah, sorry, Tommy. Not tomorrow night. I have to stay in and wash me hair. Get ready for the weekend. Then after that Odette and me watch the television. It's the only night of the week we watch it.

Listen! Have you ever seen it, it's called *Laugh-In*. Oh, Gawd! It's hilarious!'

'Yeah, yeah! I watch that too,' he said, nodding his head and laughing.

'The best bit I like,' I said, wanting to get my say in first, 'is when the aul one sits down on the park bench and this dirty aul fella comes shuffling up and sits down beside her. Then he keeps watching her out of the corner of his eye. And when he thinks she's not watching, he keeps shifting himself up bit by bit. Until he's eventually nearly sitting on her lap! Then he sits staring for a minute. And eventually he turns to her and leans in to mutter something into her ear. She pulls her head back quickly and gives him a dirty look. Then swings her handbag, giving him a clout around the snot!' Then I started roaring me head laughing, getting the picture all over again.

'Yeah, yeah, it's hilarious!' he roared, with the two of us breaking our hearts laughing. 'But now wait,' he said. 'My best bit is the dumb blonde, Goldie Hawn. She gets everything wrong and can't string two words together that makes sense when her boss asks her to do something.'

Suddenly we heard Miss Finley's voice. We looked up seeing her leaning over the banisters and shouting down to us, 'Come along up, please! This is not the time to be holding a conference! You have work to do!'

'Yes, Miss Finley,' we said together, making faces and pushing each other up the stairs.

'What about Saturday?' he whispered.

'Can't, have to go somewhere,' I said, thinking about Sister Allie. I have to report in to her every Saturday morning to collect me ten shillings pocket money, then listen to her reading the riot act after she gets her weekly report from the school and the hostel about me bad behaviour. One was over fighting with the kitchen nun's niece, Mary Murphy. She works in the Civil Service and lives in the hostel. Then having her aunt, that mad bleedin nun, chasing me all over the hostel for braining Mary, smashing what was left of me ten-shilling record on her thick bulletproof head. Jaysus! That record was brand new! I had only just bought it for meself. Then that bloody cow came flying over and scratched it. She just tore it out of the record player when Odette and me were dancing to it. She wanted to watch the television and we wanted to dance. So, as we got there first, we ignored her. The bleedin aunt tried to get me thrown out by the scruff of the neck.

But the Reverend Mother was having none of it. She even told me herself that she has a soft spot for me. So not only did she not throw me out but she even gave me the ten bob I had paid for the record, agreeing Mary was definitely in the wrong for losing the head and scratching it in the first place. I showed her the evidence, letting her see the two halves, pointing out where the big scratch was. The mad nun wanted to know what was being done about her poor niece, Mary's, skull? I could have given her brain damage, she complained. I said she already had that. The Reverend Mother told her Mary was a bit of a bully anyway. It would do her no harm to get a little rough and tumble. That did it! The mad nun has been after me ever since. She spends all her time compiling a list of complaints against me as long as her arm. Then gets on the phone to Allie. Sister Allie is sick to her back teeth hearing your woman screaming down the telephone at her.

Yeah, but Jaysus! I won't ever forget the day I had to go in and see her after I got back from me little holiday scutting around England. When I walked into her office, who was sitting down but none other than the doctor himself, the Consultant, Doctor O'Hara! He sat in a chair while Allie stood beside him with her face fixed, looking frozen solid, and her nose pinched like she was definitely getting a bad smell. On the other side of him stood two boys, one about my age and the other about a year younger. I suppose they are his sons. They were wearing navy-blue school blazers, with their lovely head of brown hair cut in a short back and sides look. Very old-fashioned. They stared at me, looking like I was something really interesting, but at the same time at bit shocked. Like they had been told I was definitely on me way down to hell. With all the carry-on of me, I didn't like this one bit. The cheek of Allie bringing the doctor in to sort me out!

'Come along in!' he barked as soon as me head appeared around the door. 'Now! Am I right in hearing you went off without telling one living soul that you went on a mission to get yourself murdered HITCH-HIKING AROUND ENGLAND? What in all that is sane and normal, and—'

'Good!' the nun said, jumping in to help him.

'Good and proper,' he snorted, 'possessed you to do such a thing? I think we need to get her assessed for brain damage!' he said, looking at the nun.

She shook her head up and down like mad, agreeing with him, making it look like she was having a fit.

'There's nothing wrong with my brain!' I roared.

'That's it! Enough out of you. This behaviour has to be nipped in the bud! Sister and I have discussed it. You will get no pocket money for one month!' he snorted, blessing their agreement by bowing his head at Sister Allie, and she bowed back to him. Then the pair of them stared at me, waiting to hear what I would say.

I said nothing, feeling me chest heave up and down with the rage. Then I let fly! 'OK! Stick your money up yer—'

'Aahhh, aaah! No! Don't say it!' he roared, waving his finger at me. 'Believe me, young lady, you won't see a penny more pocket money for the next three months! And further consequences will follow if you don't amend your ways! Well, have you anything to say for yourself?' he said, barking at me.

'No!' I muttered.

'Well, you could try an apology for all the worry you have caused.'

'Sorry . . . I got caught!' I said, making for the door in an awful temper.

'DON'T BANG THAT DOOR SHUT!' he shouted after me.

I grabbed the door, giving it an almighty swing, then caught it before it slammed shut, closing it quietly. Then went on me way, wondering what I was going to do for money for the next month. I wouldn't be able to go out anywhere, that was for sure. I had no bleedin money!

* * *

I came up onto the landing, still lost in me own thoughts, dozing. Suddenly I saw Miss Finley fussing. 'Where is she?' she puffed, turning away suddenly, making for the stairs and bumping into me.

'Sorry!' I said.

'There you are!' she roared. 'What on earth kept you? I called you up here ten minutes ago!'

'Ah, yeah! Sorry about that. I was, eh, fixing me shoe,' I said, looking down at me black patent shoes.

'Come along with me! We have wasted enough time.'

I followed her into her office, wondering what she wants. I hope I'm not in any trouble!

'Now!' she said, closing the door and leaning into me, giving me all her attention. 'Today you are to go down to Grey House Manor. You know where that is?'

'Yes, Miss! I was there once before on a message for you.'

'Yes, good. Now! This afternoon you are going to start on the switchboard. You will need that if you work for a large business. You need all-round experience. So, for the next week you will concentrate on getting your typing speeds up on the electric typewriter. Your shorthand speeds – I will be giving you dictation non-stop! So you better get moving on that over the weekend. I want you to sleep, eat and think shorthand.'

'Oh!' I said, feeling me face falling. There goes bang to me getting out anywhere. 'But I have to go and see Sister Aloysius on Saturday morning! So—'

'So!' she interrupted. 'You can get your exercise and fresh air then. You need that! I wouldn't stand in the way of you getting that. But I want you to get your speeds up! Now do you hear me?'

'Yes, Miss!' I muttered, knowing full well there was no way out of it. She has a knack of knowing when you didn't do what you were supposed to do.

'Now I have some news for you!'

I looked up at her, holding me breath waiting. I could see the glint in her eye. It must be something good.

'Next Friday, tomorrow week, you will be going for a job interview for a junior secretary.'

Me heart nearly stopped with fright and delight!

'A job! Does that mean I will be leaving here? That I'm finished me course?' I said, still holding me breath.

'Yes! That is, of course, if you succeed in getting the job! So make sure you have your best frock and polish your shoes,' she said, looking down at me black patent shoes with all the scratches on them. 'Do you have something better than those?' she said, looking down at me shoes and pointing.

'Well, I have a pair of lovely gold sandals!' I said, getting all excited about what I would wear.

'No! You better polish them up,' she said, looking down at them again, not thinking much of them. 'Now, don't wear make-up! Make sure you are well groomed. Have a nice shine in your hair. No jewellery! You don't want to give the wrong impression. Stand up straight and keep your hands down by your sides. And don't sit down until you are asked. Smile and be polite. Don't speak until they speak first. Just say, "Good afternoon, Mister so-and-so." Politeness and good manners go a long way in getting a good job! Don't be forward. State your skills calmly and politely. Then keep quiet. For goodness' sake don't start telling him your likes and dislikes. Sometimes the less you say the better.

'Now! Have you understood all that? This is good advice, Martha. Listen well! A boss wants someone he can rely on. Not a giddy silly girl who will make life difficult for him. Remember! You are there to do a job. He is paying your wages. You would do well to always remember that! Now, off you go.'

'Oh, thanks, Miss Finley! That is great news altogether!'

'Right! Good girl! Off you go. Hurry! They are expecting you! Don't waste time.'

I was off out the door and down on the street making for Grey House Manor. I flew and skipped along the road not able to believe I was actually going to be working in just over a week! Gawd, I hope I get the job! Course I will. What do they want? I'm as good as any for the job! They must only want someone starting. So that's me!

I rang the doorbell at the manor and looked around while I was waiting. Jaysus! This was some house in its time. Imagine having all these grounds and that big folly over there! I knew what it was. The last and only time I was here before I asked a man working in the grounds. That was to give relief to the poor in the area, he said, during the famine. The lord of the manor would pay men to build it, giving them a shilling a day for their labour. It is called a folly because it is going nowhere and is good for nothing. The pair of us stood looking up at the big stone tower reaching what looked like to me hundreds of feet into the air. It has stone steps up to it and you can look through the gaps that look like windows. But it had steps in only one storey. The rest gets very narrow as it goes up.

'Yes?' a grey-haired woman holding glasses on her nose said, leaning out to look at me.

'I'm from the secretarial school. Martha Long is my name. Miss Finley sent me over. I'm going to be working on the switchboard today. Someone is going to train me.'

'Oh, yes! Come along in.'

We went through a long wide hall with a big staircase going up from the middle. But we passed that and continued down a narrower hall into a huge big room with a very high ceiling. The floorboards are made of oak, with nothing covering them. They looked very dull and old, with all the polish long gone off them. I followed her over to a big switchboard standing against the wall. Our footsteps made a rumbling sound on the floorboards, that seemed to bounce off the walls. The room sounded very hollow, like it was a big old castle, or something that was haunted. Like people had run away and left it empty. Nobody wanted to stay here. I wonder if someone was murdered here, or died?

Yeah, of course they did. Lots of people would have died in this house. The owners and their families for one. But still and all, I wonder if maybe someone hanged themself or something. This house doesn't settle too well with me! There's a bad atmosphere! Like it's waiting to get you! Jaysus! I looked around seeing the big empty size of it. I could see dark corners where the light didn't shine, even though the light was on, hanging from the ceiling. Ah! For the luv a Jaysus! Would you ever stop yer carry on? Yeah! I thought, trying to steady me nerves that for some reason where getting the better of me. It's only me imagination.

'OK! Sit down here like a good girl and I'll show you how to operate the switch,' the woman said, pulling out the chair for me to sit down. 'Now! Put these earphones on your head,' she said, fitting them around me head and fixing them on me ears. When she was satisfied I had them on right, she said, 'OK. Look at the board.'

I looked at a big board with holes where plugs with long red cables plug into. 'Yes!' I said, shaking me head after getting a good look at them.

'OK. All this front row at the bottom are telephone lines. You have ten lines. When one of them rings, you will hear it and a red light will show up. Take one of these lines and plug it into the ringing line. Flick this switch here!' she pointed, showing me switches. 'Flick that on and speak through your earphones. Say "Good afternoon, Grey House Manor. May I help you?" Listen to the name and refer to this list up on the wall beside you. It gives the names and codes. See this here? Well, that corresponds to the board. Flick the switch and put them on hold. Plug in one of these cables to the board and say, "Telephone call for you!" Then flick the switch and they will be connected. Have you got that?'

'Yes, I think so,' I said, going over one by one what she had told me.

'Good girl. I will hang on until you take one call. Then I will let you take over on your own.'

'OK!' I said happily.

We both sat staring at the bottom of the board, waiting for it to ring. Then it lit up and started making a loud ringing noise. I grabbed one of the plugs and put it in the wrong hole in me excitement. 'Hellooo!' I said, hearing nothing.

The woman pulled it out and put it sitting in the right line. Then

I heard a woman's voice. 'Put me through to Tom McSweeney's office, please. Mister Craning on the line for him!'

'One moment, please!' Then I referred to me list and went down the names finding the number, and grabbed another cable and plugged it into the right hole after searching for the number. 'Phone call for you from Mister Craning,' I said, then flicked the switch, leaving them talking to each other.

A thought entered me head that I could ring the lot of them and have them all talking to each other. Me nerves got the better of me with that thought. Jaysus! Don't start getting up to your devilment here! That would be suicide! Yeah! One side of me would love that! But then there's lots of other mad things I could do! Jaysus! Where do I get me madness from?

'OK,' the woman said. 'I will leave you to it.' Then she was gone out the door, leaving me sitting here with me earphones in, staring at the exchange board waiting for it to ring and hoping I wouldn't lose the run of meself and do something stupid! Dear God, help me to be good. It's terrible when I get mad ideas into me head! Just let me calm down, God, and not want to have them all shouting to each other because I plugged them all in together!

Then I remembered the Reverend Mother one day, taking me out for an outing. We went up to Jervis Street Hospital to visit her poor niece. When we got there, the young one – she was at the university, the Reverend Mother was explaining to me, as we both arrived in the ward – had her two legs strapped up in the air.

The Reverend Mother was nearly in tears when she was telling me the whole sorry story. Her sister, the young one's mother, got a tyre puncture on her car. And when the young one stepped out of the car, she was thrown straight into the air! I looked at the young one staring at the two of us talking about her as if she wasn't there. She had such a tragic look on her face that suddenly – whatever came over me – I burst me heart laughing! I nearly got sick at the shame of it but the more I looked at the young one and then at the nun with her eyes looking so sad, the more I laughed. I got hysterical and had to run out of the ward. Yeah, I think that must be an affliction I have. It's not that I'm laughing at people, but something just gives inside of me! Like now! Wanting to do something for the devilment of it! Right! It's time to act me age! No more nonsense! I'm a woman now!

26

I checked me hair in the bathroom mirror, then stood up straight to make sure me frock was hanging right, then looked down to examine me black patent shoes. Yeah, the half bottle of Ponds cold cream for your face did wonders for the shine on me shoes. I kept at them, polishing and putting more cream on until they looked like glass. Me frock is lovely and crisp, and the white linen collar is nearly blue it's that white. I bought meself a tin of spray starch and sprayed it on when I was ironing the frock. It was well worth the money. It came up looking like nearly new again. Right! Time to go!

I ran back up to my room. Have I got everything? I thought, looking around at me bed. Do I need to bring a notebook for dictation? No, that's it! Let them supply one if they ask. I picked up me shoulder bag and took a deep breath, thinking of all the things the teacher warned me about. Then I checked to see I had the address. I better say a little prayer. Dear God, please grant that I get the job! I will definitely do me best in all things that I do from now on. With your help, God! Then I took off down the stairs and out the door, heading for me job interview.

'Hold the door for me!'

I looked back, seeing Odette struggling out with two huge suitcases.

'Where are you off to?' I said, eyeing the big heavy-looking suitcases.

'Home,' she puffed, picking them up, getting weighed down with the weight of them, trying to make it down the stone steps without breaking her neck.

'Are you leaving?' I roared, getting a fright with the sudden thought of losing me friend.

'Don't be daft. I'm just going home for the weekend.'

'So what's all the suitcases for?'

'Ah, them! That's my dirty washing. I have every stitch I own jammed into those suitcases. Except for what I'm wearing on my back. This lot will keep the mother happy and occupied for the weekend doing her "I'm a slave! Everyone takes me for granted! I'm only a mother! Don't mind me! You all carry on enjoying yourself! I'll just crawl over here into this little corner I made for myself, and lie down and die quietly, without anyone even noticing!" Jesus! My mother missed her calling. She would have won Oscars for her performances.

'Anyway! All she has to do is sort it out! She will leave the washing and ironing of it to the cleaner when she gets in on Monday morning. So, I'll hump this lot all the way home, leave it with her, then pick up a fresh batch of clothes all ready, washed, pressed and waiting for me. Just one case for that! The other one is for provisions. I'll get that stuffed with everything she has in the larder. Lumps of cheese, the hard stuff, I love that. A big tin of biscuits! Have you a preference?'

Before I could get a word out, she said, 'I like the mixed Jacob ones! Anyway, we won't go hungry. We'll have something lovely for our tea on Monday night when I get in! The father will make sure I want for nothing anyway! He always insists I'm looking pale and wan. Fading away from starvation. Naturally I play it to the hilt. Damning the nuns for not feeding me! I need a few more quid on top of my allowance,' she said, looking worried thinking about it.

'So I better sprinkle the talcum powder liberally on my face just before he picks me up from the station. I want the consumptive look! That should make him dig deep into the old wallet!'

'Jaysus! You're desperate, Odette!' I laughed, really getting enjoyment out of her.

'But, sure, I can't help it! I'm spoilt rotten! What else could you expect?' she said, snorting at me with her eyes bulging out of her head. 'But seriously, Martha! Jaysus! Money is running through my hands like water these days! I don't know where it's going,' she moaned, raising her big blue eyes and shaking her head, staring into me face.

'Well, you are always out on the tear, Odette! Eating in cafés, if you wouldn't be minding!'

'Look who is talking!' she roared, pointing her finger at me. 'Who was it that spent ten bob on that one single bloody record?'

'Ah, but I got me money back from the Reverend Mother!'

'Oh, Jesus! Don't mention her. I barely scraped past her the other night! She had the door locked just as I came steaming up the steps! I could hear her jangling off with the keys, locking me out for the night! I nearly took the door off the hinges. I lunged at it, using my body as a battering ram, banging and roaring my head! I sounded pitiful,' she said, making her eyes go sad, feeling the terrible pain of that fright all over again.

I roared laughing at the faces she was making. 'Yeah? What did she say when she let you in?'

'Oh, I told her I was stuck in the university library. They locked me in. I was hidden in an alcove needing absolute peace and quiet for my studies, I droned on. Me believing every word I told her was the truth, the whole truth and nothing but the truth. Nobody noticed me when it came to locking-up time, I told her solemnly.'

'Did she believe you?' I said, listening and taking it in.

'No! She said I was very imaginative! So I got away with that one! It was so outrageous she had to laugh!' Odette screamed, laughing her head off.

'Right!' I said. 'Listen! I'm off now for me job interview!'

'Oh, darling! Best of luck! All the luck in the world!' she said, putting her hand on me face and stroking it. Then she grabbed me in a tight hug!

'Mind me starched white collar!' I roared, worrying she might put dirty smudges on it.

'You'll have no problem!' she laughed, stepping back to get a look at me and rubbing me collar in case she stained it, but only making it worse. 'They'll snap you up! Take it as a given! So relax, just go and have a chat and take it for granted. Of course they will offer you the job!'

'Do you really think so, Odette?' I said, not sure what to expect. I had never been inside an office before, looking for a job.

'Yeah! Go on! Get going. Don't be late. I better get moving, too, if I want to catch this train,' she said, stooping down to pick up the suitcases.

'OK! Have a lovely weekend, Odette. And thanks for the advice.' Then I rushed over and gave her another hug, grabbing her neck while she tried to hang on to her suitcases.

'Jaysus! Mind the neck! I don't want to drop dead from strangulation. Not until Father's around anyway! He might even drive me back to Dublin. Jesus! These suitcases are heavy! Bye! I'm off!' Then she was gone, struggling down the road to catch the bus and get over to the train station. I stood waving and watching her. Gawd! She is the best friend I ever had. I really am so happy. What a great life I'm having! Then I turned around and headed off to go for me first job interview as a junior secretary.

Ah, this is the place! It's not too far at all from the hostel! I looked up at the big old stone archway over the lane, seeing a sign saying 'BRAGGS & SON. Suppliers. Co. Ltd'. Then I looked down the lane, seeing a van getting loaded up with stuff. Right! Here we go. I walked down the lane, looking to me right in at a big old building. It had stone arches over the high wide doors. It looked to me like it was a stables at some time. It was stacked high with boxes, and people were going in and out with papers in their hands, looking very busy. Two men were loading the boxes into the back of the lorry.

Me eyes peeled around the end of the lane, seeing it blocked by a big high stone wall, black from age, with bits of moss growing out of it. A two-storey house that looked like it had well seen its day and was just about ready to collapse took up the whole left side of the lane. The window on the ground floor was held open with an empty milk bottle. The front door was wide open. Jaysus! They sure spare the money when it comes to spending anything on this place, I thought, staring at it with me mouth open, feeling very disappointed it was not something like you get in Fitzwilliam Square. Ah, well, never mind. You have to start somewhere!

I walked over making for the door and I could hear voices through the open window. Suddenly a girl appeared out the door. 'Hello! Are you looking for someone?' a young one with long fair hair down to her shoulders and bright blue eyes asked me, looking all excited at who I might be. She looked about my age, seventeen. Another one came out behind her. She looked about in her twenties.

'Who is it, Lucy?' said the black-haired older woman, with little beady eyes and brown teeth. She was nearly my height, just about an inch taller. 'Yes! Do you want something?' she said in a common voice, trying to be posh.

I didn't like the look of her. There was something very sly about her and she was pushy. I straightened me shoulders and looked down me nose, saying, 'I have an appointment with Mister Braggs. Where will I find him?'

'Which one? There's two! Mister Braggs Junior is in his sixties, and his daddy, Mister Braggs Senior, is well in his eighties,' the older one said, sniggering to the younger one.

'The boss!' I said, seeing them laughing at me.

'Upstairs!' the older one pointed, only standing back a little to look down at me from head to toe, giving me a dirty look like she was superior.

'Thank you!' I said, squeezing past her and making for the rickety stairs. I don't think them two and me are going to be best pals, I thought, feeling even more disappointed.

I stood on an old landing with bare floorboards that someone had decided to paint around the edges. It must have been some time in the last hundred years because the paint only showed a little lighter than the black floorboards. There's two doors. I looked at the one on the right, then the one on the left. I knocked on the right.

'Come in!' an old man's voice croaked.

I turned the roundy black doorknob that was probably brass

sometime in its life. I pushed in the door and closed it quietly behind me, looking around at a big old room with a low ceiling that only left me with about a foot over me head. It was nearly touching the bare floorboards, with a faded old threadbare rug thrown in the middle of the floor. Two desks sat in a corner, one each end of the room. Me eyes lit on a tall skinny man with a white dying-looking face and a few bits of white fluffy hair. He came rushing himself over to me, smiling.

I watched as the hair blew around his head, brushing against the ceiling. He came towards me, saying, 'Come and sit down here!' in a high squeaky voice, sounding just like a woman. He waved me into a big old hard-back chair, with bars that wrapped around you when you sat into it. I sat down in front of an old man sitting behind a big leather-top desk. He watched me every move I made, taking me in with his sharp grey eyes under big bushy eyebrows that sat under a mop of thick white hair. We stared at each other as the son rushed around the place, fussing and getting bits and pieces together for our meeting. Then he went running down to the end of the room to grab a seat for himself and hike it back up, planting it down beside the daddy. Then he dropped his hands in fists, resting them on his lap, and heaved his shoulders, giving a big sigh. And smiled, waiting for the old man to begin.

I lifted me shoulders quietly, taking in a deep breath slowly, not letting him see that, and waited.

'OK!' he said, holding a letter out in front of him. 'Martha! Martha Long!' He dropped his head, leaning a bit over to me.

'Yes, Mister Braggs,' I smiled. 'That is my name.'

'Good! Seventeen! Is that right?'

'Yes. Sir!'

'This is your first job, Martha?'

'Yes, Mister Braggs. I'm just starting now as a junior secretary.'

'What are your speeds?'

'Sixty on an electric typewriter,' I said. Well, I thought, they will be when I get to master that electric thing!

'How is your shorthand? What speed do you have?'

'Eighty words per minute at the moment, sir. But I will build that up.'

'Good!' he said, shaking his head, thinking. 'George! Tell Miss Benson to come in to me. Meanwhile, give the girl a notepad.'

George leapt up and ran to a big old press standing against the wall near the window that looked out onto the yard. 'Here we are,' he said, handing me a brand-new shorthand notebook with a new yellow pencil.

'Thank you,' I said, smiling up at him. 'But it is OK, I don't need that,' I said, pointing to the pencil.

'Oh! You have your own,' he muttered, turning away and putting it back in its place in the drawer.

'I want you to take a letter, Martha. Then go into my secretary's office and type it up for me.'

'Yes, certainly, Mister Braggs,' I said, pulling the new Parker pen out of its box in me shoulder bag.

He looked at me pen and raised his eyebrows, letting his reddish-blue lips move in a smile.

'Dear sirs, with regard to your letter of the tenth inst. It is most unfortunate we cannot fulfil your order, due to a delay of shipping stranded at sea. We regret this most sincerely, blah blah! Got that?' he said, looking at me waiting with me hand paused in the air just in case he had something else he wanted to say.

'Yes, sir!'

'Good! Miss Benson, would you take this young girl into your office and let her type out a letter for me,' he said to a small thin woman coming in the door wearing a long, heavy navy-blue skirt with a white blouse embroidered on the front. She had a cameo brooch pinned to the top button of her blouse and wore black lace-up high heels. Gawd! They are really, really very old fashioned, I thought, looking down at them. Her hair was stone grey and tied up in a bun. She looked very frail, with her neck hanging down and her head looking sideways at us. But she had a very gentle way about her. She kept looking from me to the old man, then back to me, keeping a lovely smile on her face.

'Yes, of course, Mister Braggs!' she breathed, lifting her head around to me and smiling, looking at me with the most lovely pair of blue eyes. I haven't seen anything like them for many a long time. Even though they were faded now, you could still see she had been a real beauty in her time.

'Come along with me, dear. I will take you to my office. You can use the typewriter there,' she said, turning to make out the door.

I followed her into the room opposite. This office was a bit smaller. Two matching long, narrow mahogany filing cabinets with brass handles stood against the far end wall, with the same window on the left, looking out to the yard.

'Come over here, dear,' she said quietly. 'You can sit down here and use this one.' She lifted the cover of an old typewriter. I stared at it. 'You have used this before?' she said, wondering why I was staring.

'It's the same one I learned to type on!' I said, smiling at it.

'Yes! The old Underwood. I started on one of these myself!' she laughed. 'Goodness! That's not today or yesterday!' she smiled, shaking her head at remembering so many years now gone past.

'Yeah, I like the old Underwood,' I said. 'We're on first-name terms! I call mine back at the school "Dilly"!'

'Really?' she laughed.

'Yeah, because it's so slow it dilly dallies! Takes its time about getting the keys moving.'

'Oh, you are a scream!' she said, dropping her hand gently on me arm.

'Right! I better get moving,' I said, pulling out a chair and sitting at the desk, dragging the typewriter closer to the edge. Then I put down me notebook and read over me shorthand. OK! Ready!

I slipped in the paper and lined it up, wanting to make sure to get nice margins, then started blasting away. 'Finished!' I said, whipping it out of the machine and reading back what I typed.

Miss Benson leaned over me shoulder to get a look, reading it. I waited.

'Not one mistake in the typing!' she said, taking in a deep breath.

'You are well trained!' she said, putting her hand on me shoulder and resting it there.

'Thanks, Miss Benson,' I said, standing up and grabbing me bag.

'Take it in to him,' she said. 'Good luck! I'm sure he will be well pleased.'

'I hope so!' I laughed.

Me heart was hammering in me chest as I knocked on the door, waiting for him to call me in.

'Enter!' he said.

'Here you are, Mister Braggs. I have finished.'

He took it out of me hand, saying, 'Take a seat.'

I watched his eyes flying up and down the page, holding a pair of glasses with only a handle – the kind that you don't wear on your face. 'Hmm!' he said, sighing and putting down the letter. Then he sat back in his chair and him and the son looked at each other. 'Why do you want to work here?' he suddenly said.

Me heart flew, getting caught unawares! 'Well,' I said, thinking. 'Because you are looking for a junior secretary. I can see, straight away, I would learn a lot from this firm. I would expect to start at the bottom. There are people here with more experience than me. I could learn from them. Because, you see, I am very anxious to learn as much as I can. I want, someday, to be your right-arm man! So much so that you know when you are not here the business will tick away because I know what I'm doing. I will by then have learned all there is to know about this firm!'

I saw the old man's eyes light up, then look at his son and wink. The pair of them nodded to each other, bowing their heads together at the same time. Then the old man leaned across the desk, putting out his hand, and stood up saying, 'Welcome to Braggs & Son. You have the job! We are one of if not the oldest established firms in the business. We have been going for one hundred and fifty years!'

I stood up smiling, saying, 'Oh, thank you very much, Mister Braggs Senior, and you!' I said, nodding over to the son. 'I won't let you down.'

'No! I don't think you will!' the old man said. 'I think with that attitude of yours you will go far. Yes! I believe you will! Start on Monday morning. Nine a.m. sharp. The hours are from nine to half five. Your starting wage will be four pounds a week. You'll get a raise when you get more experience, start to move up the ladder. Now! Can you use a switchboard?'

'Yes, Mister Braggs.'

'Good! Start on that! Goodbye now!'

'Goodbye!' I said, with me face plastered in a smile. 'Thank you!' I said to the son as he held the door open to let me out.

He smiled and said quietly, 'Goodbye', then shut the door behind me.

I floated down the stairs feeling light as air. I got the job!

The two girls came flying out of the office downstairs. 'Have you come about a job?' the young one said, with her blue eyes dancing in her head. The older one stood behind her, leaning forward holding her breath, waiting to hear.

'Yeah!' I said, looking up and down at the two of them.

'Did you get it?' the older one said.

'Yes! I got the job!'

'WHAT?' she roared, then looked at the young one with the pair of them going into shock. Their mouths were locked open and their eyeballs sprung out on stalks!

'But that means—' said the young one.

'Yeah! Tricia didn't get it! She was waiting to hear. So now we know!' moaned the older one, dropping her mouth, letting her nose lengthen.

'Oh, well! Hard cheese,' sighed the young one, wriggling her shoulders and looking at me.

'So! When are you starting? Monday, I suppose,' she sighed.

'Yes! Bye! See you then.'

'Not if I see you first!' the older one mumbled.

'Cows!' I muttered under me breath. I knew that big one was trouble! Who cares? Yipppppee! I got the job.

A girl came out of the warehouse, and stopped. 'Hello!' she said, holding a batch of papers in her hand and making for the office.

'Hello! Do you work here?' I said.

'Yes! Why? Are you getting the junior's job?'

'Yeah!' I said, smiling all over me face.

'Oh, great! My name is Nina. What's yours?'

'Martha.'

'Hello, Martha,' she said, shaking me hand.

'Are you over in the office too?' I said.

'God, no! Work with those two hags?' she said, waving the papers in the direction of the office. 'Never! I look after the deliveries and the factory end.'

'Them two girls don't seem friendly,' I said, looking into her pale face with the freckles and the short curly ginger hair. She is well built and she has a lovely figure, I thought, letting me eyes take her in. Her chest stuck out in two big points, and her legs were bare and lovely and long, and they had a nice shape. She was wearing brown leather Roman sandals, with the leather straps going up around her legs. She has on a lovely miniskirt with brown and white and purple colours running through it, and a light orangey-red shirt on top. I stared at the lovely gold studs in her ears, thinking she is really good looking.

'Take no notice of Lucy and Carmel,' she said, twisting her face in a smile, looking over at the window, seeing the two of them staring out at us with their heads pressed together. 'They are a pair of eejits. Especially Carmel. She's loud and pushy. That one has a chip on her shoulder. She thinks everyone is out to get her, so she gets them first. Lucy is her little echo! She parrots everything Carmel says.' Then she said, staring into me face, 'Why? Did they say something to you?'

'No! I was just wondering. It's just they said something about one of their friends or something. They were hoping she was going to get the job. '

'Who? Oh, that must be Carmel's cousin. She was hoping to get her in here but there's no chance of that! Mister Braggs is not stupid! One Carmel is enough for this place. She's common as muck.

That one goes around thinking she's something she's not. God help you having to listen to those two! Carmel never stops bragging! I wouldn't mind but she has nothing to brag about! Anyway, better get back to work. I wouldn't put it past those two to run up and tell Mister Braggs I'm time-wasting,' she laughed. 'When are you starting here?'

'Monday,' I said happily.

'Great! I will see you then. Bye!'

'Goodbye!' I said, rushing off up the lane, dying to put distance between them two and meself, then enjoy the thought of me getting a good job at last.

Suddenly me heart started flying, when it hit me – I'm now going up in the world! I'm going to be working as a secretary! I took off skipping down the road, doing an Irish jig, dancing sideways with me hands on me hips. First me left side, then twirling to me right. A man coming towards me carrying a big brown leather briefcase tried to step around me. 'Hello there! Isn't it a lovely day to be alive?' I shouted, grinning up at him.

He snorted, laughing back at me, then moved around me, still watching me with a big laugh on his face. He's lovely looking, I thought to meself, with the big bluey-grey eyes and the lovely dark hair all slicked back with hair oil. He was wearing a lovely suit. Probably married! I thought, giving him a big grin, flapping me fingers at him in a wave. He nodded his head at me and winked, waving back at me, then turned and went on his way, stopping to look back at me again. We both laughed, then took off, going about our business.

'Oh! I polished and I polished and I polished that brass! Now I AM THE ADMIRAL OF THE QUEEN'S NAVY!' I roared, flying down the road. I didn't know any of the words of the song but that didn't stop me singing me head off, thinking I'm going to be like that young fella who worked his way all up through the navy, right to the top. When he only started as a little cabin boy! Yep! Outa the way, world! Gimme room! Here I come! I'm on top a the world, Ma! It's lovely an airy!

I turned off Baggot Street, hearing shouting and roaring. It sounded like a crowd chanting. When I hit on Fitzwilliam Square, a crowd of protesters were marching along the road humping posters in the air, waving and chanting.

'Down with fascists!' one lot shouted.

A gaggle of women with Afro hairstyles blowing about three feet into the air shouted, 'Freedom for women! We want our rights! Allow contraceptives! Equal pay for women!'

'Down with fascists!' screamed the students.

'More pay for the working man!' screamed a shower of aul fellas. With the lot of them all taking it in turns to get their bit in!

Jaysus! The bleedin protesters are at it again. 'Ger outa me way, yeh big hairy eejit! Have youse nothin better to be doin?' shouted an old woman, slapping a fella with her shopping bag when he blocked her way on the footpath. He was a student wearing a big hairy jacket with no sleeves and tight purple bell bottoms that flared out at the end. His hair was massive! It looked like a big curly bush, and he wore a pair of red-tinted sunglasses, trying to make himself look like an American hippie from San Francisco, where all the flower-power people come from. That lot are always talking about tripping out on LSD drugs and losing your mind. Flying out windows without a parachute and getting themselves killed stone dead, splattered to mash on the ground.

Them Beatles fellas, that music band, started all that! With their long hair and their 'guru'! He's supposed to be a wise man. Or whatever they call that old Indian fella that's robbing them blind. Wise man, me arse! He's wise all right! Taking all their money! Now everyone is on the move to India, wanting to meet the Beatles' guru!

'Make love not war! Free love!' everyone is now shouting, copying them Beatle fellas. That dirty-looking hairy Indian fella must have told them that. Free, me arse! There's always a price to pay! Hippies, me arse! Them students don't know they're born! I tried being a hippie for a day, walking around with flowers in me hair. Sure, they only talk a load a rubbish! 'Down with the middle classes! Out with money! Everyone should have the same!' Fucking eejits! No one's the same. Some people spend money faster than they can breathe! They drink the money! Throw it away! Equal? Maybe if they said we should look after each other – take care of the old and ailing and the mothers with young children. Or that we should be all treated the same. But what in the name a Jaysus are the students talking about? Throw out the establishment? Down with everyone? Gobshites!

27

I arrived in ahead of everyone else. Wanting to get here early. The front door was open and I stepped into the hall and pushed open the door on the right. I walked into a little office with the window on the right, where they have to use an empty milk bottle pushed under it to keep it open. I looked around, seeing two desks – one at the far wall, beside a door leading out into a passage; the other desk was stuck just inside the door, making it a squeeze to get into the room. Another desk stood against a wall beside the window. A small version of the telephone switchboard was planted above that, hanging on the wall.

Ah! This must be the switchboard I'm going to be working at. A big megaphone with a switch next to it stood on the desk beside the switchboard. That must be for calling people, I thought, thinking I might get to have me voice blasting all over the place when I need to call someone!

I sat down on me chair to wait. I could hear footsteps on the ceiling overhead in the hallway. That must be the Mister Braggs! They probably get in early every morning to open up the business. Gawd, this room is very cramped, I thought, looking around at the typewriters sitting on the other desks. They're electric, very modern. They must do typing as well.

The sun suddenly beamed down and shone in the window. Jaysus! There's no air in this place. I looked at the window, seeing the empty milk bottle. Right! Use that to keep the window open. I lifted the window, trying to keep it open with me shoulder, and balanced the bottle on the frame. It started to slip. Jaysus! It's going to land out the window and smash on the ground. I grabbed it just in time, stopping it slipping, then got it balanced. OK! I let go, seeing it hold. The lovely fresh air came pouring in through the gap. That's better.

Suddenly I heard voices coming down the lane, and the sound of laughing. Two girls appeared and one of them was Nina. I rushed around and out the door. 'Hello, Nina! Morning to you!' I said, waving from the door and smiling.

Nina smiled and came rushing over to me. The other girl looked over at me and smiled, giving the two of us a wave, and disappeared into the warehouse. 'How are you? So, are you all ready for your first day?' she said, smiling and looking at me from head to toe. 'I love your skirt and blouse! Those sandals are lovely! You look great!' she said, admiring me good white skirt and shirt that was me best outfit!

'Yeah! I wanted to look me best on the first day,' I said, looking at her lovely Mary Quant frock with all the different colours of the rainbow. It was about ten inches above her knees, showing off her legs. 'That frock is gorgeous on you, Nina. It really shows off your figure,' I said, standing back to admire her. 'It makes you look very feminine – all woman, as they say.'

'Will you stop? If you were a fella, I would think you were after a date with me!' she said, laughing and giving me a dig with her elbow.

I roared laughing. 'Well! Do you have a boyfriend?'

'No!' she said. 'Do you?'

'No!'

'A pair of spinsters!' she said, dropping her face, then laughing.

'Where do you go dancing, Nina? Do you ever go dancing?'

'Don't have time – or the money,' she said.

'Oh! Why is that, Nina?'

She took in a deep breath. 'I have to get home, Martha. Me mammy is not well. She's depending on my little sister, Maureen, to look after her until I get in. She's in a wheelchair,' Nina said, dragging the dust with her foot, staring at the ground. 'She got sick after me little sister was born. They're all depending on me. I'm the only breadwinner. So! Now you know!' she said, looking straight into me eyes to see how I was taking that.

I could see a defiant look in her stare, daring me to look away, thinking she's not as good as the rest of us because they have hardship! They're not well off.

'Jaysus! I think it's great the way you're all managing!' I said. 'Your little sister must be very good. Do you know what, Nina?' I said, lowering me voice, not wanting to let the wrong thing come out of me mouth and not say what I mean. 'I think when you have your mammy and your little sister, that's all that matters! It's great the way you all look after each other!'

'Yeah, that's what I keep telling myself,' she said, shaking her head.

We heard voices coming down the lane. 'Oh! Trouble!' she snorted. 'I can hear the hags coming! Watch yourself with them, Martha. Carmel can be one nasty bitch. Give her no information that you should keep to yourself. She'll only twist it against you!'

'Yeah, don't worry, Nina. I'm well on to that one! I read that in her straight away!'

'OK, I better get into work or I'll be told to collect my cards,' she laughed, turning to head off into the warehouse. 'I'll see you sometime during the break. Come over to me!' she said, talking back over her shoulder, then disappeared into the dark of the warehouse.

I rushed back in and sat down at me switchboard, waiting for it to ring. I didn't have to wear earplugs. This one had a telephone to speak through.

'Oh! The new girl is here!' Lucy said, looking at me with her eyes wide and a grin on her face, talking to Carmel.

I turned around in me chair to look at the two of them with a smile on me face. 'Morning, Carmel, Lucy,' I said, looking from one to the next.

'How do you know my name?' Carmel snorted, with her mouth hanging open and an accusing look in her eyes, narrowing them like I had just robbed all her money.

'Sorry! I should have told the boss, Mister Braggs Senior, not to tell me your name,' I said, keeping a smile on me face.

'Huh! Did he mention me?' Lucy said, hoping he did.

'Yeah, he said I would be working with two lovely girls!'

'Did he?' Lucy said, whipping her head to Carmel. The big one cocked her eye, trying to read me! I kept me face straight!

'Yes! He said he had a fine staff working here, especially the two girls working down in the office. Carmel is very efficient!'

She lifted her chin, moving her face, and slid her eyes on the typewriter, lifting off the cover and looking at it like she never saw it before. 'Well! This office wouldn't run without me!' she said. 'I mean how can you do anything if you don't have the requisitions typed up?'

'And me!' roared Lucy. 'I do the same work as you, Carmel!'

'Yes, I know you do. But I'm head office girl! I'm the one in charge here!' she said, giving her chest a thump with her fist.

Lucy wasn't too happy about that. She shrugged her body and wriggled her head, making it look like she was dancing. 'Well, if you say so!' she snorted, not at all happy.

'So, what age are you?' Lucy said, taking the cover off her machine and looking at me, leaning on it with her hands in her face.

'Seventeen. What age are you?'

'Seventeen as well! Oh! We're the same age!' Then her face collapsed, then lit up again with an idea. 'That means I'm no longer the junior! You are! So you have to make the tea for them upstairs!'

'OK!' I said.

'Yippee!' she said, throwing her hands in a fist in the air.

Then it hit me! 'I'm a junior secretary! What are you, Lucy?'

'Well, I'm the same,' she said, after thinking about it.

'What speeds do you have in shorthand?' I said.

She wriggled her head and started shoving paper into her machine. 'I do Dictaphone. You don't need shorthand any more,' she said, lifting her nose in the air.

'Ah, so you didn't do shorthand,' I said. 'So, with all due respects,'

I said, imitating Miss Finley, 'that means my status is higher than yours, Lucy! You make the tea!'

'You're not even typing!' she roared. 'You're only sitting there at the switchboard!'

'Since when was that a secretary? I am a secretary!' I said quietly, lifting up me nose and picking up the phone to make sure it had a whirring sound. Wishing it would ring so I could look important!

'Girls, stop fighting!' Carmel said, leaping up and rushing out the back door. 'I'm going to have a word with Jimmy about Friday's last two requisitions.'

The telephone rang! I tore up the receiver and dug in the plug, saying in my best voice, 'Gud oftar noon! Eh, I mean . . . Gud mor nink! Braggs and Son! Mey I help phew?'

'Yes! Put me on to Junior, please. Mister O'Keefe calling.'

'One moment, please.' I looked up the son's number, seeing which line was his, then plugged it in, putting the caller on hold so he couldn't hear me. 'Mister Braggs! Mister O'Keefe wishes to speak to you.'

'Good! Put him on, please.'

I flicked the switch, saying, 'Putting you through now to Mister Braggs Junior!' Then connected the pair of them and hung up, putting the phone down, and examined me nails.

'Huh! You would think you were working for the American president the way you talk on that phone!' Lucy snorted at me.

'Well, I might be one day, Lucy! You never know! Reach for the moon and you'll hit the stars! That's what I believe!'

'Tch! Huh! I have no idea what rubbish you are talking!' she snapped. 'I'm getting down to do my work. This is very important! Without this getting done, nothing can move! So don't talk to me again. I'm very busy!' she snorted, stabbing at the keys on the machine, making it fly. 'Oh! Rotten egg!' she snorted, staring and leaning into her machine. 'Now you have made me make a mistake!'

I ignored her and picked up me phone again, wondering if it might be ringing but I'm just not hearing it.

Carmel came flying back in and shoved a pile of papers on Lucy's desk and another pile on her own. Then the two of them started banging away, with the two machines clacking in me ear. But it was a good sound. It meant they were busy and would leave me alone.

The phone rang. 'Peterson's here! I want to talk to Junior!'

'One moment, please.' I plugged in his extension number. It rang and rang but nobody answered.

'What do I do, Carmel? Mister Braggs Junior is not in his office.'

'Use the intercom – press the button and lift the speaker. Put it to your mouth and tell him over the air.'

Me heart lifted. First I put Peterson's on hold, then pressed the button and lifted the speaker. I could hear airwaves, like sparks and crackles and air! 'Will Mister Braggs Junior please come to the telephone. Telephone call, please, for Mister Braggs Junior!' I said, then switched off the phone, feeling very important. I sounded just like the speaker in Roches Stores. They have that going all the time. You hear the lovely voice of a woman calling all the managers and everyone working there. I always wanted to do that – get me voice blasted out on the air! Then you could tell everyone, 'Well, you know the person's voice who calls people over the intercom in Roches Stores? Well, that's me!'

Men kept putting their head in the back door and handing papers to Carmel, then flying off again. 'Get these out, Lucy,' Carmel said, lifting her head when she finished typing a batch of papers.

'Can't,' Lucy said. 'Got to finish these last few.'

'Here, Martha. Take these out to Jimmy out in the factory. He's the foreman. You'll find him in his office.'

I stood up. 'Where's that, Carmel?'

'Out through the hall and the door at the end.'

'OK!' I took the papers and went off out the door and down the passage behind the stairs and pushed in a heavy door.

The noise that hit me made me ears go deaf for a minute. Machines were flying, sending stuff rattling down a black rubber machine. Girls grabbed at them, wearing white mesh hats on their head and brown overall coats. They stacked the little packages into big cardboard boxes. Hands flew as they tried to keep up with the machine. Music was blaring out of a radio wired up to an intercom. The girls talked to each other and some sang along with the music as their hands kept busy and their heads moved from side to side, keeping up with their hands. They all stood next to each other against long wooden tables. There were rows and rows of tables, all lined up behind each other from one end of the factory to the other. I watched them as I made me way, heading over to a glass box office sitting high up over the factory. How do they keep that up? I wondered. Managing to keep their concentration while all the time watching, grabbing, packing, talking and singing all at the same time. Managing to keep that up hour after hour, day after day. I suppose you get used to it, I thought, looking up at the glass office, seeing the foreman in his brown overall coat keeping his head bent, writing. Every now and then he lifted his head to look around the factory, wanting to make sure everyone was working and things were going OK.

I walked up the stairs, feeling them shaking under me, and then I was swinging out over thin air. If the banister went, I thought, getting me heart in me mouth, I would go sailing out into fresh air, then land. I looked down, seeing nothing underneath me but miles of thin air stretching all the way down to a concrete ground. I could feel me legs shaking under me, afraid to even hold on to the banister rail in case it gave way. Me eyes were peeling on the stairs under me, seeing gaps on the stairs where I might slip through. I looked over at the hundreds of pairs of eyes looking up at me. Some of them were watching with their mouths open. They had a laugh on their face, knowing I was afraid of me life.

NO! I'm turning back. I turned around, wanting to make me way back down, but couldn't move me legs. I could feel a scream coming up through me belly and getting ready to erupt. No! Can't do that! They will all think I'm a wet nelly! Good for nothing. I took in me breath, feeling meself shaking, and turned around again slowly, then got me foot on the next rung, deciding if me time has come, then, yeah, I would fall and break me neck. So that is that!

I got me next foot up and kept going, getting a bit better with that thought! Nothing on earth will save me if me time is up! Keep going. I got onto the platform and opened the glass door into the office. 'Here you are, Mister Jimmy!' I said, putting the papers down, seeing them rattle with me hands shaking like mad.

'Are ye all right! You're white as a ghost! What happened? Did them stairs get to ye?' he said, standing up and putting me sitting down in a chair.

'Yeah! I'm afraid of me life of heights!' I said. 'I used to keep dreaming I was falling outa the bed when I was a baby!' I babbled. 'Every time I would wake up just before I hit the ground. It always frightened the life outa me!' I puffed, still getting that feeling now that it all came back to me.

'Ah, ye poor thing!' he said, half smiling and half looking worried. 'Somebody must have dropped ye when ye were born!' he said, laughing, trying to get me to laugh.

'Yeah, ha!' I said, trying to let him think I was OK now. 'Eh, how will I get back down?' I said, feeling me heart sitting in me mouth with that sudden thought.

'Well, I could call the fire brigade,' he said, lifting the telephone.

'No! Don't do that!' I shouted.

'Only kidding you!' he laughed. 'Here! Have a biscuit! The sugar will do ye good! It's great for an aul shock!' he said, holding a half packet of Jacob's custard creams out to me.

I dipped me hand in and helped meself to one.

'Take another one! Have two! Then when ye're ready to move, I'll come down ahead of ye!' Then he looked out, seeing what the girls were up to. 'Mind you, them young ones will crucify ye when they catch on ye're afraid of something. Do ye see that woman there? The one at the second row from the back. The one with the red face and squinty eyes! Fourth from this end!'

I looked along the row. 'Yeah, yeah, I see her.' She was talking away with her mouth flying up and down to the aul one standing next to her.

'Well, that one had the time of her life, drawing in the rest of them I might add. Oh, yes! She's the ringleader of any troublemaking there is to be made, I can tell ye that here and now. I keep me eye very closely on that one. She nearly cost a young fella his life. The poor chiseller nearly died of fright. She put a dead mouse in his sandwiches! How it happened was this. We had a young fella working here. The poor chiseller was no more than fourteen. He was on the deliveries van. Well, one of the young ones got a fright when she saw a mouse running past. She leapt up to him coming in the door, ready to get his deliveries. Anyway, "Christie!" she screams. "Do something! There's a mouse just gone flying past – right over me feet it went! Get the brush quick, Christie! Kill it! Look! It's over there!" she pointed, hiding in the corner. Well, Christie looked, spinning his head, seeing the mouse cowering in the corner. Well, he let out such an unmerciful roar! He started screaming for his mammy! Lepping up and down he was, hammering his feet on the ground. Then he took off out through that door there! We couldn't find him for love nor money! Straight home, he flew! The mammy had to drag him screaming back into work the next morning.

'Well, them women gave that poor young fella an awful time! The only way we could get him to even come next to the place was to let him sit in the van while the rest of them had to load it up themselves. That was supposed to be his job – loading and unloading, helping the driver. It seems the poor kid had a terrible fear of mice and rats. You would have thought he would be used to that, living in the tenements. Sure, that's all ye see! They nearly come and sit next to you and join ye at the table when ye're having the dinner!' he said, laughing and shaking his head, trying to figure out why the young fella wasn't used to mice and rats.

'Yeah, but I'm afraid of dogs,' I said, thinking about it. 'And drowning, and falling from a height! And there's dogs everywhere, you know! But I'm still not used to them! But other than that I'm not afraid of anything or anybody. Nothing else on this earth would frighten me!' I said, wanting him to know I'm not really a coward.

'Oh, I would well believe that!' he said, shaking his head agreeing with me. 'You came up them stairs whether you were afraid or not! That says something for you!'

Yeah, that's true! I thought, feeling better thinking about it that way.

'Right! Are ye ready? Let's go if ye are.' He stood up.

'Listen, Jimmy! Don't bother coming down with me. I'll be grand!'

'What? Sure, it's no bother.'

'No, really. Thanks very much for offering to help me. But I'll be grand now! I have to get over me fears.'

'Well, take it easy. Mind yerself. Go down slowly.'

'OK!' I said, standing up and making for the door. I put me foot on the stairs and went down slowly, looking straight ahead, seeing the men coming in and out through the big gates that were used for the deliveries. They were busy carrying boxes out to the lorries parked in a back lane that must have another entrance. I made it down the stairs without getting meself killed, then walked out through the factory, deciding I'm not coming back to take them stairs again even if they pay me to do it!

'Where where you? That phone has been going mad!'

'I got delayed,' I said.

'Doing what?' Carmel shouted. 'I can see now you are not going to last in this job. You were skiving off! Wait until Mister Braggs gets his hands on you!' she snorted.

I could feel the colour suddenly draining outa me face again. Jaysus! Now he's going to just think I'm a nuisance! I'm more trouble than I'm worth. Dear God! Please don't let me lose this job! I'll do what I have to do. Even if it does mean going up them stairs again. People run up and down them all the time. I have to stop acting like a wet nelly. Yeah, I might even take on a few dogs! But I'm still not going near water! Oh, no! Not on yer nelly! I can't bleedin swim!

The extension beeped. It's Junior! Me heart leapt into me mouth. Maybe he's going to fire me for going missing. 'Hello, Mister Braggs!' I croaked, with the nerves taking away me voice.

'Will you ask Lucy to make the tea and send it up? Would you come up, too, Martha? Mister Braggs Senior would like to see you.'

'Now, Mister Braggs?' I squealed, losing me voice altogether after seeing stars from the fright.

'After your tea break will be fine.' Then he hung up.

'Lucy,' I said, feeling weak all over. If I stood up I would fall down. 'Mister Braggs said you are to make the tea and bring it up.'

'No, no! No way! No will do!' she said, shaking her head, scraping her teeth on her top lip, not even looking at me but staring at her typing.

'He said you are to make it. I have to go up and see him after me break,' I said, feeling all the life draining outa me.

'Ohh! You are getting the boot!' she said, spinning her head to Carmel.

'I said so!' Carmel sang, letting her eyes light up and look down her nose at her typing with a smirk on her face.

I stood up and grabbed me bag, making me way out the front door. I leaned against the wall, taking in the sun and the fresh air. Not even a full day did I last! I thought, feeling like I was going to get sick. I opened me bag and took out a cigarette, lighting it up. Then walked up the lane to put distance between me and the factory. I suppose I can always look for another job meself. I won't say I worked here. I'll say I just left the secretarial college! Which I have. Oh, well! That's that! It can't be helped. What's done is done! Unless I explain I got a fright. I'm afraid of heights. These things can happen to anyone. But then again, I was time wasting. That's all he's concerned about.

As the teacher said, he's paying me wages to do a job. Getting the job done should only be my concern, too. Anything after that is my own business. Oh, well! There's always another day! I'll scratch this one down to experience. I went back down the lane and in the door, leaving my bag under me desk, and went out again, heading up the stairs to see Mister Braggs.

'Come in!' he barked when I knocked on the door. 'Ah! Miss Long. Take a seat. I want you to take down a letter. George, pick up a notebook there!' he said to Junior, throwing his head at the press.

I waited, letting the message get through to me. I'm not getting fired! He wants me to do a letter for him! I'm being his secretary! Oh, thank you, God! You are very good to me. Ha! Wait till I get back downstairs and let them two aul hags know what I was doing! That should put the smile on the other side of their ugly mugs!

Junior handed me the same notebook I used the other day. I whipped through the pages and got a new page, then swung me leg over, dangling me gold sandal, and waited with the yellow pencil held in the air ready to take down every word he said.

'Read that back to me,' he said when he had finished. 'Change "we will despatch" to "we will send forthwith". OK! Got that?'

'Yes, Mister Braggs!' I said, standing up.

'Take it into Miss Benson's office and get it done as quickly as you can. I want to catch the early post this afternoon. Get the address from the files. Make it for the Attention of Mister P. Owens. Write private and personal on the envelope! Then get on the phone, you'll find the number in Miss Benson's phone book. She keeps it on her desk. Tell them the letter is on the way. It should arrive in Holland by tomorrow's post. Have you got all that?'

'Yes, Mister Braggs. Type fast but accurate. Personal to . . .' I looked at me notes, 'Mister P. Owens. Written on the envelope. Find address and telephone number. Ring and say they will have the letter by tomorrow's evening post!'

'Excellent! Now get moving!' he said, throwing his hand at the door.

I flew out and started straight away. Miss Benson is not here. She must be sick! Right! I whipped the cover off the typewriter and started to hammer away. Finished! I read it back. Good! No mistakes. Then got up and opened the mahogany filing cabinet, looking to see how she does her filing system. Ah! Alphabetical company name. Here we are! Got the address, including the phone number. It's on the file. I wrote that down in me notepad. I brought the letter along with the typed address on the envelope and knocked on Mister Braggs' door.

'That letter is ready for your signature, Mister Braggs,' I said, handing it to him.

He read it. 'OK! Stamp it. You'll find the stamps in Miss Benson's drawer. Then run out and post it. Don't forget to make that call when you get back, OK?' he said, lighting his eyes on me.

'OK!' I said. 'I'm off to do that right away.'

'Oh! Just a minute!' he said, stopping me with me hand on the doorknob. 'I heard about your little drama out in the factory.'

Me heart leapt with fright. 'Eh, yeah,' I mumbled.

'What happened? Do you suffer from vertigo?'

'Eh?' I didn't know what that was. But I said yeah anyway.

'Well, there's no need for you to go running up those stairs again. Let the other two do their own work! You get on with yours. I want a secretary not a circus performer!' Then he gave a little snort, letting his face wrinkle into a laugh. 'Go on! Hurry up! Get that letter posted!' he said, waving me out the door with his head.

Ha! Now I can tell them shit rags to get off their arse and deliver their own stuff! I'm the secretary! 'Oh, the sun has got his hat on! Hip hip hip hurrah!' I sang, flying open the door.

The pair of them looked up. 'Did you get fired?' Lucy said, with her head spinning up to look at me and her eyes dancing in her head, dying to see me misery.

'Yeah,' I sighed, grabbing me bag and making for the door again. 'He said I'm to get off the premises straight away!' I said, standing for a second to see their faces.

'Oohhh! I knew it!' Carmel muttered, trying to find her voice with the shock and delight. 'I know Mister Braggs! I knew it! I said so!' she shouted, throwing her head at Lucy. 'Didn't I always tell you I knew Mister Braggs inside out and outside in? Wasn't I right?'

'Yeah, you did! Yes! You were right!' said Lucy, shaking her head up and down, thinking about it, sounding like she was saying a prayer.

'Goodbye!' I shouted. 'It was nice knowing you! Sorry we didn't get to be great pals!' Then I whipped meself off out the door, flying up the lane. When I got to the top, I let out an unmerciful scream, laughing me head off. Ha, ha! I can't wait to see their faces when I appear back in the door. Not just that! Not only am I not fired!

Oh, no! But I'm his standby secretary when Miss Benson is not around. That should put a red-hot poker up their fat arses! 'Life is a carousel, old girl! Come drink the wine!' I sang, flying down the road to the postbox.

28

J unior's line beeped. I plugged in, picking up the phone, saying, 'Yes, Mister Braggs?'

'Martha, Mister Braggs would like you to come up immediately after tea break. We need you to do some letters. Please tell Lucy to send up the teas.' Then he was gone.

'Lucy! Make the tea, please. They are waiting upstairs.'

'No! Absolutely not!' she said, twisting her nose and mouth into a straight line.

'Do it, Lucy! I've made the tea for months. Your turn, I'm going for a break. I have to get upstairs and take dictation. See you!' Then I grabbed up my coat and bag and took off out the door. I went across and leaned against the warehouse wall, lighting up a cigarette, waiting for Nina to appear.

She came breezing out. 'Oh, great! You're here! What's happening? No tea-making today?' she laughed, buttoning up her heavy coat against the cold wind blowing down the lane.

'Nope! The dopes are making it today! I'm on secretarial duty.'

'You know, Martha? I think old Braggs might offer you Benson's job when she finally retires. The poor aul thing can hardly drag herself in any more.'

'Yeah, old age is a bitch!' I said, seeing poor old Benson trying to type on her crippled hands, getting more and more gnarled every day.

'But listen! A word of warning. You need to watch out! Those two over there have the knives out for you! Carmel is sick with the jealousy! She can't stand you being the old codger's favourite girl.'

'Am I?' I said, feeling me heart lift. 'I never noticed I was, Nina!'

'Oh, you are! Believe me. Carmel used to be the centre of attention before you came. Now he hardly speaks to her. You're up and down them stairs like a yo-yo! When he wants anything, it's you he calls.'

'Honestly, Nina. How do you always seem to know so much about what's going on when you are not even working over there?'

'Ah, come on, Martha! There's nothing else to do but talk in this place. You never hang around for the gossip. You disappear up that lane every chance you get!'

'Yeah, that's the idea of breaks, Nina. Get out of here even if it's only for a few minutes. Anyway, listen, Nina! What about coming out for lunch with me on Friday? I'm paying! So you keep your hands in your pockets. What about it?'

'OK! That's really nice of you to ask me!'

'Nice, me arse, Nina! You would do the same if you had it to spare.'

'But where will we go?' she said.

'I don't know,' I said. 'I'm only used to fish and chips and eating them on the street. I only know one place but that's haunted by anarchists, students and women's libbers!' I laughed. 'I stumbled into it a couple of years ago! Jaysus! I don't want to repeat that experience! Anyway, I'm celebrating!'

'What are you celebrating?' she said, laughing and staring into me face.

'Not telling! It's a secret!'

'Ah, go on!'

'No! Are you game?' I said, looking into her face, wanting her to come. 'We'll go out for lunch on Friday afternoon! Is that OK? Would you like that?'

'Yeah, smashing! OK, then listen, Martha. There's a Chinese restaurant just up off Grafton Street. We could go there.'

'Chinese? Jaysus, no! Chopsticks? No! I like plain food. I wouldn't like the taste of something foreign.'

'Ah, go on! Give it a try! I've never had Chinese food either but it will be something different.'

'OK,' I sighed, thinking about hearing something people were saying about some of them getting closed down for serving up cat food or something. Someone said the inspectors found all the cans of Kit-e-cat sitting in the dustbin! Wonder If I should believe that?

'Right, we'll go down straight after work at lunch time,' I said. 'We'll need to be fast if we want to get back in time for work.'

'OK, Martha. Thanks, this is great. I'm really looking forward to that!'

'Yeah, so am I, Nina. See you! Better get back to work,' I said, stubbing out me cigarette and crushing it under me boot. It will be nice to celebrate me eighteenth birthday with Nina. But I don't want her knowing. She'll only feel bad one way or another, thinking she might have to buy me a present! The present for me is seeing the look of happiness on her face. Just being able to get out for a change should give her a great lift! That's good enough for me.

I walked into the office and whipped off me coat. I checked there were no wrinkles in me tights and pulled up me soft leather calf-length boots. I looked down at meself, seeing me light-brown leather tunic frock with the fringes around the edges. The style is copied from the American Indian women. The squaws! They wear these with the leather fringe for a hem. Except mine nearly goes up to me arse, showing me leather boots hugging me thighs. Yeah, I get a few looks from the fellas strutting down the road in this get-up! Right! I better get upstairs to the old men! Or himself will have a stroke shouting down the blower wondering what's keeping me! I fixed me white polo neck jumper, then grabbed up me pen and notebook, taking off up the stairs. Maybe some day soon I will be taking these stairs every morning, then clattering down in the evening. That will be good. I won't have to listen to the hags' non-stop bullshit! I can't believe the rubbish they were talking about this morning.

'Oh, look!' says Carmel, tearing up her frock. 'I bought these frilly knickers on Saturday!' showing the side of her leg and pulling at the elastic in her knickers. 'Do you like them?'

'Oooohhh! They are lovely!' says Lucy. 'Where did you buy them? I want to buy a couple of pairs like that! What colours do they have?'

'Oh, I bought three pairs. One in pink, blue and white! I bought them in Arnotts!'

'Of course! Where else?' I mumble under me breath. Dunnes Stores? Never! That is far too common for the likes of you, Carmel. I mean, as you pointed out to me when you first asked me where I live – not wanting to tell you exactly, I said, 'Down by Holles Street Hospital.'

'Oh, my God!' you shouted, making it sound like the place was on fire! 'That is really common down there! All them flats! Slums!' Then you gave a shiver! 'Daddy bought us a purchase house years ago when he came back after working and saving for years! We own our own house!' you cackled. Yeah! Silly cow! You were trying to make out you are better than me! Me! What a bleedin cheek. An she only a . . . What is she anyway? Well, I am a junior secretary! So she can stuff that up her arse with her new knickers!

Yeah! Nina told me it was only a plain box of a house anyway. One of hundreds in a new estate out in the arsehole of nowhere, miles from the city centre. You nearly have to take the country bus to get there! Cretin! Nothing worse than them who drag themself out of the gutter then they think they are better than everyone else. I've met too many in me lifetime. Bleedin pot looking down on the kettle! They offend my sense of dignity! I heard meself thinking. Then laughed. Yeah! I'm arming meself with words these days. It is most definitely offensive for me to be sitting in such lowly company. I prefer to sit with me boss. That's where me bread is buttered!

Yeah! Nina told me Carmel invited her to her house once. She didn't like the family. The mother kept running everyone down – all the neighbours. The father went on about how hard he worked, and nobody was allowed into the 'good' sitting room. That was only for show. She said in a way she felt sorry for Carmel. Sometimes I do too. I can see how proud she is. Getting out of the slums as she calls it. But still! She puts everyone down just so she can feel better about herself. Gawd love her! Daddy buying the house didn't bring them any happiness judging by what Nina said about them and seeing how miserable a cow Carmel is.

Oh, well! Here I go. Raising me way to the top! Up onto the first landing! And I am in with the ruling classes! How's about that then, Ma? Little old me, scabby Martha, is squeezing her way into the respectable! Not one of them have copped on yet, I am not of them. I come from the 'unclean', the unwashed! Yikes. Eeekk! What would Carmel say to that if she knew? Wouldn't I just love to sit her down and tell her quietly, 'Carmel darling! You have not risen in the world! Sob! Bad news! I – me – am a child of the slums! No, not just that. Wait for it, Carmel. Remember your worst nightmare? Or at least your ma's. The young one with the scabby lice-ridden head, no knickers, rob the eyes outa your head? Yeah, well, here I am! I've managed to move up and sit next to you! Isn't that great, Carmel? Carmel? Are you all right, Carmel? Jaysus! Slapping her face won't bring her around. Smelling salts, please, Lucy! Ha, ha!'

Jaysus, Martha. Cut it out! One of these days your carry-on is going to get you into trouble! Who cares? Life is a carousel!

Right! Down to business. Tights, fine! Legs, grand! With a bit of luck, old Braggs may decide he can't do without skinning his rheumy eyeballs up and down me legs! I might get a permanent fixture in that chair next to his desk yet.

I gave a little rap with my knuckles.

'Enter!'

I think I hear energy in that voice. Maybe he's glad to see me. I whipped open the door. You are on, Martha! I plastered a smile on me face, giving the Gibbs toothpaste-ad look, enjoying meself no end. He can have two looks at me legs swirling through the air as I cross them today. Poor thing is in need of a bit more life pumped into him!

'Good morning, Misters Braggs!' I said, bowing me head to each of them, feeling cheeky, happy and delighted with me life.

'Huh!' said old Braggs. 'Sit down there and take a letter!'

I squinted into the mirror, pulling down me top eyelid, drawing a line with the little brush across the top of me eyelashes. Jaysus! That black liquid eyeliner is a curse! I can't get the curl up at the end of me eye. The two of them are crooked. I look nothing like Cleopatra! I look more like someone let out of a loony bin for the day! Jaysus! Start again! The things we women have to do to try and make ourselves look irrestible. OK! That's better. Just a little bit at the end. No need for a curl. It will only end up halfway across me ear anyway. Right! Two coats of mascara and a bit of lipstick. I smacked me lips together, seeing them lovely and pink. OK! Out with the hair rollers. Yep! Very nice. Me hair fell out in shiny brown curls with a lovely red gloss through it. I brushed it out and it fell in a wave over one eye, then slicked in waves and curls down to me shoulders. OK! Here we go! Now to test out me look on the fellas! Well, only one that matters to me. Jaysus! That's a waste of time!

If only I could listen to meself. Good advice, Martha! Take it! Forgetting it already. I strained me head behind me to check me black miniskirt – very mini – was straight, then hiked on me flat, thigh-hugging leather boots, dragging them up over me thighs, then stood up.

'OK! Dressed,' I sighed, letting out me breath. I picked up me long, black, shiny coat, slipping it on. Then grabbed up me shoulder bag and whipped open the door, leaving the coat wide open to show off me legs and boots, then swung out the door, leaving the coat flapping out behind me. Heading off on me Saturday-morning visit.

I pushed in the door and walked to the reception desk standing at the big wooden counter. 'Father Fitzgerald,' the eagle-eyed aul fella with the grey baldy head said, looking down at me chest. He misses nothing that aul fella, sees everything and says nothing.

He picked up the phone and rang the priest's extension. 'There's a girl here to see you, Father. Will I show her down to a parlour? Right, so!' Then he hung up and walked around the desk, looking at me with a smirk on his face.

I pulled me coat around me, not wanting his dirty mind getting ideas looking at me.

'Follow me!' he said, strutting off down the long wide passage, heading for the parlours with his fat little squat body swinging from side to side. He has a filthy way of looking at you, that aul fella. Like he is peeling your clothes off one by one. I don't like him.

He threw open a door, flicking a sign around that said 'Occupied'. 'You can wait for him in there,' he said, showing me into a big room with a high ceiling decorated in lovely blue mouldings. The huge rose around the ceiling light is really ornate and very heavy looking. Two armchairs sat one each side of the fireplace. The fireplace here was now even more ornamental. But they don't use it any more. An electric heater sat in front, waiting for you to plug it in and give a red glow in the bars and throw out instant heat. I decided to sit down at the long conference table with a big wine tablecloth thrown over it. Tassels hung from the end of it. Me heart was flying and yet I felt a little down. I could feel the palms of me hands damp with cold perspiration. Jaysus! Me nerves always get the better of me when I come here. No, it's not the place. It's at the thought of seeing Ralph!

'Well, well!' he boomed, swinging open the door and stopping to look at me. Then he shut it firmly, checking first to see if the card was facing the right way.

I stood up, waiting for him to come over to me.

'How are you, darling?' he said gently, lowering his voice to a whisper as he wrapped me in his arms. I could get the smell of soap and aftershave. He hugged me tighter, pulling me into him, resting his face on the top of me head.

I said nothing, just listened to his heart beating and feeling the beat of my own. We were both still. Nobody moving, nobody saying anything. Then he slowly let out his breath, very quietly, and moved his face down through me hair, taking the smell of it slowly up through his nose. I was caught in that moment, hearing his every breath, feeling meself tingle and on alert for every movement of his. His face moved gently, brushing against my face. Then he lifted me face in his hand and stared into me eyes, saying nothing. I snuggled in closer, resting the side of me head on his chest. I could hear his heart beating faster. So was mine. But me mind was still, thinking nothing. I wanted this to last for ever!

He put his hand under me chin again and lifted me face, staring at me. Then he very slowly kissed my lips, letting his lips linger for a second, and lifted his head, murmuring, 'Come, darling! Sit down. Tell me all that you have been up to!'

The moment was broken. I felt me heart drop. This is it! The most I can expect.

'Come! We'll sit down here by the fire,' he said. 'It is absolutely freezing in here!'

He bent down and plugged in the heater, then dragged over the other armchair, putting the two of them side by side. 'OK! What mischief have you been getting up to this week?' he said, landing himself in the armchair and crossing his legs. Then he grabbed hold of his thick mane of glossy brown hair and whipped it back, throwing it over the side of his head. His green eyes sparkled, watching mine and waiting for me to start talking.

I let me coat fall each side of me, trailing it on the floor, and crossed me legs, seeing him lift his chin and look down at me legs! Then he looked straight at me and grinned, shaking his head!

'You do know, of course, you are teasing the men dreadfully dressed like that, don't you?' he said, leaning over to my face then landing a sharp smack on me leg.

'Jaysus! You're a savage!' I snorted, rubbing me leg. 'That stung!'

'Of course! You are very naughty, gadding about dressed like that!'

'What's wrong with me? Everyone dresses like this these days!'

'Oh, nothing wrong, my darling! I think you look delectable! But, well,' he said, shaking his head, taking in a breath through his nose and throwing his eye sideways at me. 'What is the intention when you go out dressed like that? Is it to gain attention from men? A lot of temptation for the poor chaps out there!' he said. 'Particularly, as you say – I know this – you may look, but you may not touch! Not all girls are like that, so men may not know or care. And you could find yourself in a lot of difficulty!'

'Ah, for fuck sake, Ralph! Stop giving me a lecture! I know exactly what men are like, so shut up!' I said, getting very annoyed because that's not what I want to hear.

'What did you just say?' he said, making for me.

I was up and out of the chair, flying around the room. 'No, no! I take it back!'

'Good!' he said, sitting himself back down again.

'Jaysus! Them shovels you call hands are made of steel!'

'Really, Martha! That does not become you. You have to remember you are a young lady now.'

'OK,' I said, wanting to make the peace.

'Yes!' he said, examining his hands. 'I am strong! Pretty powerful, really!' he said, flexing his arm.

'Yeah! And modest.'

'Of course! Humility is all!' he snapped. 'Now come and sit down,' he said, patting the seat beside him. 'I have things to attend to. Let's not waste more time. Tell me what has been happening. What have you been getting up to? How is the job? Have they made you managing director yet?' he grinned, showing his gorgeous white teeth, flashing his green eyes.

'No, not yet. But I'm getting there! Poor Miss Benson is on her way out,' I said, thinking about how stooped she's getting but not wanting to give up.

'Yes, old age can be very cruel,' he said, going silent, thinking about it. 'You know, that is one of my great fears,' he said quietly, looking at his hands, then lifting his head, looking into the fire.

'Why, Ralph? Sure, don't we all have to get old? It's part and parcel of life. Taking the good with the bad.'

'How wise you are! An old head! And on such young shoulders!' he said, wrapping his arm around me and pulling me into his shoulder. 'But you see, I don't want to be a burden. I would hate to lose,' he stopped to think about it, 'my dignity.'

'But,' I said, thinking about it, 'doesn't that come with humility? You were just talking about that a minute ago. No one can ever take your dignity; it is something that is part of you. Like your integrity. Or keeping a promise. The kind of things that make you who you are,' I said, letting me head fly with the thoughts, trying to nail down what I wanted to say. I was worried that he was worried about something that would come to him one day down the road.

'Humility is only given to a rare few individuals. People who are very spiritual,' he said.

'Are you not?'

'No! I'm far too self-indulgent!' he said. 'So! What is happening with your friend, Odette? Have you heard from her?'

'No,' I said, feeling me heart sink even lower at the mention of Odette. 'She's got her law degree. Now she's managed to get herself an apprenticeship in a solicitor's office in Galway. He's a family friend of her father's. So, that's that! No more Odette! I really miss her.'

'Oh, I know, darling!' he said, taking me hand and wrapping it in the two of his. 'It must be dreadful for you. The two of you were thick as thieves! My goodness! When I think of the night you both climbed in that window! You bloody fools! You could have killed yourselves!'

'Yeah, well! We got locked out, so we got the girls on the ground floor to open their bedroom window. Then Odette had the idea of me collapsing meself across from the iron bars and throwing meself at the window. She was hanging on to me legs. If I fall, she said, it was no problem. She would still hang on to me legs and swing me back up!'

He kept sighing, flying his eyes up to the ceiling and looking back at me, shaking his head. 'You are both stark raving mad. Mad as hatters! In a way it is a good thing you have both been separated. You two sparked off each other. It was a lethal combination. Both of you together spelled nothing but trouble. I should know! It was I who would have to go and sort out the jam you both got into!'

'What? Do you mean the . . . like that time on New Year's Eve last year when we went up to Christ Church Cathedral to ring in the new year? Oh, yeah!' I laughed, remembering. 'We forgot all about getting back into the hostel until it was all over! Gawd, that was still awful, though,' I said, thinking about it. 'We had to come up here and sleep on your stone steps in the freezing cold all night, waiting for you to wake up and get us back into the hostel. We knew the Reverend Mother would listen to you!'

'Hmm! I have no idea how you both managed to cling on in that hostel. I think the Reverend Mother indulged you both!' he said, half smiling. The other half was annoyed at all the trouble we got him into. That aul kitchen nun got fed up getting nowhere with Allie. As soon as she clapped eyes on him talking to the Reverend Mother, she was in like a shot, ringing him up non-stop, demanding he take me out! Ha! She's given up trying to get rid of me as a bad job. Now, she just tries to poison me!

I got a bad dose of the runs one day. She offered me a peace offering, she called it! A nice slice of apple tart cooked specially for me! Fucking bitch! She's mad as a hatter. I spent a whole day and night sitting on the bleedin toilet scuttering me brains out! Nobody else got it!

'Where are you?' he said, pulling me into him. 'What are you thinking about?' he said, whispering into me ear.

'Nothing!' I muttered, snuggling me head inside his neck.

He let his mouth drop on the side of me head, gently kissing it. 'I must go,' he whispered.

'No! Not yet!' I said, feeling a panic rise up in me. 'Don't go! Stay a while longer!' I said, lifting me head and looking into his face.

'You know I have duties. I would love to stay with you longer, my precious, but—'

'No! Say nothing!' I said, leaning me head back into his chest, trying to burrow in as far as I could get meself.

He sighed and wrapped me tighter to him, then started stroking my head and face. 'This is not good, darling. You know that,' he said, whispering even more quietly down into me face, letting his lips rest on the side of me cheek. 'I want what is best for you, my darling,' he whispered. 'My dearest wish is to see you happy!'

'I am happy, Ralph!' I said, wrapping me arms around his neck.

'No, no! Don't play games, sweetheart! Of course you are not happy. I can see you are miserable,' he said, grabbing me chin in his hand and lifting me face to look into his eyes. 'I can't give you what you want. I have a commitment!'

I dropped me eyes, refusing to look at him. Me heart was breaking. 'OK!' I said, standing up and taking up me bag. 'I'll let you go!'

He waved his hands, then dropped them by his side saying nothing. He didn't know what to say.

I turned and headed for the door.

'Come back! Please, Martha! I love you! Very deeply! But I can't give you what you need! You will find someone. Someone who will belong to you completely. I am a priest! I do not want to marry. I can't! I have vows!'

'OK,' I said, turning suddenly, making for the door, keeping me head down.

'No, wait!' He grabbed me, holding on to me tight. 'Please try to understand! I know you want! I – I would – I love you so much!' Then he suddenly kissed my forehead, holding me face in his hands, and let me go, whipping open the door, saying, 'Come on! I will see you out, darling!'

He walked close to me, wanting to lift his hand and put it around me. But then dropped his arm and let it hang by his side. 'By the way, darling! My mother sends her love. Why don't you write to her? She would love to hear from you. I gave you the address, did I not?'

'Yes, you did. So did your mother,' I muttered, feeling like I had no life in me.

'Yes, the house is locked up for the winter. She generally spends the winters abroad. It's much too bleak for her being shut up in that dark old house during the winter months,' he said, making conversation, trying to cheer me up.

'Yeah, OK. Bye! See you,' I said, waving at him, barely lifting me hand, then turning me back and heading off. Not caring where I went. Without Ralph, nothing seems worth bothering about. That's always the way it is after visiting him. The next time will be even worse. Nothing changes.

I walked through the late morning, feeling the early October cold wind driving against me coat. A gust of wind caught hold of me leather coat and flapped it against me legs, stinging me, making me realise I was cold, leaving meself open, exposed to the chilly winds. I grabbed me coat, wrapping it around me, and closed the buttons from top to bottom, pulling the belt tight around me and fastening it. Then I lifted me collar, wrapping it around me neck, heading off into town. I have spent enough time wandering, going from one side of the Liffey to the other, walking the length and breadth of the streets.

I passed the black church on me right, looking at the old shops on me left, seeing very few people in them. Haunted-looking faces from behind a counter looked up hopefully from the dark, dusty, half-empty shop as I passed, then dropped, letting the waiting go on, hoping someone would come in and buy something. Old decayed Georgian houses stood side by side with the shops next door. Parts of the iron railings wrapped around the basement were missing. Not giving much protection now to the basement. The owners had long gone, past caring. They had been carried out in a box. Their home was now shelter to the poor. One room each, more money for the country navvy who came back from working the building sites in England. He didn't drink or didn't smoke. Now he was flush with the money he saved. Enough to buy these old houses for next to nothing. It all paid off. Cracked window panes with their grey net curtains now moth-eaten hung in tatters on the windows. He still doesn't spend the money. For him, it's just keep saving and buy more!

I looked up, then stopped, seeing the pale grey face of an old man pull aside the curtain. He lifted his face to the sky, checking what kind of day he has woken to, not liking the look of it. He pulled the blanket tighter around his shoulders, covering his neck, then he dropped his eyes, locking for a second on mine. The two of us stared. Him in his world, waiting. His journey was a long one, now it is coming to an end. All his dreams are just memories. He has had his time. Now it is just the waiting. A spark of hope still flickers. All he wants is his passing will be peaceful. Some morning he may not wake up and pull the curtain, no more loneliness to face because there is no more day for him.

Now I'm waiting, him and me are connected. We're both lonely. We're like ships passing in the night. He is heading back, almost at his end. But I'm only taking off on my journey – it is not long started. Eighteen years is not a lot. I have a great power of energy surging through my veins. All my hopes and dreams pull me forward into the great unknown. The old man stares. I see his eyes ready to pull away but he hesitates. We stare more intensely. Speaking without words. His wise, tired old eyes sense the connection. Yes! We see into each other's soul. For a split second we are not alone! He lowers his head, letting me go, then drops the curtain.

I walked on, stopping at the corner, waiting for the traffic to pass. I turned me head, looking up Belvedere. There is nothing up there for me. Just rows and rows of old Georgian tenement houses. That was me old haunting grounds. Running for messages in me bare feet. Flying up into the Jesuit priest's house and ringing the bell, looking for money for Jackser. Holding me breath, hoping and praying they would give me something. It would buy us a bit of peace and save me a kicking and beating for a little while.

Suddenly I found meself walking in that direction. Then I stopped and stared up at the Jesuit house, bigger than all the other houses on the road with its high wide steps and big columns jutting out. I could almost imagine I could see the ghost of myself, the little Martha, standing up on the steps of the Jesuit house, waiting. She turned, whipping her little head with the matted hair, standing in her black bare feet with the little blue skinny matchstick legs, looking down at me. Her little white face, black from the dirt, stared at me with a puzzled look. 'Wha! Is it no good, Martha?' she said, looking me up and down, then staring into me face. 'Ye got the lovely clothes, an the good grub, an ye don't have te do no beggin any more! An ye're not watchin over yer shoulder te see if anyone is after ye for robbin. Ye don't even get kilt any more! No one is out te kill ye! Even the most important bit is ye got rid a tha Jackser fella! He can't torment ye or kill ye night an day! He can't get next or near ye! Ye're home an dry, Martha! Ye have money in yer pocket! An ye now have a good job! Ye're respectable! You're yer own person, Martha!' she said, swinging her little head up and down me, taking me in from head to toe. 'So is it no good then, Martha?' she said, looking very worried.

'No! It won't take away the pain, little one,' I said, looking down at her, suddenly feeling the terrible pain of loneliness bursting up through me, out and through me eyes. I shattered into tears, letting the salty water pour out of me eyes and nose, staring down at her, knowing she would understand.

'So ye got all tha, but ye're still painin. Because it's like the time when the lovely kind woman gave me the shillin and the hug! I would have given her back tha shillin fer just one more a them hugs. Cos ye see, fer tha minute when it lasted, wit me wrapped inside her coat, feelin meself pressed into her body, an her arms wrappin me all up, I was still. Very quiet inside meself. It was just me an her. She took away all me pain of the worry, an the dirt, an the terrible fear I would get murdered stone dead by Jackser. She liked me, Martha. Just me! Nobody else did, but she did! She didn't want anythin offa me. She thought I was somebody, even though I was dirty! Yeah! Just all for meself! She liked me. All me pain went away! The heat flew aroun through me body. I was cosy an warm, an in outa the dark an the wet, an the storm, an anyone tha wanted te do me harm. That's wha it was like, Martha! So! Ye're still lookin for tha. Someone te make ye feel ye belong te them. Is tha it?' she said, waiting for me answer, looking at me with pain and loss in her eyes, yet thinking, hoping, there's always something.

'That's the way it is, little one,' I said, nodding me head down at her. 'Everything has changed but nothing changes. I still pain like you! I'm still you, little one, underneath the grown-up me.'

'Yeah,' she said. 'I know tha!'

She stood staring at me with her mouth hanging open, trying to take in what I had told her. I could see her thinking. Then she said in a whisper, 'It will be all OK! You look lovely!' she said, looking me up and down admiringly. 'But yer face is all dirty! Is tha from the stuff ye put on yer eyelashes, Martha? Te make them look nice?'

'Yeah!' I said, sniffing and smiling at her.

'Well, it doesn't look nice now! Ye look a bit like me! All tha black stuff is streamin down yer cheeks! Ye better wipe it offa ye!'

'OK! You're right,' I said, opening me bag and reaching in to take out me little powder compact with the mirror. 'Jaysus! Look at the state of me!' I laughed.

'Yeah, wipe it off. Make yerself look nice again,' she said, looking out for me like the little granny she always was.

I took out a packet of tissues and spit on one, wiping the black streaks away gently, then powdered me face with the little powder puff.

'Now ye look grand!' she said, lifting her chest and trying to stretch herself, looking up at me. 'Wha are ye goin te do now, Martha?'

'I don't know,' I said, feeling half dead inside meself.

'Listen! Why don't ye go off an do somethin I would like te have done?'

'What's that, little one?' I said, bending down wanting to hear what she would do.

'Why don't ye go an spend some of yer money tha ye have in yer pockets? Go in te one a them nice warm cafés an buy yerself somethin lovely te eat! Ye can do anythin ye want now, Martha. So don't be goin an forgettin tha!'

'Yeah! You are so right!' I said, feeling me heart lifting. 'OK! Goodbye, little one!' Then I turned me back, looking around once more, seeing the ghost of little Martha vanishing slowly, going back into the mists of long-ago dark days. I moved on, walking away, leaving her little ghost to roam around these streets, living the only life she's ever known. I headed off in the direction of Parnell Square, to make me way down to O'Connell Street.

29

'**E**venin paper, Miss?' the little young fella said, snapping it folded and holding it out to me.

'Yes, thanks, love!' I said, handing him the money and taking the newspaper from him, then heading into Cafolla's café on O'Connell Street. I pushed in the glass door, looking around. The place was nearly full with Saturday shoppers all getting stuck into their plate of fish and chips. Ah! No free tables, I thought, flying me eyes up and down the red shiny tables with the long red-leather seats facing each other. Little jukeboxes made out of glass and steel hung on the wall next to the tables. I spotted a space just inside the door, with a good view to the people and traffic all going up and down the street outside. I moved in next to a woman and her friend, leaning across the table talking to each other. It looked to me like they were ready to go. They had their coats in their hands and were having a last-minute discussion about what shops they wanted to go to next.

'Let's go into Cleary's,' said the older woman with the new perm in her hair. 'I might find a nice frock there!' she said, looking at her friend, who looked a good five years younger. She had less wrinkles on her powdered face and her short curly hair wasn't as grey as her friend's. 'Do ye like the way I got me hair done this time?' said the older woman, feeling it gently with her hand and looking a bit worried at her friend.

'Oh, God, yes! Didn't I tell you the softer perm was nicer? It takes years offa your age!'

'Really? Do ye think so?' the older woman said, letting a smile break out on her face, and her grey eyes lit up, getting all delighted with herself as she ran her hands slowly around her head, barely touching it for fear it might pull the perm out.

'God, yes! Ye're lookin marvellous!' said the younger one, standing up and twirling a pink nylon scarf between her two hands, then wrapping it around her neck. She leaned down to the seat and picked up her heavy grey overcoat, putting it on. Then buttoned it, shaking her shoulders to get the coat settled. The other woman moved out of the seat and put on her beige coat, gently pulling it across her shoulders in case she tossed her new perm.

'Are we right?' the older woman said, looking around as they picked up their handbags and shopping bags. Then she peeled her eyes over the table with the remains of their fish-and-chips dinner, then down at the seats, saying, 'Do we have everything?'

'Yeah come on!' said the younger one. 'Let's get a move on before the shops get packed. Then they followed each other out the door, leaving me with the two seats all to meself.

'What can I get you?' said the waitress, leaning across me to collect up all the dirty plates.

'I'll have a fresh cod and chips, and a pot of tea and a plate of bread and butter, please, thanks!'

The waitress loaded up the plates beside her and whipped out her little notebook, writing down me order. 'Right! I'll get that for you,' she said, whipping up the dirty dishes and taking off to the kitchen with them.

I opened me paper to see what's happening. Then I decided to have a look for the flats to let first. I'm looking for a bedsit. I don't want to share with anyone. In any case, I haven't anyone to share with even if I wanted to. Oh! I might be in luck today! Here's something – 'Bedsit to let. Within walking distance to City Centre. Fifteen-minute walk to O'Connell Bridge'.

Jaysus! That's sounds just right! I better move on that fast. Before anyone else beats me to it. I grabbed open me bag and tore out me little notebook and Parker pen, then wrote down the phone number. As soon as I have me dinner, I'll run across the road to the GPO, the post office, and phone up about it. Maybe I'll strike lucky this time. Every time I ring up, it's either gone, or gone by the time I phone and get the address and get there.

I turned right, leaving the River Liffey at me back, and climbed up a steep hill. Yeah, this is the place. I looked up at the house, seeing it sitting on its own with a line of older houses going down from it almost to the end of the hill. It looked well kept. It's a three-storey – a ground floor with windows looking out onto the front, a middle level and a top level. This looks nice.

I went up the steps and pressed the doorbell, then waited. Hope it's not gone. He didn't say on the phone how much he was asking. Well, I'll soon find out. A man looking like he's in his fifties, with grey wavy hair and bits of black still showing, opened the door.

'Are you Mister Byrne?'

'Yes!'

'I rang you about a while ago. Is the bedsit still vacant?'

'Yes, it is. You are?'

'Martha Long.'

'Oh, yes! Come on in, Martha. Follow me. It's the first floor upstairs.'

I followed him through a hall and climbed the stairs, seeing the place was nice and clean. We came onto a little landing with a door in front of us and another down a little passage. The two rooms would share the same middle wall. So you can hear all the neighbour's goings on! He opened the door into a nice little room. It's bright and airy, I thought, looking at the big window straight ahead of me looking into the street. A big old wardrobe sat against the left-side wall, with a small table and two chairs under the window. In the right-hand corner beside the window was a little area with a two-ring cooker and a sink for washing. A single bed was pushed into the corner behind the door.

'This is it,' he said, after giving me a few minutes to take in everything.

'Yeah, it looks OK. It will do me grand. But the next question is, how much rent are you charging every week?'

'Two pounds ten shillings,' he said. 'The cooker is electric and you have a little blow fan heater to warm the place up. The meter's under the sink. It costs a shilling. So if you don't want the meter eating up your money, my suggestion is go easy on the cooker and the heater. It eats up the power. I'm just warning you, mind.'

'Yeah,' I said, hearing this.

I thought about how much I was earning. Four pounds a week. That would be two pounds ten shillings out of that for the rent, leaving me one pound and ten shillings left for food, electricity, cigarettes and anything else I need. Just as well I can walk from here to work. I can walk down the hill and across the Liffey and up by Doctor Stephen's Hospital, and down into Thomas Street, down through the Liberties, passing me old home where I was born, and just keep going. Past Christ Church, down Lord Edward Street, Jaysus! I'm still miles away from up off Baggot Street! It will take me a good hour or more to get in to work! But I'll just have to work out a good route.

'Yeah, two pounds ten shillings is grand,' I said. 'I'll take it.'

'I thought you would say that!' he laughed. 'The rent is cheaper than most places. I just want good tenants. I have me own business close by, so I'm not depending on this place,' he said, looking for the keys for the bedsit and throwing two keys held together in a ring, landing them on the table. 'I just want the first week's rent now. That means a week in advance. You don't pay the last week you leave. By that I mean on the last day. I collect the rent every Friday morning. So just leave it out there on the table for me. I'll let meself in to collect it.'

'So, today is Saturday. Do you want me to pay you now?'

'Yes! Otherwise it will be gone. Somebody will take it!'

'Oh, yeah! I know that. So does that mean when I give you the money now, the bedsit is mine?'

'All yours!' he said, grinning and dropping his head, then lifting it again. I counted two pounds and ten shillings out of me purse and handed it to him.

'Here you are!' he said, picking up the keys from the table and dangling them to me, dropping them in me hand. Then he was gone out the door, leaving me standing in me very own, very first place I ever had to meself.

'Jaysus! Just like that! That was fast!' I puffed, swinging me head around taking another look at me new home.

I went over and looked out the window, seeing an old Protestant church and graveyard. It's lovely and quiet here. You wouldn't hear a pin drop. Right! What do I do now? I rushed over and pulled back the blankets. Two blankets and a mattress. Oh! I'm going to need sheets and another few blankets. Then I went to the press and shelves lined under the sink and cooker. One little pot! That's it. No knives, forks, spoons, cups, plates – nothing. Oh! I have a frying pan. That will come in handy. Right! I will need to sort out stuff I'm going to need now I will start to pay me own way. I only had to pay two pounds a week towards the cost for the hostel. The total they charge is four pounds! That's very expensive. I only earn four pounds! Anyway, if all else fails here, I'll always have the two pounds ten shillings a week for me rent. If all comes to all, I can sing for me supper and do without the heat! So it's grand. I can get by. I'll move in here tomorrow. I'll have to buy a knife and fork and spoon and plate today. I'll get them in Cleary's. Just as well I managed to go easy on me money. Now I have the few bob put by. It all came easy. 'Oh, one day I am up in the air! Then I'm flat on me arse!' I sang happily. 'Yep! Life is a merry-go-round! I'm off me arse, rubbing away the pain! Leaping back up on the carousel! This is all mine,' I sighed feeling very contented. I slowly closed the door behind me, looking at me room until the door shut. Then made me way down the stairs. I looked in at a half landing, seeing a door open. I pushed the door in further, seeing a big old bath with a geyser over the sink. Then me eyes clapped on a meter for putting money in. I suppose that takes a shilling or two. Well, put by a shilling a week for that. I better add that to me outgoings!

I went down the hill and followed the river, then lost it going down Benburb Street. I could see the women hanging around the army barracks, talking to the soldiers on guard duty with their brown uniforms and black boots, standing each side of the entrance with their rifles held against their legs. A couple of women came mooching down the road, looking up and down, seeing if there was any business waiting for them. Jaysus! Poor women having to go out and do that! They must have a houseful of children at home waiting to be fed. Well, they certainly had no luck when it came to getting a husband. They must be married to a shower of wasters! Shiftless bastards. Men like that should have their what-nots cut off, then handed them back on a plate. 'Here's yer oats, darling! Ah, Jaysus! Sorry! Isn't tha terrible! Sure you won't be needing them now! Lookit! I cooked them for yer dinner!' That would spread the word fast enough! No lazy idle bastards! Ha.

I turned right again, ending back up on the Liffey, then kept walking, making me way past all the second-hand shops selling old furniture. Adam and Eve's Church – plenty of big old churches down along here. Past the four courts – halls of no justice! For the big nobs who want to fight it out but not for the poor. They go around the corner to get lagged, charged in the Bridewell, the district court. Here we are, back down to O'Connell Street. I crossed over the bridge making me way up to Cleary's, seeing people waiting under the clock for their dates. You can tell them a mile away. The fella is standing in his best Crombie coat, with the hair combed back and half a bottle of olive oil poured over it. You can smell the Old Spice aftershave a mile away! He poured half a bottle of that over himself too after he gave himself a good shave using a new silver Gillette blade. He stands with his hands dug into his pockets, slapping his feet from one foot to the other, trying to keep out the cold. Then his head is swinging up and down the street, looking for a sign of the 'bird' he asked out. He's trying to remember what she looks like, because he was a bit under the weather, had too much to drink, by the time he met her at that dance. *Jaysus! I hope she turns up! I don't want to have had to go to all this trouble for nothing! I even washed under me arms when I dipped me head under the running cold tap in the sink.*

I pushed in the doors and made straight for the basement. That's where they keep all the household stuff. Priests out on a mission to get themselves a new black shirt made for the priests' department.

Desperate nuns, looking haunted and hunted, made straight for the women's, looking for the special vests and very long navy-blue knickers, and the outsize pure cotton granny nightdresses. We all collided with each other as I went on my mission.

'Sorry, Father!'

He bows, waving a limp hand, giving me benediction. 'OK, dear!'

'Sorry, Sister!'

'No, my fault!' she smiles. Then we're off again. Me to hunt down the makings for building me very own first nest!

OK, that's enough! These things are a lot dearer than I thought they would be! Pity! I still need to get a lot more stuff, I thought, making me way back up the stairs and out through the doors. So, what did I get? Let's see, I got the cutlery and a sharp knife for cutting things. I bought meself a lovely big kitchen mug – white with blue stripes around the rim. Oh, yeah, and very important, a teapot! Jaysus! I would get nowhere without that! When all else goes wrong, have a cup of tea. Now! I still need to get me hands on sheets and a pillowcase for the bed. The price of them in that shop would break a bank! No, what I'll have to do is ask the Reverend Mother. She'll be delighted when she hears I'm going. God knows she's been dropping enough hints!

'Oh, Martha my dear!' she smiles every time she claps eyes on me. 'Any news yet about you getting a nice little flat? The girls here are always looking for someone to share with them. I do believe three of them at this very moment are looking for a fourth. The more the merrier!' she laughs, leaning into me. 'You get a better class of flat and you have plenty of company. In fact, it is essential to have as many girls as possible. If you fall out with one, then you always have another girl to speak to! Ha, ha!' she roars, getting hysterical and going purple in the face at her own joke. 'Why don't you have a word with them?'

'Yeah, Mother! Smashing idea!' I puff, then clear off, not giving it a second thought. Me and a shower of culchies? Never! Not over my dead body. That mad nun must have been getting at her. Right! I'm sure she'll settle on giving me a few sheets and blankets. It's a cheap price to pay to get rid of me! Oh, yeah, she will, and as many as I can carry. It's going to be freezing at night with the wind blowing up the Liffey. I certainly won't be getting carried away, blowing meself into a heatwave, using that little fan heater. Oh, yeah, luckily I noticed them in the shop – couple of towels. The price of them! Jaysus! I would need to own a bleedin bank. So I'll ask the Reverend Mother for them as well. That mad aul nun will probably go mad and start doing the can-can, whipping up her habit and flying out her legs, with the big navy-blue knickers hanging down to her knees, when she hears I'm gone. Ah, sure! Let her have her enjoyment! I went in me own good time. Oh, yeah! Soap! I'll need to buy that, and tea, sugar, milk and bread. And good butter. I'm not living on margarine! That's only for paupers! Just as well I was saving me money. You never know the hour or the day when you may need a few bob. I know that only too well.

So! That's the last few bob I'm spending on meself for many a day to come, I thought, looking at the big Cleary's paper bag dangling in me left hand. Still an all, it was worth it. Buying meself them new blue jeans and them lovely desert boots! They'll be lovely and warm on me in the winter, with me multicoloured teddy-bear's jacket worn over them. Only thing is, I better not wear the boots out in the rain. Suede doesn't mix too well with water! Still, I look lovely in them.

OK! I think I'm all sorted. I'll move meself into the bedsit tomorrow. It's going to take me all day. First thing is, I think what I'll do, I'll bring down the stuff for the bedsit and then go back for me suitcase. So, say an hour each way. Add another hour, then a bit more. Ten hours should get me sorted. I will buy the food and put everything away. Then make the bed and get meself ready for work on Monday.

I'm going to have to leave around half past seven in the morning if I want to get to work on time. But I'll see after Monday which route is best. I'll work it out as I go along. God! I can't believe I have me very own place to go to! So long as I pay me rent I can come and go as I please with no one to tell me different! This is what I have waited all me life for – living me own life! Now it's like a dream come true!

I sighed with contentment as I made me way around Trinity College. Pity Odette is not here to see me. She could have come and stayed with me every now and then, maybe even stay for the weekend.

I could feel the heat beginning to drain outa me with that thought. I was starting to feel cold and lonely inside. It would be lovely to have someone to share things with. But there's no one waiting for me. Father Ralph's face appeared in me mind's eye. A pain cut through me chest, a longing to be wrapped inside his arms and listen to him talking quietly, whispering that he cares about me, that I mean something to him.

I looked around, seeing people making their way, heading down to Grafton Street. They looked well dressed, the moneyed people. Their heads were lifted with their eyes pinned straight ahead, having the picture of getting themself somewhere. They might have people waiting for them. Then they will go off somewhere and do things together with a friend, I thought, looking up at a woman as she brushed past me, letting her long navy-blue wool coat brush against me face. I could get the whiff of expensive perfume. Jesus! Will this pain ever go away? It keeps catching me unawares. No! Stop, Martha. You are so well off now, you don't know you are born. My God, life is very good to me. I have got meself, now, where I always wanted to be. Now it can only get better and better. Just think! God knows how far I will get if I just keep working hard and pushing ahead! There will be nothing to stop me.

30

I worked me way through the Saturday crowds, trying to hurry meself over O'Connell Bridge. I looked back, trying to see the time up on Cleary's clock. People bashed into me as I slowed down.

'Will ye ever mind where you're stopping!' an aul one roared, pushing me outa the way.

'Sorry, Missus!' I said, moving meself on without being able to get a look at the clock. I ran across Westmoreland Street just as the lights were going red. The traffic took off before they even hit the red. That dozy-looking policeman standing up there in the middle of the road must be gone to sleep, I thought, diving out in front of a fella on a scooter. He swerved around me, nearly hitting the other two on their bicycles.

'Bleedin road hog!' I shouted after him, then headed meself on about me business. Making straight for CIE, the bus and rail company office.

Gawd, this is a great idea I have. It only hit me after a while, when I woke up this morning. Yeah, take meself off somewhere and do something different, like going off down to the country for the day. It will be good to get out of the city. I've never seen what the countryside looks like. I only did that once before. When I went on the train with all the other poor kids from the city centre. The holiday home was run by the Legion of Mary women, and it was all organised by the St Vincent De Paul. They're the society who help the poor. I went off down for the holiday of me lifetime. It was magic from heaven. That's where I first got the idea that life could be so great. I had a real bed to sleep in, with lovely bedclothes. The food was gorgeous. I even got time to play. That was where I first got a taste of something I never knew existed. Love! I got a hug from a woman. She reached down to me with her face lit up in a smile. The light in her eyes as she looked at me was pure love and gentleness. They said to me, *Little one, you are somebody!* Me! A little snot rag. A bastard nobody wanted. Someone . . . who people would say, 'Listen! Look what's here! Watch your purse! Move away, you will catch disease.'

But she swooped to gather me up and bury me in her arms. Then I was disappeared inside something very powerful. The suffering instantly vanished. The pain was gone. I was at peace. She had reached inside me, tapping into the most powerful force on earth. It flickered, then died away. But I had felt it. I knew it could heal – bring an exquisite sense of joy. Now I'm forever haunted with the pain of trying to find it again. 'Dear lady,' I whispered. 'Wherever you are now, I hope the almighty God showered a million blessings down on you. I won't ever forget you for showing me that glimpse of love.' It had lain deep inside me, ebbing away until it was just a memory. Now Ralph has woken it and it's burst into life.

I sighed, feeling down in meself. Ah, there's no point in getting lost inside meself again. I suppose I'm feeling let down because I can't see Father Ralph today. It's left a huge hole in me that only he can fill. But he's too bleedin busy! Well, OK, never mind. I'm going to enjoy meself. He's not the centre of me life. Huh! Like hell he's not! Anyway! I'll just buy the cheapest train ticket they have. Anywhere in the countryside will do me. Just so long as I get to go somewhere. I'm fed up wandering around the town on a Saturday, seeing the same old faces. You might not know them. But they all look the same after a while. This will do me a world of good. I want to feel I'm on the move. Doing a bit of travelling. Like I'm going on holiday or something. Even if it is only for the day. Pity, though, I can't go up to the north of Ireland. But now they're having a war up there. They call it the Troubles! But Jaysus! Throwing bombs at each other is a bit more than just troubles!

It was only beginning to start up the first and last time I went up there. Jaysus! I had what I thought was a marvellous idea. I took meself off up one Saturday on the train, just like now, thinking it would be lovely to see the North! I heard it's very English looking – the very same as if you were living in England. Well, I thought that sounded great.

I landed in Belfast and was just wandering out of the train station, getting ready to stop and ask someone where all the fancy shops were with all the latest fashions. I just made it down the road when a row broke out. People were standing around shouting and cursing at a load of policemen. I stopped to get a look. The police were nothing like our gobshites. These ones had big black boots and carried big guns.

'Go on oura dot! Yeha B'Special bostards!' the crowd roared.

More people joined in, moving in closer to the B'Special bostards. They moved back, then moved forward, walking in a straight line and holding up their guns! Suddenly, outa nowhere, bricks started flying through the air, landing on the skulls of the B'Special bostards. That did it! They had enough. They drew out their batons, opened their mouths, showing big horses' teeth, and shouted, 'CHARGE!'

I took in a sharp breath, pumped up me lungs, swung me head in the direction I just came, then, with me arms pinned back and me legs goings like pistons, I managed to make it back to the train station and was sitting on the train just as it was heading back to Dublin.

'Right, here we go! There's your ticket, but you better run. You only have seven minutes to get from here over to Amiens Street Station. The train will be pulling out, and you'll be left behind. You won't get your money back. Not our fault if you miss the train,' the ticket office man said, standing behind his counter and giving it a quick slap to make it sound like he was playing the bongos!

'Yeah, right, lovely! Thanks!' I puffed, shaking me head up and down, taking in him giving me the bad news after he took me money and waved the ticket at me. Me eyes peeled on the ticket he wasn't in a hurry to hand over. I snapped it outa his hand, shouting, 'Bye!' Then I was gone, tearing open the door and lashing out, straight across O'Connell Bridge, firing meself under the cars, ducking and flying onto the footpath. I flew down Eden Quay, passing all the buses stopped at the terminus with their engines left still going. I tore past, gasping in lungfuls of black smoke steaming out the back of the buses. I flew on, wheezing and gasping, feeling me lungs were being torn out with a red-hot knife. Jaysus! Have to give up the aul smokes!

'WAIT!' I screamed, coming to a stop in the middle of the road with me hands held high. I made a mistake. The truck was coming too fast. Me whole being went on red alert. I moved slowly, walking sideways across the road, all the time keeping me hands in the air and me eyes on the driver, then slowly peeled them down, seeing the size of the lorry as the big black rubber wheels slid towards me, with the brakes screaming for mercy and the rubber burning, tearing into the road. I could nearly taste the metal as it roared on top of me. I closed me eyes, holding me breath, and the world stopped. I was deaf, blind, mute! Everything was blocked out!

Then I opened me eyes, looking up at the big cab of the lorry! Me nose was nearly tipping it. The burning heat poured out and straight up me nostrils, letting me think me nose was on fire. Missed me! Jaysus! Help, Mammy! Me heart is stopped. I turned me head to the footpath and took off again. I steamed into the train station and spun around. Then I spotted an aul fella wearing a uniform with a cap on his head. He was blowing a whistle and waving a flag. I went screaming in his direction. 'MISTER! Which one is the country train?'

'That one just pulling out! You missed it!' he said, waving his flag at the train as it moved off in a puff of black smoke with its hooter going.

I came to a skidding halt, staring after it, gasping for breath with me mouth open and me eyeballs hanging out seeing the wheels going faster, trying to get up speed. Then I whipped me head back to the aul fella. He was grinning at me and waving the flag like mad at the train. No, no point in asking him to stop the train. He wouldn't give ye the steam offa his piss! Ah, holy mother a Jaysus! That's cruel! After all me running! And only by a hair's breadth! Me brain thought about this for a split second, then me eyes lit on the train again, beginning to gallop outa the station, making a huge song and dance about it with smoke belching and wheels flying, hooting its horn, screaming it's leaving. And all without me!

I'm not having that! I threw back me head, straightening me shoulders, and pumped me arms, skidding into a run, then took off with me legs flying like pistons! I built up steam, keeping up with the train, then grabbed hold of the handle on the door and yanked, slamming it open. I gasped another gust of air in me lungs, getting an extra spurt, then timed meself and held me breath, getting ready for a flying leap! And I was on, swinging outa the door, then banging it shut. I heard shouts coming after me, with the aul fella cursing me. So I pulled down the window to get a look out and see the face on him. He was stopped halfway down the platform with the whistle in one hand getting bounced up and down to his mouth. The other hand was lifting and dropping the flag, with him not knowing whether to wave or blow. I gave him a big wave, showing him me two thumbs and closing one eye at him, winking. Then it hit him.

'Ye haven't got the bloody sense ye were born wit!' he screamed. 'If ye're not kilt stone dead be that train, ye will be if I ever get a chance to get me hands on ye again! By Jaysus, you'll be one sorry young one!' he roared, waving his rolled-up flag at me.

I kept nodding me head, agreeing with him, driving him mad, then seeing him hopping up and down with the rage on him. I pulled me head back in the window and closed it up, thinking, Ah, he was only raging I might end up under the wheels, getting meself mashed stone dead. Then he would have to bring the whole train to a halt, causing mayhem. We probably only have two! Yeah! Bet that's all we have, I thought, thinking about that for a second. So, well, when the second one gets in tomorrow, or whenever it manages to limp back. Holy Jaysus! The whole train system would come to a standstill, judging by all the gnashing of teeth and the nervous collapse of the girls in the hostel when they finally manage to stagger back from the arsehole of nowhere and land back in the big city smoke after taking the train. All the same, I used to think I could put that to good use. I could bring out an empty suitcase with me when I knew I would be out late, then appear back, banging on the door at whatever time I like. I could say, standing with the empty suitcase in me hand, 'The train broke down in the middle of nowhere! I'm only getting back now!' Then they would have to let you in! Only problem was they knew I didn't live in the country! So that was out for me!

Bloody hell! I hope that aul fella is not waiting for me when I get back off the train tonight! Jaysus! There'll be killings! Ah, well now! To hell with him! Isn't it a bleedin pity about him? If he had taken his time with that flag and not been so fond of the whistle, he wouldn't have ended up getting himself all excited about nothing. Now he's probably on his way over to Jervis Street Hospital to get his heart attack seen to! Not to mention I wouldn't have nearly lost me limb and life! I could have strolled onto the train at me leisure, like a real proper lady!

I wandered down the train looking for a seat. Ah! Here's a free one next to the window. I sat down happily, dropping me shoulder bag on the seat, then took off me teddy-bear fur jacket and folded it carefully, putting it over me bag on the seat beside me. Lovely! Me eyes peeled out the window, seeing the city crowded with the people all falling over each other with the lot of them in a hurry to get their shopping. Not me! I sighed with contentment. I'm free as a bird and going off on me day's holiday. I shifted meself for more comfort, sliding out me feet, and folded me arms, letting me head drop back, then looked across at a fella and his young wife. She was wearing a wedding ring.

'That was some going!' he said, throwing his head sideways at me and laughing. 'You must be related to Ronnie Delaney! That's the fella who got a gold medal in the Olympics!' he muttered, leaning his left eye to the wife, making it look like she was thick and himself was very intelligent altogether. I didn't like him. So I lifted me cheeks in a smile, keeping me lips clamped shut, then dropped them again and threw me eyes to the countryside flashing past. Well, it's not really that fast, because the train is old and it's doing its best. But it coughs and loses its wind, slowing down every time we hit something that looks like a little climb. Me belly started to rumble, watching the pair of them in front of me take out a flask and pour Bovril into two cups. The steam lifted into the air and curled over to me, going straight up me nostrils. Gawd, that's lovely, wonder if they'll offer me a drop? Pity I wasn't nicer to your man. Then the woman lifted her shopping bag and took out a big parcel of greaseproof bread paper that you get your sliced bread wrapped up in when you buy it in the shops.

I watched as she held out a big ham sandwich, offering it to the husband. He took one look at it, with his eyes following her every movement, and his hands at the ready, then grabbed it and shoved half in his mouth, filling it, and started to munch away, giving a quick look out at the scenery for his better enjoyment. Then she slowly took a sip of the hot drink, and half the size of his mouthful, and started to munch, waving it at him, saying, 'I got this ham in the pork butchers! They put lovely seasoning on it. Isn't it lovely?'

'Oh, yeah!' he muttered, shaking his head up and down, looking at the sandwich, then at her, giving her a smile without opening his mouth. Then he suddenly leaned into her, planting a kiss on the side of her head because he missed her mouth! She bent down to rescue a crumb of ham landing in her lap. Then he went back to his making short work of the rest of the sandwiches, leaving half of what was in his mouth sitting on the side of her head. I gaped, keeping me mouth open and not breathing, watching and hoping they might lean across to me and say, 'Would you like a sandwich? Go on! Take one, we have plenty to spare.' No! I'm not going to hit lucky with them hungry fuckers! I moaned to meself, watching as she rolled up the empty bread paper and put the cork back on the now empty flask. Ah, Jaysus! Would you credit the meanness of them two miserable aul pigs? You would think they would at least have offered me one sandwich. I was right about them!

No, not only do I not like them but I now wouldn't piss on them if they were on fire! Pity they didn't choke! I snorted, giving him a dirty look when he caught me eye. Gawd! I'm dying with the hunger! I could feel me insides beginning to get smaller, trying to eat itself alive with the starvation on me.

Right! No more tormenting yourself thinking about grub. Think of the lovely fish and chips I will get meself when we get to the country. Ah, Jaysus! It just dawned on me! They might not have fish and chip places in the country. They probably never even heard a them! Yeah! That's right! They only eat bacon and cabbage! That's how they end up with all the red necks! It's all them good steaks they eat seeing as they have all the cows! Ah, now I'm really fed up. Maybe this wasn't such a good idea after all.

I sighed out me wind, dropping me head back to looking out the window, seeing nothing but trees and grass, and cows idling, happily munching away. Then I spotted a farmer woman coming into me sights. She was standing in a farmyard, wearing an apron wrapped around her and a pair of wellington boots with the tops rolled down. She was swinging a metal bucket and throwing stuff out of it at a crowd of chickens. I watched, craning me neck as they all came tearing over. Suddenly she was smothered from head to toe in chickens. They took off, flapping their wings in the air, landing on top of her. One chicken was on her shoulder, then another one leapt, diving for the top of her head. Jaysus! I never knew chickens were that dangerous! I didn't get a long look, because the train hit a hill and we went flying down. Further on, I saw another aul one that looked nearly identical except for the woolly hat on her head to keep out the cold. She was leaning herself on a big farm gate talking to an aul one in a heavy coat with a long apron hanging under it and a pair of wellingtons that matched her own. That aul one was supposed to be heading somewhere, because she was leaning on a bicycle. But she looked like there was no hurry on her.

Suddenly the train jerked and we all shot forward. Then there was an unmerciful screech. The iron wheels skidded along the tracks, throwing up sparks, and the driver was hopping off his hooter, making the horn go mad! People who were dozing shot up their heads, saying, 'What's happening? We're stopping! But we haven't arrived yet!' Then we looked out the window. But no, we didn't stop. We were still moving straight across a railway crossing with a farmer on one side standing with his bicycle and a big stick in his hand, wearing the rolled-down wellingtons and a long coat tied around the waist with twine. He pulled the cap off his head, looking very worried as we shot past his cow. It was stopping for a piss on the railway track. I looked, seeing gallons of golden hot steaming piss pouring down. The cow moved on slowly, still pissing, managing to pass out of the way of the train. It had huge eyes and stared back at us as we barrelled past with wheels screeching and smoke pouring everywhere and the driver dancing on his hooter! The cow roared after us, opening its mouth and dropping its big pink tongue, letting out a terrible moan, sounding like she was really disgusted we had disturbed her in the middle of doing her business.

The train roared into the station, letting go with everything it had. The wheels did their screaming, the steam poured out, covering everyone and everything in smoke. The hooter went and the engine panted, sounding like a pack of Red Indians, working up a war dance. We were stopped. Then the doors were flung open and people started jumping down.

The two people in front of me stood up and stretched. Then the man grabbed his coat, putting it on. 'Ready?' he said, looking at the wife as he bent down and lifted their shopping bag. 'Come on, love, we're here!' he said, hopping from one foot to the other, getting impatient with her.

'Take your time, Joe! I have to get me coat on,' she moaned, getting annoyed with him now.

'Ah! I'm going!' he said, moving off, hoping she would get a move on and follow him fast.

I stood up and put on me coat. Jaysus! It's great to have your freedom and not have to answer to anyone. Am I glad to be here on me own and not have to please anyone, I thought, seeing the woman muttering her annoyance as she rushed after the husband. I bet they end up with a fight before the day is out. Serve the eejits right for not offering me a bit of their picnic!

31

I stepped off the train, following the crowd all making for the outside. Oh! First I better find out what time the train leaves for Dublin this evening. 'Excuse me, Mister!' I said to a man heading into the little ticket office. He was wearing a railway uniform. 'What time do I have to be back here to catch the train going home to Dublin?'

'Six o'clock, no later,' he said. 'It leaves then. You better get here around quarter to six just to be safe.'

'Thanks, Mister!' Then I was gone, heading out the station and making to see how the culchies live.

Suddenly a fella roared up on a big black motorbike! He came to a stop, turning the bike around sharply, facing the way he came. I watched as a fella jumped off the back then tapped the driver on the back, saying, 'Thanks for the lift, Ulick! See you back in Dublin.'

Me breath caught in me chest staring at it, and him! He was wearing brown-tinted sunglasses and he had nice wavy, carroty-red hair cut up around his ears and curling down his neck. But it's not his looks that interest me! He's OK looking. No, it's the black leather jacket he's wearing with the matching leather boots fastened with buckles around his legs. With him looking like that, sitting on the huge motorbike with big silver handlebars coming up into the air – looking exactly like the motorbike yer man rode in that great film I saw once. It was called *Easy Rider* and, Gawd, yer man here is the image of him. So is the bike!

Without thinking, I said, 'Hey! That's a smashing motorbike you have there!'

He was just about to lift his foot, and was turning his hand on the gears, gunning the engine into a roar, when he suddenly stopped and looked at me, saying, 'Would you like to go for a spin?'

Before he had time to draw the next breath I was sitting on the back of his motorbike, saying, 'Yes please!'

'Where would you like to go?' he said, without smiling, and throwing his head to one side of me, waiting for me answer.

'Eh, anywhere you like,' I said, not knowing where the hell I had even landed.

'OK! Let's go! We'll take a run around the town.'

'That will do lovely!' I said happily, delighted to get meself a lift on the back of a bike with a fella that looked like Henry Fonda, or whatever his name was. Even the bike was the same.

We took off and flew around the town. I didn't see much. I'm too busy hanging on. This is just great. I could feel the power of the speed under me arse and legs, and the wind blowing me hair out behind me. I could even get the smell of yer man's leather jacket. He felt real manly under me hands, grabbing him by the shoulders. Not like a skinny young fella. He is definitely well built. So, at least I got noticed by a proper fella. Then we were back, whizzing up to the entrance to the station. People were still spilling out and stopped to stare. They must have seen the film too. I felt like a little bit of a film star meself.

'Thanks for the spin,' I said, throwing me leg back and climbing off the bike.

'Are you from Dublin?' he said, just as I was about to go off on me business.

'Yeah! I came down for the day. Is there anywhere good to eat?' I said, looking at him.

'If you like, I'll take you to a café in the town. You can get fish and chips there. Is that what you want?'

'Yeah, exactly that! You just read my mind,' I laughed.

'OK! Get back on and we'll go there!' he said. 'I'm down here with friends for the weekend. We are all heading back this evening. If you like, you can come back to Dublin on the bike with me. It should be more fun than the train, even if it is a whole lot colder,' he said, smiling without opening his mouth.

'Yeah! Smashing! I don't mind. Anything for a bit of adventure.' Then I hopped on and we were off again.

He slowed down outside a café that said 'Mario's Fish and Chips'. I could get the smell and me mouth watered. I was nearly weak with the hunger.

'Right!' I said, watching his leg draw back and click on the stand. Then he stood up, brushing back his wavy hair with his hands and followed me into the café. A load of young ones and young fellas stopped what they were doing to look up and watch us. The young ones took him in and the young fellas stared at me from head to toe with their mouths open. I could see the girls nudging each other and fixing their hair, giving yer man the eye. I felt very glamorous altogether and I started to wriggle me arse like Marilyn Monroe, thinking I was the greatest-looking thing since sliced pan.

'What do you want?' he said to me, still wearing the sunglasses.

'Eh, fresh cod and chips,' I said, looking up at the counter.

'Do you want to eat here or will we take them outside?'

'Let's go outside,' I said, looking around seeing no free tables.

'These are for you,' he said, handing me a big parcel of white paper. I opened it, seeing a long brown battered fish and a bag of chips smothered in salt and vinegar. I looked to see what he got. Ah! He only has a bag of chips. This must have cost him all his money. I dragged me bag around me shoulder and dipped in looking to see what I had in me purse.

'Here! My share of the grub,' I said, handing him two half crowns. 'Take that five shillings.'

'Ah, no! Keep your money. It was me who invited you!' he said.

'No! If you don't take the money, then I'm going to feel under compliment to you! Take the money,' I said, pushing his arm.

'OK! This is definitely me getting off lightly!' he laughed, showing his teeth that could have looked whiter.

I stared at them. Ah, well! You can't have everything, I thought, swallowing me disappointment down with a chip. Then he took off his sunglasses, taking the glamour with them. He wanted to see his chips. I stared, seeing him put them away inside his jacket pocket. Then me eyes flew back to his face. Me own face was falling and I stopped chewing on me chips. Ah, Jaysus! His eyes are – what would you call them? – flat looking. Not to mention his face looks longer now. And all without the sunglasses.

Oh, who cares? I sighed, thinking he's just a fella anyway. I'm not interested in looking for a boyfriend. Anyway, I have Ralph!

'What do you do?' I said, making conversation. I was only interested in the bike really. When he put on the sunglasses and we took off on the bike, then it was grand. We gave the impression we were really with it! Well, he did! People would make the same mistake as me, thinking I'm with someone that looked like a film star. Then people would be jealous! All wanting to be me with the lovely-looking fella on the lovely-looking motorbike!

'I'm a clerk for an engineering business,' he said, looking at me, examining me face to see what I was like and really made of.

I gave a little nod, giving him the impression I was not really bothered whether he liked me or not. That wasn't really hard, because without the bike and the sunglasses he wasn't exactly any girl's fancy! At the same time I wanted him to think I was a nice person. But laid-back. Very sophisticated!

'What's your name? Mine is Ulick!'

'Martha!' I said.

'What do you do, Martha?' he said, looking really interested at me, smiling.

'I'm a junior secretary!' I said, giving the air of someone who was born with a silver spoon in me mouth!

'Oh!' he said, with his eyes lighting up, very impressed I was a somebody.

'How many brothers and sisters do you have?' I said, thinking again about what I thought of him. Ah, he's real nice, really. He did want to spend all his money on me! That tells me he's very kind.

'I'm the only child,' he said.

'You mean you are an only child?' I said, wondering how that could happen.

'Yeah!' he laughed. 'They only have me to fret about!'

'Gawd! You must be really spoilt, Ulick,' I said, wondering what it was like to be him – an only child!

'No! I'm not spoilt,' he said, dropping his mouth and creasing his forehead, thinking about it. 'But Mammy is very strict. She tries to keep me wrapped in cotton wool!

Mammy! I thought. Calling her that to me at his age!

'How old are you?' I said, thinking he must be at least twenty-two or -three.

'Nineteen. How old are you?'

'Eighteen! So that means we are nearly the same age!' I said, delighted and yet a bit disappointed. He looked really big, well built. I thought he was older, more like a man. Not a young fella, really. I'm not interested in them. Or older fellas, come to think about it. No, just the one and only Ralph. The be-all and end-all of me life as far as I'm concerned.

'What part of Dublin are you from?' I said.

'South County Dublin. Mountain Hill.'

Oh! That's very respectable, I thought to meself. At least he's not a gurrier!

'What about you? Where do you come from?'

'Oh, I'm living close to the Phoenix Park. Just down near the River Liffey.'

'Oh, that's very close to the city,' he said. 'What does your father do?'

'Nothing,' I said. 'He's dead!'

'Oh, sorry! So, it must be hard on your mammy, having to manage on her own.'

'No, she's gone too,' I said, thinking of the book I came across not long ago. It was written by a fella by the name of Oscar Wilde. He wrote a lot of books. Anyway, for a change me and Odette went to the Gate Theatre one Saturday afternoon. She said I needed to further my education. It was a great idea. Well, the idea was Ralph's, really. He insisted we go. He said it would keep us out of trouble. 'Besides, you need to further your education, my love!' Those were his exact words – the 'my love' bit. Still sends a rush of heat flying around me body.

Christ! What was I thinking about? Oh, yeah. The play was called *The Importance of Being Earnest.* He was an orphan found dumped in a handbag. I loved every minute of it. Me and Odette crunched and sucked our way through a big bags of sweets and laughed our heads off. People kept looking around at us and tut-tutting! Then they had the cheek to tell us to be quiet! Their mad whispering with the rage on them was worse than our sucking and crunching! Anyway, what was I thinking? Oh, yeah! Oscar, or the people in the play, said, 'To lose one parent is unfortunate! But to lose two is careless!' Then I sighed, enjoying me memories, and batted me eyes, opening and closing them, to come back to Ulick! The poor fella was rambling away to himself, not realising I wasn't listening.

'So, what about the rest of your family?'

'What family?' I said, losing track of where we were.

'Your brothers and sisters? Do you not want to talk about it?' he said, shaking his head and looking a bit ashamed.

'No, there's nothing to talk about, Ulick. There's just me. I was reared by my grandmother.' I nearly said Grandmam'ma! 'So, she's dead, and now I have me own flat. Well, it's a bedsitter!'

He nodded his head, listening. I thought he was really interested in hearing all about me. But that's all the information he's ever getting outa me!

'OK! Maybe we should get moving,' he said, wrapping up the empty chip papers, rolling them into a ball and walking back into the café to leave them on the table.

'Gawd! You really are well trained,' I said, thinking he must come from a very respectable home.

'Yes, my mother is house-clean mad. She follows me around the house with a dustpan and hand brush,' he said, not looking too happy about it.

I laughed, liking the sound of her.

'Come on! Let's go and see what the gang is up to! You can meet my friends. They are sitting in a pub a couple of miles down the road from here,' he said, throwing his leg over the motorbike and waiting for me to jump on.

We flew down country roads, with the branches of big old trees hanging over them, making it look a very dark and lonely place in the late October winter. 'Duck!' he shouted, and I bent me head into his back as he leaned the bike into hairpin bends, dropping the bike sideways, nearly tipping the handlebars on the ground as it whizzed past us at a dizzying speed. I went with his movements, leaning with him. Then he would flip the bike, straightening it up, and jerk his hand, going into a higher gear. The bike rocked and we hit into the wind, letting it take our breaths away as we roared into a straight road, feeling we were like gods! Nothing could touch us. We would live for ever. The open road is ours and the world belongs to us.

I could see ahead an old country pub sitting nestling under a mountain. There was nothing around for miles but rocks and gorse and the lonely sound of a cow crying to be taken home. Ulick slowed down and pulled up beside four other motorbikes. Jaysus! I hope this lot don't think themself Hell's Angels! I'm not interested in troublemakers! We could hear noisy singing. It sounded like a load of fellas getting a bit rowdy. I hope this wasn't another one of me bad ideas, I thought, beginning to feel me nerves going.

'Come on! Let's go in!' he said, walking ahead and holding open the cottage-looking front door.

I hesitated.

'Don't worry! They're just enjoying themselves. You'll like them,' he said, seeing I was nervous. 'It's a bit spit-and-sawdust but we like it. That's the reason we came all the way out here,' he said, walking in with me following behind.

I walked into a dark stuffy little cottage, with a long wooden counter and plain hard well-worn stools with three legs lined up against the bar. The smell of paraffin oil sent shudders down me spine. It reminded me of when we first moved in with Jackser. He used to light the little room we lived in with a paraffin lamp. I shook me head and blinked, chasing away them pictures of long ago, then looked around, seeing who was here. Two aul geezers with caps on their heads and old coats that had seen better days rested their turned-up wellington boots on the bar of the stools. They looked around, holding a big pint of black Guinness with half of it drunk and some still left on their mouths. They gaped at us with their mouths open, then turned their backs, wriggling their shoulders to get more comfort for ignoring us. I heard one mutter to the other, 'Bejaysus! Musheen! Dhere's more a dem queer sorta people just come in on top a us!'

'Take no notice, don't you now,' muttered his friend, sounding very experienced on what to do when you were in danger of losing your life! I felt a bit ashamed, not wanting to be in the company of people that worry others.

Ulick made his way over to the one and only table, pushed into the end of the little room. I looked down at the floor, seeing what he meant about spit and sawdust. The cement floor was covered in sawdust. A metal bucket full of the stuff stood next to a fireplace with a few sods of turf smouldering away. Every few seconds it threw out a belch of smoke, nearly suffocating the room. A big brass paraffin lamp burned on the counter and another one burned over a shelf, throwing flickering light down into the corner where a crowd of fellas sat with one girl between them. They were singing a rowdy song. I listened to the words. 'An engineer told me before he died! A hum diddly I diddly I dee dee. He knew a girl with a ahem so wide that she could never be satisfied. A hum diddly I diddly I dee dee!'

'Cut it out!' shouted Ulick. 'You are terrifying the local natives!'

'HURRAH! The wanderer returns!' they shouted, waving their arms in the air and banging their feet and their hands on the table all at the same time.

'Oooh! He has been woman hunting!' one fella with a big black beard said, staring at me with his eyes going wide and laughing.

'Take no notice of them,' Ulick said to me, laughing. They all stared at me with their eyes taking me in and big laughs held on their face, waiting to hear what was going on.

'Listen, everyone! This is Martha. I met her at the railway station when I was leaving off Sean. She's coming back with us to Dublin!'

'Ohhhhh, you naughty boy!' they roared, starting the roar low, then bringing it up to the ceiling. 'What will Mammy say?' they laughed.

'Don't mind them eejits, Martha,' Ulick said to me, pointing at them with his forehead creased and a laugh on his face. 'They're nice fellas, really.'

'How're ye, Martha?' the big fella with the black beard said, half standing up and leaning his hand across the table to shake me hand. 'I'm Arnie!'

'Yeah!' they all roared. 'AN ENGINEER TOLD ME BEFORE ME DIED! AHH HUM! DIDDLY I DIDDLY I DEE DEE! HE KNEW A GIRL WITH A AHEM SO WIDE THAT SHE COULD NEVER BE SATISFIED. A HUM DIDDLY I DIDDLY I DEE DEE!'

'STOP! SHUT UP, the lot of you,' laughed the girl, shouting at the lot of them.

'Arnie is an engineer, or at least he will be when he gets his degree,' Ulick said, nodding to Arnie, who was giving me a big smile and looking a bit shy now that all eyes were on him.

'Yeah! A big hairy engineer,' a tall skinny fella with a mop of red carroty hair said, leaning across to him, then saying, 'Arnie, you'll never get that girl engineer in your class if you don't get rid of that beard.'

'Me and the beard go together,' he muttered, stroking it down with his hands.

'Hello, Martha! I'm Sophie,' the girl sitting next to Arnie said. 'Take no notice of this lot!' she said, throwing her eyes from one side to the other, taking them all in. 'They're fellas! What more can I say?'

'Yeah!' I laughed, nodding me head, agreeing.

'Nice to meet you, Martha! I'm Owen,' the tall skinny fella said, standing up to shake me hand.

'Yeah! He's hoping to get wings and start flying!' a fella sitting next to him said. They all laughed. He could take the easy way and go tripping on LSD, then they all started singing, 'LUCY IN THE SKY!'

'Don't mind them!' Owen said. 'The cider is rotting their brains. I'm stationed down in Baldonnell, in the Air Corps. I'm a trainee pilot, for me sins,' he said, with his face going red. Then he looked down and examined his nearly empty glass of cider.

'Ritchie!' a tall dark-haired fella said, standing up quickly and shaking me hand.

'What do you do, Ritchie?' I said. 'Seeing as the rest of them said what they were doing,' I laughed.

'Architecture, or at least me mammy hopes I will!' he laughed, hearing the rest of them give a big laugh. 'Yeah! I'm a student, Martha.'

'And the last fella is Evan!' said Ulick, laughing, as a fella lifted his hand giving me the V-for-victory sign.

'Peace, man,' he said, looking very serious.

They all cracked up, spitting their drinks down the front of their jumpers. 'Ha, ha! He's still at that lark! Wait till we tell you, Martha. Your man there, Evan, went around all day trying to pick up a bird! He was trying to convert the local young ones into making love not war. Giving them a load of malarkey about him being a hippie. He thought by wearing his mammy's scarf on his forehead would get them eating out of his hands.'

I looked at the multicoloured scarf tied around his forehead. 'Did it work?' I said.

'No! The mammies chased him outa town. That's why we all have to hide out here. The fathers are searching for us right this minute, carrying shotguns!' they laughed.

I laughed, getting the picture of him with the long skinny face and the desperate look in his eyes. He reminded me of a puppy wanting to be picked up.

'He's never had a girlfriend!' Arnie said, taking a sip of his cider, half laughing and half serious. 'No! He keeps sending all the wrong signals! The girls head for the trees when they see him coming.'

'Do you know something?' Owen said, thinking, looking around at the lot of them then up at me. 'He once asked a girl would she like to get married. But just in case they were not compatible maybe they should have the honeymoon first! He was deadly serious!' Owen said, shaking his head, choking on his drink and spilling it, trying not to laugh.

'Aw, come on, fellas! Enough is enough!' the hippie said, looking around at them with his face pained like it was hurting him. His eyes got very watery looking. I felt sorry for him. I shook me head, laughing. 'I'm Evan!' he muttered, looking up at me then dropping his eyes, picking up his cider.

'Right, boys and girls! I think we should start hitting the road!' Ulick said. 'We need to make a start before the light goes. We don't want to be travelling these roads in the dark! Come on! Drink up and let's go!'

'What? We haven't even started!' Arnie roared, looking around at everyone's nearly empty glass.

'No, don't be mean, Ulick! You just want to miss out on the next round because you know it's your turn!'

'What? Feck off, the lot of you! I wasn't even here while you lot were filling your gut! I was taking Sean to the station while you lazy lot had a party!'

'Aw, come on, Ulick! Look what you got yourself! If I had known she was floating about, I would have been at the station like a light,' said Arnie.

'Hear, hear!' said the other fellas, banging their glasses on the table.

I felt me face going red, seeing them all looking at me like they thought I was a great find.

'Yeah, so stop moaning,' said Evan.

'Look! You haven't even offered Martha a drink yet! Where's your manners, boy?' shouted Arnie. 'Come on, Martha. I'll buy you a drink,' he said, jumping up, making for the bar counter, then sitting back down, saying, 'Only I feel sorry for Ulick. He would crack up without me! Sorry, Martha. You need to be very intelligent to get through to Ulick. He's not blessed with too much brain power between the ears.'

'Come on! For Christ's sake, lads! It's time to get moving. I want to get back home before it gets too late!'

'Ah, yeah! Will we go, lads? Otherwise his ma will be phoning the police,' said Owen.

'And the fire brigade,' snapped Arnie. 'Yeah! She'll want an all-out search for him! Right! Let's get going,' he said, standing up and stretching. They all wore jeans and leather boots. I watched as they sorted their stuff out and pulled on black leather jackets. All the jackets had little medals on them, even the girl's.

She saw me looking. 'These are from the Isle of Man motorbike races – the TT races. We go over there every year,' she smiled, walking over to me with a helmet under her arm and holding her black jacket by the collar to show me.

'So, you go to motorbike races?'

'Oh, yeah!' she said, shaking her lovely head of long brown hair and looking at me with her gorgeous greeny-blue eyes. 'We're in the motorcycle club. There's a big event coming up. Clubs from all over Ireland and England meet. They have different competitions for all classes of cc. That's the size of the engine in the bikes. It will be held down in the country.'

'Oh, yeah, that sounds good!' I said, thinking it would be nice to go travelling and be with a crowd.

'OK! Let's get moving,' Arnie said.

'Who are you with, Sophie? Which one is your boyfriend?'

'Ritchie!' she said.

'Oh, he's nice!' I said, watching as she tied a scarf around her neck and zipped up her jacket, then pulled the left flap across, snapping it shut all the way up. Then she pulled the silver buckle at the end of the jacket and pulled it tight, fastening it. Then she whipped on her helmet, hammering it down, and pulled the leather strap across, tightening it.

'Ready, Sophie?' Ritchie said, coming up behind her and putting his hand on her back, leading her out the door.

'Bye, Martha. Prepare yourself for a freezing run back to Dublin!' she said, giving me a smile and looking at me clothes. 'You need the right gear. Like this,' she said, slapping her leather jacket. 'Otherwise you freeze to death. Sit in behind Ulick and keep your head well down. Let him cover you,' she said, looking serious.

'Yeah, OK! Thanks, Sophie,' I said, waving at her heading out the door.

'Goodnight!' they all shouted to the men resting their arms on the counter. The owner, an aul fella with snow-white hair and not a tooth in his head, lifted his big bushy eyebrows and muttered 'G'luck' outa the corner of his mouth. The others nodded their heads without saying anything and not looking around, just giving a quick eye to the door as everyone followed each other out.

'Here, Martha! You wear this,' Ulick said, reaching down to land a motorbike helmet on me head. It looked like one of them big round iron things the deep-sea divers wear when they are going to the bottom of the ocean.

'Ah, no thanks! It's all right. I'll wear me hat,' I said, pulling up the hat on me fur jacket.

'No, you need to wear this if you are getting on the bike,' he said, putting it down on me head and giving it a bang to get it to sit properly.

'But, sure, that's yours, Ulick! What will you do?'

'Never mind me! You wear this,' he said, pulling the leather strap across me chin. 'OK?' he said, looking at me to see if I was looking OK. 'Pull up the zip on your jacket. You need to keep the wind from getting inside you.'

'Yeah, right,' I said, watching him wrap a woolly scarf around his face, just leaving his eyes free. Then he zipped himself up and we were off out the door.

The rest of them were all sitting with the motorbikes, firing up their engines. They turned looking at us, waiting for us to get on, then we could all take off. Ulick threw his leg over and snapped the bike stand back, then started his engine and I hopped on behind him, sitting meself down into the well-padded leather seat. He had both feet on the ground, revving up the engine. Then Arnie took off and Owen followed. Evan roared up behind them. We waited while Ritchie moved off, tearing to catch up because the group had disappeared – gone bombing up the road, leaving a trail of smoke behind. Then we took off. The bike hesitated while Ulick changed gears. Then our heads lurched back and we took off like a rocket roaring into the dark night, getting smothered up by the pitch black of the countryside. All I could make out was the lights of the bikes letting us see a few feet ahead. Shadows danced out in front of us, making me think we were going to hit something. It was only the shapes of the trees dancing around the narrow roads in front of the light. The roar of the engines was the only sound to be heard.

I lifted me head into the wind, feeling the icy blast tear at me cheeks, rattling my face and trying to rip out me eyeballs. I dropped me head, burying in down the side of Ulick's back, and wrapped me arms around his waist, feeling the power of the speed as it tried to tear me off the bike. Jaysus! We're going at an almighty lick! Any second now we could be killed stone dead. The only thing between us and that is the two wheels and the metal frame holding us up! Yeah, this is the life! She flies like a bird! Oh me, oh my! I sang in me mind.

We flew through little villages with maybe only a couple of cottages and a pub. It looked like a shop as well. One side had tea and cornflakes in the window. The other side showed a fat little leprechaun sitting on a barrel of Guinness! This village was so small that if you blinked you would miss it. Then we hit a town. I knew it was because it had a church, two pubs, a little post office that sold groceries, and a hardware shop. That would be for the farmers, I suppose.

Three young fellas were sitting sprawled on a bench outside the little church. They had their necks buried inside their overcoats and their hands dug into their pockets trying to beat the cold. When we came roaring past, their heads snapped, following us, taking in one bike at a time. They moved their heads slowly, doing it together. Then they whipped their heads back to get a look at us – doing it so perfectly, it looked like they had only one head. They watched us without saying a word. We were the last to roar out of the town, leaving only the silence behind and the smoke to show we'd been there.

32

W e roared out of the countryside, seeing the bright lights of the city ahead of us. The last trees and hedges faded away into the darkness as we flew past the first street lamps sitting in a no-man's-land between town and country. Everyone continued together, making their way across the River Liffey, heading for the South Side. I was frozen solid. Jaysus! Where is he going? I live up at the Phoenix Park. Ah, let it go! I can remind him when he stops the bike. I'm too cold now to bother moving a muscle.

We reached the South Side and stopped at the traffic lights just after the cats' and dogs' home. Arnie turned around, giving a wave. Then he turned right and was gone, disappearing into the empty streets with a cold damp fog hanging close to the ground. I suppose he was heading for the comfort of his home. That's the place to be on a night like tonight, thawing out over a hot drink and toasting your toes by the fire, I thought, thinking of me own bedsit.

One by one, everyone peeled off until it was just Ulick and me. Then he slowed down as we turned right into a row of houses.

'We're here!' he said, stopping the bike and pulling the scarf off his face. I hesitated, wondering if I would ever be able to move again. Jaysus! I'm too stiff! Someone's going to have to carry me over to the heat and melt me down! I lifted me leg, feeling it stiffen, then stood up, watching him lift the bike onto the footpath and wheel it into the front of the house. A big black car stood in the drive. I looked up at the house, seeing it was an old house with a big storm porch in front. The inside was red tiles, with a lovely coloured lamp hanging down to give out light. The front door had half glass that looked like church glass. Ulick saw me staring at the house as he parked the bike in the corner, well away from his father's car. 'They were built in the 1920s,' he said, walking stiffly over to me.

Just as he was about to put the key in the front door, it opened. 'Ah! You're back, Ulick, love,' a woman with a big smile lighting up her face shouted. She was wearing a yellow apron tied around the front of her, with strings going around the back. Then the smile was wiped off her face at the sight of me. She stopped talking, leaving her mouth hanging open to take me in.

'Who did you bring home?' she said after getting her voice back and pulling the door open to let him in, then holding it shut a bit in case I followed him home and wasn't invited.

'Oh, yeah, Mammy! This is Martha. Come on, Martha,' he said, coming back out to grab me by the arm and drag me into the house. The mammy looked out to see if there was anyone else coming, then banged the door shut to keep out the cold damp night. The lovely heat hit me as I made me way, following Ulick down the hall.

'Here, Ulick. Take off them boots and leave them in the hall. I only polished that floor this morning,' she said, looking down disgusted at his big leather boots. He flew outa the kitchen, whipping his leather jacket and scarf off, throwing them up on the hall stand for hanging your coats up. Then he dropped his boots under a shelf kept for all the outdoor shoes. I waited for him while the mammy rushed into the kitchen, saying, 'Daddy! Ulick is home safe and sound. He's brought a girl with him.'

I heard a mumble. Ulick turned around and smiled at me, checking to make sure I was still behind him and not gone running back out the door. He was looking in a hurry to get into the kitchen. I hesitated, not wanting to be here. The mammy looked like she wasn't in the mood for visitors, especially a young one.

'Come on! Let's go inside. Me mammy really has taken to you,' he said.

I looked at him. 'How the bloody hell can you tell that?' I said, suddenly, without warning, beginning to lose me rag. I wanted to go home. Not have to please his mother.

'Well, she does,' he said, not looking too sure.

'Is it because she let me in?' I said, feeling peevish, knowing I was creating a bad impression with him, letting him think I was always cranky. But I'm cold and tired and hungry. 'OK!' I said, hating to go where I'm not wanted. Especially when I'm not invited. I gave a big sigh, letting out me breath, and followed him into the kitchen. I looked around, seeing a lovely big kitchen. It had a big window looking out into a garden. But the curtains were drawn against the night and I couldn't see the garden.

'Hello!' a tall man wearing glasses said, smiling up at me from an armchair by the fire. He was wearing slippers and he had a pipe stuck in his mouth. The fire was roaring hot, banked up to a golden glow of red-hot coals.

'Sit down!' his mammy said to me. 'What did you say your name was?' she said, looking at me and grabbing a dishcloth to lift a heavy pot off the gas cooker.

'Martha.'

'Oh, I like that name!' she said, grabbing two big bowls and spooning a lovely brown stew out of the pot using a big serving spoon. 'Here! Get that into you,' she said to Ulick, sitting at the table with his big spoon ready.

He looked at his, saying, 'Great! Thanks, Mammy! Just what the doctor ordered. I could eat a scabby babby!' Then he whipped the spoon into the bowl of stew and started to wolf it down, then stopped to grab his mouth. 'It's hot!' he moaned.

'Take it easy, Ulick! You'll burn the mouth off yourself. Tut, tut!' she said, shaking her head to me and making a face much as to say *I don't know what I'll do with that child*. Then she handed me a big bowl of stew, the same as his.

'No!' she said, changing her mind. 'Move your hands and I'll put it down for you. The bowls are hot. I had them warming in the oven.'

Then she opened the oven and took out a big black tray with little cakes. 'Oh, Mammy! Did you bake today?' he said, dropping his head down to his dinner then whipping it up into his mouth, letting his head fly back to the cakes, wanting to grab at them all at the same time.

'Yes! I did a lot of baking today. I baked an apple tart. Hang on! Have some soda bread with that stew. It's just out of the oven,' she said, fixing the hot cakes on a wire rack to cool them, then rushing over to a long wide press behind the daddy in the corner, going the length of the wall. 'Would you like some of this?' she said to us staring over to see what she had, bringing back a lovely brown crusty-looking loaf of bread and landing it on the bread board with a big kitchen knife sitting next to it.

'Yes, please, M'am!' I said happily, beginning to feel better with the heat and the good food.

She sat herself down in the other armchair beside the fire opposite the daddy. 'So! What was the weather like?' she said to Ulick, watching him make short work of the bread after he polished up what was left of the gravy with it. Then she stood up, seeing we had finished the dinner, and lifted the tea cosy off the teapot sitting on the table. I watched as she poured out two mugs of tea and handed me one then gave Ulick the other. Then she lifted the cakes off the wire rack and tested them to make sure they were not sticking to the rack, then grabbed up a big fancy cake plate and loaded them on, piling them all on top of each other.

'Here! Try them. I put jam and almonds in these ones,' she said, putting the plate in the middle of the table.

'No, the weather was great,' he said, stuffing his mouth with one cake after another.

'Did you wear them two thermal vests I bought for you? They are meant to keep your chest warm and dry. Especially when you go off gallivanting on that bike down to God knows where! They end up in the middle of nowhere!' she said, looking at me, shocked. Not able to take in how they could all be so brainless.

I nodded me head, listening.

'Right in the heart of the country, Martha. I mean, what would he do if the bike broke down?' she said, looking very worried over at him.

He ignored her and kept his mind on getting through the cakes. So she just shook her head, looking very sad, and sat watching the fire crackle and hiss. Then she remembered what she had started out saying. 'I hope you did!' she said, leaning herself forward to get a better look at him. I could see her eyes narrowing and she had a suspicious look on her face. 'Did you?' she said, getting ready to be annoyed with him.

'Did I what?' he said, sticking his fingers in the crumbs left on the plate then shoving them in his mouth, licking his fingers, nibbling away at nothing.

'Tut! Didn't I just ask you? Did you wear them warm thermal vests I left out for you?'

'Yes, Mammy, I did! Don't worry,' he said, giving his eyeballs a quick flick to the ceiling, not wanting the mammy to see. Then he creased his cheeks in a quick laugh over to me.

'He's very delicate!' she said to me, nodding her head quickly up and down, knowing this to be a fact. Then she threw her eye over to him and back to me, making sure I knew who she was talking about.

'He is?' I said, creasing me eyebrows, looking shocked at that news.

'Oh, yes! When he was a baby, he got very sick on us! We thought we were going to lose him. I can tell you it was touch and go, for a while.'

'Yeah, well, he's a credit to you now, with the size of him,' I said, smiling at her, then looking at the size of him.

'Oh, yes!' she said, still thinking about it. 'Isn't that right, Daddy?' she said, looking over at the daddy reading his newspaper.

'What? Yeah, right! Oh, yeah!' he said, shaking his head up and down trying to work out what she said to him but in an awful hurry to get back to his newspaper!

'Have you had enough to eat?' she said, looking over at our empty plates and the empty cake plate with not even a crumb of bread left. We polished off the lot. Ulick was grabbing away, shovelling it all down his gullet, so I stopped being polite and helped meself, grabbing at everything before he got a chance. At one stage there was only one cake left on the plate. We both grabbed for it at the same time.

'Go on! You have it!' he said, pulling back his hand and jamming them into fists against his stomach.

'No, you have it, Ulick!' I said, not wanting to be seen as a savage.

'No, no, you take it!' he said, not really meaning it.

So I decided to grab it, saying, 'OK! Thanks. If you're sure.'

He watched it going into me mouth, then smiled at me, thinking he was being very manly. Ah, Gawd! He really is very nice! I thought, looking at him sitting there watching me eat.

'There's more stew if you want it,' the mammy said, jumping up and going over to the pot to take a look.

'No thanks, Mammy! I've had enough of that. What about a piece of that apple tart if you're not saving it for tomorrow?' he said, looking hopeful at the press.

'Oh, go on then!' she said, making for the press and taking out a lovely big crusty brown apple tart with burnt sugar on top. Me mouth started watering. Jaysus! Ulick has the life of riley. Who could ask for a better mother and father than he has? They just live for him! I wonder does he know how lucky he is? I suppose he does. He never put his ma down when the fellas were making a joke of him being a mammy's boy. Yeah, I'm glad I met him. It will be great to go out and do things together with him. Maybe he will be me first boyfriend. Well, friend! I'm not looking for a fella like most people would think it. No, but I sure did land on me feet today when I met him.

'Would you like to do something next week?' Ulick said as I climbed off the back of the bike and looked up at the window of me bedsit. It looked a bit lonely. The curtains were open and it was pitch black, probably freezing now. But still and all, a tingle went through me. That's all mine! I have me own place to go to! No more wandering the streets, looking for somewhere to get in out of the elements. God, I'm so lucky!

'So, what do you think?'

'Sorry, what did you say, Ulick?'

'Would you like to go out with me next Saturday?' he said, looking very nervous and playing with the helmet in his hand, not wanting to look at me in case I refused.

'Yeah! Why not?' I said. 'When? Saturday?'

'Yeah! Say Saturday,' he said, with his eyes lighting up.

'Yeah, OK! What time?'

'I'll pick you up here around three o'clock,' he said.

'No, that's fine, but not here. Meet me under the clock outside Cleary's on O'Connell Street. OK, Ulick?'

'Yeah, but it's no bother to come here.'

'No! I won't be here,' I said. 'I always go into town on a Saturday.'

I didn't want to tell him that's my morning for going to see Ralph. I never miss a Saturday unless Ralph says otherwise. 'I won't be available,' he says. Then me heart drops right down into the ground. I end up going around for the next two weeks living for me next visit. Fuck! It drives me mad. How did I ever get into this state? Yeah! Me whole life revolves around him. I even think about things I'm going to tell him! Jaysus! Where did I go to? Me, meself! And what have I become? I thought, feeling very annoyed with meself at being so dependent on him.

'OK!' he said. 'I'll see you next Saturday outside Cleary's. I better go now! Mammy will be waiting for me to get home. She doesn't rest easy until she knows I'm back safe and sound,' he laughed. But I could see he was serious.

'Yeah! Thanks for everything, Ulick. I really enjoyed meself today. Especially when we went to your house. You have a lovely home. Oh, and tell your mammy for me I said thanks very much for being so kind to me. I really appreciated that. Yeah, and don't forget to tell her as well I think her cooking is gorgeous. She's a great cook!'

'Yeah, I'll tell her that!' he said, laughing, delighted I liked his mammy.

Yeah, I thought. I can sense deep down she doesn't like me. But still and all she is a very good woman and Ulick is very lucky to have her for a mother. I watched as he sat himself on the motorbike and jammed on his helmet. Then he revved up the bike and took off, roaring down the hill, disappearing out of sight, going home along the Liffey.

33

I washed up all me dinner dishes, leaving the frying pan to last. Then I wiped around the cooker and cleaned the sink, rubbing to bring up a bit of a shine, then looked at the table. I rinsed out the cloth in the sink, getting it all wet again, and wiped down the table, pushing in the two chairs. I looked around, seeing if everything was all nice and tidy. Me eyes lit on the bed, made the way I used to see the nurses in the hospital make the beds with the corners tucked in making an envelope, they called it.

Lovely, everything is grand and tidy. That's gives me a great sense of having order in me head. When things are in a mess, it makes me feel very insecure. A bit like the feeling of being stranded. I don't know where I am. I looked at the wall in the corner around me bed. I had three birthday cards stuck on the wall to decorate it. They are me memories, the cards people gave to me since I first started having me birthdays. I only started collecting them after I left the convent. Two is from Ralph; one is from Odette. Me heart dropped for a minute, thinking about her. I wonder how she is? She must be nearly a solicitor by now! We said we would write to each other, but we only wrote once. Then the time passed and I suppose we just forgot. But I still remember her.

Me eyes peeled to the lovely green tapestry hanging on the wall over the length of me bed. I always rest me sights on that, seeing the woods and trees, with the deer stopping for a drink by a little river. I got that for ten shillings, along with a few more things. The kettle for one. I need that for boiling the water to wash up the dishes. Yeah, it was one Saturday afternoon. Me and Ulick went into the Dandelion Market for a ramble, over in Stephens Green. The fella selling the stuff wanted thirty bob. A whole one pound and ten shillings. I bargained him down, telling him if he was serious about making a few bob, then take the ten shillings; otherwise, let it sit there for the moths to eat. Then we'll all be losers: I won't get the stuff and he'll go home without any money in his pocket. Ulick and me nearly got into another one of our big fights over that. He gave out because he thought I was robbing the poor fella. Poor, me arse! Ulick has no idea about anything. Money goes through his fingers like a little child let loose in a sweet shop with their pocket money. I snorted to meself, thinking he drives me mad, he's so bleedin childish.

Yet I wouldn't want to be without him. Him and me and Sophie and her boyfriend Ritchie are the best of friends. We do everything together. We're always going off somewhere – camping, or doing something. The funny thing is, they have been together for years, even though Sophie is my age exactly and Ritchie is Ulick's age. But them two never fight. Not even an insult! Where as me and Ulick – Jaysus! There's always skin, teeth and hair flying. Usually his! That's why his ma hates me. He's gone home with too many lumps and bumps! She keeps telling him to keep away from me but he doesn't listen. He never listens to his ma anyway! I think the two of them have to go through their act together. She follows him around the house when he's packing up all the stuff to go camping. 'Ulick! I'm telling you here and now! You are not going out that door!' He ignores her and just gets on quietly getting the stuff together. 'Your daddy said he's going to stop you, Ulick!' she snorts.

Then when he's ready and the stuff is all loaded up on the back of the bike, sitting on the back rest with the big bar going up at the end – he ties all the stuff onto that – then goes back into the house with the mammy still following him, giving out like mad. Then when she sees him all ready, wearing his black leather-looking rubber trousers over his jeans, and we're all wrapped up for the rain with me wearing me new leather jacket I bought to go with the bike – I used the last of me savings to buy that. Anyway! The mammy knows she lost! Then she starts rushing and fussing to get him into his woolly vests. 'Ulick! Come back! You're not dressed properly! You'll catch your death of pneumonia!'

We're gone off down the road, spluttering and banging out blue smoke. The timing is always going on the bloody bike. Then it starts backfiring! People think the Protestants have arrived down here to bring the Northern war to our side of the border! Fuck! We nearly got arrested one day. It happened as we were passing the policeman directing the traffic on O'Connell Bridge. The motorbike gave an almighty bang – backfired right into his face nearly. It sounded like someone had fired a gun. The copper leapt with the fright, staggering back with his hands still in the air thinking someone had shot him. Then he got his senses back and whipped his big culchie head on us. He started shouting at Ulick. 'One minute, lad! Sthop right dhere dis minnet! Why have you no silencer on dat bike? Show me yure insurance papers!' Then he whipped out his little black book and started writing down poor Ulick's details. 'You'll be getting a summons from me!' he barked. 'For disturbing the peace! Now get on with the pair of you, before I arrest you altogether!'

Ulick went mad with the worry his mammy would find out and have a canary! Ha! That was a great laugh. For once it wasn't me causing the trouble!

Right! I better keep going. Now, what's next? I better sort out me money for the week. I opened me bag, and took out me purse with all me money. Right! I get paid four pounds a week for me wages. Now, I better leave out of that two pounds ten shilling for me rent. Put that to one side. Now, what's next? There's the six single shillings for the electric meter. Put that in the little cardboard box under the sink. Keep it handy for when the meter goes. Right, what's next? Twelve shillings and sixpence for me dinner. That's two shillings and sixpence a day. It's grand and handy I can get on the queue down on Camden Street and get a three-course dinner every day, Monday to Friday. The queue is long but it keeps moving quickly.

Gawd! Yer man that runs that place is on to a good thing! The

lot of us, all the paupers, some I think are even down and out
– anyway, we keep moving behind each other, then we are in the
long aul dusty hall. It's an old tenement house nearly at the end of
Camden Street. You go up the stairs slowly, because the queue keeps
moving. Then you are on the landing, standing outside what looks
like an empty room. It was probably the sitting room sometime in
its lifetime. Anyway, we stand on the landing, waiting our turn to
go in. It gives us time to gape at the aul fella in his little scullery.
He only has a four-ring cooker but he has big pots of cabbage going
on one ring, a big pot of potatoes cooking away in the other, then
the frying pan is going like the clappers getting our rissoles ready.
That's a lump of mincemeat with a bit of chopped onion thrown in.
Then it's rolled up in a ball and flattened out. Then he slaps them
on the pan and puts one on a plate, a bit of cabbage from the pot,
two potatoes, and just keeps going.

There is a little door off that. And his son grabs the plates and
comes out through the eating room. He walks up and down long
tables pushed against the wall, going all the way around the room,
with long benches each side of the table. Then we shuffle in while the
first lot shuffle out. We all push in beside each other, with people the
length of the table, all of us facing each other. Then the son brings
our dinner, no questions asked – just plops them down, serving us
all at the same time. Then he goes back to the top where he started
and grabs up the empty plates and gives them a bowl of jelly then a
cup of tea. Nobody speaks. We are all hungry and in a hurry to get
back to work. Some of them go back out onto the streets, doing their
mooching. They are the homeless. We are all finished at the same
time. He collects the cups and takes our half crown – two shillings
and sixpence. Then we rush out and the next lot rush in. Everyone
keeps moving. Nobody even looks at each other.

I think I'm the only office worker to go in there. They are mostly
men and a few women who look a bit down on their luck. Well,
it suits me grand. I get fed – otherwise I couldn't afford to feed
meself properly. The cooker eats up all me shillings. Anyway, buying
the food to cook it would cost more. Yeah, there's only one thing,

though. Me tastebuds are very well tuned in to what I'm eating. So is me sense of smell. So I'm definitely sure that mincemeat is gone off! In fact, I know it is. I said it to the young fella one day. He looked at me plate and said, 'Well, it can't be all that bad! You've eaten most of it,' he said, with the two of us staring at the bit of rissole left sitting on the plate.

I was hoping he might not charge me the full price. 'So, are you going to charge me for that?' I said, watching him start to make off with the bit of me dinner.

'Course I am. Who do you think we are, the St Vincent De Paul?' he said, snorting down at me.

'Right! Gimme back me dinner!' I said, snatching the plate back outa his hand.

Right, so where was I? OK, five bob for cigarettes, have to spare them. Then one shilling and sixpence for savings. That leaves me a total of five shillings left for bread, butter, tea, sugar, milk and cornflakes for me breakfast. Then the odd egg for me tea. Plus I have to buy me dinner and cook it on the Saturday and Sunday. Hmm, five shillings doesn't get me far. No wonder it's one slice a bread a day. That's for me tea. I have to spare everything. Go easy on the milk. The box of cornflakes does me for the week. A half-pound of butter does me for two weeks. Oh, well, at least I don't have bus fares. I walk everywhere!

Right, that's that sorted out for the week. Now, what's next? Get me clothes ready for work tomorrow. Monday – beginning of a new week. Right, what will I wear? Me jeans and a jumper. No one sees me anyway. I'm in that office all on me own. But it's grand. There's no women around to torture me. Especially after that last job! Them two fuckers got me fired! That Carmel one and that little creep Lucy. She wouldn't make the tea. The pair of them were jealous because I was the junior secretary-in-waiting, hoping to get promoted – become the full-time secretary! Yeah, they kept laughing and jeering behind me back. Then I lost the rag and ended up getting into a pushing and shoving match with Lucy. She pushed

and I shoved, giving her a box for good measure! Fired on the spot.
Her daddy played golf with Braggs Junior! That's how she got the
job in the first place. Anyway, I'm much better working for a crowd
of men now anyway. There's only three of us women. Me in one
office, the old woman in hers, doing the books, then the secretary.
She's gorgeous! A very plain-looking woman from the back of the
beyonds in the country but she makes up for it by having the beauty
shine out through her eyes.

I love her! We have great gas together. She sneaks down to my
office and we sit nattering away like mad. I can't leave me office
because I'm on the switchboard. Plus I'm at the beck and call for
any one of them fellas who want a quick letter sent out. They're all
stone mad. Well, one of the partners is! There's two of them. But
the first one spends his time roaring at me for losing his call. Didn't
get his letter out! I just sit and munch on the secretary's bull's eyes
she gives me to suck. She loves them. I hate them. But better than
nothing. Anyway, I just let him go mad. Roar and shout until he
turns blue!

He's very old but huge looking. Well built. He has eight sons. They
all work in the business when they're not gallivanting out enjoying
themself. Jaysus! They're a pack of lunatics! All screaming at each
other about who's in charge! Oh! Forgot! There is one who doesn't
work in the business. He's not well. He's a little slow. But Jaysus,
him and the wife! When they hit the office, he dumps her with me.
She sits there whining while he rushes off telling me to mind Mo!
'I'm going down to talk important business with my daddy!'

'Yeah, OK! But it will cost you, Felix! I want six of your
cigarettes!'

The shouts and screams outa him, roaring he's going back to tell
his daddy I'm robbing him! Well, fair exchange is no robbery. He
has me making mug after mug of coffee for the two of them. Plus I
have to mind her. Stop her crying after him! So we usually bargain.
I manage to squeeze three or four cigarettes outa him. Then we're
all smiles again. OK! That's me sorted out for the week.

34

I looked down at meself, seeing I look gorgeous! Well, I hope I am. I can't do any better than this. I stooped down, stretching me black soft-leather boots with the flat leather soles. I got a hold of the top of them and pulled them over me knees, letting them rest on me thighs, then felt me short white minifrock sink into me body, showing every curve I have. Gawd! This was a great buy. I bought it for a Christmas present for meself. I left a shilling every week for them to put it by for me until I had the whole lot paid off. It was well worth it. I pulled down the zip at the front, showing a little of me chest. Just a peek! It zips from me ribs right up to me neck. But you don't zip it up that far. The whole idea is to show a bit of what you have. Yeah, the collar is like a Chinese one. It stands up. Ohh, but it is so light and silky. It feels lovely and soft and light sitting on me skin.

So now, with me thigh-length black boots, me short silky white frock and me brown hair hanging around me shoulders, and me Cleopatra eye make-up – the black eyeliner and loads of mascara – Jaysus, I'm ready for anything! Yeah, Martha. The idea is to look any man's fancy! Better still, get dirty looks from the women! Then you know you're really looking grand! But who cares about all that? I'm doing meself up for Ralph. I can't wait to see him.

I opened the wardrobe and pulled out me long black maxi coat with the belt. It nearly goes down to me ankles. But that's how you wear them. Long coats are very fashionable. So today I want to look me very best. Ohh, I love Saturdays! That's the day when I see Ralph. Well, in the morning time. Then he has to go about his business. Then for me, the day feels like it's over. Even though it may be only about one o'clock. He has to go off and have lunch with the other priests, then I wander off to get me bits of shopping. I go down to Moore Street to bargain with the butcher for two nice gigot chops. They're the cheapest. Then a few vegetables from the dealer women. You can't bargain with them aul hags. They would eat you alive! So I just watch to make sure they are not sticking me with the rotten ones. Then I do rear up and tell them to shove them up their arse if they won't give me me money's worth! So that's me dinner for the two days, Saturday and Sunday. Then I wander about and usually meet Ulick in the evening on the Saturday, if we haven't fallen out!

Right, keep moving. I pulled out the long wool yellow scarf that wraps around me neck and goes down to me toes. I bought that at Christmas as well. To go with me maxi coat. It's lovely and warm and I'm looking in all the fashion. I buttoned up me coat and wrapped the belt around me, then threw the long scarf around me neck, wrapping it twice. I let one side hang down the front and the other down the back. I picked up me bag from the bed and made out the door and down the stairs. Then I was off down the hill, feeling me heart going like the clappers with the excitement of seeing Ralph again. I breathed in through me nose, getting the early-morning fresh air into me lungs. Gawd! It's great to have the spring arrived. Well, nearly. It's only the beginning but soon it should start to get warmer. Ohh, how lucky to be alive, I sighed, feeling on top of the world.

'I'll tell Father Fitzgerald you're here,' said the aul fella, holding the door of the parlour open for me.

'Thanks!' I muttered, then he shut the door behind him and I heard his feet walking down the very long passage back to the switchboard. I made straight for the long mahogany table under the big window looking out onto the street. The glass was fogged up at the bottom half, so you couldn't see in or out. I rested me back against the table and opened me bag, taking out a packet of cigarettes and lighting one up. I took in a deep drag of the smoke into me lungs.

Jesus! How long am I looking at these rooms? I thought, looking around at the big room with the high ceiling and the bookcases with religious books telling about the lives of different saints. But I associate this place with Ralph. So the one is the same as the other to me – happiness, tears and snots when we have blazing rows because he seems distant or tells me something I don't want to hear, like I make difficulties for him, whatever that's supposed to bleedin mean! I hope today is not one of them. It puts me into a terrible mood for the rest of the week. I end up feeling he doesn't care about me.

Jaysus! Me nerves are going. Then it hit me I was holding me breath. I started to walk slowly up and down, trying to think. So, what do I want? Where is this getting me? How long has this been going on? Too long. I suppose it started that first moment he put his arms around me. It felt like something I had been waiting all me life for. He was so gentle. He looked at me like I really mattered to him. Yeah, since that first time when I was sixteen. But there is no one else in this world like him. I meet fellas all the time but none of them interest me. I don't bother going out with them. Even Ulick. He's just a friend. Nothing more than that. Christ! There's a part of me wanting to run, telling me to stop acting the eejit! What the hell do I want from him? That thought worried me. I couldn't drag meself to answer. Me mind kept flitting away from it. But I should face up to it – use me head. I used to be good at that until I started losing it over Ralph! So, what's the answer? I used to want him to be a daddy. But now I want to hear him say he will spend the rest of his life with me because I am the most important person in his life, just like he is for me. Nothing else matters except being with him. Jaysus, Martha! You have two hopes: Bob Hope and no hope at all! But stranger things have happened.

The door whipped open and me head shot up. He looked around at me, then shut the door, checking the occupied sign was on. Then he made his way over, slowing down to stare at me. I took in a deep breath, lifting me shoulders. I could feel me heart going like the clappers. Yet one part of me shut down as I watched him coming closer to me. I was afraid he would turn me away, tell me he didn't want to see me any more, or be cold!

I stared down the length of him, hearing the squeak in his new black soft-leather shoes. His black suit was spotless, the trousers pressed within an inch of their life. I stared at the big white collar around his neck, telling me he was off bounds. That's what made me shut down, knowing that was a good reason to walk away. Then I looked into his face. He looked nervous, a bit pale. And his green eyes stared at me, taking in not just me but searching my soul, like he was trying to reach something deep in me.

'How are you?' he said, almost in a whisper, wrapping his two arms around me, burying me with his body. I could feel how strong he was and his chest was wide yet he was soft. His heart was beating fast and I could hear his breathing and me own. We stayed still, just feeling each other's warmth and letting the blood flow through our bodies, feeling like we were one and the same person. We were together yet we were each listening to the other's life force. In that moment, we were living for each other. Nothing else existed. Then he lifted himself back and took my two hands in his, holding me to him and letting his green eyes take me in. His eyes lowered, looking the length of me, then up again, looking into me face. I stared up at him, seeing him breathe in and out through his nose. It sounded like he was out of breath. I loosened me hand and opened his, closing me hands tight around them, feeling them warm and dry. Then I let go and wrapped me arms around his waist, saying, 'I missed you! Did you miss me?' I said, looking up at him grinning, wanting him to think I was joking. But I'm not!

He stared at me without saying anything, still looking deep into me. Then he gave a bare nod of his head, whispering, 'Yes, I missed you!' His hair fell into his eyes and without thinking I reached up and lifted it gently, pushing it back out of his face so I could see his eyes. He didn't grab my hands and take them away. Sometimes he would do that when he thinks I have overstepped the mark. Or he would push me away. Now, suddenly, he wrapped his arms around me, pulling me closer to him burying his face in me hair.

Happiness leapt up through me chest and I pulled me arms free, wrapping them around his neck.

'You smell lovely!' he whispered, running his face through me hair and around to me face. Then he lifted his head to look at me. 'Your hair smells so fresh,' he said, feeling it gently with his hands, running them through me hair, looking very intently, staring and letting my hair run through his fingers like he was examining it.

'Yeah, I wash it in Clinic shampoo! The cheapest stuff!' I laughed, pulling away to look at him.

'No,' he said quietly, still very intent, locking his eyes on me. 'It is your very own scent, darling. Unique to you. Wonderfully pleasurable!' he said, grinning at me with a glint of mischief in his eyes. Then he held me at arm's length, staring at me like he was thinking. 'What will you do today?' he said. 'Do you have anything planned?'

'No, why?'

'What about your friends? Ulick, is it?'

'Yes,' I said.

'Will you be meeting him?'

'No! We've fallen out!' I said, not remembering if that was true or not. Anyway, he had no place here! I didn't want to talk about him. He's only a fella, I snorted to meself, annoyed he was even getting a mention.

'Hmm,' he said, thinking about this. 'I hope you are both behaving!' he suddenly said, letting his green eyes stare daggers at me for a second. 'Particularly that young buck!' he muttered, looking like he was clenching his teeth.

I laughed, saying, 'Ah, come on, Ralph! You know me better than that. He has the hands smacked off himself! I'm well able to handle him! Fellas are all the same,' I said, sniffing. 'They are always on the look out for their oats!'

'Their what?' he laughed, waiting for me to say it again.

'Their oats! You know!'

'Yes, of course I know. It's just amusing to hear how you describe it.'

'Give me a hug,' I said, not wanting to keep me hands off him.

He held me loosely in his arms and took in a deep breath, saying, 'Wait here. I'll be back.'

'No, don't go! Where are you off to?'

'Wait, darling! Don't panic. I'm not leaving you. I'll be back.'

Then he was gone out the door and vanishing down the corridor. I could hear his shoes squeaking, then fading away in the distance. Jaysus! He's going to come back and tell me he has an appointment, he must go! I could feel me heart sinking. Why do I put meself through this? Jaysus! One of these days I am going to give meself such an almighty kick up the arse. God knows it's long enough coming! I snorted. It almost feels childish! I can't make head nor tail of what I am doing, or what the hell is going on with me. It's like one minute I'm nearly wanting a father, then the next I'm looking for him to be a husband. Well, maybe in another while. Not just yet! Oh, fuck! I wish I had never found out about love. I was better off without it. If he comes back in that door and tells me he's got to go, I'll swing for him! That will be it! I'm going to tell him to fuck off!

I could feel the heat of me rage calming down now that I knew I meant it this time! No more messing. I'll get over him! Right! I picked up me bag and fixed me coat, tightening me belt. It wasn't open anyway. Then the door opened and he walked in. I looked at him. He was wearing a heavy sheepskin coat and he had a lovely wine soft wool scarf wrapped around his neck. I could see the little label. It said 'Hermès'. That's a very expensive scarf, I thought, staring at it. You buy them in Brown Thomas. Hmm, wonder where he got that? Then it hit me. Fuck, I knew it! He's going out! OK, that's it, enough is enough. I got only about ten minutes this time, if even that. He barely spoke two words to me.

'So, Ralph! You are going out!' I said, gritting me teeth with the rage.

'Yes, my darling! We—'

'OK, that's it!' I roared. 'Ralph Fitzgerald, you can go and fuck yourself! I'm off out of here! Don't expect to see me back. What do you think I am? Some snotty-nose kid? A sixteen year old you can treat like a child? Well, I've had it with all this messing around, you!

I'm a woman, not a child! So, out of me way and let me pass!' I said, shoving past him, heading meself for the door.

'No, wait! Oh, really, you are so silly!' he said, making a grab for me.

I made it out the door and he lunged after me, grabbing me by the arm, then catching hold of me and wrapping his arms around the front of me, walking me back into the room, marched between his legs. Then he lifted his leg, slamming the door shut with his foot.

'Oh, you are so lovely!' he said, hanging on to me with one arm wrapped around me to stop me escaping. Then with the other, he stroked me cheek, looking down into me face and smiling. He whispered, 'Darling! I was going to suggest we could spend the day together!'

'Who? You and me?' I puffed, getting outa breath, thinking I was hearing things. Yet me mind wouldn't take it in.

'Yes! I thought perhaps we could go somewhere. Take a drive. We could stop and have some lunch.'

'Where?' I said, with me head whipping up to look at him, seeing he was really looking at me like it was only him and me. That suddenly he saw me in a different way for the first time ever. I wasn't really interested in hearing where we could eat. I wanted to ask him a million questions. Why has he changed? What's happening to him? But that's the only thing I could get out of me mouth.

'We can go where ever you choose!'

I could feel the colour draining outa me face with the shock. One minute I was making me mind up to get the hell away from him. I was feeling a cold anger inside meself, not wanting to be acting the fool, chasing rainbows. Then the next it sounds like he is telling me he really wants me!

'I don't care where we go!' I said, looking at how handsome and terribly manly he is. He looks so different with that coat and the scarf wrapped around his neck. You wouldn't think he was a priest now that the collar was out of sight.

'Where would you like to eat?' he said. 'Any preference? So long as it is not the Ritz,' he said. 'I don't think I can stretch to that!' he laughed.

'We don't have the Ritz here, do we?' I said.

'No, of course not! Oh, you are funny!' he laughed, grabbing me in a hug.

'Come on! Let's go!' I said, grabbing his hand, making for the door. I was afraid something would go wrong.

'Take it easy, darling,' he whispered. 'A little bit of decorum is required. Remember where you are!'

'OK!' I said, feeling chastised and letting go of me breath because I kept forgetting to breathe.

We walked down the corridor and past the reception desk. The aul fella was missing. Ralph pulled open the heavy door and held it for me, letting me spring through. Then he bounced ahead of me. I watched, seeing his lovely silky brown hair flopping around his head. The light hit me eyes, making me squint after the dark inside the parlour. I took in the fresh air, feeling light as air. I kept staring as he opened the driver's door and leaned across to open the passenger door for me. I tried to make the moment last. I still can't believe here I am going off with Ralph instead of the usual way of just leaving on me own, feeling me happiness is over for another week. I always feel lonely somehow. Then it fades, getting lost deep inside me as I go on about me business, getting on with me everyday life. But now he's taken me out! Maybe I'm dreaming! Ah, Jaysus! I'll kick meself right up the arse if that is only what is happening. I might even pack me bags and go off to England or somewhere! Oh, I would have to get a few bob first!

Jaysus! No, I'm not dreaming! Me heart leapt with the happiness! I felt like me insides was going to melt! I stopped taking me time and rushed around the car, pulling the passenger door open, and sat in. Then I lifted me legs, swinging them in, slamming the door shut. My coat fell open as I stretched me legs then crossed them, letting my white silky frock ride up, clinging to my legs, showing off my leather knee-high boots. I saw Ralph throw his eye down, taking in my legs with the white shimmering frock clinging to my thighs. Then he swung his head back to take another look, seeing was he right the first time. He lifted his head to the road, drawing his chin up, breathing slowly and quietly through his nose, saying nothing. Then he started the car and took off, whipping the car into the centre of the road, making the other cars stop. Then he spun the wheel around, going off in the opposite direction. Ah, we're heading up towards town. I'm not going to ask him where we're going. He might say something that would spoil things. Like, 'Yes, after lunch I will let you go on your way', or something terrible like that. Anyway, I don't want to know anything. Let him go where he wants to take me.

'Gawd! You really drive fast, Ralph. You are bloody fearless when it comes to taking on other drivers!' I said, looking up at him, grinning, knowing we wouldn't crash because he's very quick to see what he's doing.

He turned his head slowly, looking at me, giving a grin. 'Do you find it thrilling, my love?'

'Yeah, providing we don't get killed,' I said, watching his hands slam the gears up and down, then latch onto the steering wheel, making the car rocket ahead when the road was clear.

'Yes, it is a weakness of mine. In my Cambridge days I used to roar around in fast cars. It was all part of being a young buck. We terrorised the county, driving through the countryside at alarming speeds!' he grinned, shaking his head, thinking he was terrible.

'Did you drive a sports car?' I said, looking up at him, not able to get over how handsome he is.

'Of course, my darling. I needed to cut a dash,' he said, grinning at me then winking slowly, looking back to the road.

'Did you have girlfriends?' I asked him with me heart in me mouth.

'Yes, of course! I was not a monk, you know.'

'Oh!' I said, feeling me heart drop, getting a terrible feeling of jealousy inside me.

'What?' he said, twisting his head down to get a look at me, grinning. 'Don't be jealous, darling,' he smiled. 'I was saving myself for you!'

'You were?' I nearly roared, feeling me heart take a leap out of me mouth!

Then he went for the gears again, closing his face down, saying, 'We must concentrate on the driving,' he said, facing his head on the road as we steamed up behind the traffic on O'Connell Street.

We drove over O'Connell Bridge, heading past Trinity College, making for the South Side. I opened me bag and took out me cigarettes, saying, 'Do you want a cigarette, Ralph?'

'Yes, hang on, darling. I'll just pull over here.'

We stopped on Sandymount Strand, beside the big houses opposite the sea. Then he switched off the car engine and hopped out of the car. I watched as he pulled off his coat then sat back in the car, throwing it on the back seat. Then he reached up and opened his dog collar, whipping it off, then rushed out of the car again and went around to the boot.

He dropped in the collar and took out a big dark-green wool sweater and pulled it over his head, then jumped back into the car, slamming the door shut. 'That feels better,' he said, letting out his breath in a long slow sigh.

I stared at the jumper, admiring it, thinking I would look lovely in that meself. 'Where did you get the jumper, Ralph? It suits the colour of your eyes,' I said, smiling up at him.

'I can't remember these things,' he said, not bothered about it. 'My family insist on keeping me well kitted out. I keep telling them to stop. It is not necessary. But you ladies never listen to a man!' he said, grinning at me.

I leaned across him and had a look at the label. 'Ah, yeah! I knew I recognised something like that. It's Christian Dior. They have them in the men's department in Brown Thomas. I love that shop. But I would never be able to buy meself a hanky in that place. Anything there would cost me nearly a year's wages,' I said, looking mournful.

'Darling, you look beautiful, Brown Thomas or not!' he said, looking at me and smiling.

'Really?' I said, feeling delighted he thinks I'm looking lovely.

He nodded his head up and down, saying, 'You are lovely, you know!'

'I think I will take me coat off too, Ralph,' I said, moving to open the belt and the buttons.

He watched as I tried twisting to get me long heavy coat off. 'Wait! Let me help you,' he said. 'Lean forward.'

I leaned me head and he slipped the coat off me shoulders, then lifted me arms, letting the coat drop. Then he put his hand across me, catching me under my left arm, and lifted me like I was a feather. Then he slipped the coat from under me and threw it on top of his, left thrown on the back seat. I sat back down and pulled me frock under me and crossed me legs. It made no difference. You could still see the whole way up me thighs almost to me knickers. The frock was too clinging.

'Cigarettes!' he suddenly said, and twisted around to grab at his coat and pull out his lighter and a packet of twenty cigarettes.

'Very posh!' I said.

'What? These?' he grinned, holding out the cigarettes.

'What else?'

'You have seen nothing yet, ma cherie!' he said, grinning at me, showing his dimples and sparkling white teeth. He lit up two cigarettes and handed me one.

'Oh, this reminds me of the time when I went hitch-hiking around England. A priest I met there in Coventry when I went to Mass, he was on his way down to London and he took me with him. All the way down, Ralph, he kept saying, "Light me up a cigarette and have one for yourself!" I spent me time puffing two cigarettes all the way down to London. I was nearly sick by the time I landed,' I said, getting the picture all over again, and started to roar me head laughing.

'You didn't tell me that one!' he said, looking at me with a long face on him.

'Yeah, well, I'm telling you now! What are you getting so ratty about?' I snorted, puffing on me cigarette and looking over at the sea.

'Darling, you are such a contradiction!' he said quietly, pulling me hair out of me eyes.

'Why? Why do you say that, Ralph?'

'You have such street sense, yet it is not a naivety with you but an innocence!'

'Is that a compliment?' I said.

'Yes! You know the worst in people yet you see only the best!'

'Well, the devil takes care of his own!' I laughed.

'No, your great allure is your spirituality.'

'Me? Never! What do you mean?' I said, wondering if we were thinking the same thing. 'I'm not all that religious.'

'You are full of goodness!' he said, looking at me. 'You have a pure heart.'

I felt meself getting red in the face, thinking that was a lovely thing he just said. Then it hit me. 'Wait a minute, Ralph! When I was in the convent, I once managed to get me hands on a book from the nun's library. Because I used to clean the convent, you know that?'

He nodded his head, listening to me.

'Well, it was called *Abelard and Heloise*. He was a monk and she was his student. Then she became even more clever than him. The two of them ended up having an affair. Then the uncle of hers found out and cut off his, eh, you know!'

'Yes, I do!' he said, listening and smiling.

'Well, then, she wouldn't give him up! And as he didn't have his credentials any more . . .' I held me story, seeing Ralph throw back his head and roar laughing. 'Wait! Let me finish. You know what he did, the good-for-nothing toerag?'

'Yes,' Ralph muttered, shaking his head and smiling, saying, 'go on!'

'Well!' I said, continuing me story. 'He managed to persuade her to go into a bleedin convent! Become a nun! For the love a Jaysus, Ralph! The next thing I know is, you'll be hatching up some plan to get me into the enclosed order of Carmelite nuns with a bleedin vow of silence! You'll do anything to get rid of me!'

'Absolutely not! The Carmelites? They would not dare! What? You a nun? Good God! You would have them all closed down in no time! They would all go barmy!' he roared, throwing his head back and laughing himself stupid.

'I'm not that bad! I could be a nun if I wanted to!' I snorted.

Then he stopped laughing and looked at me, 'Really, Martha! It is impossible. They would never have you!'

'Why bloody not?' I shouted, thinking he was looking down on me. 'So, you think I'm not good enough, is that it?' I said, blowing smoke in his face.

'Don't do that!' he said, pushing away me face and opening the window. I opened my side and stuck me head out the window, wondering if I should grab me coat and leave him to his big ideas about himself. Fuck him, if he thinks he's doing me any favours! In fact he is. Just the thing to get me moving well away from him!

'In fact, if you must know,' I snorted, whipping me head around to glare at him, 'I wouldn't be a fucking nun if they paid me! So stick that up yer arse! And furthermore! Try walking in my shoes, without your fancy life and your fancy schools and all the other fancy fucking things you had in your life! See how far you would get! One day, Father Ralph Fitzgerald! Just you wait and see! I will show you and your like! I knew it! People like you. Fucking do-gooders! It makes you feel so superior to help little snotty-nosed street kids like I was! But I'm not that any more!' Then I reached into the back and grabbed me coat. Fuck him! I don't need a gobshite like him!

'What are you doing?' he said, catching me waist as I reached round to grab me coat and scarf. 'Please, darling! Don't get upset,' he said, grabbing and snatching the coat out of me hands and moving over to pull me into his arms. 'You are so sensitive! It was a joke! The whole bloody thing was nonsense!' he tried to laugh, seeing I was stone cold. 'Come on! Let's not fight! I would not dream of wishing to willingly hurt you!'

'Yes, you did! You hurt me! I know you think I'm one of your bleedin charity cases!'

'No, no! Stop it! Of course you are not! Oh, my heavens!' he said, raising his head to the roof. 'Why must you always take up what I say as wrong? Don't be silly! How is it possible I should look down on you? Why would I even think that way? Really, darling, you have no real idea of just how worthy you are. I hold you in very high esteem. Look at me, Martha!'

'No! I don't believe a word out of your mouth, Ralph!'

'Stop! Now you are hurting me!' he said. Then he was sighing. 'Come to me!' he said, moving closer to me and wrapping his arm around me shoulder and the other one around me back, then pulled me tighter into him. He leaned over my seat, saying, 'Look at me.'

I looked up into his face, seeing his eyes hurting.

'Don't fall out with me. I know you can go running off on a tangent! Listen to me, darling. I want to say this.' Then he paused. I watched his face, seeing him hesitating. Then he cleared his throat and whispered, 'I love you more than you know! So very much.'

'You do?' I whispered, looking into his face and smelling his breath. It smelled of toothpaste. 'I love you too, Ralph!'

'Yes, I know, my darling,' he whispered.

We just stared at each other. Waiting. Feeling the intense pain of wanting to be closer. I could feel the tingling come off him. It felt like the car was charged with electricity. I could almost hear it. Then he moved his head, burying his face in my hair, and let his lips barely touch my neck. Then he slowly moved his face to look at me again. I could feel his hands tightening on my back, stroking me with the palms of his hands. And I reached up to lightly put my hands around his neck, holding him gently. Then he moved his hands up my back and around my sides, stroking me very gently. Then suddenly his lips touched mine and locked. His hand dropped to the side of my seat and I felt meself lowering down as the seat went back. He moved his leg across to my side and spread himself over me. Then his mouth moved around to my neck, drawing it close to my ears, then around to my throat. Then he lifted his lips to mine again. An electric bolt shot through me. Our mouths started opening so fast, yet I could feel it in slow motion. Power surged through me, meeting his. We flowed, with our bodies reacting, wanting to match this power as it moved with the speed of light, shattering me into millions of little pieces, sending me hurtling through infinity. Attracted like a magnet to fuse with what is Ralph, our bodies melted into each other, wanting to become one. My soul his and his mine.

Suddenly we tore back from each other, staring in shock! I could see the colour drain out of him. I felt meself shaking. I couldn't get a breath. He felt the same because he suddenly breathed, 'Good God!' as he stared, holding himself rigid with his eyes locked on mine, still staring in shock. I just stared back at him. Not able to take in what just happened all in the blink of an eye. One kiss! His arms opened, grabbing me to him again, wrapping me in his body. He buried his head in my neck, kissing me, whispering, 'I love you, my precious darling! More and more my love for you grows. I don't want to lose you! This is impossible! I never intended we should act on it.' Then he pulled away, saying, 'We really are making an exhibition of ourselves, my love! And in broad daylight!' He laughed, trying to shake off the shock of what just happened.

I felt dazed, saying, 'Yeah, we have a bit of a cheek.' I laughed, feeling all shaky. The two of us looked around to see if there was anyone gawking.

'Come on! Light me up another cigarette and let us get out of here before they call the guards.'

'Yeah, right!' I said, saying, 'It might even make the evening headlines in the paper: "Priest and woman found behaving in an indecent manner in broad daylight on Sandymount Strand".'

'Don't even jest!' he said, laughing. 'I would have to take up medicine again!'

'Yeah! What would your mother say?' I said.

'Oh, she is pretty broadminded. Besides, I am an adult. She would respect that!' he said, dropping his head and looking at me with a twinkle in his eye. 'We all have the great gift of free will, my precious! We must take responsibility for our own actions!'

'Yes, I know,' I sighed, wondering if he was going to patronise me and start giving me a lecture.

'Where is that cigarette?' he said, smiling over at me again, hearing me sigh.

'Oh, yeah! What did you do with the cigarettes, Ralph?' I said, looking around.

'Try the glove compartment!'

'No! Ah, here we are!' I said, diving into the back seat.

He looked at the great show of leg I was giving and said, laughing, 'Get thee behind me, Satan. I hope you don't wear that dress when you are with that young buck!' he said, sounding very annoyed again.

'Ah, I told you, Ralphie, darling!' I said, grinning. 'I can handle him. He gets nowhere with me!'

'You are very attractive to men, Martha. I should know,' he murmured. 'Make sure you do!' he said.

'Do what?'

'Not let that fellow go messing about with you! You are far too precious to throw yourself away on someone half-baked!' he said, getting very annoyed altogether.

'Jaysus, Ralph! What do you take me for? The only person I am interested in is you, if you must know!'

'Yes, darling! But I just want you to be careful. Men can be very devious in getting their way.'

'Have a cigarette!' I said, lighting up his and putting it into his mouth.

'Listen, sweetie,' he said, talking with the cigarette in his mouth, letting the smoke get in his eyes. 'Why don't we head into the country? Would you like that?'

'Oh, yeah! That would be lovely.'

'Yes, then. Let us go!' And he tore up through the gears and we took off out of the city.

35

Before long I was looking out the window seeing green fields and hedges.

'Oh, peace, blissful peace!' he said, taking in a big breath, saying, 'Living in the heart of the city has its drawbacks. The constant din of traffic and the massing hordes, not to mention smoke belching out of chimneys, can be quite overwhelming sometimes. One can have a sense of being trapped.'

'Yes, one can!' I drawled, imitating some of his mother's friends.

'You are naughty!' he said, landing a slap on me leg.

'Ralph, you are exactly now where I want you – behind that wheel – and I can do what I like to you, so watch yourself!' I said, warning him with me eyes looking daggers at him.

'Are you threatening me, darling?' he said, smiling.

'Yes, most definitely!' I said.

He looked in his mirror, then pulled the car over to a stop and switched off the engine, pulling up the handbrake. Then he lunged at me, grabbing hold of me and lifting me up and smacking the side of me arse. Then he locked me in a bear hug and kissed my cheek, saying, 'No more threats!' Then he switched on the engine and we took off again.

'Jaysus! That was vicious!' I said.

'Nonsense! It was the principle! Showing you who is boss! I gave you a little pat, that is all! I treat you like delicate china!'

'Me arse!' I said.

'Yes, and that too!' he laughed, whipping his head over to me with his green eyes sparkling with mischief.

We whizzed past woodlands, high up on a hill. I looked, seeing they were on both sides of the narrow country road with paths leading up to them. I opened the window all the way down, getting the lovely smell of pine. 'They look lovely,' I said.

'Yes!' he said, looking up at them. Then he started to say in a beautiful soft voice, 'The woods are lovely, dark and deep, But I have promises to keep, and miles to go before I sleep. And miles to go before I sleep.'

'Where did you hear that, Ralph? It's lovely.'

'Yes! A man going home on horseback. He finds the woods very inviting,' he smiled, showing his teeth and looking at me like he really was happy to be with me. 'It was written by an American, Robert Frost.'

I moved over closer to him and wrapped me arm around his waist. He lifted his arm and pulled me into him, letting me rest on his chest. I watched the road as he steered. I have never felt so contented or happy in my whole life!

We came to a little village. I looked around, seeing no shops but a couple of houses hidden behind high walls. Ralph pulled up outside a big house with a little low entrance. I could see a glass box outside with what looked like a menu.

'Here we are, darling. Take your coat. We can walk in the gardens.'

'Is this a restaurant?'

'After a fashion,' he said. 'Some of the greatest poets and writers have taken refreshment here and stayed on. It is a very old country house going back to the seventeenth century.'

'How do you know about this place, Ralph?'

'I know a lot of things, my sweet!' he grinned, putting his coat on and pulling me with him. 'Come on! Let's go inside!' he said, doing his usual running act, always managing to get ahead of me. Then he hopped in the porch and held the door wide open for me.

We walked into a long hall with a table holding letters and all sorts of bits of stuff. I looked at the hall stand with a silver walking stick and hats and coats and scarves sitting on it.

'Leave your coat here,' Ralph said, pulling off his and helping me out of mine. 'We can come back later if we decide to go outside.' Then we walked into a big dining room that looked a bit like his mother's. It had a huge gilt mirror over a big old marble fireplace. A big sideboard with silver dishes and embossed covers were sitting on top.

'OK, let's continue!' he said.

We walked back out to the hall and went into another room. It was a sitting room with a big bookcase and cosy-looking armchairs beside a roaring red-hot fire. A man was sitting reading the newspaper. He had a monocle in his right hand and he was looking through it, reading the newspaper. He lifted his head when we came in. 'Good afternoon!' he said, looking at Ralph, then he lowered his head to me. I said the same, then Ralph moved over to the two big old French doors and went out into a garden. It was lovely. You couldn't see all of it, only bits. You had to walk around big bushes, passing flowers and a rockery with a fountain. The sound of the water pouring down on the old black granite rocks was lovely and peaceful.

'This is beautiful!' I murmured, taking in the lovely fresh smell of the shrubs and trees, and getting the scent of flowers.

'Yes! I thought you might like this,' he said, walking on ahead of me, wanting to see what there was to see.

The garden went for miles. 'Gawd! Who would believe this is all here, hidden from the road?' I said.

'Yes! It is wonderful. They have managed to retain the original. It has been in the same family for centuries,' he said.

'Have you come here before, Ralph?'

'Yes, of course! Not too often, but yes, I like this place. OK! Shall we go inside and see about getting some lunch?' he said.

'Yes, please.'

'OK, darling. Let's move back inside,' he said, putting his arm around my waist. Then we got to the French doors and he let me go. I could feel cold, like there was something missing when he let go of me. I followed up behind him after he led me through the door and took off.

'Let's go this way!' he said, making further into the house.

We ended up in another dining room with round heavy mahogany tables and old well-padded dining chairs to match. A white linen tablecloth covered the tables. They were set for the lunch.

While we were having a look to see what was happening, a woman with grey soft hair waved around her head came in behind us, saying, 'Oh, good afternoon! Are you lunching?' she asked, smiling at us.

'Yes, that would be nice. A table for two, is that possible?' said Ralph, swerving around to take in the tables. We could see two old ladies at one table near the end of the room. They barely looked at us. They were too busy leaning across the table, muttering to each other. An old gentleman and his wife were at another table down the far end. The room was big but it looked smaller because it was packed with little tables and armchairs. They are up beside a big window that goes the length of the floor nearly, showing the gardens. There is a garden room attached where you can go and sit and read. Even this room has books and lamps.

'Perhaps you might like to sit over here,' she said, bringing us over to a little alcove with a table and two chairs.

'Yes, that would be fine,' Ralph said, marching after her. He pulled out the chair next to the wall and held it out for me. Then he took the one on the outside, sitting close to me. I could feel the warmth of his legs on mine as we sat side by side. It made me tingle all over and I had a buzzing in me chest. Never did I ever feel so alive and happy in me whole life. I wanted to rest me hand on his leg but I'm always afraid of overstepping the mark and upsetting him.

'I shall get you a menu,' she said, giving us a big smile, then going off to get it.

'This is like being in someone's home!' I said, looking around delighted.

'Yes, that is exactly what it is, Martha. That lady to whom we have just been speaking, she is the owner.'

'Oh, yeah! Right enough! You would know she is a lady,' I said.

She was back in a flash. 'The soup de jour,' she said, 'is consommé!'

'That will be fine,' said Ralph.

'What about you?' she asked me.

'Eh, yes, that would be lovely,' I said, imitating him.

'The rack of lamb is to be recommended,' she said.

'Yes, I will have that,' he said. 'What about you?' he asked, looking at the menu. 'You can have fish – trout, baked,' he said.

'No, I will have the same as you,' I said, watching me diction.

'OK,' he said, 'the lady will have the same.'

'Very good!' she said, giving him a big smile and nodding at me, giving me one too.

'Would you like to see the wine list?' she said, looking at him.

'No, that won't be necessary. I shall have a half bottle of house red, please.'

'Very good,' she said, then took off.

'What about me?'

'What about you?' he said.

'Well, you didn't ask if I wanted a glass.'

'No, because you are not going to start drinking. At least not just yet. Wait until you are older – mature. When you can handle it.'

'OK! I was intending to do that anyway,' I said. 'But I don't like to be taken for granted.'

'That will never happen to you, my darling,' he said, slipping his arm round my shoulder.

'By the way, what the hell is consommé?' I said.

He laughed. 'Clear soup!'

'Oh, right!'

'You are funny!' he said, pulling me close and kissing my forehead. 'I do love you so, darling!' he said, looking at me with his beautiful green eyes looking nearly sad yet happy. It was like he wanted to cry! But I didn't understand where it was coming from.

I put me arms on his neck and pulled him to me and kissed his face, letting my lips rest on him. 'I love you too, Ralph!' I said.

Then he pulled away and picked up his silver knife and ran his finger over the handle, looking like he was worried and thinking about something.

'What's wrong, Ralph?'

He shook his head, looking up at me. 'Nothing, darling! I am just thinking how wonderful it is being here with you. Now, in this place, at this time! It is a memory to be cherished by me.'

'And me! I cherish every minute I am with you! You know, Ralph. You have no idea what goes on in my head when I can't be with you!'

Before he could say anything, the lady came in carrying a big wooden tray with a white linen cloth covering it. She handed me a royal patterned plate, with a matching bowl sitting on it. I moved back and she put it down in front of me, then gave Ralph his. Then she put a basket of bread on the table. I saw the little glass dish with rolled butter and helped meself to a piece of brown bread with a thick crust. 'This is home made!' I said. 'They didn't buy this in the shops.'

'I should think not!' he said. 'They have a very fine cook here.'

'Who did you come here with, Ralph?' I said, feeling worried he might have taken a woman.

'My family, friends of the family, that sort of thing,' he said, helping himself to the bread and plastering it with butter. 'Come on! Eat while the soup is hot,' he said, shaking his head at me soup.

'OK!' I picked up the spoon, tasting the brown, watery-looking soup. 'Hmm! Delicious!'

'Yes, it is good!' he said.

Then she arrived with his half bottle of wine and poured it into a long, bubbly-looking glass.

'Would you like an orange juice?' he said to me.

'No, I'm fine, thanks!'

'Is that OK for you?' she said, waiting for him to taste the wine.

'Perfect!' he said, nodding his head. Then she was gone.

'Do you want pudding?' he said, when she took away the dinner plates.

'No, I don't like pudding. What would I be doing eating black and white pudding when I've just had a lovely dinner?'

'Oh, you silly sausage! I meant sweet, dessert, ice cream!'

'Oh! So why didn't you just say that?' I said, feeling a right eejit.

'Here is the menu,' he said, sipping on his wine. Then he got up and went outside, saying, 'Back in a moment, darling. I've left my cigarettes outside.'

'Hey! Don't you go running off and leaving me with the bill!' I laughed.

'Oh, you are too clever for me,' he laughed, flicking his hair back out of his left eye then taking off out the door.

I looked around, not believing what was happening to me. I was afraid to think what it might mean. Afraid to hope! Never have I ever been so happy or believed I could ever feel so loved. But I'm afraid. Nothing is sure! The only thing I am sure about is I will love Ralph all the days of my life. Nothing will ever change that. I know some things about meself. One of them things is that I never trust anyone! But I would trust him with my life. Yet, I sense, somehow, all is not well. Something is going to happen. I can feel it in me bones. Never mind, Martha. Right now is what is important. Just enjoying the sheer happiness of being with him. I must have done something really good to deserve this!

I looked up, seeing him appear back in the door. Me heart just turned over. Gawd! How can someone be that handsome? Even men stare at him, never mind women. I see the way they all turn to look at him. His manners are out of this world. Then when he speaks, it's like listening to beautiful music. Jesus! I never thought I would lose me head and me heart over a man. You sure don't know anything about yourself until you're put to the test. I'm learning a lot of things I didn't know about life. I used to think I knew everything – at least about people. I could read them like a book. Now I can't even understand meself.

'Sweetheart, are you listening to me?' he said, lifting me face to look at me.

'What? Sorry, I was miles away!'

'Yes, I can see that,' he laughed. 'What were you thinking?' he said, bringing me head close into his shoulder and whispering.

'Nothing. Just empty thoughts,' I said, landing me hand on his leg.

He looked down, then put his hand over mine and lifted it, kissing me hand. An electric jolt shot through me, making me melt.

'I would doubt that. Darling?'

'What?' I said.

Then he pulled me into him and breathed, 'My desire is to fill up that empty space. Allowing my heart to act as a balm. To slowly ease the pain of the scars you bear. I would dearly love to see you brimming with happiness,' he murmured, really quiet around me ear. Then he sighed and said, 'So, would you like something else? Pudding?' he laughed.

'No, thanks!' I laughed.

'OK. Shall we take a walk in the garden? Or would you prefer to move on?'

'Let's move on!' I said.

He drained the last of his wine and stood up. 'OK. Let me settle up the bill. Here, take these cigarettes and wait for me. Take a seat over by the window, if you like.'

'OK,' I said happily, making for a chair by the window and looking out at the garden.

We got back into the car and he drove on. He looked very happy.

'That was the best dinner I ever had in my life,' I said, deciding to watch me diction.

'No, darling. Not the best, I'm sure. But certainly the best ambience!'

'What's that?'

'Oh, everything. The place, the atmosphere, the company!' he laughed, showing his dimples, with his green eyes sparkling.

'Yes! It could have been the Queen's palace. It would have been all the same with me if you were not there,' I said, looking mournfully at him.

'Oh, my precious,' he sighed. 'What if we—' Then he stopped.

'Go on! Say it, Ralph! What were you going to say?'

He just shook his head and reached out to pull me to him, nestling me under his arm, with me head on his shoulder. 'They grow up in the most delightful way,' he sang, almost to himself, under his breath, in a French accent.

'Ralph,' I whispered, lifting my head to look into his face.

'Yes, my love?' he said, whispering down to look at me quickly and squeeze me, then looking back at the road ahead.

'When . . .' I hesitated to ask him. 'When did you decide you loved me?' I asked, holding me breath.

'Oh, my goodness!' he said, taking in a breath and thinking. 'I think I have always loved you. Right from the beginning. You were a fiery little thing. Oh, heaven help us, those tantrums of yours!' he said, laughing. 'They got you into so many scrapes.'

'So did you ever want to turn your back on me and tell me to go away?'

'No! Never!' he said, slowly shaking his head, staring ahead at the road. 'I loved you. You needed me. I used to think of you as "Martha, my little Rosebud". Thorny but exquisitely beautiful once you matured. You would one day unfold like a beautiful rose coming into bloom.'

'Ralph,' I said, letting him barely hear me.

'Yes, my sweet one?'

'You are very handsome,' I said, looking into his face.

He gave a big smile, showing his dimples, with his eyes twinkling, and I stared at his gorgeous teeth. They are so straight and white. 'Thank you, darling for that very nice compliment. But I should hope my looks alone would not be the reason for you loving me. That is quite an accident of birth. No achievement on my part. It is the luck of the gene pool. I probably got my attractive looks from a rogue ancestor! Probably one who went around ravishing all the local native beauties!' he said, laughing.

'Oh! Did you have rogue ancestors?' I said, thinking I can't imagine him having criminals in his family.

'Well, everybody does, do they not?' he said.

'Yeah, I suppose so,' I said, thinking the lot who come after me when I have children – well, hundreds of years down the line from them – they can all tell each other they had a robber for a great-granny. Me! 'Do you know of any of the rogues going back in your family, Ralph?'

'Well, we did have one who used to chase butterflies out in Africa. Oh! Way back. Over a hundred years or so. He lived with the local natives. Right old rake he was too, judging by all the accounts given about him. He had several wives, with one waiting for him back in England. He refused to return home unless he could take his wives with him. Naturally, that was out of the question!' Ralph laughed, throwing his head back and letting a roar outa him. 'He was quite the drinker too. So when he died, the family wanted him returned home. Naturally, they needed to find a way to preserve him. It was weeks of travel then. Not like today. You can fly. So, do you know what they did with him?' he said, looking to see if I could figure it out, waiting for me answer with a big grin on his face. I couldn't think, so he said, 'I shall tell you. They pickled him in the local brew he had invented and packed him off home.'

I started roaring me head laughing and he was laughing too. 'Stop, darling! We will crash,' he kept saying, tapping me on the side of me arse. But we carried on laughing. 'Yes,' he said, getting over his laughing. 'He really was quite batty, poor old chap.'

'I know the first time when I decided I love you,' I said, looking up at him, smiling, feeling shy.

'Oh, when was that?'

'When you first took me to your mother's house.'

'Oh! Oh, yes! I remember that. You were like a little kitten on a red-hot tin roof. You kept fidgeting. Quite the little bag of nerves, poor thing,' he said, laughing. 'My mother quite adores you, you know.'

'Does she?'

'Oh, yes. She found you terribly amusing. It gave her something to report to her friends. She would spend hours on the telephone, regaling them of tales about you, giving them a blow-by-blow account of your latest reign of terror over those poor unfortunate nuns in that hostel. You were such a little horror. You would trot off to see my mother, giving the latest account of your very naughty escapades. It kept them all highly entertained,' he laughed.

'Yeah, the worse one was when Allie found out I had told the nun in the hostel a pack of lies, letting them all think I was somewhere when I wasn't. Remember the time, Ralph, when I got stuck outside, locked out all night?'

'Don't remind me!' he muttered.

'Yeah! I ended up right in the middle of the anarchists when they started their riot over the Troubles in Northern Ireland. I was only hanging around watching what was going on, then the bricks started flying. I was right in the middle, standing between the police and the anarchists, watching and gaping. Then they all charged at each other. Bricks started flying out of nowhere. I leapt straight into the arms of a man standing at the park railings opposite. It turned out he was a detective watching what was going on. Anyway, I kept screaming, "Save me, save me!" He turned away from the crowd, burying me head with his arms, leaning down to protect me inside his coat, saying, "Oh, a damsel in distress! This must be my lucky night!" He kept laughing but I was bloody tortured with the fright!'

'Do you want an answer to that?' Ralph said, looking down at me.

'No! Anyway, I took off, hiding in the park opposite, shivering on a bloody bench all night. When I finally got back into the hostel the next morning, I told the nuns I had stayed with your mother. Allie found out when she rang you, then all hell broke out! You didn't have to tell her, you know!' I said, lifting me head and pulling away from him, getting annoyed all over again, this time at the memory of the loss of me pocket money. 'Jaysus! Her and that doctor kept using every excuse to hang onta me money, Ralph. Most of the time I was flat broke. Marooned without a bleedin penny in me pocket,' I snorted, feeling he was half to blame for that one.

'Well, darling, they were trying to instil within you some discipline. You won't get far without it, you must know that?'

'But you didn't have to open your mouth, Ralph! You could have kept quiet.'

'No, I could not! I, too, wanted to know where you had spent the night, my darling. I was terribly concerned about you. So were they, the sister and doctor.' Then he took in a breath, saying, 'Oh, what a tangled web we weave, when first we practise to deceive. Goodness, you played merry hell with the lot of us,' he laughed, thinking about all me carry-on.

'I miss your mother!' I said, feeling the loss of her because she wasn't around any more.

'Well, darling, you could be there with her right now if you had taken up my sister's offer to take you back to live with her in England. Remember when you met her that first week you were staying with my mother?'

'Yeah, I remember. She said I could go to school. She would even get me a private tutor to help me, and her own daughter, Charlotte, would help me. She's the same age as me!'

'Yes, she has just completed her A levels. Now she's gone to start life at Oxford.'

'Oh! What's she doing?'

'Law,' he said.

'Your sister is a doctor, isn't she, Ralph?'

'Yes! A professor of medicine. She teaches student doctors,' he said, lifting his head and dropping it, keeping his eyes on the road.

'But Charlotte decided not to follow in her footsteps?' I said, looking at him.

'Yes! That is quite right,' he said, lifting his head up and down. 'She has followed her father into law. He lectures in law.'

'Oh!' I said, thinking maybe if I had gone to live with them would I have been able to become a barrister? I always fancied meself strutting around doing me stuff in a wig and gown. Just like Odette's mother wanted her to do. Anyway, it would have made a change from always being on the other side. Up in court arrested for robbing! Oh, well! I will get where I want to be all in me own good time.

'So, darling! Why would you not go with her? You would have been very happy. She would have treated you well. You would have become a member of the family. That is what we thought best for you at the time! Why did you resist the idea?' he said, looking down at me.

I hesitated, then said, 'I didn't want to leave you. I loved you.'

'What? So! That is the reason?' he said, shaking his head. 'Well, if I had known that, I would have picked you up, given you a good spanking, then taken you there myself and deposited you in your new life, brooking no nonsense from you!'

'But you just said you loved me too, Ralph!'

'Yes, of course I did. What has that got to do with anything? You were a child! I loved you as a child! I wanted what was best for you! For heaven's sake, Martha. What the bloody hell are you thinking?'

'Don't curse at me!' I snorted, moving meself well back into me own corner. I stared out the window, feeling raging. Huh! So he wouldn't have missed me! Well, fuck him too!

'Oh, darling! Come on! Move over beside me,' he said, reaching his arm over to try and pull me to him. 'Oh, really! Let us stop this nonsense. We are arguing over piffle!'

'So!' I suddenly exploded, not understanding where he was coming from. 'When? How?' I was trying to think. I wanted to say, 'Why did you kiss me!' but I said, 'So, when did you change?'

'What do you mean?' he said, looking at me confused, with his eyes not understanding.

'Now! Today, when you kissed me.'

'Oh, yes!' he said, taking in a slow breath through his nose. 'When did my feelings towards you change?'

'Yes!' I said, waiting with me mouth open to hear what he would say.

He stared ahead, thinking about it, drawing air in though his nose. 'I suppose,' he said, looking at me and grinning, 'it was around the time you met that young buck!'

'Why do you always call him that, Ralph?'

'Well, that is what he is! He spends an awful lot of time sniffing around you!' he snorted.

'But, sure, you don't know him! You never met him.'

'It was not necessary, darling. I do not need to. I have been listening very carefully to what you say about him. I was not impressed. He is not suitable for you. You would eat him alive, poor chap!' he laughed, roaring his head off. 'But the question of when my feelings started to change for you?' he said quietly. 'Well, I had thought, my concern was that he would hurt you. I was simply being protective of you. Nothing more. Then you started to disturb my dreams,' he said lowering his voice even more, making it a whisper. 'Yes, it was quite disturbing. Particularly when you began to haunt my waking moments. I would hear the laughter of a girl and look around thinking it may be you. I would look into a crowd as I walked through the city, hoping I might meet you,' he said, sounding very serious, looking sad.

'You walked along O'Connell Street?' I said, disappointed I never met him.

'Of course, you silly goose! What do you think I do? Live in an ivory tower?' he laughed.

'Pity we never met!' I said, thinking it was always only ever in the parlour or out in his mother's house when I would bump into him. They were the best times! I would sit beside him getting a lift home, then wait patiently for a hug just before he let me out at the hostel.

'So you were jealous?' I said quietly, looking at him, smiling. Feeling my heart bursting out with happiness, flying around me. I leapt across the seat, plastering meself into his arms, mooching me head on his chest to get the closest spot, then wrapped me arms around his stomach.

'Yes, my dearest loved one,' he said, happily and quietly, wrapping his arm around me, snuggling me into him. 'I realised then my love had deepened into something more. I loved you as a woman. A very young woman. Much too young, really,' he said, shaking his head, not looking very happy. 'But my need for you is very strong, darling,' he said, taking in a deep breath. 'You are very lovely. You enrich me with your goodness, your warmth, your laughter. You have so much love within you! It shines out like a beacon! I love you for all this – your naughty sense of humour, your boldness. You are so enduring! How could I not but love you? My precious Martha, you are unique! I cannot but love you. Yes, I have fallen in love with you,' he muttered, dropping his head, then looking out his side of the window, not wanting me, really, to hear this. But letting me know anyway!

'The shock of knowing I wanted to keep you all to myself – it has taxed every ounce of my strength. My life has been turned on its head. I am used to an ordered life. This has toppled everything into total confusion – my life as I have known it, my commitment as an ordained priest. I do not take my vows lightly, Martha,' he said, making it sound like he was giving out. 'These are all things I hold very dear.'

'Is that why you were not available every time I came to see you recently?'

He nodded his head, saying quietly, 'Yes! I was frightened of losing control. I needed time to think. I want to do what is best,' he said, looking even more serious. 'It is a dreadful decision for both of us. We cannot allow it to just take its own course!'

'What do you mean?' I said, getting worried.

He said nothing, just looked around, seeing where we came to.

36

We came to another woods with a path up to it. He pulled into the path and drove into a little area and parked near the trees. 'Shall we get out and take the air? Walk up through the woods?' he said, leaning back and getting my coat. 'Here! Wrap up, darling. It's getting chilly!'

'OK! Yes, let's go.' I jumped out of the car and wriggled into me coat then belted it up.

'OK!' he said, pulling up the collar of his sheepskin coat, then leaning into me to pull up the collar of my coat. 'We must not let you catch cold!' he said, grinning at me.

'Why do you always say we, Ralph?'

'Oh, that is the royal "we". Victoria, the Queen, would say "We". By that she meant "Me",' he laughed. '"We are not amused," she was wont to say, meaning I am not amused.' Then he wrapped the scarf around his neck. 'Let us go!' he said, grabbing me hand and pulling me up the hill.

I laughed as he dragged me along, letting him do all the work. 'If you don't walk, I shall be forced to carry you!' he said, looking at me like he was threatening.

'Yeah! You and what little army?' I said, snatching me hand away and diving well away from him.

'Oh, come on, darling! Let us take a walk,' he said, half laughing, watching me getting ready to run across the forest, daring him.

'Nope! Catch me if you can!' I said, shaking me head.

He lunged for me and missed. This time I was wide awake. I took off, looking back to see him haring up behind me just about to reach his hand out and grab me. I held me coat and ducked back under his arm and I was gone again. 'You won't catch me, mate! I'm far too quick for you!' I warned, feeling meself getting hysterical with the excitement of him nearly catching me and not wanting him to. I tried not to laugh and let him catch me and win. He was quick as the wind, but I was faster on the ducking and diving. 'You're not bad for an aul fella,' I shouted, getting near a tree.

'You will pay for this outrageous insult,' he said, laughing, slowing down to judge which way I would move.

He looked very determined. I flew around the tree and he came from me left, reaching out to grab me. I screamed with the laugh and the fright in me. Me heart was going like the clappers. I was determined he wouldn't get his hands on me. I ducked and he slipped. That gave me the advantage to tear up the hill and keep going. I looked back to see him stampeding up behind me. I heard a scream coming out of me and ducked to the left without knowing where he was behind me. Then I looked, not able to see him. Me head flew around, looking at the trees and bushes. Jaysus! Where did he get to? I moved slowly, backing away from the tree. I heard a branch crackling and whipped me head around. Suddenly he was barrelling down on top of me.

'Got you!' he roared, putting his arms wide, not letting me escape. I went backwards with the fright, screaming just as he lunged, catching me with his two arms, wrapping them around me waist. We ended up piled on top of each other. He went down, twisting himself to stop me hitting the ground and him landing his weight on top of me. But he was still holding on to me. I twisted meself and ended up rolling away from him, trying to get to me feet.

'You,' I panted with the laugh, 'didn't get me yet.' I was nearly up and he reached out his hand, trying to get to his feet.

'Back here! You! Wench!' he said, grabbing a hold of me coat and pulling me back just as he was getting to his feet. I lost me balance and started falling backwards again, screaming, 'Ahhh! Lemme go!'

He went down but wouldn't let go of me. I was laughing and panting, keeping me eyes ahead of me, wanting to escape. Then he went down and I rolled with him. I started screaming with the laugh. He couldn't keep hold of me.

'I told you,' I said, laughing me head off, 'you were an old man!'

He rolled himself around, giving up trying to get to his feet, saying, 'We'll see about that.'

Suddenly he shot out his arm, grabbing a hold of me coat, dragging me to him. Then he rolled on top of me, pinning me down. 'Got you, my little beauty!' he said, with a mad gleam in his eye like he had just won something really marvellous. 'Now who is the old man?'

'You!' I screamed, laughing like a hyena.

'Fifteen lashes with a feather, M'lud!' he roared. 'What is that you say, M'lud?' he said, looking up at an imaginary judge with his eye cocked and his head tilted, listening.

I screamed laughing.

'Spare the rod, you say, M'lud? Pleasure!' he snapped. 'So be it! TLC it shall be!'

'What's that?' I said.

'Tender loving care! M'lud's order! Could I not ravish her first, M'lud?' he asked the imaginary judge again with his face looking hopeful. 'No! M'lud says out of the question! Doddering old fool! Sorry, darling! But you may ravish me!'

'What? OK!' I said, making to push him off me.

'You little minx!' he said. 'How dare you take advantage of an old man like me?' he croaked, sounding just like an old man. Then he picked me up and wrapped me in his arms and started going mad, making fast little kisses all around me neck and face, spinning me around, laughing, saying, 'My God! Enough! I need to get my breath.'

I was still out of breath, too, from all me running and laughing.

Then he rolled away from me and started panting, trying to get his breath. I could feel me heart rattling in me chest, trying to get me breath too.

'Naughty girl!' he muttered in between pants.

'Geriatric aul fella,' I panted.

'Oh, dear! You will regret it,' he warned, still waiting for his breath to come back. Then we just stayed quiet, listening to our breathing, with me feeling the damp earth under me. But it was soft and smelled lovely. I felt a sense of great peace. Somehow the earth under me and the forest around me made me feel nothing in the world should worry me. Time here just stands still. This forest just goes on living, growing and being here without too much fuss and bother and worry. Nothing really is that important. Here, this place has gone on for hundreds of years. It will still go on when I am long gone.

I felt me heart slow down and rolled off me back to look at Ralph. He was lying flat out with his arms spread down by his sides, looking up at the clear evening sky, then letting his eyes roam around to the trees with their branches hanging over the paths and their wide trunks losing their bark. He took in a huge sigh, turning his head and resting his eyes on me. I said nothing. Just looked at him. He put out his hand, saying, 'Come closer, darling. Lie beside me.'

Me heart lurched and I rolled meself over, snuggling into his chest, and his arms wrapped around me. I listened to his heart beating in his chest. It was strong and steady.

'You know, my love. I was just thinking about that first time I met you.' He shook his head slowly, looking up at the sky, not really seeing it. 'You were just a little waif! So bedraggled looking. But there was something in your eyes. Yes, you were exhausted, but you had a fire burning in them. It moved me. I was quiet taken by you, even then. I knew you were unique. Do you know, I look at you now and you are developing into a lovely young woman. Darling, you have come so far in such a short time. What has it been? Two years? Yes, now look at you. You look wonderful. I see you blossoming, more and more. You are maturing.'

'Ralph?'

'Yes?' he said.

I hesitated to say what I wanted, so I kept quiet.

'Tell me – what is it you want to say to me?'

'I don't know,' I said, very afraid to hear the answer.

'I shall get it out of you,' he said, swinging me on top of him, then rolling me to the other side of him. Then he lifted himself up on his left side and looked down at me. 'Tell me!'

'No!' I laughed.

He took my arms and pinned them above me head, then leaned into me. I could feel me heart starting to hammer in me chest. Then he let himself go more and leaned his chest on me. 'My God!' he whispered, letting go of me arms and wrapping his hands in mine, still pinned above me head. 'I never thought I would ever experience anything like the way I'm feeling right now,' he breathed.

I found me voice and said, 'What are you feeling. Ralph?'

'It takes my breath away,' he whispered. 'Darling, I love you so very dearly. It is hard to articulate the words that will help you understand. It is so important to me you do understand. I cannot give you what you need. You have years ahead of you! Darling, you are not ready to make a commitment. Even were I to ask you to marry me! Darling, I am very tempted! So close! Yet you are not mature.'

I felt meself going cold. This is not what I want to hear. I started to pull away from him.

'No, no, please, darling, I beg you! Listen to me,' he said, moving himself over me so I couldn't move. 'This is not what you need. It is part of a commitment. You are not ready for that. I couldn't do this to you. It would destroy you! I love you much too much to take advantage of you.'

I turned me head away, not wanting to hear.

'Oh, please, darling. You mean so much to me. Don't turn away from me. Listen to me. Do you not know just how much I dearly want to make love to you? Now! Right this minute! My God, the need is so overpowering! But what would it serve? It is not just the act itself! For you, it would mean giving yourself entirely to me. It is the same for me. It would be a commitment for both of us, because we love each other. But you are not ready for this kind of relationship. I would hurt you, darling. I understand you better than you think. I know you! I have watched you grow. You are becoming a wonderful young woman. I can't take that from you. I will not rob you of your future! It is not with me, darling. We could be married. I have a deep yearning for you, to take you all for myself. But you are too hurt! You are so vulnerable. You have never experienced love or affection.

In time, you would outgrow me. You have not fully matured yet, Martha. I brought you out today—'

'Yes! Why did you, Ralph? Why are we here?' I said.

'Because I wanted us to be together!' he said, sounding like he was ready to cry. 'I needed you to know just how much I love you. You have experienced just how powerful my feelings are for you. So, you know now I am not rejecting you. I am showing you how deep my love for you is by letting you go. You must see this! Martha, I need you to allow yourself to be free from me, move forward with your life. Do this for me, please, darling, because I want only the very best for you. My precious darling! It is almost my gift to you. How else can I prove my love for you? Tell me, darling! Do you want me to make love to you?'

I wanted to say yes but I couldn't.

He said nothing, just thought about it. Then he said quietly. 'Yes, it would be so very wonderful to lose myself in you. To take you, right here, this minute. Make you mine. The act would be blissful, while it lasted. But what should we do then? Making love is very sacred, darling, I tell you! It means a commitment, otherwise what? It is hollow. You would feel cheated. Neither of us is able to make a commitment. Do you see what I mean? Do you believe I love you, Martha? Speak to me!'

I couldn't open me mouth. I felt numb.

'Oh, I never thought I would love like this!' he said, pulling me to him and burying my face in his neck. 'You are not ready to make a lifetime commitment. This is crazy! It is bloody nonsense. I don't know what I was thinking,' he muttered. 'Will you let me release you? You need to help me, too, darling! It is almost impossibly difficult for me to let you go but I must!'

'Ralph?'

'Yes?' he said, holding his breath, looking at me.

'Your mother was very young when she married, wasn't she?'

'Oh, sweetheart! That was so different then. They were different times! She had come from a loving family. She had a husband who was totally committed to her! They had no difficulties standing in the way. It is not the same for us, darling! You are unique! You are too strong to settle for what I have to offer you. It would stifle you. Marriage is not for the faint-hearted. There is so much of you waiting to be released. You have so many gifts. You need the freedom to grow. You need to mature, to develop. You must be able to stand on your own feet. These demons you are tortured with now, they will diminish as you grow more secure. You will gain confidence in yourself, then you will make a decision not out of desperation, because you are desperately seeking love and affection, but because it will be your own choice! This is the gift I want to give you by letting you go. I want you to take your place in the world. You will do this by your own endeavours. I am not good for you. You don't need me now. Darling, it will be very, very hard for you, I know. Also for me too! But it will be nothing like the pain you would endure if we went down this route, OK?' he said. His face is so close to mine, his breath whispered on my face.

'No!' I said. 'I belong with you,' I whispered.

'Oh, darling, please! This is the right thing to do!'

'Ralph?'

'Yes, sweetheart?'

'I want you to kiss me!' I said.

He stared at me. I heard the silence as he held his breath. I held mine, staring back at him, waiting. I could see the longing in his eyes as he searched mine, seeing the same thing.

'Please! I need you to,' I whispered.

'Why, darling? I have explained all this.'

'Yes, Ralph, and I heard you.' I hesitated, trying to find the words I wanted to say. 'I may never find love again,' I said, staring into his face.

'Darling, of course you will!' he smiled, stroking my face and hair with his hands.

'No, you don't know that. I want to feel what it's like to have kissed someone I love with all my heart. I need to know! It is important to me.' I didn't say I wanted to take away the picture of being raped by men when I was a little child. To carry a new picture. Knowing what it was like to touch and be touched by a man who loves me. So instead I just told him, 'I want to know what love feels like, Ralph.'

'Darling,' he sighed, shaking his head. 'You don't need that to prove my love,' he whispered.

I said nothing, just stared into his eyes, hoping he would not reject me.

I felt it was a battle of wills. He wanted to walk away from me, believing it was the best thing for me and himself! I believe being with him is the only thing that will ever matter to me. He stayed staring at me. I stared back, without moving my face. He knows everything I have to say. Everything I think. The decision is his.

'But it won't stop there,' he said.

I said nothing. Then I said, laughing, seeing he was now keeping quiet, 'Well, we can't do much sinning, Father! Not with your big heavy coat and mine between us. That should stop us getting up to any real mischief!'

He grinned at me, landing his finger on me nose. 'Tut tut! Don't look at me with those flashing eyes. You will tempt me!'

'Ah, come on, Ralph! Give us a kiss. The coats will protect our virtue.'

He roared laughing, saying, 'Oh, you really are a naughty little wench!'

'Brute!' I snapped back. 'You refuse to ravish me! But on the other hand . . . Wait, move over. Let me get my hands back.'

'What?' he said, leaning away from me and looking to see what I was doing.

'Now, if I was to do this, we may have a better chance of confessing something interesting in the confession box!' I said, flicking open the belt of my coat and flying open the buttons. Then I grabbed the buttons on his coat, opening them.

'Stop! You are a bloody Jezebel!' he said, roaring laughing.

'Well, you know your man Oscar Wilde? He used to live in the house around the corner from my hostel!'

'Not personally, darling. He was a tad before my time. But, yes, what about him?'

'Well! You know I trot meself off down to the library every now and then?'

'Quite right, too! A bit of literature will do you no harm!'

'Shut up! Pay attention when I am speaking.'

'You little horror! Apologise at once! You do not tell me to shut up!' he said, grabbing me arms and pinning them over me head.

'No, definitely not! I'm loving every minute of this, you brute!' I said, giving him a big grin and blowing him a kiss. 'Now let me say what I want to say.'

'Tell me!' he said, resting himself on me and staring with a smile on his face.

'I was reading a few of the books he wrote.'

'Like what?'

'Well, I started with a fairy story—'

'"The Happy Prince",' we both said together, laughing our heads off, with him bowing his head at me, knowing what I was going to say. Then I went on to other things he wrote, like *The Picture of Dorian Gray*. Oh, and lots of other stuff he wrote.

'Gawd! He was really decadent, Ralph! He had a brilliant mind! But it ran like a sewer!' I snorted.

'Oh, I am impressed, darling! Oscar Wilde! And a new word – "decadent". All in the same sentence. My, you are coming along.'

'Don't be such a patronising bastard, Ralph. We can't all get our education in a private school. The library is good enough for me.'

'Oh, darling! Please forgive me. You know I am very proud of you. I was teasing!' he said, leaning down and kissing my nose.

'Yes, well! Be quiet, and listen. Before you land yourself in even bigger trouble.'

'I am hanging on, waiting to catch every pearl of wisdom dropping from your rosy-red lips, my love!' he said, with his eyes lighting up, keeping his face dead straight.

'Ye're a right bleedin Don Juan,' I snorted, laughing.

'Martha, my love, you grow more interesting by the minute. Hmm, you must tell me about that book,' he laughed, flicking his eyebrows up, grinning at me, then giving me a peck on the lips.

'Be quiet! I'm trying to tell you something.'

He took in a big sigh, trying not to laugh, saying, 'Of course, darling. On with your tale. Tell me about the "bold Oscar Wilde". What did you learn?'

'Yeah, right! So, anyway! Oh! What the bloody hell was I going to say?'

'You were going to tell me something about the decadent old boy, Oscar!'

'Oh, yeah! I remember now! Do you know what he said?'

'No! Not until you tell me,' he said, grinning at me.

'OK! But first, move over to me. I'm bleedin freezing in this bloody frock.'

'What did he say?' Ralph whispered, wrapping his arms around me.

'He said,' I whispered back, looking into his face as he bent over me, '"I can resist anything but temptation." So,' I said, putting his hands inside me coat and around me back, then running me hands under his jumper, 'now opportunity presents itself, Ralphie, darling!' I said, grinning at him.

'You are absolutely incorrigible and utterly adorable,' he said, pulling me arms out of the sleeves of me coat, then whipping his own coat off his back.

'Now, move down and lie on this,' he said, spreading his coat out on the grass and lifting me like an empty bag, plastering me on top of it.

'Oooh, lovely!' I said, wriggling on his sheepskin. 'It's lovely and warm.'

'Yes, darling! But I still think you need me to keep you warm,' he said, slipping his arms around me back and shoulder, then sliding over on top of me.

'Oh, this is even better!' I breathed, wrapping me arms around his neck and back.

I held him tight, feeling his hot breath on me face as he stared, with his face just inches away from me.

'You are so soft,' he whispered.

'Kiss me!' I sighed, feeling like my bones were turning to putty.

'Oh, Martha,' he breathed, letting his breath wash over me in a heavy sigh.

I watched his face moving closer to me, seeing his eyes drawn to my lips. His mouth brushed again mine. 'Oh, darling! We must stop,' he moaned as his body sank into me and his hands tightened around me, drawing me hard into him. Then he covered me with his body, lying stretched over me.

I ran my hands under his shirt and slowly stroked his back, feeling my body reach up to strain into him. Then I felt myself melt as my body opened up, letting his weight sink into me. I could feel his muscles strain, sinking deeper into me. Then he moved his leg between mine and opened my mouth with his lips, clamping his down to breathe a roaring fire tearing through me. A deep sob escaped me as an intense liquid pleasure surged through me. I felt his tongue slide around my mouth and catch mine. Then he drew me to him like he was really going inside me, searching, making his way steadily to my soul, then letting go and drawing me back tighter into him. I started spinning away, sighing out his name over and over again, feeling more alive than I ever felt in my whole life.

His hand moved inches from my breast and his head moved down to kiss me as he pulled the zip of my frock down. 'I love you so much,' he breathed, lifting his face, looking into my eyes. 'Darling,' he whispered, 'we dare not! I cannot turn back! There will be no return. Please! I am very close to making love to you. Help me! It will horribly complicate our lives. You will be hurt! We both will,' he pleaded, his eyes looking very pained, staring deep into me.

I said nothing. Just stared back at him, listening and taking him in. I could see he was turning very pale. He was shaking with the effort to stop himself. I could feel his heart hammering into me chest. Jesus! He really is afraid. He meant all them things he said. So it would be wrong. I'm only going to end up making him suffer. I'm asking for trouble, and I'm not even being fair. He did try to explain to me. It's really me he wants to release him. To just let go, walk away from him. So this is the end. There is no more Ralph, not for me anyway.

I could feel the life going out of me. I suddenly felt very cold and empty inside. I closed my eyes, nodding at him.

'Don't,' I whispered, looking into his face and shaking me head. 'We better stop,' I murmured, then closed me eyes, not wanting him to see me pain.

I stayed still, hardly breathing, waiting for him to move away from me. Then I turned over and reached for my coat. I stood up, putting it on and buttoned it up, taking me time pulling the belt tight. Then I looked at him lying down, resting on his arm, seeing him watch me every movement. Me heart turned over with the pain at the loss of him. I love him so much. I reached down and picked up his coat. 'Put this on, Ralph! You'll catch cold.'

He dropped his head, looking at the coat, then took it out of me hand slowly, muttering, 'Thank you, darling.' He stood up and buttoned his coat, then sat back down again and lit a cigarette. His hands were shaking as he lit it. He dragged on the cigarette, inhaling it deep into his lungs, then let his head drop back, blowing the smoke into the air. 'Take this, darling,' he said, holding the cigarette out to me. 'Come, sweetheart. Sit close to me,' he whispered, looking up at me, letting me see his pain and loss.

I couldn't move. I felt rooted to the spot.

'Come on, darling. It's lonely without you next to me,' he muttered, taking me arm and pulling me down beside him. Then he lit a cigarette for himself and lay down, resting himself on his arm, smoking and looking into the distance. His eyes weren't really seeing anything. He was trying to make sense out of what is happening.

I turned me eyes away from him. It's late in the evening, I thought, hearing the quiet of the forest as it settled down for the night. It felt like a very lonely place now. I was sitting close to the man I would give my life for, yet I feel more lonely now than I have ever felt in me whole life. He is gone from me. Me world feels like it has ended. Nothing will ever be the same.

He stuffed out the half-smoked cigarette hard into the earth, making sure it was well out, with no more sparks to be seen. Then he picked it up and flicked it away into the forest. 'Are you all right, darling?' he said, turning around to look at me with his head resting on his arm.

I said nothing, just dropped me head, staring at the earth.

'My God, you look haunted!' he breathed, letting his breath out slowly. 'What have I done to you? You are just a child, not quite yet a woman really. I have hurt you. It is unforgivable,' he whispered, staring at me with a pained look in his eyes. He reached out with his arms, pulling me to him, holding me in his arms and rocking me. 'Please forgive me. I am so sorry to have been the one to cause you more pain. I feel you have suffered more than enough already. I dread to think what may have hurt you so badly. You never say but I know you carry some terrible scars. When you smile, you try to cover up the pain. But I see it, Martha. When you are in repose, you are not aware I am watching you. Your eyes look so haunted! There is an air of terrible loneliness about you in one so young. I sometimes find myself asking the question, what must you have seen? What is it that haunts you so? Darling, please share it with me,' he said, pulling my chin up to look at me.

I stared into his eyes, seeing he really does love me. Yet it makes no difference now. He is going to leave me. I will be all on me own, without him. So, what's there to talk about? I could feel an annoyance coming into me chest. Talk! Does he really think I am going to ever tell him anything now? No, there's nothing more to ever talk about. So I just said, wanting him to let go, 'Ah, don't worry about me, Ralph. I can look after meself,' I said, not caring any more. But there's no point in him worrying himself. 'Look, Ralph. Everyone gets hurt. It's just part of living. Some more than others. But try telling the people who have less than yours! Well, they will soon tell you where to get off. Everyone thinks their pain is worse than others. So, we all get hurt along the way. You have too, Ralph! Anyway, it could always be worse. We could be dead! I always look at it like this, Ralph,' I said, looking at him, 'I heard someone say once, when I was a child, "I thought I was badly off because I had no shoes, then I saw the man with no feet!" I've always managed to get by, Ralph. Tomorrow is always another day! Things can get better,' I said, seeing him staring at me, looking like it was the end of the world for him too. Jaysus! I hate to see him worrying himself for nothing. He's too good, really. He tried his best for me. What good can it do him anyway? Yeah, he's so good! That's why I love him so much! Fuck, if it's raining pennies, I'm over on the sunny side of the street! I thought to meself. Then I went back to me own thoughts. The pain inside me was getting worse. I couldn't get a grip on it. The lonely feeling at the thought of facing into nothing was making a hole in me insides. Ah, I thought, trying to keep meself from the worry, so what? Happiness never lasts, I thought. Come on! You knew that. You even felt it earlier on. It was a warning that something was going to happen. You bloody knew! Now, wipe your snots, Martha. Dust yourself down! See what's next around the corner! Life can be a bowl of bleedin cherries!

Something caught in me chest and a sudden gush of tears started to erupt out of me. I wanted to burst out crying. I was already beginning to feel the emptiness waiting ahead for me even as Ralph held me tight, trying to drive away the pain at the feeling of a terrible loss. A thought kept going through me head, driving me heart into breaking: it's all gone. There is no love waiting for me. He's going to leave me! It's just me and the world again, without any Ralph. I will have to go back, trying to find a safe haven. So, that's it. Fairy stories happen only in children's books. Ralph and me were never going to be together. I knew that all along, deep down inside me. Pity I don't have the sense to listen!

Just as suddenly as I reached up and caught a star I ended up drowning at the bottom of the ocean. Now I feel dead inside. I mooched away from him, resting with me head on his stomach. Then he gathered me up in his arms again, holding me tight, whispering, 'Let me hold you, Martha.'

He held me with both his arms wrapped around me, stroking my hair with one hand and keeping me pressed tight to him. I rested me head under his neck and me arms lay on his chest, with his right arm supporting me from the damp earth. I lay still, feeling the time slipping away, knowing this is just the waiting for the last bit of happiness to fade away. Then he would let me go out into the cold without his arms to protect me. A song came into me head. I heard a lonely little inner voice start to sing. It sounded so very sweet and haunting, as only a child can sing. Her voice lifted as she sang, 'Sand can get into yer eyes, but only people make ye cry. Do I know where hell is? Hell is in goodbye! Heaven is hello for ever, I'm comin te stay, my love! I was born under a wanderin star. Snow can burn yer eyes, but only people make ye cry! Mud can make ye prisoner, an the plains can bake ye dry. Pain can freeze yer heart up, an only love will make it melt! I was born under a wanderin star. Home is made for comin from, for dreams of goin to. I was born under a wanderin star. A wanderin, wanderin star.'

I stayed still, listening to her voice fade away into a lonely little cry. She sounded so desolate. Be still, little one, I said back to her. I'm not crying. It's OK. I don't feel anything. Then I thought to myself. Yes, I will probably wander for the rest of my days, looking for another Ralph!

'We must move, darling!' he said, starting to take his hands away. He stood up, taking me with him. 'Take these keys of the car, darling. I will be with you in a minute. Just give me a few minutes. Will you do that?' he said, looking down at me.

I stared into his green eyes. They were like green pools of water. He took out a cigarette, then lit it and gave me the packet. Then he turned his back and walked away up the path. I stood staring after him, watching him slow down. I waited to see if he would look back. But he didn't. I saw him drop his head in his hand, then take a white handkerchief out of his pocket, and he was wiping his eyes. He's crying! I thought. I don't understand. Why is he hurting me and himself? I know he does love me! I am sure of it! So why? I turned me head to the car and walked towards it, taking out one of Ralph's cigarettes and lighting it. I inhaled it into me lungs and kept it there, wanting comfort from the burning smoke in me chest.

We drove back to Dublin in silence. He was lost in his thoughts and I had mine. I didn't notice the miles flashing past until we reached the hill to my bedsitter. He pulled the car up outside the door and switched off the engine. 'I don't understand!' is all I could whisper inside the dark car. The light from the street lamp threw shadows across our face. His eyes were so sad looking. It gave me a little comfort to know my pain was not all for nothing. He did love me.

'Yes, darling, I know you don't. But you will in time,' he whispered.

I pushed open the door of the car and just before I moved out I looked over at him. He was staring at me like his heart was breaking. 'So, no more visits to come and see you then?' I whispered.

'No, darling,' he said quietly, shaking his head. 'No more visits.'

'Goodbye then, Ralph.'

'Goodbye, Martha.'

I walked up to the front door and hesitated before putting the key in the door. I looked, seeing he was still sitting there, looking at me. Then his arm moved and he switched on the engine, then turned the car around slowly. I stopped to watch him go. He slowed down and looked at me, then he blew me a kiss, very slowly, and moved off, going down the hill. I stood on the steps, watching until there was no more sight of him. No more Ralph! I thought, then I turned and put the key in the door and pushed it open.

The hall was dark and there was a smell of someone having a fry for their tea. I could hear the sound of a radio and the voices of the two people who lived on the ground floor. They were having their tea, the two of them together with the radio for company. I walked through the dark hall and up the stairs, not bothering to put on the light. When I turned the key and pushed in the door to my little room, it didn't look very welcoming. The cold air hit me. It looked and sounded like no one lived here.

I shut the door and sat down on the bed and opened me bag and lit a cigarette, then just stared out through the window into the dark night. 'I can't understand, Ralph,' I whispered, looking across to the empty dark church on the other side of the road, seeing the tombstones standing out against the street lamps. All their troubles are over, I muttered to meself. They're not missing much. You get a helping of happiness in this life, then it ends in the blink of an eye. After that, you pay with an awful lot of pain that goes on and on until it is time for the happy day to come around again. Is that all I am living for? When will I ever be happy again, God? Will it be as long coming as the last time? Or maybe that is the last I will ever see of it? God, I wish I was out of me misery. I can't bear the pain any more. There's nothing left for me to hold on to. I knew my happiness was too good to be true. Happiness never lasts! I always knew that. But I had nothing to lose. I could reach for the moon and hit the stars. Well, I did, God! I reached out and grabbed hold of a star! But me and it went plunging straight down into hell! So, now what, God? What do I reach for now? Me star fell out of the heavens, taking me with it.

37

I passed the shop at the end of Thomas Street and turned down past St Patrick's Hospital for the people suffering with mental problems. I looked over, seeing the high walls and the big entrance gate. Jonathan Swift started that place for himself! The poor man was suffering from madness. I bet there's saner people locked up there than there is out here. I feel like going over and asking them to let me in. I might have more in common with people in there than I have out in the world. I just want to be left alone. But people keep asking me what's wrong with me because I've stopped bothering about them. Even me mad boss had to get his spoke in. Now every time he comes to me office door and shouts in at me, I say nothing. Sometimes I don't even bother to look at him. 'Are you all right?' he said to me, two days ago. 'You're not yourself.' He stood nearly hitting the height of the door frame, he's that tall, waiting quietly with his mouth open to hear what was wrong. I said nothing. Then he coughed and said quietly, 'Will you get them back on the phone for me, Martha? I got cut off. I think there's something wrong with the bloody line. Will you do that for me? Like a good girl,' he muttered quietly, adding that bit.

I thought about Ralph. I couldn't get his face out of me mind, or the smell of his skin, or the feel of his touch. He just keeps haunting me. How could he ever think I would be happy without him? I know he meant what was best for me. But he doesn't know me. Not really. I'm a bit like the duck that hatches out of the egg. The first thing it sees, that is what it loves. It clings, even if it is an old shoe. Well, it was a bit like that for me with Ralph. I never trusted anyone. But he is the first person in my life I have loved. He loved me back. Therefore, for me, I could never replace him. How could I love someone else when I don't let them get close enough to try? I let him get close, because he was the first. But there will never be a second. Everyone will always be second best to him, if at all!

It's nearly two weeks now. This is Thursday. To hell with it! I can't accept it! There is a lot of truth in what he said. But I have the final say about what decisions I make. I am an adult! What's the difference between eighteen and eighty? They have been around a lot longer. Then again, I accelerated me way through life. I think in a lot of ways I'm more well up than a lot of people twice my age! But it is true what he says, I sure am behind a lot of people half my age, children, when it comes to looking for acceptance. Yeah, I know I'm behind there. But I could catch up. That would come with having a close relationship, surely? He said he knew me. But how could he? He has never been me. How could he know what it feels like to go around all your life with a pain deep inside you? A feeling of being empty, like it aches all the time. You have an idea what might help it. But you don't really know what it is. Then along comes him and in no time at all he starts to pour something inside you. Suddenly you know what was causing it. You had a hole in your heart. He pours a certain amount in. He calls it love. Now you know. But the hole is only getting little drops at a time. It leaves you aching with the pain. But now you know what to ask for. You know where to go and who to ask. He is the one that carries the cure. Your heart will only open for him.

You spend all your time dreaming about it. Thinking how to try and get more, because he is very sparing with it. Then one day he pours the lot in with a kiss. It tells me he is going to give me all his love. I will never be empty again. I will never have to endure that pain no more. My heart overflows with all the love. It feels a bit much all of a sudden. But then he keeps it there, keeping my heart well filled up with love. Then, just as I think with all that love in my heart I am so very special, I am filled up with all this love. The most wonderful man I have ever met in my whole life has picked me to be the most special person in his life. Me! Who only a few years ago was a scabby little toerag, running around barefoot and in rags, the little nobody bastard that scattered everyone in all directions. One look at me and they all gave me plenty of room when I crossed their path. Just in case they caught something or got robbed. Then, just when I'm about to start thinking, *How're ye, Missus? Remember me? Take a good look! Yeah, it's me all right. All you respectable looking-down-your-nose gobshites! I told you I would get here! Now get outa me way and mind me silk frock.* Then, before I could take in me next breath, in a terrible few minutes he empties it all out again. He takes it all back, letting it all pour out into that damp forest earth. The life in me just drained away. Then, while I'm bleeding from the pain, numb from it, he is telling me I will be grand now. I can go on me way, because he gave me all his love. But I was left more empty than I have ever felt in my whole life! He broke me heart to smithereens, because he took it all out too quick! He never gave me a chance to get used to being loved. My soul never made it back out of that forest. It stayed behind, watching, confused, waiting for me broken heart to mend.

Now I have no way to go but stay at the bottom, living in an empty dark shell. The holes in me let in all the cold. My heart is freezing with the pain. I have no way to climb back out again. What can I do?

I thought about it, then I made up me mind. Well, he did all the talking last time! I said barely anything. I went into shock. So, now I think I should have my say. If he says he doesn't want me, that it is not just a question of what is right for me, then I will accept it. There's no point in flogging a dead horse. Right! So that's it! I've made me mind up. So, as there's no time like the present, I'm going to find a phonebox and ring him straight away.

'Hello! Eh, yes! Can I speak with Father Ralph Fitzgerald, please?'

'Who?'

'Father Fitzgerald!'

'Oh, he's not here any more.'

Me heart leapt with the fright. What's he talking about? 'So he's not living there any more, did you say?'

'Yes, that's what I said.'

'Where can I contact him then, please?'

'Oh, he's left the country altogether!'

'Where's he gone to?' I nearly screamed, getting hoarse with the shock, hearing me voice going.

'He's gone away. Probably to England. I don't know! They don't tell me their business,' he snorted.

'OK,' I said, feeling me legs going from under me. 'Oh! When did he go away?'

'Last Thursday.'

A week today. I hung up the phone without saying anything. I could hardly get a breath. Gone! He's gone and left me? No, Jesus! No! How can that be happening? How do these things happen? I had everything only a short while ago – friends, Odette, living with Ralph's mother, the housekeeper, Ralph. Now it's all gone, vanished as quickly as it came! Who can I turn to now, God? I can't turn to you. You give things then you take them away. Why didn't you fuckin leave me alone and not give me anything. I would have fended for meself! I will never trust you again, God! This is too much to bear! I need somebody, God. I can't take it on me own any more!

You showed me what I was missing. Now I want that! How can you expect me to keep going without anyone to go to? Ahhh! I hate you, God! You can't exist!

I made me way over the King's Bridge, seeing the prostitutes walking up and down. I wonder do they not get lonely, having men who don't care about them? Who do they turn to? Someone that knows they are on the game wouldn't think very highly of them. So, do they have anyone? I felt like asking them. But that's only a mad thought! It's not my business. But I need to know. Who do you turn to when there's no one you care about and no one cares about you? What do you do?

Keep walking, Martha. First one step, then the other. Go home! Sleep and get up for work tomorrow. I looked over the wall on the bridge, seeing the water flowing along the River Liffey. It would be over in what? How long does it take to drown? Never mind. Save that for another day. I can do it but I can't undo it! The world is full of people like me. Them prostitutes, for a start. They are not having an easy time of it. So, yeah, hang on, Martha. Save that luxury for another day. I can end it whenever I like. But I can't bring meself back.

38

I heard the motorbike engine revving up outside the window. Ulick! Jesus! Not him again. 'Go home and just leave me alone,' I muttered, sitting on the side of me bed smoking and looking at nothing. I couldn't move. Every day when I get home from work, I just dump me coat and bag and sit on the bed or sit by the window watching it get dark. This reminds me of my mother when I was little. She used to do the same thing. Just sit and stare. It must be in the blood. I heard a little stone hitting the window and looked up. Jaysus! If that eejit breaks the window! He's stupid enough to do that!

I got up from the bed and walked over to the window. He was staring at the door, hoping it would open. Poor Ulick. He should get himself a proper girlfriend. Someone who will appreciate him. Then it hit me, and I gave a laugh. It sounded very empty to me ears. Yeah, Ralph! I'm beginning to sound just like you! I found the word for you. It's called altruistic! Yeah, maybe I'm becoming altruistic! Next thing you know, I'll be going around in sackcloth and ashes like the mad saints long ago! God, the fucking country was riddled with them. The 'Land of Saints and Scholars', me arse! Yeah, so I can cross priests off me list. They're going on me hit list along with the nuns. Fucking Eleanor! She turned out to be a sleevin! All over you when you were giving her something!

Ah, shut up, Martha. Listening to meself would give an aspirin a headache. I'll go down and let that fella in. It's better than listening to meself going mad! I opened the door, seeing him sitting on his bike. Jaysus! Talk about faithful, loyal! Well, you can't beat him for that. Only thing is, now that I look at him I can't bear it. Seeing him is a reminder all over again of Ralph. When I wasn't with one, I was out with the other! Except he's only a boy in a big man's pair of trousers. Am I that desperate? Yes, I am.

'Hello, Ulick! Sorry for not answering the door. I was flat out on the bed.'

'Where have you been?' he said, seeing me with his eyes lighting up. 'Gawd! You look terrible.'

'Thanks, Ulick. I know.'

'Here! I brought you a present,' he said, rushing to the back of his bike and throwing his arm at a television sitting there all strapped up to the backrest.

'Oh! What are you going to do with that?'

'I told you. It's a present for you!'

'Me? A television?'

'Yeah, it will be great. We can watch it together.'

'OK! Bring it upstairs. Can you manage on your own, Ulick?'

'Yeah, easy,' he said, hefting it into his arms.

He hauled it up the stairs and I waited with the door open.

'Where will we put it?'

We? I thought. I hope he's not getting ideas about making my bedsit a home from home. I don't want him thinking he bleedin owns me! I'm not that desperate! I stood back watching as he hoisted it on top of the wardrobe.

'We don't have the rabbit's ears, but not to worry,' he said. 'We can use a clothes hanger. Have you got one handy?'

'Yeah,' I said, opening the wardrobe.

I sat on the bed as he messed around with it, looking very intent and busy. Then the aerial was sorted and he switched it on.

'This is a very old one. Mammy and Daddy have bought a new colour television.'

'Very swanky!' I said. 'Colour!'

'Yeah, this is black and white.'

The sound of hissing came on and I sat back on the bed with me back against the wall. The hissing went and a picture started to emerge. It was funny shapes and lines and more hissing.

'Hang on! We'll get there,' he said, fiddling around with the knobs. 'You'll only get the one station, Telefís Éireann.'

'OK! So long as it's not all in Irish!' I said. 'Then it will be no good to me. I don't speak any foreign languages!'

He laughed. 'Glad to see you still have your sense of humour!' he said. Then suddenly gave a roar. 'OK! We have it working.' Then he stood back to watch the fuzzy picture.

The man, or whoever he was, kept getting stretched then flapping back to normal.

'Ah! The picture keeps disappearing,' he said, sounding downhearted.

'Never mind, Ulick. You did your best.'

'No wonder Mammy and Daddy went out and bought a new one!'

'Is that why your father's hair turned grey?' I said, feeling peevish.

'Jaysus! Leave him alone, Martha. He's done nothing on you! It's back. We have the picture!' he roared.

I watched, seeing real people. And what looked like a real film should actually look like. 'Yeah, great. Thanks, Ulick.'

He took a flying leap and landed on the bed, bumping me into the air and hitting me head against the wall. 'Jesus! You can be so thick, Ulick!' I said, rubbing me head and spitting me venom on him.

'Sorry! Let me rub it.'

'No! Keep your hands to yourself!' I said, slapping him away.

He sat down gently beside me and we settled in to watch the television box. Then cartoons came on.

'Looney Tunes!' he screamed, hopping up and down on the bed, bouncing me around again.

'For fuck sake, Ulick. One more bang off that wall with my head and yours will be going straight through that window!'

'Sorry!' he said, dropping his eyes like a six year old.

I snorted, thinking this is a pain in the arse.

'But I love cartoons!' he said.

I don't believe it. I never heard in me whole life an adult saying that, I thought to meself, wondering if there was maybe something missing in him because I never took much notice of him before. Me mind was always elsewhere, thinking about Ralph. Damn you, Ralph! You self-righteous bastard. I picked that word up from Sophie. But it describes Ralph, thinking he can think for the pair of us.

'I better get home,' Ulick said, stirring himself out of the bed.

I had nearly dozed off. The first time in weeks I had felt still, not having the silence of the room and the walls closing in around me. Occasionally I would hear the sound of a voice as people passed the window or a car drove past. That was even lonelier, reminding me I didn't have anyone I belonged to or they belong to me. I sat up here night after night, staring at the shadows on the wall thrown in from the streetlights outside as the evening crept into darkness.

'No! Don't go!' I heard meself say.

'What? But I have to go home,' he said, looking at me with a half smile and puzzled at the same time. 'Sure, we have to get up for work in the morning!'

'Yeah, I know. But just for a little while longer. Come on!' I said, patting the space beside me on the bed.

He hesitated, then said, 'OK, But I'm really punched-out tired.'

'Yeah, sorry! I know you are, Ulick.'

'Just for a little while, OK?'

'Yeah, right. Not too long. No, not too long,' I said, feeling the relief flying around me chest. I couldn't bear to be on me own any more.

He mooched down beside me and pushed me into the wall.

'OK, have you enough room?' I said, seeing him take up half the bed.

'Well, we could make more room if I turn on me side,' he said, reaching to get a hold of me. He planted his kisser right on me mouth and I wanted to jump up and push him off the bed. But I said nothing. Me desperation at keeping him just a little longer was more important.

His hands started to ramble. I felt meself tensing, then I went off somewhere. Who knows where I'm gone? But I could feel his hands rushing and his fingers were roaming. It's not so bad, really. He is me boyfriend! I'm just coming around to that idea. Yeah, he's a nice fella, really. Very kind. Who needs love? That's for jokers! It doesn't really exist. If it did, I would have found it by now. No, this is what matters. Having someone around I am used to.

Ulick lifted his face, looking at me. 'Will I?' he said.

Ah, isn't he good? He didn't take advantage! He asked me first! I nodded me head. Yeah, anything that will keep him here, I thought, as he went all the way into a place where there used to be a soul. I wonder does he hear the echo of the emptiness inside me? There is nothing there, Ulick! I am still waiting to be filled up again with something that filled my soul with fire and passion and life and wonder and awe and . . . then it ended. He crept out of my life like a thief in the night. It was all for my good he told me. Yes, Ralph, I know you believed that.

He was finished for himself. I felt like giving him a pat on the head. It was that or cry and scream and roar for me mammy. Where are you, Mammy? I'm lost! So, this is my lot. It is now, for me, fair exchange is no robbery. I trade with Ulick the benefit of enjoying my body in exchange for him keeping away the haunting loneliness that plagues me when he is not around. The time flies, then he is gone! But for at least a couple of hours I am with someone who wants to be with me. I am not alone! He knows my ways and I know his. He sees it from his point of view. *I am with my girlfriend. We do the normal things like have sex. That's what you do when you love each other. She loves me. I love her. It keeps the world going round!*

I wonder how much them prostitutes earn? Poor Ulick. He should have a girlfriend. Cut it out, Martha. Think business!

'Was that good?'

'What? Was what good?' I said, looking at Ulick's red-hot face from all his exertions.

'Did you enjoy it?'

'Oh, yeah!' I said, remembering now. 'Yeah, smashing, Ulick! You are very passionate!'

'Yeah, I'm getting good at it!' he said.

'Oh, yeah, definitely!' I said, nodding to keep him happy but desperate to get back to where I was. Back to business! Now, where was I? Oh, yeah, money-making schemes! Ah, Jaysus, no! I might catch disease! I'll have to come up with something else. I can't go on working for peanuts! Then I remembered to ask something.

'Oh, by the way, Ulick, are you sure that method works?'

'Oh, yeah! I read it in a book. It's called the "Billings Method".'

'Oh, yeah! I remember now what you called it. So, let me see, halfway through your cycle you are fertile! Meaning pregnancy! Not a good idea! It gave me the shivers just thinking about it. But we're all right. We're using this Billings Method. So if we abstain – Jaysus! I sound like a priest!'

'Yeah! Don't worry! I'm keeping track!' Ulick said, giving me the nod.

I lay back, going back to me money-making schemes, feeling very reassured. Where would I be without him! I sighed.

39

I pushed open the door into the hall and picked up a letter addressed to me. I looked at it, seeing the English postmark. I rushed up the stairs and put the key in me door and flew in, throwing me bag on the bed and pulling off me coat, landing it on top. Then I sat down to read the letter: 'Dear Miss Long, we have great pleasure in informing you your interview for the position as shorthand typist has been successful. Your starting salary will be as follows £ . . .' Me eyes skinned to the next bit. 'We will also pay your boat and train ticket once a month to return to Ireland—' Who gives a damn about Ireland? I'm never setting foot back here again. There's nothing here for me. '—We hope you will enjoy working with our bank.'

Lloyds Bank! I got the job! 'I'm going to be working in a bank in London!' I screamed at the room. It has listened to enough of me moans over the past couple of months, it must make a change hearing me sing a different tune!

Right! I have four weeks to get sorted, give in me notice at work, then let the landlord know I will be leaving. Four weeks. I get paid on a Friday. I can travel over on the Saturday and start work on the Monday. Jaysus! I'm going to have to look up temporary accommodation until I find me feet. I better get busy using the phone at work. Right! I can phone London from there. By the time they get the bill I should be well gone!

Ralphie! My darling man. The great love of my life! Our paths may yet cross again! In fact they bloody will! We have unfinished business to settle. While you were over there, getting yourself lost, probably in the great city of London, I was marooned here on my little island of saints and scholars, with the might of the Irish Sea keeping us safely apart. Well, I will be sailing there very soon! You will be getting a surprise visit from me, Amen!

I made me way down the hill and over the King's Bridge, then I hurried down the quays, walking along Usher's Island. Here we are again, I thought, looking up at the few remaining old terraced Georgian houses. I walked up the stone steps to the second one. It was directly in front of the River Liffey. I pushed in the hall door, closing it behind me. The light in the hall was very weak. It was just one bulb hanging from a long flex, swinging out of the big ornate rose in the ceiling. I looked down, making sure not to break me neck going up the old stairs. A door faced me as I arrived on the landing. I knocked, then waited, feeling me heart up in me mouth. I could hear the beat of it in me ears. Dear Jesus! Please grant that the news won't be bad.

'Come in!' an old man's voice lifted, coming through the door.

I pushed the door open into a big old room. Tall mahogany glass cases covered one wall, groaning with books. The room was stuffed with papers and medical instruments all sitting on top of presses and side tables. A long black leather examination table stood at the right side of the wall. I looked over, seeing an old man with a mop of silvery white hair sitting behind a big old desk. It was covered in papers. He looked up at me with little glasses sitting on the end of his nose.

'Doctor Barnes, I'm Martha Long. You told me to come back tonight. You would have the results of the pregnancy test. I left them into the Rotunda Hospital as you told me to do!' I hesitated, not knowing what more to say. I felt sick in me heart.

'Ah, yes! Come in and sit down,' he said, pointing me to a big old stuffed leather chair sitting right in front of the desk.

'I have the results back for you,' he said. He wasn't smiling. He rooted around and came up with a piece of paper. 'Yes! Here we are, Martha,' he said, getting up to walk around to my side. 'I'm afraid the results are not good. You are pregnant, my dear,' he said, taking his eyes up from the piece of paper and looking down at me with a very kind smile, then patting me shoulder. 'I take it you are not married?'

'No, Doctor.'

'Tut, tut! Poor girl. What age are you, Martha?' he said, bending down to me.

'Eighteen, Doctor!'

'Oh dear, oh dear!' he said, sighing heavily and shaking his head. 'What will you do? Is there anyone you can talk to who will help you?'

I shook me head.

'Well, you can have the child adopted. There are convents around the country. You can go to one of them and have the baby. Then, when it is born, you can hand it over for adoption. My nephew, who is also a doctor, he and his wife have recently adopted a child from a convent. There are homes for unmarried mothers. No one will ever know. The whole thing can be kept secret,' he said. 'Look, I have details here from when my nephew made all his arrangements. You should go in as soon as possible to see them. They will arrange everything for you. It is the Catholic Protection and Rescue Society, South Anne Street. It is run by a priest. He will organise things for you, make all the arrangements for you to go into the home. I would suggest you don't delay. You are already two months pregnant. In another few months you will clearly start to show your condition. It would not be wise to allow this to happen in a small town like Dublin. It is a lot smaller than people think,' he laughed.

'OK, thank you, Doctor. How much do I owe you?'

He shook his head. 'No charge! You keep what little money you have in your pocket, child. You will be needing all the funds you can get. Look, I wish you the best of luck.'

'Thank you, Doctor,' I croaked, walking out the door not knowing what day of the week it was any more.

I walked back to me bedsit. It serves me right! What was I thinking? Gone from the frying pan straight into the fire. Now I will have to give up my bedsit and me job. So, that's it. I blew everything away just like that. I certainly won't be taking up that job in London. Not now! That's gone for good! Jesus! Jesus! Why was I so stupid? For what did I do it? I hurt meself. That's what I did. Well, you did want to drown yourself on the King's Bridge over the River Liffey! Remember back that evening, around two months ago? You thought you put it off, but did you? You sure used up all that anger, Martha.

Now what? Lose the opportunity of a lifetime working for a bank in London. Lose me job here. Lose me home, me bedsit. That's the end of everything. Jesus! To put the final curse on it.

I never stop getting sick. From the minute I wake up, I'm throwing up anything that's in me stomach. Morning, noon, night and day. These days I'm always running to work because I'm not on time. Then I'm stopping to retch up me guts, then start running again. Why would I do such a thing so stupid? Because I am stupid, of course! Now, you have given yourself a right kick up the arse. Let that be a lesson. There's no need to learn things the hard way, fucking eejit!

'So, that's it, Ulick. I'm giving up the baby for adoption.'

There's no way I'm repeating me ma's mistake, I thought. Ireland is no place for an unmarried mother. Don't I know that just too well? I want my baby to have nothing but the best. I could offer the little mite nothing. I don't even earn enough to keep meself. Anyway, you can't have a child in this country without having a husband. They would run you out, just like they did to me ma.

'I'm giving up me bedsit and me job, Ulick. Naturally I won't be seeing you again. What's the point? We have no future. So, I will be going away to the convent when I am six months pregnant. I know I'm pushing it, but, well, I don't want to be stuck in the convent any longer than I have to be.' I stared at him, waiting to hear him say something.

'Yeah, you are right, Martha. It is the best thing for everyone!'

'Yeah,' I said, thinking I will just have to start all over again. If I could get some money, I would head straight for the boat to England the day I hand over me baby in the convent. I have a better chance of starting a new life over there. Anyway, there's nothing left in Dublin for me now.

40

I closed me suitcase, then lifted it and put it on the floor. Then picked up me coat and put it on. It still fit me, barely. All me clothes do! But it's a bit of a squash! It must be all the weight I keep losing. I never did stop vomiting. Even though I'm now six months pregnant. 'Oh, well,' I sighed, looking around at me little bedsit. Me eyes peeled all around the room. No! I've left nothing behind. Everything I own is in this suitcase. I walked over and put the two keys on the table, then walked back and picked up me suitcase. Here we go again. Always on the move. Homeless again and jobless. But the big difference is I'm older, eighteen. I'm wiser. I've certainly learnt me lesson well. And I am qualified to take on the world!

'Goodbye, little home! I was happy here,' I whispered, looking at it for the last time. I opened the door, shutting it quietly behind me. Then I walked down the stairs and out through the front door.

I stood on the doorstep, looking over to the little churchyard with all the tombstones facing out onto the quiet narrow road, giving a silent reminder our time will come too. This moment is all we have. I sense deep within me it is very precious. Yet a tiny part of me wants to trade this time, just to never have to wake to a pain like this again. I have a terrible feeling in my heart. No matter what the outcome of this will be, my life has changed course, and I don't think it is for the better. I think it will be many, many a long day to come before I ever feel real peace again. But I know one day it will come. Nothing lasts for ever. Not even pain. My last moments with Ralph floated into my mind's eye. When he reached out his hand to pull me to my feet, it was the last time we ever touched.

'It is over!' he had said. It felt like it was over for me, too. I had reached the great joy of finding love, through you, for a brief time, I got a glimpse of the hidden me, the might of the love that hid sleeping deep inside me. When it woke, I sensed its power. I could move mountains, feel intense peace. I knew for what I was born. To love. I had arrived home. My demons were vanished. I was somebody. You loved me. I knew who I was. I loved you beyond life itself. Then it ended. The light went out. I fell into the dark. You left me without hope. The one thing I brought with me when we first met, along with my half-empty suitcase. I had very little. But I had my dreams, and a burning belief, man, is not all bad. But you went away, taking that from me. You did not love me, Ralph. I know what love is. Nothing tears it apart. I love my mother, because we were once connected by her heartbeat. She brought me into being. Then she gave me birth. She is what she is. She is my mother. I will never stop loving her. No more than I can ever stop loving you, Ralph. With all my heart and all my soul. Because this is how I love. But I will never love like that again. Because my love is precious. It lasts a lifetime. There is only one Ralph. But you were a man of straw. The coward does it with a kiss. It hid the knife, Ralph, you used to cut my heart out. But my love lasts a lifetime.

I looked down towards the Liffey, hearing the sound of a horn as a barge made its way down the river. It was the only sound to break the silence of the early-morning quiet. It brought me back from my thoughts. I lifted my face to take in a breath and it came out in a sudden sob. Jesus! Stay with me! I'm going to need you very close.

The day suddenly woke with the bells ringing out loud and clear from across the Liffey. I listened, hearing where it was coming from. A sound I knew from long ago in the days of my childhood. It was Christ Church Cathedral. I was born just around the corner and down the hill, in the very heart of the Liberties of Dublin, the ancient part of the city, where all we true Dubliners come from. St Patrick's Cathedral broke in, adding its joyous tones, followed by the rest of the churches all around the city, all calling the people to prayer. I imagined in my mind's eye people and children waking to the sound and turning over to listen. Sunday morning, it is time to start the day. To get up and go to church and give thanks for a day of rest and all the gifts they have been blessed with – a loving home and children, with a husband to walk through life with.

These people I am now running from. They will not forgive me for my sin. My baby will be a bastard. I will be seen as easy prey for lecherous men. Women will not associate with me. I am not a respectable married woman. I am a whore! So, I'm going to hide in the convent especially for girls like me. But the rat-bag nuns needn't bleedin think they are getting any work out of me. I am too well up to them. Cheap labour! They can go and get stuffed for themself! Sparks will fly, little nuns, if you think you can rub me up the wrong way! Ha, they need me as much as I need them! So, fair exchange is no robbery! I will loll about, smoking meself to death, biding my time until my little baby arrives. Then you will see a clean pair of heels. From then on I am taking a perpetual vow of chastity! I am going to become a professional virgin! Haunted and hunted.

Damn you, Ulick, for being Ulick. Did you not, when you first looked into my face to ask permission to enter, see there was no one there? Did you not see the emptiness in my eyes? Or as I know it was, you didn't mind playing with an empty shell! You are young and want to sow your wild seeds. Well, they have taken root in me. Something precious came out of my stupidity and your wild oats.

I went down the hill for the last time, carrying all me possessions in one suitcase. Heading, one last time, to cross over the King's Bridge. I will then turn right for Heuston Station to take the train. Then I take a bus that will take me into the heart of the country. It is very quiet there, the priest said. There is no need for me to worry. Nobody will ever find out, because the convent is not close to many living people. I'm to take a little bus when I get off the train. The bus will carry me all the way to the gates of the convent – the home for unmarried mothers somewhere in the country.

MA, HE SOLD ME FOR A FEW CIGARETTES

MARTHA LONG

Born a bastard to a teenage mother in the slums of 1950s Dublin, Martha has to be a fighter from the very start.

As her mother moves from man to man, and more children follow, they live hand-to-mouth in squalid, freezing tenements, clothed in rags and forced to beg for food. But just when it seems things can't get any worse, her mother meets Jackser.

Despite her trials, Martha is a child with an irrepressible spirit and a wit beyond her years. She tells the story of her early life without an ounce of self-pity and manages to recreate a lost era in which the shadow of the Catholic Church loomed large and if you didn't work, you didn't eat.

Martha never stops believing she is worth more than the hand she has been dealt, and her remarkable voice will remain with you long after you've finished the last line.

ISBN 9781845963132
Available now
£6.99 (paperback)

'A remarkable personal and literary achievement for the author and an unforgettable experience for the reader'

– *Irish Independent*

'A born survivor, Martha is undoubtedly also a born storyteller'

– *The Star*

MA, I'M GETTIN MESELF A NEW MAMMY

MARTHA LONG

Aged thirteen, Martha is rescued by the courts from the clutches of her evil stepfather, Jackser, and her feckless mother, Sally. After numerous arrests for shoplifting, a judge rules that she is to be sent to a convent school with the instruction that she is to get an education.

Her initial relief at escaping the abuse and neglect she suffered at home is, however, short-lived, as she soon realises that there are many forms of cruelty in this life. As she says, 'You can have a full belly, but your heart can be very empty.' Ostracised by the other children for being a 'street kid' and put to back-breaking work by the nuns, she leads a lonely existence, her only joy coming from the books she devours and her mischievous sense of humour.

Desperate for love and a little place where she feels she belongs, despite all that she has suffered Martha retains her compassion for others and still continues to hope for a brighter future when she will be free to make her own way in life.

ISBN 9781845964498
Available now
£6.99 (paperback)

'A born survivor . . . a born storyteller . . . a heartbreaking true story'

– *Trisha Goddard*

'[Martha's] humour, verve and inextinguishable spark of hope always shine through, which is what makes her book so appealing'

– *Irish Independent*

AVAILABLE FROM ALL GOOD BOOKSHOPS, MAINSTREAMPUBLISHING.COM AND RBOOKS.CO.UK

MA, IT'S A COLD AUL NIGHT AN I'M LOOKIN FOR A BED

MARTHA LONG

In this latest instalment of Martha Long's real-life account of abuse, deprivation and cruelty at the hands of her mother's partner, Jackser, and the establishment, Martha is sixteen and her time at the convent school is up. Martha is free, but alone and vulnerable. She can't look back – only horror waits there – so she must start again, hiding what her life has been.

With no friends, family or safety net, she sets out with nothing but a suitcase of old clothes and a burning ambition to shake off her impoverished past. Trained by the nuns to work as a domestic, she finds a place as a skivvy in a miserable household where she is reminded of the terror Jackser brought into her life.

Soon she is back on the streets, searching for work and a bed to call her own. With a fire burning in her belly, she vows, 'I will work hard night and day if I have to, but one day I am going to be somebody.'

However, the world will not be kind to Martha, and as people turn her away, predators wait in the shadows.

ISBN 9781845965822
Available now
£6.99 (paperback)

'Martha Long has a talent of interlacing her tragic life story with humour . . . a fluently written and absorbing memoir, which will horrify and inspire'
– *Ulster Tatler*

'An ultimately uplifting story which salutes the strength of the human spirit'
– *Irish World*